VIRGINIA HISTORICAL GENEALOGIES

VIRGINIA
HISTORICAL GENEALOGIES

by

John Bennett Boddie

CLEARFIELD

Originally published
Redwood City, California, 1954

Reprinted for
Clearfield Company, Inc. by
Genealogical Publishing Co., Inc.
Baltimore, Maryland
1990, 1996, 1999, 2005

Library of Congress Catalogue Card Number 54-3721
International Standard Book Number: 0-8063-0042-6

Made in the United States of America

PREFACE

This book is dedicated to the memory of my dear wife, Pearl D. Boddie who died July 17, 1951. She helped in gathering and typing material and a promise was made at that time to dedicate the book to her. Her picture is the frontispiece.

The State Library of Virginia has microfilms of the Colonial records of all the counties in Virginia, except Surry, the very county whose early records I wished to consult. Mr. Barham, the county court clerk, would not permit the Church of the Latter Day Saints of Salt Lake City to microfilm the county records. Copies of their microfilms were later deposited in the State Library; hence the absence of Surry's records.

The reason this is stated is that it was my hope to confine this work to that county, and add another volume as a follow-up to "Colonial Surry" as promised. I was unable to do so. Hence the name "Virginia Historical Genealogies."

Genealogy of families long in this country and in England is really "history". The history of some families herein extend back through the wars of England from the time of William the Conqueror to the period of the Commonwealth, and in America from 1607 to the present day. Religious movements, persecutions and the vicissitudes of the old world which brought many people to our shores are recounted herein.

The rooms allotted to visitors at the Virginia State Library are large and commodious. It is an ideal place to work. The late Mrs. Mary J. Pollard, head of the Archives Department, had a very thorough knowledge of Virginia history and genealogy and was of the greatest assistance. I am deeply indebted to her, Mrs. Bass, Mrs. Nugent, and others in the Library for their help.

The most complete genealogical library in the United States is Newberry Library in Chicago, and I am grateful to Mr. Joseph Wolf, head of the Genealogical Department, and Miss Chase, his assistant, who were of invaluable assistance in suggesting and producing needed books. I have known Joe since he was a boy and consider him one of my most valued friends to whom I owe much.

A library that will be very important for historical research is that of the Genealogical Society of Utah at Salt Lake City. They have microfilmed the early records of many of the Colonial States,

such as Virginia and the Carolinas. Also under the direction of
Mr. Archibald F. Bennett, Secretary, they are busily engaged in
filming the records of old England, including the wills of the Pre-
rogative Court of Canterbury which extend in some instances
back to the thirteenth century. These wills are the backbone of
English and American genealogy.

Thanks are due to Mr. Alphus L. Walter, Chief of the Stack
and Reader division of the Library of Congress for his kind permission to visit the stacks of the History and Genealogy department. Also to Mrs. Mary Isabel Fry of the Huntington Library
for permission to use their rare books.

The nearest library to my home is at Stanford University,
where I visit frequently and wish to thank Mr. R. C. Swank,
Director, for his courtesy in giving permission to use the library.

The Genealogical and History department of the Public Library
of San Francisco, under the auspices of Miss Bruner, Mr. Dillon
and Mr. Lee Lewis Burtis is one of the best in the West, and I
wish to thank them for their aid.

Most readers will be familiar with the laws of inheritance prevailing in Virginia during Colonial times. However, it is hoped
that it will not be amiss to mention a few that were ascertained in
this search.

Under the law of primogeniture, as the name indicates, the first
or oldest son inherited all the real property of a decedent in the
absence of a will. If a father wished to divide his property among
his children it was necessary for him to make a will specifically
designating the property he wished to bequeath to each of them or
to any other person. If an eldest or only son was not mentioned
in the will, he inherited all the property not bequeathed. Because
of this, some few testators, where they had an only son, often bequeathed property, usually personalty, to their daughters without
mentioning the son. When a person died intestate his or her personal property was usually divided, one-third to the widow or
widower, and the balance was distributed equally among the children. This rule also prevailed in South Carolina, where women
had no property rights. (See division of Barrick Travis estate.)

Real property could not be conveyed by a nuncupative or oral
will. (N. N. G. B. 2-109) See Gregg family herein, where one
Nicholas Bulbrooke of Stafford did verbally, upon his death bed,
give to Thomas Gregg, Jr., 200 acres of land. It was held by the
land office that "said verbal will is not good in law to devise land."
Jacob Smith Sr. on his death bed in Fairfax County, in 1753, made
a desperate effort to divide his property among his children, for
he provided that all his realty be sold, converted into personalty
and then given equally to all his children. This was not done, as
his real property, less widow's dower, was inherited and sold by
Jacob Smith Jr., his eldest son.

A wife's personal property before marriage became the property of her husband for the payment of his debts, regardless of a pre-nuptial contract that the property was to remain her own.

In a case in Charles City County, when a testator provided for the emancipation of his slaves, it was held that regardless of his wishes the slaves became the property of his heirs, for there was no law in Virginia at that time that permitted the freeing of slaves.

Some few families herein trace back to early times in England when the use of coats of arms prevailed. Oftentimes these coats were mentioned as having a label, a crescent or a star for difference. These were to distinguish the different members or branches of the family, as follows:

Eldest son bore a label.
2nd   "   "   " crescent
3rd   "   "   " star
4th   "   "   " bird (martlet)
5th   "   "   " ring
6th   "   "   " fleur de lis
7th   "   "   " rose.

The eldest son dropped his label on succeeding to the family coat, but younger sons retained their individual designation and passed them on to their descendants. Where an armiger had no sons, his daughters could quarter his arms. Several generations of marriages to heiresses can bring a large number of quarterings to a family.

There are five colors mentioned in Heraldry: gules, (red); azure, (blue); sable, (black); vert, (green); purpure, (purple). There are two metals: gold, (or); and silver, (argent). Then there are certain "ordinaries" which include, for example, the cross; the fess (a bar); the chevrons, etc.

In the 17th century the word "cousin" in wills meant nephew or niece, and "nephew" and "niece" meant "cousin". (See will of Benjamin Reade). "Son in law" usually meant "step son". "Daughter in law" was sometimes used for "step daughter", although it was often used to designate the wives of sons. This can usually be told from the context of the will. The phrase "father in law" or "mother in law" does not seem to have been used. They were often called "loving friends", and these words were also used for "nephew" or "niece"; the phrase, however, did not always mean that a relationship existed. (See Hayden 300.)

Families are not arranged herein in alphabetical order but are placed together in the order of their relationship with one another. Several pedigrees leading back to Royalty are shown. They are not given as anything unique or unusual, for nearly all Virginia families who came over in the 17th century connect with royalty somewhere along their line. The only difficulty is in correctly tracing their descent.

Unfortunately, there are many persons who sent in their immediate family records whose names and families will not appear in this book. Another volume on the families of Surry and Sussex is in course of preparation and it is hoped to finish them in the near future. If the Surry records had been filmed, they would have been in nearby Salt Lake City, which would make this task much easier.

Mr. Lundie W. Barlow of Boston, Mass., and Mr. James G. W. MacClamroch of Greensboro, N. C. conducted an extensive research on the Barham and Warren families in England and kindly shared their findings with me.

Many persons have contributed records of their immediate families, which I appreciate. Mr. Henry Legare Watson of Greenwood, S. C. furnished information concerning the Smallwood, Smith and Watson families in South Carolina, as did Mr. Milledge Louis Bonham, of Hamilton College, Clinton, N. Y. Mrs. Glen E. Miller of Ridley Park, Pa. contributed an extensive account of the Butler family in Virginia and the Carolinas.

Others to whom credit is due are Mr. Hugh Wagner Stallworth of Nashville, Tenn.; my esteemed cousin Capers J. Perryman of Montgomery, Ala.; Burrell Marion Ellison, Jr.; of Lancaster, S. C.; Mr. Sydney Rhodes Prince of Chevy Chase, Md. Mrs. P. W. Hiden of Newport News, Va., one of Virginia's best and most accurate historical writers, kindly reviewed many of the pages herein and offered valuable suggestions; to her I am deeply indebted. Mr. W. A. Graham-Clark of Washington, D. C. furnished the chapters on the Clark and the Flood families, and also contributed to the ones on the Gray and Ruffin families. Dr. B. C. Holtzclaw of Richmond furnished the chapter on the Norwood family and contributed towards the Jones family. Mr. Archibald Stuart Hall Smith of Scotland Neck, N. C., and Mr. Edward Devereux Smith of Atlanta, Ga. furnished information about the Smith family. Mr. John Butler Sledge of Durham, N. C. furnished the information concerning his family, as did Mr. William Haywood Ruffin of the same city. There are many others I should thank, and it is hoped to remedy this in the next book.

A genealogical work of this nature is never complete, as further research brings out new material. I would appreciate any mistakes or inaccuracies being brought to my attention, so they may be corrected in the next volume.

John B. Boddie

2318 Sunmor Avenue
Mountain View, California

TABLE OF CONTENTS

FAMILIES

CHARTS

EXPLANATION OF ABBREVIATIONS

A.C.	Alumni Cantabrigiensis, by Venn.
A.O.	Alumni Oxoniensis.
A.P.R.	Albermarle Parish Register.
B.J.	Journals of the House of Burgesses.
Brown	Brown's Abstracts of Somerset England Wills in 6 volumes.
Burgess	Revolutionary Soldiers of Virginia, by Burgess.
Chapman or C	Mrs. Blanche Adams Chapman's Abstracts of Elizabeth City County, or of Isle of Wight.
C.P.	Cavaliers and Pioneers (Abstracts of Virginia Land Grants) by Mrs. Nell M. Nugent.
do.	Ditto; meaning the same reference previously shown.
D.A.B.	Dictionary of American Biography.
D.B.	Deed Book.
dsp.	Died single person.
dvp.	Died before parent.
D.N.B.	Dictionary of National Biography.
E.	Essex.
Foster	Alumni Oxoniensis, by Foster.
Fleet	Abstracts of Virginia County Records, by Beverly Fleet.
G.E.C.	The Complete Peerage, by G.E. Cokayne.
G.B.	Grant Book.
Harl.	Harleian Society Publications.
Hasted	Hasted's History of Kent County, England
Hayden	Virginia Genealogies, by Hayden
Heitman	Historic Register of Officers, American Revolution, F.B. Heitman
Hotten	Original Lists of Immigrants to America, by Hotten.
I.P.M.	Inquests Post Mortem.
J.H.B.	Journals of the House of Burgesses.
K.G.	King George County, Virginia
L.B.	Land Book at Virginia State Library.
M.C.B.	Magna Carta Baron.
M.C.G.C.	Minutes of Court and General Council.
M.	do.
N.N.	Northern Neck Land Grants.
N.E.G.R.	New England Genealogical and Historical Register.
Nash	Nash's History of Worcestershire, England.
O.	Orders.
O.B.	Order Book.
P.B.	Patent Book.

P.C.C.	Prerogative Court of Cantebury Wills, England.
P.G.	Price George County.
P.R.	Patent Rolls of England.
P.W.	Prince William County.
R.	Register of Parish.
Reg.	do.
R.B.	Record Book.
S.	Stafford County.
S.P.	St. Paul's Parish or Parish Register of Stafford County.
sp.	Single Person.
S.P.R.	St. Paul's Parish Register, Stafford County.
S.P.	Calendar of State Papers of England.
S.P. Col.	Calendar of State Papers, Colonial.
Sweeney	Abstract of Rappahannock Wills, by Sweeney.
T.	Tyler's Magazine.
Tyler's	do.
V.B.	Vestry Book.
Vic. His.	Victorian Histories of the Counties of England.
V.	Virginia Historical Society Magazine.
V.M.	do.
W.	William and Mary College Quarterly, Series (1) and (2).
W.M.	do.
W.B.	Will Book.

Abbreviations are not uniform because some chapters were written before Dr. Swem's Index was published using T.W. and V. to designate the above magazines. Also, other persons contributing used other forms of abbreviations which were not changed.

VIRGINIA HISTORICAL GENEALOGIES

STONE, SMALLWOOD AND SMITH FAMILIES

Maryland and South Carolina

Governor William Stone was born in England about 1603. It is stated by some authorities that his place of birth was in Northamptonshire. However, from the records of his family in England, it would seem that he was born in Lancashire. The Northampton tradition may have resulted from the fact that he came to Maryland from Northampton County, Virginia. It is very difficult to place the old English homes of our early immigrants. Governor Stone's family home is known because his uncle, Thomas Stone, haberdasher, of the City of London, the 31st day of July, 1647, made his "nephew, Captain William Stone of Maryland, my true and lawful attorney to collect a debt from Thomas Weston, formerly of London, ironmonger. " (Md. Arch., Vol. 4, p. 377).

Thomas Stone of London recorded his pedigree upon the Visitation of the Heralds to London in 1634, as the Stones were an armorial family and such families were then required to register their pedigrees in order to establish their right to bear arms. This pedigree shows that the Stone family was domiciled at "Carr House" near the village of Bretherton in the Parish of Croston, Lancashire. Their arms were "Per Pale or and Sable a Lion rampant counterchanged".

The pedigree begins with Thomas Stone's grandfather, William Stone of Twiston in Lancashire, which was near the Yorkshire border. He married Elizabeth, daughter of John Bradley of Bradley, another armorial family. The only child shown in the pedigree was Thomas Stone's father, "Richard Stone of Carr House", married to "Isabel, daughter of John Girdler of Carr House". This statement is verified by referring to the printed records of the Parish Church of Croston, January 12, 1572. John Girdler was from Carr House Parish, Doncaster, in the West Riding of Yorkshire, and it is probable that Richard Stone's home, "Carr House", was named for Isabel's old home in Yorkshire.

Richard Stone made his will the 13th of March, 1605, as follows:

> "Rychard Stones of Carrhowses within the Lordshippe of Bretherton, Co,, Lac., husbandman. To be buried at the Parish Church of Croston. After my debts and funeral expenses are paid my goods to be divided into

three equal parts, whereof I give one part to Isabell my wife. The second part I give to my children, John, Thomas, Andrew, Matthew, Mary, Margery and Katheryn Stone equally amongst them.

"The third part of my goods whatsoever I give to John Stone, my said son, and my greatest chest and the greate table in my dwelling house, my almery and dishbord, my plough, my harness and other implements belonging to husbandry.

"I give to Thomas and Andrew Stones, sons of Robert Stones, 12 d. To John Stones, son of the said Robert Stones, 3 sh. To Hugh Stones, son of the said John Stones, 3 sh.

"The rest of all my goods whatsoever I give to my daughters Mary, Margaret and Katheryn Stones equally amongst them.

"Whereas I have one lease and grante of my Right Worship full Sir Peter Legh, Knight, of one messuage or cotage, with the lands belonging and appurtenances lying in Mugh Hoole Co., Lanc., which is in my occupation. My will is and I give the said lease, etc., to my wife for life, she to pay all rents for the same.

"I give one close of lande, parcell of the same messuage and commonly called Marshreades, to the said Katheryn my daughter, to have and hold the same from and after my decease, and the decease of Isabell my wife, for the life of the said Katheryn if the term so long continues, she the said Katheryn paying all rents for the same.

"I give the same lease, messuage, cottage and other premises after the several deceases of me, Isabell my wife and Katheryn my daughter, to Henry Stones my son for the residue of the time of the said lease.

"I make Isabell my wife and John Stones my son, Exors., and I make Thomas Smith, Supervisor. Teste, James Hey, Hugh Hey, James Smith. (Proved in the C. C. C. the 24th of June, 1606, by Isabell the relict).

"Debts owing by me: To Robert Jackson surety for my son Robert. To the late wife of Richard Marston surety for the debts of my sons John, Henry and Matthew. "

Thomas Stone, of London, his son and uncle of Governor William Stone of Maryland was baptized November 12, 1580, in the Parish Church of Croston. In 1647 he forwarded a deposition in a law suit to Maryland in which he stated that he was then "68 years of age or thereabouts", which would verify the above date.

John Stone, who was Richard's eldest son and heir, inherited "Carr House", but he does not seem to have prospered as much as his younger brothers, Thomas and Andrew, who journeyed from home to become merchants, for an inscription still existing in raised letters on a stone in the doorway of Carr House reads, "Thomas Stone of London, haberdasher, and Andrew Stone of Amsterdam, merchant, both builded this house at their own charges giveth the same unto their brother John Stone, Ano Domini 1613". (Victoria History of Lancashire, Vol. 6, pp. 102-3)

This nearby church of St. Michael in Hoole has a font, which is of stone and octagonal. It was the gift of John Stone of Carr House and bears this inscription, "Deo Donum Johanus Stone an Dom 1633."

Research has not definitely proven which one of Richard Stone's sons was the father of Governor William Stone. Tradition has it that John was his father and this may be true, as the children of Thomas and Andrew are known.

An article in the Maryland Historical Magazine, Volume 14, Page 157, states that the governor was a son of "Captain John Stone who was killed by the Pequod Indians in a battle on the Conneticut River". This has been repeated frequently. However, the above "Captain Stone" arrived in Massachusetts from Virginia in 1632, when he was killed on board his vessel by the Pequots, (Mass. Hist. Soc. Coll, 3rd ser., Vol. 6, p. 158). This date eliminates him as the father of Governor William Stone as it has been shown that John Stone, the brother of Thomas Stone, made a gift to the church in Hoole, England, in 1633.

William Stone came to the Eastern Shore of Virginia before 1633 as he was a justice in Accomac in that year. He also served as Sheriff of Northampton after it was cut off from Accomac. On the 4th of June, 1635, he was granted 1800 acres in Accomac, at Blunt Point for the transportation of himself, his brother Andrew Stone and 34 servants. These grants were usually dated several years after the arrival of the grantees.

Captain William Stone married Verlinda Graves, daughter of Captain Thomas Graves, Burgess for Smythe's Hundred in the General Assembly of Virginia, 1619.

When Leonard Calvert, Governor of Maryland, died, he designated Thomas Greene, a Catholic, as his successor. Lord Baltimore, however, removed Greene from office in 1648 and appointed Captain William Stone in his place. What influenced Lord Baltimore to appoint Stone, a Protestant of Virginia, to this office is not recorded in the history of the times. It is conjectured that this was a political move on the part of the noble Lord in order to appease the growing enemies his Catholic Province of Maryland had made in England's Protestant and largely

Puritan Parliament.

William Stone served as Governor of Maryland for some years. He was the leader of the Cavalier forces against the Puritans at the Battle of the Severn, March 25, 1655. (17th Cent. pp. 64, 72) This was the first battle fought between Americans on American soil.

Governor Stone patented 4,000 acres of land in Charles County, which he called "Poynton Manor". He died in 1660 and this was inherited by his oldest son Thomas. John, his third son, was given 500 acres at Nanjemoy. Except for being married three times, John seems to have led an uneventful life. He was a justice of the county court in 1670, 1687, and also represented Charles County in the General Assembly from 1678 to 1688.

John Stone's first wife, according to a deed in 1676, was named Elizabeth, last name unknown. She was the mother of Thomas (1677-1727), and John (d. 1702), Matthew (1679-1750), his third son, was by a second wife, whose name is also unknown, as Matthew is spoken of as being a half brother of Thomas and John. John, Sr., married, thirdly, in 1684, Elinor, daughter of Walter and Elinor Bayne of Charles County by whom he had Walter, Elinor and Elizabeth. (Md. Arch. Vol. II, pp. 587-596)

The Bayne family was in Maryland as early as 1637. Walter Bayne represented St. Mary's County in the General Assembly on the 21st of March, 1641, and in April, 1650, (Md. Arch., Vol. I, pp. 116-284) His brother, Ralph Bayne, a merchant, died in 1655, and willed Walter all of his property in Maryland and Virginia. Walter's first wife was Mary, daughter of Randell Revell, and second wife was, Elinor, daughter of Thomas Weston, member of the Maryland General Assembly, 1641.

Thomas Weston was a London merchant. He, together with John Peirce, obtained a grant of land in Virginia, Jan. 12, 1619/20, from the London Co. In 1622 his ships the "Charity" and the "Swan" brought over about 60 men who settled at what is now Weymouth, Mass. The Puritans objected to his settlement and Weston returned to Virginia where he served in the House of Burgesses in 1628. (24V238) He patented 650 acres in York county, Feb. 9, 1637. (C.P. - 80). He is said to have died in Bristol, England, in 1647. His estate in Maryland was settled by John Hansford of York, Va., who exhibited his will in the Provincial Court of St. Mary's, July 15, 1648. (Md. Arch.). His plantation in York which descended to his daughter, Elizabeth, who married Roger Conant, was sold to John Hansford.

John Stone died in 1697. His will contained a bequest of 400 acres called "Durham" to his daughters, Elinor and Elizabeth, but this was his wife's property, having been bequeathed to her by her father, Walter Bayne, and as she married again it appears that Elinor and Elizabeth Stone never received "Durham", but that it became the property of their mother's last husband, John Beale.

There was a defect in Walter Bayne's title to Durham, which resulted in a long law suit in the Maryland courts. This suit covers many pages in the "Proceedings of the Maryland Court of Appeals, 1695-1729".

The court found that the said "Elinor Bayne, the devisee, in the year 1684 was then of the age of 17 years. She intermarried with one John Stone, now deceased. That the said Elinor was covert of the said John Stone by the space of 16 years and then the said John died in 1697. About 18 months afterwards she married Hugh Tears who died about a month after his marriage, that she, June 22, 1700, married John Beale the defendant by whom she had Richard and John Beale. "

John Beale, Sr., recovered Durham and soon sold it, for Daniel Jenifer, Surgeon, of Charles County, made his will in 1728 and gave his son Daniel part of a tract called "Durham" bought of John Beale. (Md. Cal. Wills, Vol. 6, p. 117). It is evident that Durham, although bequeathed to them by their father, never came to the two sisters, Elinor and Elizabeth Stone.

The above Elizabeth Stone, daughter of John, married about 1704, when she was 16 or 17 years of age, Peter McMillion of Charles County. Peter died soon afterwards, his will being probated July 27, 1706. On July 2, 1708, as Executrix and Relict of Peter McMillion, she and her second husband, Pryor Smallwood, were granted administration upon her first husband's estate.

It might be said here in passing that John Stone was the great uncle of Thomas Stone, who achieved immortality through signing the Declaration of Independence, and also of John Hoskins Stone, Governor of Maryland, 1794-1797.

Pryor Smallwood was the fourth son of Colonel James Smallwood of Charles County. Colonel Smallwood was High Sheriff of Charles County in 1694, Lt. Colonel of militia in 1700, and a member of the Maryland Assembly for Charles County from 1692 until his death in 1714. (See article on Smallwood family by A. L. Keith, Md. His Mag., Vol. 22, p. 139).

Pryor was born about 1680, for he made a deposition in the Charles County Court in 1722 in which he said he was 42 years of age and a son of Colonel James Smallwood. (Charles County, Lib. M. No. 2, Fol. 122). He and his wife, Elizabeth, August 9, 1720, sold to Daniel Bryan of Stafford County, Virginia, a tract of land called "St. Bridgetts".

Pryor Smallwood also held land in Stafford, for on April 3, 1724, he and his wife, Elizabeth, sold to George Mason of Stafford for 5 shillings, 200 acres known as "Cockpitt Point, north on Marsh Red Bank, east on Potomac River, south along Potomac

River for a breadth, thence into the wood, being bounds expressed
in ancient patent. Witnesses, William Talifero, Richard Hubbard". (Stafford D. B. 1724, p. 92).

Pryor Smallwood died in 1734. His will was dated February 23,
1734, was probated March 29, 1734. The inventory of his estate was presented in court, August 7, 1734, by Ledstone Smallwood, his brother, and Matthew Stone, the surviving brother of
Pryor's wife, Elizabeth. They signed as "next of kin" to the
heirs as required by Maryland Laws. (Charles County, Lib. M.
No. 2. See Index).

Children:

I. William Smallwood, youngest son, was given 200
acres, part of "Christian Temple Manor" in his
father's will. In 1753, Bayne held 200 acres in this
same manor.

There is not a record of any deed from William to
Bayne in the Charles County deed books from 1734 to 1768,
nor is there any record of his will or the administration
of his estate in Charles County or the Maryland Calendar
of Wills.

William Smallwood was the executor of the will of
William Travis in Stafford County, Va., in 1765. (See
Travis of Alamo). William Travis stated in his will, "my
intent and meaning is that if my wife Margaret Travis
should hereafter marry, that then my said loving children
with their estate left them by me shall be put in care and
management of my loving friend William Smallwood, and
further do appoint my loving wife, Margaret, and my
loving friend Mr. William Smallwood, my whole and sole
executor and executrix."

The term "father-in-law" meant "step-father" in
those days. Very often, but not always the use of the
word "loving friend" designated some degree of relationship. For example, Raleigh Travers made his will in
Stafford in 1749 and appointed his "loving friends" Sarah
and Travers Cooke, his executrix and executor. Sarah
was his sister and Travers his nephew. (Hayden 300).

In those days nearly all widows married soon after
their husband's death and their second husband administered on their first husband's estate. It was probably in
anticipation of this that William Travis desired his children to be put in the care of William Smallwood. Lucy
Travis, William's youngest daugter, born Dec. 16, 1762,
was under three years of age. It is hardly possible that
he would risk to have his children taken from their mother
and placed in the care of only a "friend". It seems possible

therefore that Margaret, wife of William Travis, was a daughter of William Smallwood. The name "Smallwood" was "handed down" in the Travis family for several generations. The old Scotch saying, "He is no friend of mine", is said to mean, "He is no kin".

Inasmuch as William Smallwood was appointed co-executor with Margaret Travis, it seems probable, under the circumstances, that they were father and daughter.

William Smallwood was living in King George in 1782 for he furnished supplies to the Revolutionary Army in that year. (4 T 65). He probably migrated after the Revolution.

II. Bayne Smallwood, (1711-1768), was given all of his father's remaining land; except Pryor's daughters, Anne and Elizabeth, were to have use of "Bayne" commonly called "My New Design", while single. (See later).

III. Anne Smallwood.

IV. Elizabeth Smallwood.

V. Hester Smallwood, m. (1) Jacob Smith; (2) Edmund Linton; (3) Wayman Sinkler; (4) Thomas William Wells. Her only children of whom there is a record were: 1. Jacob Smith, Jr., (1735-1805) who married Sarah Butler and removed to South Carolina; 2. Smallwood Smith, (1738?-1781) who married Elizabeth Marable Jones in South Carolina and was killed in the Cloud Creek Massacre 1781. (See later).

Bayne Smallwood who married Priscilla, daughter of William Heabard of Stafford County, Virginia, had seven children, and died in 1768. His daughter, Elinor, married Colonel William Grayson, one of the first two United States Senators from Virginia. Bayne's eldest son, William, was a noted general in Washington's army. His brigade fought with distinction in the Battles of Trenton, Princeton and Germantown, and Camden in South Carolina. In 1785, William Smallwood was elected governor of Maryland and served three consecutive terms.

Hester, the above daughter of Pryor Smallwood, and aunt of Governor William Smallwood, married Jacob Smith of Fairfax County, Virginia. This is proven by the fact that on June 4, 1736, Bayne Smallwood, as Executor of his father's will, shows in his accounts that he delivered a negro girl bequeathed by Hester's father, to Jacob Smith, her husband. (Md. Mag. Vol. 22, p. 169).

Jacob Smith patented land on the north side of Bull Run in what was then Stafford County, Virginia, January 15, 1724. This land later fell in Prince William County (1731), Fairfax County (1742), and in Loudoun County (1757), as each county, respectively, was cut off from the other.

He made his death bed will in Fairfax County, December 9, 1749. This was a verbal or nuncupative will, and under English law only personal property could be bequeathed by a nuncupative will. Evidently wishing his property to be divided equally among his children, he endeavored to convert all of his property into personalty. He directed that all of his lands and negroes be sold, and that the money arising from such sale be divided equally among his children that were then in being and an expected child. The above phraseology would indicate three or more children, and according to the law of primogeniture then in effect in Virginia, only the eldest son would inherit the land. It will appear later that his wishes in respect to this division were not followed. (Fairfax, Bk. A, p. 404; Bond, Bk. A, p. 396; Inv. Bk. A, p. 411; Bk. b, p, 40, estate acct.; B, p, 54, additional Inv.; B. p. 40, estate account to Nov. 21, 1753.)

On November 21, 1753, Hester Linton, Administratrix of the Estate of Jacob Smith, deceased, and her husband Edmund Linton filed an account of the estate. She seems to have lived happily with her second husband for nearly ten years. He died intestate in Loudoun County in 1759. The inventory of his estate was recorded in Loudoun, November 13, 1759, and same was signed by Benjamin Grayson and Nathaniel Grigsby. (Loudoun Bk. A, p. 20).

Nathaniel Grigsby, one of the above signers, later moved to South Carolina in a colony with the Smith's and other persons. He married Elizabeth Butler, a sister of Sarah Butler, who married Jacob Smith, Jr.. Jacob was a son of Hester and stepson of the above Edmund Linton.

Hester waited over a year before she married the third time. She married Wayman Sinkler of Dettinger Parsh, Prince William County, Virginia. These contracting parties each had separate estates and children of their own, so they made a pre-nuptial agreement, November 19, 1760, which provided that, "in case the said Hester should survive the said Wyman Skinkler, then that at and immediately after his death his whole estate shall descend and pass according to his last Will and Testament - all of his debts to be charged to his own estate - that the estate of said Hester Linton shall remain the absolute property to be used at her discretion and to descend as she sees fit". (Loudoun Bk. B, p. 92).

Wayman Sinkler lived less than two years after his marriage to Hester Smith Linton, for he made his will as of "Cameron Parish in Loudoun County" on April 12, 1762, and same was probated July 13, 1762. He left his seven children by a former wife, "all my land in Prince William County", and made his "loving wife Hester" and brother John Sinkler, joint executrix and executor of his will. (Loudoun Bk. A, p. 59).

Hester married Thomas William Wells before June 12, 1764,

for on that date, "Jacob Smith, orphan of Jacob Smith, deceased, came into court and made choice of Enoch Grigsby for his guardian, with Robert Sanford as his security". The court ordered that certain trustees "divide the personal estate of Jacob Smith, deceased, and allot to the said Jacob Smith, the heir, his part, * * * and that they lay off and allot the dower in the lands of Jacob Smith, deceased, to Hester Wells, the wife of Thomas William Wells and report same to the court". (Loudoun, Order Bk. B, p. 361).

Enoch Grigsby was a brother-in-law of Jacob Smith, Jr., as he had married Mary Butler, a sister of Jacob's wife, Sarah Butler. Two Grigsby brothers married two sisters, for as stated before, Nathaniel Grigsby married Elizabeth Butler, sister of Mary.

On November 21, 1769, Jacob Smith, Jr., and Hester Wells of Cameron Parish, sold to Landon Carter, Jr., a tract of land, which had been "granted to Jacob Smith, deceased, by the Proprietors, of the Norther Neck by a patent dated January 15, 1724, * * * lying on the North side of Bull Run". This deed was witnessed by Smallwood Smith, a brother of the above Jacob Smith, Jr.

This was the last known transaction of Hester and her sons in the Loudoun County records. Soon after selling this land it is very probable that they set out on their five hundred mile journey to the rich bottom lands of the Saluda River in South Carolina. Accompanying them were their relatives and neighbors, the Grigsbys, Enoch and Nathaniel; James Butler, and his three young sons, William, Thomas and James; and perhaps Barrick Travis; Edward Watson, and many others, for it was customary for these migrating settlers to travel in large parties, as their long journey would take many weeks.

This colony of Virginia settlers arrived in South Carolina not long before the outbreak of the Revolution and the Smiths, Butlers and Grigsbys served in the American forces. The official records of South Carolina show that they received pay for militia duty as follows: Jacob Smith, 13 £, 1 shilling, 5 pence; Smallwood Smith, 26/10/0; James Butler, Sr. and Jr., together received 39/16/5; William Butler, son of James, Sr., received 222/15/8 1/2 as lieutenant and captain; Thomas Butler, his brother, received 40/5/10 1/4; Enoch Grigsby received 7/2/10 as lieutenant. (See index stubs indents Book R-T and U-W.)

The American sympathizers were called "Whigs", the British sympathizers were called "Torys", and the strife between them was very bitter. It has generally been considered that the Tories of the Revolution were wealthy inhabitants of our chief cities, who opened their purses to the British, in the interest of maintaining the status quo, but did little fighting. However, the Tories of the Carolinas were not city "softies" but were mainly recent arrivals,

who lived in the Carolina Highlands and were loyal to the King.
Like their Highland ancestors they were used to fierce fighting
and forays.

The most notorious Tory family in the Ninety Sixth District
was the Cunningham family, said to consist of seven brothers,
who came from Scotland by way of Augusta County, Virginia, and
settled at Island Ford on the Saluda River in 1769. Major William
Cunningham, one of the brothers, first enlisted with the Whigs and
served in Captain John Caldwell's company in the Fort Charlotte
Expedition in 1775. He claimed he had been promised a commission as a first lieutenant and because he did not receive this appointment he left the company and came back to the Ninety Six
District.

Upon his return a bitter neighborhood strife arose. The
leader of the Whigs was Captain William Ritchie, who had been
with Cunningham in Caldwell's company. He sent word to Cunningham that he would shoot him on sight.

In 1778, while Bill Cunningham was away in Savannah, Ritchie
gathered a party, and under circumstances of great atrocity, if
the Tory accounts are to be credited, killed Bill's brother, John
Cunningham, who is said to have been lame and an epileptic.

As soon as Cunningham heard of the killing of his brother, he
walked all the way from Savannah to the Saluda Country, where
he found also his father had been badly treated by Ritchie's men.
He went over to Ritchie's house and shot him down, making good
his escape afterwards to the British.

He enlisted in the British army and was given the command of
a troop of horses. Then he proceeded to vigorously enforce Lord
Cornwallis's order, "that all persons should be executed as trai-
tors, who after having taken the oath of allegiance to the King, had
been found in arms against his majesty".

He followed the example of Sumpter and Marion in secretly
penetrating behind the lines of the opposing forces, but unlike
those leaders, who conducted their forays upon the principle of
civilized warfare he carried fire and sword into the back country.

For his fierce fighting and many butcheries, he soon was
known throughout the Whig country as "Bloody Bill". In the Fall
of 1781, he set out from the garrison at Charleston with a force
of three hundred men to raid the Ninety Six District and bring in
needed supplies. He crossed over the Saluda River and went to
Mount Willing in what is now Saluda County. This was where
Captain James Butler lived. Bloody Bill burned and destroyed
considerable property in the neighborhood and carried off a large
number of horses and cattle. Captain James Butler had refused to
accept the terms of Sir Henry Clinton's proclamation issued after
the fall of Charleston in 1780 and had been confined in irons in
the Ninety Sixth jail and at Charleston. He was asked by his neigh-

bors to lead a force after the Tories in an endeavor to recover their stolen property, but pleaded that the hardships of his recent confinement had unfitted him for duty. He finally consented to go, provided they would elect another commander, and Captain Turner was chosen. They set out under Turner's command and overtook a detachment of the Tories in Lexington County and recovered some of their cattle.

THE CLOUD CREEK MASSACRE

On their way back home this force stopped at Cloud Creek, a branch of the Little Saluda River, in what is now Saluda County, and without posting any sentinels, camped there for the night. It is said that Captain Butler urged them to adopt ordinary military precautions, but not being disciplined troops and subject to mili-regulations, no one would take upon himself the burden of being a sentry.

The Tory detachment they had pursued reported to Bloody Bill, their commander, and upon receiving the report of their defeat, he rallied his entire force and started back in pursuit of the Whigs.

Early on the morning of November 7, 1781, the American camp was located and surprised. The entire party, about one tenth as strong as the opposing force, took refuge in an unfinished log house.

Cunningham surrounded the place and demanded their surrender. Smallwood Smith was selected as a messenger to parley with him. Cunningham's first questioned who was in the party. Smallwood began to name the members of his party and upon reaching the name of James Butler, Cunningham halted him and advised that young Butler must die. Cunningham said the reason was that young Butler had been in a party of Americans, who killed Captain William Radcliffe, one of his friends. He refused to give any terms that would release Butler from slaughter. Young Butler, however, hearing of Cunningham's animosity towards him, and believing that if they surrendered he would be killed anyway, determined to fight. "Exclaiming that 'he would settle the terms' he fired his rifle, through a window, killing a Tory named Stewart. This concluded the parley, and young James Butler fell with a mortal wound, while kneeling to pick the flint of his gun for a second shot. The expiring boy called his father to his side, handed him his rifle and told him there were yet a few balls in his pouch."

After young James's death, the whole party, seeing that the odds made fighting hopeless, surrendered.

"It is said that after the surrender, Bloody Bill, at a meeting of his officers, advised and ordered the massacre of the whole party. It was then that Captain James Butler, Sr., caught up a pitchfork and defended himself, until his right hand was cut off. One man, Bartley Bledsoe, was spared as a compensation shown to Henry Etheredge a few months before. All the others were butchered. Mrs. Sarah Smith, sister-in-law of Smallwood Smith, and sister of Captain James Butler, with other women, wives, mothers and sisters of the slain, went the next day with their negro servants, dug graves and buried the dead as decently as possible. Lot, a negro who belonged to Smallwood Smith, told long afterwards that he helped bury three men, and the he saw a Tory strutting about, wearing a coat of his master's that had been cut with swords." (Chapman's History of Edgefield County, 1897, p. 69).

Jacob Smith, Jr., son of Hester (Smallwood) and Jacob Smith, Sr., born 1735, died 1805, served in the Revolution in South Carolina (Stub Indents, Book R-T, p. 298, #661). He first settled at a place, which he called "Mount Willing", but later moved to his plantation "Winehall" which was inherited by his daughter, Sophia Bonham, mother of James Butler Bonham. This place is now owned by Mr. F. P. Matthews of Saluda, South Carolina, whose wife kindly sent the following inscriptions from the graveyard to Mr. H. L. Watson of Greenwood, South Carolina:

"In memory of Jacob Smith, who died in the year 1805, age between 65 and 70, this memorial is erected by his affectionate daughter Sophia Bonham."

"In memory of Mrs. Sarah Smith, relict of Jacob Smith, who died in the year 1817 in the 76th year of her age. She was a kind and benevolent Christian. This memorial is erected by her affectionate daughter Sophia Bonham."

As stated before, Jacob Smith, Jr., married Sarah Butler, sister of James Butler killed at Cloud Creek, and daughter of William Butler of Prince William County, Virginia. Their children were:

I.   Luke Smith, m. Elizabeth Lamar and had a daughter, Sarah, who married Rhyden G. Mays; and a son, Jacob Smith (1799-1853) who married Matilda Youngblood (1807-1849).

II.   Sophia Smith, m. James Bonham (see later).

James Bonham was born near Frederick, Maryland, May 1, 1766, and died in Saluda County, South Carolina, November 27, 1815. He was the son of Absalom Bonham of New Jersey, who moved to Lincoln County, North Carolina, and was resided there in 1790.

James was living in St. Bartholomew Parish, Georgetown County, South Carolina in 1790, but moved and settled on Red Bank Creek, Edgefield County (now Saluda) soon afterwards. His first wife was Mrs. Hannah Whitsell Lewis, a widow, whom he married at St. James, Georgetown County, March 29, 1787. His second wife was Sophia Smith, daughter of Sarah (Butler) and Jacob Smith. Jacob was brother of Smallwood Smith, killed at Cloud Creek.

Children: (of first wife)
I. Ann, b. May 4, 1793, m. James L. Butler.
II John Witsell, b. December 18, 1795, m. Sarah Pou.
Children: (of second wife)
III. Sarah Marcy, b. February 3, 1799, m. John Lipscomb.
IV. Jacob Absalom, b. November 3, 1800.
V. Simeon Smith, B. April 6, 1802, m. _____ Wardlaw.
VI. Malachi Mark, b. November 30, 1804, m. Mary Ford.
VII. James Butler, b. February 20, 1807, killed at the Alamo, March 6, 1836. (See Travis family for an account of his death).
VIII. Elizabeth Jemima, b. August 9, 1809.
IX. Julia Ann Rachael, b. October 9, 1811, m. Dr. S. W. Bowie.
X. Milledge Luke, b. December 25, 1813, m. Ann Patience Griffin (See later).

Milledge Luke Bonham, born December 25, 1813, near Red Bank, South Carolina, died August 27, 1890, was Colonel of the 12th U. S. Infantry, in the Mexican War; Brigadier General C. S. A., 1861, commanded Beauregard's centre at first Bull Run; was Governor of South Carolina 1862-64; married November 13, 1845, Ann Patience Griffin, daughter of Ann (Butler) and Nathan Lipscomb Griffin, b. 1829, died October 11, 1894.

Children:
I. Sallie Butler, b. January 9, 1847, d. May 4, 1862.
II. Richard Griffin, b. May 24, 1849, d. February 15, 1887.
III. Sophie Smith, b. February 13, 1851, m. Robert Aldrich.
IV. James, b. May 24, 1853, d. February 8, 1884.
V. Milledge Lipscomb, b. October 16, 1854, m. Martha Aldrich, sister of Robert. (See later).
VI. Unnamed infant, b. May 27, 1856.
VII. Ann Elizabeth, b. 1857, d. 1921.
VIII. Julia Ellen, b. 1859, m. Dr. George E. T. Sparkman.
IX. Nathan Griffin, b. May 9, 1861, d. July 5, 1864.
X. Mary Rebecca, b. May 25, 1863, d. July 5, 1864.
XI. William Butler, b. May 14, 1866, m. Marie Graves.
XII. Thomas Seymour, b. September 13, 1868.
XIII. Patience Griffin, b. April 10, 1871, m. Gladsden E. Shand, Sr.

> XIV. Francis Pickens, b. March 13, 1873, m. Georgia
>   Watson.

Milledge Lipscomb Bonham, 5th child above, married October 24, 1878, Martha, daughter of Martha (Ayer), and Judge Alfred Proctor Aldrich, born September 28, 1856, died July 13, 1923. On March 2, 1925, Judge Bonham married Lillian Carter of Anderson, South Carolina. Mr. Bonham was elected Judge of the Tenth Judicial Circuit of South Carolina, 1924-1931, and Associate Justice of the Supreme Court, 1931.

Children:

> I. Milledge Louis, b. February 21, 1880, m. December 22, 1904, Odelle Austin Warren, b. June 28, 1879, in Talbot County, Maryland, daughter of Mary, (Price), and the Rev. Patrick Thomas Warren. Dr. Bonham obtained an A. M. Degree at Columbia in 1910, Ph. D, in 1911; was associate-professor, professor and head of Department of History at Louisiana State University, 1912-19; head of Department of History, Hamilton College, Clinton, N. Y., 1919, to present time. He served as a sergeant-major, 1st Batallion, 1st S. C. Infantry, Spanish-American War. (See Who's Who in America). One child, Luke Warren, b. February 25, 1922.
>
> II. Proctor Aldrich, b. August 28, 1883, m. Margaret Rion.
>
> III. Martha Ann, b. August 31, 1889.

Smallwood Smith, son of Hester (Smallwood) and Jacob Smith, married Elizabeth Marable Jones, daughter of Francis Jones, whose will is shown in Edgefield will Bk. A., p. 336.

Smallwood received a grant, July 8, 1774, of "Two hundred acres in Colleton (later Edgefield County now Saluda) on Richland Branch, the waters of the South East side of Saludy River, bounding northeast and northwest on Smallwood Smith, northwest on Jacob Smith, the other sides on vacant land".

As heretofore shown, Smallwood Smith fell in the Cloud Creek Massacre in 1781. His widow married, secondly, Frederic Sisson, who evidently in 1790, was living on Smallwood Smith's old plantation, patented by Smallwood in 1774, on the Red Bank Creek, next to Mumford Perryman, Barrick Travis's son-in-law.

Frederic Sisson died two years later for he left a will dated March 5, 1792, and probated Steptember, 1792. (W. B. A., p. 37). In this will he mentions his wife, Elizabeth and his "two stepsons, Marston and Wiley Smith, and stepdaughter, Mary Smith. Mrs. Elizabeth Smith-Sisson married the third time, Henry Ray, and died in the summer of 1817. Her will was dated July 3, 1817, and was probated September 5, 1817. (W. B. A., p. 388). In her will she mentioned her granddaughter, Talitha Burton, daughter of her daughter, Mary, who had married William Burton.

William Burton lived below Old Ninety Six or Old Cambridge on the Charleston Road, and his house is shown on the map of Edgefield County Drawn by Major William Anderson for Mills' Atlas, which was reproduced in Chapman's History of Edgefield. William Burton died in 1816, as his will was dated May 12, 1815, and was probated May 6, 1816. (W. B. A., p. 387).

He mentions his mother-in-law, Mrs. Elizabeth M. Ray, in his will and several children among whom was his daughter, Talitha Burton. Talitha Burton, daughter of William Burton, and his wife, Mary Smith, and granddaughter of Smallwood Smith, was born August 7, 1807. She was married to Johnson Sale, a son of John Sale, Sr., and Rebecca Johnson Sale, on August 16, 1827. She died August 9, 1836. Johnson Sale was born near Old Cambridge, September 12, 1805, and he died at his home at Phoenix, South Carolina, October 26, 1868, and is buried at Damascus Church near Phoenix. His wife is buried in the Sale family burying ground. He was a planter and merchant at Phoenix.

Children:

I.   Julia Annis Sale, b. August 29, 1829, m. Nathaniel Henderson, April 21, 1846, d. January 27, 1847. No issue.

II. James Smith Sale, b. April 1, 1831, died August 13, 1834.

III. Josephine Rebecca Sale, b. June 25, 1833, at half past eleven o'clock. (See later).

IV. Joseph William Sale, b. June 25, 1833, twin of above; did not live long.

Josephine Rebecca Sale, daughter of Johnson Sale and his wife, Talitha Burton, was born June 25, 1833, at half past eleven o'clock. She was married November 27, 1849, to Doctor Adolphus Kerr Watson. He was born January 10, 1826, and died June 22, 1853, at 4 P. M., is buried at Andrew Chapel near Cokesbury, South Carolina. She died May 30, 1892, and is buried at Damascus Churchyard.

They had children:

I.   Johnson Sale Watson, m. Charlotte Louisa Moseday. (See later).

II. Elihu Legare Watson, b. June 5, 1852, d. July 15, 1852, and is buried at Old Rehoboth Church in Greenwood County, the original site.

III. Talitha Adolphina Watson, b. July 31, 1853, d. September 24, 1853, buried at Andrew Chapel Church, near Cokesbury.

Josephine Rebecca Sale Watson married second, John E. Lake, on January 5, 1858. He was of the Newberry family of that name. He died May 8, 1862, and is buried in the old Sale family burying ground.

Children:

    I.   Joseph Lake.

    II.   Josephine Lake, twin of Joseph, b. February 23, 1859, d. May 4, 1859.

   III.   Elizabeth Lake.

Johnson Sale Watson, son of Josephine Rebecca Sale Watson and Doctor Adolphus Kerr Watson, was born at Phoenix, South Carolina, November 6, 1850, at 7 A. M. He was married to Charlotte Louisa Moseley, daughter of Dr. Charles R. Moseley, of Greenwood, South Carolina, September 10, 1873. Johnson Sale Watson died February 7, 1905. Charlotte Louisa Moseley Watson died November 19, 1921. Both are buried in Greenwood. They had one son, Harry Legare Watson.

Harry Legare Watson, editor and proprietor of "The Index Journal", Greenwood, South Carolina, was born at Phoenix, South Carolina, July 11, 1876. He was married June 27, 1900, to Ella Dargan at Phoenix. She was born September 27, 1877.

Children:

    I.   Lavinia Harris Watson, b. April 26, 1901, d. April 26, 1901.

    II.   Louise Montague Watson, b. January 4, 1903.

   III.   John Dargan Watson, b. May 23, 1905.

   IV.   Elizabeth Sloan Watson, b. February 26, 1908.

    V.   Johnson Sale Watson, b. March 5, 1910, d. January 23, 1912.

   VI.   Rachel Stokes Watson, b. July 12, 1912, d. July 12, 1912.

  VII.   Margaret Josephine Watson, b. January 11, 1916.

 VIII.   Ella Virginia Watson, b. April 2, 1918.

CAPTAIN BUTLER'S COMPANY

Captain Butler's company of volunteers according to pay from Sept. 1, 1781, to March, 1782, including 182 days. (D.A.R. Mag., Jan. 1945)

Sterling Turner	Capt.	70 d.	Abner Corley	70 d.
William Butler	Lt.	70 d.	Amos Richardson	70 d.
William Sisson	2nd Lt.	70 d.	Zacharias Corley	70 d.
John Corley	Lt.		Robert Davis	70 d.
Fredrick Sisson	Qm.	70 d.	Peter Foy	70 d.
Daniel C. Jones			George Mason	70 d.
Thomas Butler			Benjamin Bledsoe	70 d.
James Allen			Joseph Nunn	70 d.
Russell Wilson			Handley Webb	70 d.
Dunn Fort			Daniel Jones	38 d.
Nathaniel Corley		70 d.	Hezechiah Watson	38 d.
Samuel De Loach			Cato	70 d.
Lewia Clark			Harrison	60 d.
Sherod Corley			Harrison	60 d.
Abner Corley			Humphreys	30 d.
Zacheus Corley			Burrows Whittle	60 d.
John Berry			Sherard Corley	20 d.
James Edson			John Smith	38 d.
Joel Paggett			Thomas Davis	30 d.
Josiah Pagget			James Butler, Sr.	70 d.
Josiah Warren			James Butler, Jr.	70 d.
John Wilson			Burdet Eskridge	70 d.
James Troop			Zachariah Davis	70 d.
Zakiriah Watson			Smallwood Smith	70 d.
Richman Watson			Gideon Nicholson	70 d.
William Watson			John Douglas	70 d.
Samuel Williams			Bartlett Bledsoe	70 d.
			Matthew Jones	70 d.

BUTLER

of

Yatton Co., Worcester; Sharnbrooke, Co., Bedford;
Little Burch Hall, Essex; Kent Island, Maryland;
Westmoreland and Stafford Counties, Virginia; and
South Carolina.

This family originated in Worcestershire, England, where it
is found soon after the conquest. It seems to be clearly traceable
from father to son from the time of KING JOHN, (1199-1216) down
to this day.

The arms of this family were "argent on a chief indented
sable three covered cups or". These arms are still extant in
some of the ancient churches in Worcester. (Habington's Survey
of Worcester", see index).

Pedigrees of this family are shown in the Visitations of Worcester (1569, Harl. Vol. 27, p. 30); of Bedfore (Harl. 19); of
Essex (Harl. 13, p. 365). The first two pedigrees extend back to
the time King John and can apparently be verified.

A branch of this family became possessed, through marriage,
of the manor of Barham, Teston Court, Kent, and an account of
this family is given in Hasteds, History of Kent which will be
quoted (Vol. II, p. 291).

Hasted says, "This family is descended from Thomas Pincerna
who lived in the reign of King John, and sealed with a covered cup,
with this inscription, as appears by old deeds of the family, en-
circling the seal, -- 'Sigillum Thomas Pincerna', probably from
his being chief Butler to the Prince. Whence his successors
assumed the name of Butler or Boteler. His descendant was
Robert Le Boteler, called in a Latin deed without a date, Robertus
Pincerna, as is supposed likewise from his office; and he had
issue three sons; Robert, called in Latin deed without a date, 'Le
Boteler', Thomas; and William who was a priest.

"John, son and heir of Robert, lived in time of King Edward I,
and by Anne Hanbury, had John Boteler, his son and heir who was
living in the 5th and 45th years of King Edward III, (1332-1372)
and married Margaret, daughter and heir of Froxmere, by whom
he left issue Nicholas Butteler of Yatton, who by Jane, daughter

and heir of John Butler of Droitwich in the county of Worcester, had William Butler of Yatton, who lived in the time of King Henry IV, and by Margaret, daughter and heir of John Wibbe of Feckingham in co. of Worcester, left issue William Butteler of Droitwich, Esq., who married Elizabeth Bradwell of Worcester and had one son, William and a daughter, Phillippa married to William Newport, which William Butteler, the son, was of Droitwich. "

In a window of the North Isle of the Parish Church of St. Andrews, Droitwich, are the arms of Froxmere "Sable a bend between two arms extended, argent". In the west windows of the same Isle (4th) are the arms of Butler. "Gules, a chevron between three cups covered or", (Nash 1 p. 319).

William married Jane, daughter and heir of Backecott of Co. Worcester, gent., by whom he had George Buttelet, who removed his seat to Sharnbrooke in the Co. of Bedford. He left issue by Mary, his wife, daughter of Richard Throckmorton of Higham-park in Co. of Northampton, three sons, John, his Heir, Peter, and Raphael and two daughters; Catherine, married to Gilbert Martyn of Barford in Bedford, gent., and Margaret who died unmarried in 1566 (see also Vis. of Bedford Harl 19). (26 W (1) p. 123) (Burkes Peerage 1938, p. 2417).

Sharnbrook, to which place the above George Butler removed his seat, is a parish in Bedforshire, nine miles northwest of the town of Bedford. The parish contains a village and a manor of the same name.

Thomas Grey, Marquess of Dorset, died seized of the manor of Sharnbrook in 1530. He was a descendant, through maternal lines, of Albert of Lorraine, who held the manor of the King in Chief in 1086. In 1543 his son Henry Grey alienated tha manor to George Boteler who died in 1551. His estate passed to his son John Boteler, who in 1614 was succeeded by Sir Oliver Boteler, his eldest son and heir. His descendant, Sir William Boteler, was created a Baronet in 1641 (Vic. His. of Bedford, III, p. 88).

In the north chapel of the Church of St. Peters in Sharnbrook is a fine Jacobean mural monument, with the Boteler arms, "three covered cups, " enclosed a brass band set up by Sir William Boteler with a pedigree of the family on it. (Do. 89-94).

As stated above, George Butler married Mary Throckmorten, daughter of Richard Throckmorten of Higham Ferrers, Northampton. Richard was the second son of Sir Robert Throckmorton, K. B., one of the Private Council of Henry VII, who died while on a pilgrimage to the Holy Land. His first son and heir was Sir George Throckmorton, who had a son Clement.

Clement Throckmorton, in 1553 was granted the custody of his first cousin, John Butler of Sharnbrook, by the following order: "Grant to Clement Throgmerton, esq., of the custody of the manor of Templehill in Sharnbrook, Beds., with the issues to the

yearly value of 14 £, 7s, 3½d in the Kings hands by the minority
of John Butler, son and heir of George Butler, decd., who held
of the King in chief, also of the custody and marriage of the heir"
(P. R. Ed. VI, 1553, Vol. 5, p. 1).

Richard Throckmorton, grandfather of the above John Butler,
was Seneschal of the Duchy of Lancaster 10 Henry VIII. He mar-
ried Joan, daughter of Humphrey Beaufo, of Bereford, Warwick.
Their second son was Gabriel Throckmorton, ancestor of the
Virginia family of Throckmorton, and their second daughter was
Mary Throckmorton, who married George Butler of Sharnbrook.
(Burke Peerage 1949, p. 1986).

11. John Butler, or Boetler, of the Parish of Sharnbrook, Bedford, and of Thobie, Essex, son and heir of George Butler, who
died 1551, married (1) Cressett, daughter of Sir John St. John of
Bletsoe, Bedford; (2) Mary, daughter and co-heir of James Gedge
of Essex, surveyor to Queen Mary (Harl. 13-365). John Butler's
will was dated September 1, 1612 and proved at London January
20, 1613. (P. C. C.) The pedigree of St. John of Bletsoe is given
in the visitation of Bedford 1634? (Harl)

Children of first wife
    I.   Oliver Butler of Sharnbrooke, Bedford, married
        Anne, daughter and heir of Thomas Barham of
        Barham-Court county Kent, who carried the manor
        of Barham-Court in Kent to her husband, to which
        place he removed and was knighted by James I at
        Whitehall August 1604. He died in London November
        22, 1632 and is buried at Teston.

        William Boteler, his third son; heir to his brother,
        Sir John Boteler, who died August 2, 1634; resided at
        Barham-Court. He was created a Baronet by Charles
        I, July 3, 1641, and lost his life in the fight between
        the King's forces and those of Parliament, at the Battle
        of Cropedy Bridge, June 29, 1644. (Hasted II, 291)

        His title became extinct on the death of his great
        grandson, Sir Phillip Boteler, 4th Baronet, January
        22, 1772. (Complete Baronetage, Cockayne, Vol. II,
        p. 97)
   II.   John Butler of Littell Burch Hall, Essex. (See Later)

Children of second wife
   III.   Captain Nathaniel Butler, member of the Council for
        the Virginia Company; Governor of Bermuda, 1619-
        22; in Virginia during winter of 1622-23; author of the
        "Unmasking of Virginia," published 1623; Governor
        and Admiral of the Bahamas 1638-41 (Brown Gen. II,
        p. 836).

IV. James
V. Elizabeth m. John Cornelius of London, merchant;
VI. Sarah m. John Jeffrey of Essex. (Harl. 13-365).

12. John Butler of Littell Burch Hall, Parish of Roxwell, Essex, married at Roxwell, December 27, 1599, Jane Elliott, (baptized at Roxwell June 22, 1576), daughter of Joan Gedge and Edward Elliott of Newlands Hall. An account of the Elliott family is given in Morant's Essex (Vol. p. 54). It seems that Edward Elliott married Joan, daughter and co-heir of James Gedge (d. Aug. 22, 1555) These two families were therefore related. Edward Elliott died December 26, 1595. (Harl. 13, pp. 49-191-192). The Elliotts of Westmoreland, Virginia, associates of the Butlers there may be of this family.

Children of Jane and John Butler:
    I.   John, bapt. at Roxwell, Essex, December 7, 1600, came to the Isle of Kent, in Chesapeake Bay, Maryland, with his brother-in-law, Captain William Claiborne, about 1637. While in Maryland, on May 26, 1640, John Boteler made a deposition relative to affairs on Kent Island in which he gave as 39, which agrees with the above date of birth. The deposition was as follows, "Johannes Butler de Insul Kent in provincia de Maryland, gen. estatis 39 Annor, aut eo circeter natus in fra Pochiam de Roxwell in Com, Esseq, gen." Same is signed "John Boteler" (Md. Arch. V., pp. 212-220).
    II.   Thomas Butler, (no. 13) m. Joan Mount Stephen, widow (See later).
    III.   Jane
    IV.   Sarah
    V.   Elizabeth, m. William Claiborne of Virginia (See Claiborne).
    VI.   Cressett
    VII.   Martha
    VIII.   Ursula

13. Thomas Butler (also "Boteler", name spelled in various ways both in England and Maryland) married Joan Mount Stephen, widow. The records of the Draper's Company of London give the following information; "Thomas Butler, Haberdasher, son of John Butler and Jane Elliott, of the Parish of Roxwell, Essex. Jane Elliott, daughter of Edward Elliott. Thomas Butler married 16, January 1625/6 at St. Magnus the Martyr London, Joan Mount Stephen the widow of Nicholas Mount Stephen, citizen of St. Martin Ludgate". (Will P. C. C. 93 Clarke) (56 V -459).

Thomas Butler and his brother, Captain John Butler, are found residing on Kent Island in 1637. There are no records preserved before that time, so they may have arrived much earlier, for the first permanent settlement of white men within the present boundaries of Maryland was made on Kent Island in 1631. William Claiborne, formerly Secretary for the Colony of Virginia, had received a grant of this island from the King when it was considered a part of Virginia. In 1632, the King granted a charter for Maryland to Cecil Calvert, Lord Baltimore, which charter contained within its boundaries the Island of Kent. Baltimore refused to recognize Claiborne's rights. Claiborne tried but could not obtain recognition from the King, so there was nothing left for him to do but fight it out with the Calverts.

Among those settlers who came to the Island and acted as mariners and traders for Claiborne were Captains Thomas Smith and John Butler, (or Boteler), also Thomas Butler, brother of the last named. Claiborne is referred to in the records as a brother-in-law of Captain John Butler. Claiborne married Elizabeth Butler, sister of the two Butler brothers.

Claiborne's chief aids or supporters in his war with Governor Leonard Calvert, brother of Lord Baltimore, were Captains Smith and Butler. He sent them to Palmer Island for the purpose of making a friendly agreement with the Susquehanna Indians. Governor Calvert feared that the result of these negotiations might be that the Susquehannas would join with Claiborne in attacking his colony at St. Mary's. The question came up in Council as to what should be done to prevent Smith and Butler from carrying out such plans, and Hanley, one of the Councillors, thought nothing should be done in view of Lord Baltimore's doubtful title to Kent Island. Butler and Smith, however, had no such plans of invasion. They had been traders with the Susquehannas and the trade had been very lucrative.

In 1637, Claiborne, called back to England, left Smith and Butler in charge of the island. While Claiborne was away Cloberry and Company, wealthy London merchants, of which firm Claiborne was a partner, sent over George Evelin as Commander of the Island. He returned from St. Mary's to the Island and the inhabitants, numbering about 120 men able to bear arms, were assembled. "There the astonished traders and planters listened to Zachary Mottershead, one of Governor Calvert's chief men read aloud the provisions of the Maryland Charter." (Semmes "Captains and Mariners", p. 149).

Later while Evelin was himself addressing the Islanders, Captain John Butler spoke up and asked him "whether he was agent for Cloberry and Company for the Marylanders". Evelin replied he was agent for both. Butler and Captain Thomas Smith, however, were loyal to Claiborne and refused to support Captain Evelin in his cowardly surrender of the Island. Governor Calvert ordered Captain Evelin to arrest Butler and Smith and bring them to St. Mary's to answer for the crimes of sedition and piracy but the warrant could not be served because the Kent Islanders would not permit their arrest. (Md. Archives, Vol. 10, p. 4).

Governor Calvert then decided to use force. Armed with a cutlass and placing himself at the head of twenty musketeers he landed his men on the Island, suprising a fort which had been erected by Claiborne's men and easily capturing Captain Thomas Smith. He then sent an ensign with ten musketeers to Butler's plantation called "The Great Thicket" to arrest him.

On the 14th of March 1638, Captain Thomas Smith was brought before the bar of the Assembly at St. Mary's and there faced by all of his enemies he was ordered to be hanged. Calvert wrote to Lord Baltimore that he had not called "Mr. Butler to trial because I hope by showing favor unto him to make him a good member ... that Butler might be the fitted man to command Kent Island".

Captain Butler, however, refused to accept a commission or appointment under Calvert and died on the Island in 1642, his will being probated on April 1st of that year. He made his brother, Thomas, executor. The will has been lost. (Md. Archives, Vol. 10, p. 128).

Thomas Butler, brother of the redoubtable Captain John had a small plantation and a family but had lived a less exciting life. In March 1637, Thomas Butler, together with Edward Thompson, who later married his widow, signed the election returns in Kent Island, at which time Richard Thompson was elected Burgess. Richard Thompson represented the Island in the first General Assembly of Maryland in 1637, and continued in office until his death. (Proceedings of the Assembly, Vol. 1, p. 31). In 1642, Thomas Butler and Edward Thompson were levied upon to pay the charged of Richard Thompson's election to the House of Burgesses. In September 1642, they are shown in the lists as inhabitants of Kent Island (Proceedings of the Assembly, Vol. 1, pp. 143, 168, 169). Thomas Butler's name is also spelled "Boteler" in the records. In 1640 Thomas Butler of Kent Island demanded 600 acres due him for transporting himself, wife, and two children, and Capt. John Butler payed to have confirmed to him lands he holds by grant of Capt. Wm. Claiborne. (Burns, "Early Settlers of Maryland", p. 21).

About 1644 in Maryland, a period of dissatisfaction with the Government began to manifest itself. Protestants and Dissenters either suddenly became poor or went on tax strikes. A long list of persons on the Island are shown to be tax defaulters. Among them in 1644, was Thomas Butler, from whom Giles Brent, acting on the behalf of the Governor, demanded 600 lbs. of tobacco as taxes, or an attachment would issue. In 1644, Thomas Butler appears on the records as suing Richard Smith for 1000 lbs. of tobacco and John Powell for 500 lbs. (Md. Archives, Vol. 4,

pp. 100, 136/7, 211, 234, 236, 269, 302, 307). Butler was
dead before January 16, 1646-47, for on that day it was alleged
in court that 100 acres of land late in the tenure of Thomas Butler, deceased, was delinquent in rent to the Lord of the Manor,
(the Governor) for the past three years at a yearly rental of two
barrels of corn and two capons. (Md. Archives, Vol. 4, p. 43).

Thomas Butler, Edward Thompson, and Richard Thompson
and many other Protestants who had upheld the claim of Virginia
to the Island of Kent were proclaimed in 1644 enemies of the
Catholic rulers of Maryland. Although Thomas died during these
troublesome times, his family later with many of their neighbors,
"escaped" or removed to Virginia. (Md. Archives, Vol. 5, p. 80;
W & M Quart. XVII, p. 58).

By February 10, 1646, Joan Butler, widow of Thomas Butler,
had married her neighbor, Edward Thompson, for on that date
Leonard Calvert, the Governor, bound himself "to deliver unto
Mrs. Jone Thompson for the use of Thomas Butler, deceased,
his children, two cows, and two calves three months old some
time in June". (Md. Archives, Vol. 5, p. 15). While this record
in itself does not prove a marriage yet sixteen years later in
Westmoreland County, Virginia, the records recite that Edward
Thompson had previously married the widow of Thomas Butler.
(West. Orders, 1, p. 79).

The Thompsons soon moved to what is now Westmoreland
County, Virginia, taking with them the orphans of Thomas Butler.
Westmoreland was then a part of Northumberland, and a suit
concerning these same cows and calves appears in the Northumberland records six years later. On September 20, 1652, Edward
Thompson, sued Mrs. Margaret Brent, representing the Governor of Maryland for failure to deliver these cattle. The order of
the court was as follows:

> "Whereas, it doth appear unto the court by the testimony of
> John Hallowes that there was an order issued against Mrs.
> Margaret Brent for the payment of two cows and two calves
> .... unto the children of Thomas Butler, that the said Mrs.
> Hallowes took out (of Maryland), the Court doth order that
> the said Mrs. Brent shall deliver unto Edward Thompson
> at his now dwelling house for the use of the said children
> the said cows, etc. " (Northumberland Orders 2, p. 5).

On the 20th of September, 1653, an order of satisfaction of
judgement was entered in this case.

Before this order had been entered, John Hallowes, later a
Burgess for Westmoreland, on January 30, 1650, had obtained a
patent for 1600 acres of land on the west side of Curriman Bay
and south side of the Potomac River in Northumberland, now
Westmoreland, "for the transportation of Edward Thompson,
Jone Thompson, Thomas Butler, Christopher Butler, William

Butler, John Butler, John Hallowes", and others. (Cavaliers and Pioneers, Nell M. Nugent, p. 207. See also David W. Eaton's excellent "Historical Atlas of Westmoreland", p. 67). This would seem to prove that the four Butlers were the young orphans who were still waiting for their cows and calves. From ages given later, John Butler was then 13 years old in 1650, and he afterwards calls Christopher "his younger brother".

The Butlers were proud people even in those days for Captain John Butler, uncle of the orphans had refused to accept a patent from the hands of the Governor. This is proven by the testimony of one Roger Baxter, given in the Kent County Court House in 1656, in which he states that he was "50 years of age or thereabouts" and several years ago "that there came upon the Island one Francis Posey and quartered at your deponent's house, wherefore he asked this Posey whether or no he intended to dwell upon the Island. He answered 'no' he was come upon the Island to receive of John Abett 700 lbs. of tobacco and 7 barrels of corn for the use of the then secretary. Further I asked the said Posey for what Abett owed this sum to the secretary. He told me it was for Captain Butler's plantation which Abett had bought. I asked him why the secretary should do this with the plantation being it was given by will to Mr. Thomas Butler. He said it was confiscated to the Lord Proprietor by reason that Captain Butler would have no patent under his Lordship." (Md. Archives LIV, p. 196, John Butler's will is lost.) (Northumberland Book 1, p. 43).

The two brothers, John and Christopher Butler, are often mentioned together in the early records of Westmoreland because they were under age and in the guardianship of their father-in-law, Edward Thompson. On April 15, 1657, Edward Thompson agreed to give John and Christopher Butler "The Long Point Necke", but if they wished to leave it to let their father-in-law have the refusing of it before another. John Butler agreed to build a "twenty foot square house, a tobacco house and if a crop is raised to my younger brother 300 lbs. of tobacco." (Bk. 1, p. 93). John relinquished his bargain with his father-in-law on account of his inability to carry out the contract on December 18, 1657. On June 21, 1658, John Butler deposed in court that he was 21 years of age. Therefore his career can be followed through the records, as his age given heretofore coincides with his age given later.

Children of Joan and Thomas Butler:

14.   I.   Thomas, m. Jane, widow of Captain Alexander Baynham and daughter of James and Dorothy Baldridge. (See later).

II.   John Butler, d. 1684, m. (1) Ellen, widow of Francis Burwell; (2) Martha, before 1643; (3) Sarah, executor of his will, 1684.

III.   William, m. Joanna Ward, relict of John Ward.

IV.   Christopher, m. Margery, moved to Stafford County. As "Christopher Butler of Westmoreland" he was granted 339 acres on the branches of Pope's Creek in Rappahannock County, north side of Rappahannock River, bounded by land of John Payne, William Underwood, and others for the transportation of 7 persons. (Rappahannock Bk. 671-76, p. 304-307). On August 11, 1675, as "Christopher Butler of Stafford" he appoints his loving brother John Butler of Pope's Creek to acknowledge sale of part of this land to John Elliott.

    Christopher served on a jury in Stafford, March 12, 1690, in the case of Brent vs. Darrell. His will was probably among the missing records of that county.

V.   Nathaniel, m. (1) Mary Adgee; (2) Sarah. On April 21, 1684, the will of Nathaniel Butler was probated by Mrs. Sarah Butler, "one of the executors named". She relinquished in favor of Christopher and William Butler who assumed management of the estate during the minority of the executors (Bk. 1675-89, p. 335).

14. Thomas Butler II, probably the oldest son of Thomas I, is mentioned first in the list of the four brothers brought by John Hallowes into Virginia before 1650. He is the ancestor of the South Carolina Butlers. On May 16, 1660, he makes oath that "no land has been taken up by him" and receives a grant of 700 acres for the transportation of 14 persons. (Order Bk. 1660-62, folio 8). March 23, 1664, he patented land "on south side of Appomattock Creek; n. e. upon land of Mr. Thomas and James Baldridge; s. e. upon land of Daniel Kitson n. w. to land sometime in possession of Mr. Johnson and the land of Mr. Alex Bayneham, 175 acres by a former patent and 216 acres for transportation of five persons. "(C. P. p. 432). On April 29, 1670, Thomas Butler, Sr., assigns all this patent of his to John Butler. (Deeds and Patents 1665-77, p. 68). On November 15, 1660, Thomas Butler assigned 60 acres of his patent of May 16, 1660, to James Harris, and also he sold 250 acres of this same grant "lying on the south side of Appomattox called 'Little Browne' next land of James Harris and Richard Browne. " (Order Bk. 1660-62 folio 21; Deeds and Patents 1665-77. p. 65).

    Thomas Butler married Jane, widow· of Captain Alexander Bayneham and daughter of James and Dorothy Baldridge. James Baldridge also came from Maryland where he had been sheriff of St. Mary's County, and a member of the first General Assembly in 1637. (Archives, Vol. 1, pp. 2-10) Dorothy Baldridge in her will made March 11, 1662/63, probated November 2, 1662, names her son-in-law, Thomas Butler, her executor. She also provides that "a bowle and chalice be sent out of England this shippin, and that my executor shall pay two thousand pounds of tobacco and caske for them. I give the said cup or bowle and chalice to the Parish Church of Appomattock, to celebrate the communion forever. It is my will that my name be engraved on the said bowle and chalice". (Deeds and Wills, 1, 11. 188-9). One wonders if this gift ever arrived. Alexander Bayneham was a Burgess for Westmoreland in 1653 and appears last in the records about 1658. Thomas Butler died early in 1678 for his widow, Mrs. Jane Butler, on February 27, 1677/8, was appointed administratrix "cum testam't annexed" of Mr. Thomas Butler's estate. (Orders, 1675-89, p. 105). The record of his will has been destroyed, but two of his children are known. They are Joshua Butler who was mentioned in 1662, as a grandson in the will of his grandmother Mrs. Dorothy Baldridge. The other son was Thomas Butler, Jr., who had reached his maturity before Thomas Butler, who signed as "Senior" during his later years, had passed away. Jane Butler married a third husband, John Berryman who died before April 28, 1680, for on that day the court entered a judgment in favor of "Mrs. Jane Berryman, relict of Mr. John Berryman, decd. who intermarried with the relict of Thomas Butler, decd. for 13,258 lbs. of tobacco out of the said Butler's estate". (Orders 1675-89, p. 183). Her fourth husband was Joseph Harvery whom she married before October 26, 1681. (Orders 1675-89, p. 231).

Known children:

I. Joshua, son of Thomas II, and grandson of Thomas I, moved out of the county. He bought land in Stafford County on Aquia Creek from William Chaplin, October 4, 1706. (W. B. 1699-1709, p. 305). He died in King George County about 1725. Joshua Butler had a son Joshua as evidenced by the following records: "July 28, 1735; Joshua Butler and Grace Ripley, planters, of Hamilton Parish, Prince William County, convey to Thomas Turner of Hanover Parish, King George County, surgeon, 283 acres of land which was granted to Joshua Butler, father of said Joshua Butler in 1715 and adjoined Charles Emmont and Russell. (Deed Bk. 4, p. 497).

15. II. Thomas, III. (See later).

III. John, who was assigned land in 1670, may be another child.

15. Thomas Butler, III, son of Thomas II, first appears in the

records in 1673 when he leased from Francis Gray 125 acres of land in Washington Parish being half of 250 acres, the other half being sold to Meridith Price. (Deeds and Pat. 1665-77, p. 159). On April 4, he bought 200 acres from Henry Orkell, cooper, of Stafford County, for 5000 lbs. tobacco; and on 27th of April, 1707, Nathaniel Gray of Washington Parish, for 1800 lbs. tobacco paid by Thomas Butler, sells to Thomas, James and Elizabeth Butler, sons and daughters of Thomas Butler, 125 acres "formerly leased to the said Thomas Butler by Francis Gray, father of Nathaniel, whereon said Thomas Butler is now seated". (Deed Bk. 2, p. 80; Deeds 4, p. 153). On May 26, 1703, he bought land in Sittenbourne Parish, Richmond County, and on May 25, 1704, land from Meridith Edwards and wife, Anne.

Thomas Butler made his will May 2, 1714, (W.B. 5, p. 317) as follows: "to my son William Butler 100 acres where he now lives; to my son James Butler that tract of land where I now live unto my son James during his life and then to my daughter Elizabeth Baker. I give to grandson Thomas Butler son of John Butler 200 acres of land being part of a tract where Stephen _____ now lives, the other where Katharine Butler now lives. I give to John Butler and James Butler, sons of John Butler 200 acres to be divided between them in case they die to Anne Baker, daughter of Elizabeth Baker; to my daughter Elizabeth Butler all of her mother's wearing apparel, etc.; to grandson Thomas Butler young mare etc., the residue divided between James Butler and my daughter Elizabeth Butler".

Children:

I.   John, m. Katharine Price. He predeceased his father, his will being probated January 28, 1712, as follows: "To George Purvis one heifer, ... to William Butler of 'Cutler' one sow; to Richard Cogins 100 lbs. tobacco due me, residue to be divided between wife Katharine and children. My brother William Butler to be co-executor with wife. If wife cannot keep the children, brother William Butler to have my oldest son Thomas Butler; brother James to have my son John Butler, and John Baker to have son James Butler." (W.B. 5, p. 12).

    Meridith Price, grandfather of the above children, made his will 14 April 1708 and mentions his daughter Katharine and son-in-law John Butler. Katharine, wife of John Butler, deceased, made her will dated November, 1730, probated April 26, 1743; mentions sons James, John and Thomas, "cozens" Sarah Anderson and Thomas Price and two brothers William and James Butler. (W.B. 9, p. 305). This will was presented in court by James Butler, Jr., and objected to by Thomas Butler, the elder, who entered a cavet; James Butler, Sr., was named executor and Thomas Butler then withdrew his objections. John and Katharine Price Butler had issue:

1. Thomas, on May 2, 1734, of Washington Parish, sold to John Wright, Jr., 150 acres west side of John Weedon's run, part of a patent to Anthony Beard, dec. who sold same to Thomas Butler, the elder, 28 September 1688, who by will bequeathed same to his grandson Thomas Butler.

2. James, made his will 27, January 1749; left land on "Irish Necke" to wife Ann and then to son Thomas, mentions also son James, daughter Mary, other married daughters and grandchildren. (W. B. 11, p. 429). James Butler, Jr., August 2, 1736, sold to John Popham 100 acres where he now lives, north side of land of large branch which divided the line of Thomas and John Butler, etc. (B 8, P, 412).

3. William, son of John Butler and Katharine Price, made his will April 26, 1720, probated September 29, 1731, mentions son Price; other sons under 18 not mentioned by name, cozens James and Thomas Butler, daughters Elizabeth and Mary.

4. John, willed 100 acres by grandfather Thomas.

II. William IV, son of Thomas III, son of Thomas II, son of Thomas I, was executor of his brother John's will in 1712. He is also mentioned in the will of his sister-in law, Katharine Price Butler in 1730. He evidently moved out of the county.

16. III. James, m. Katherine _____. (See later).

IV. Elizabeth, deeded land by Nathanial Grey in 1707.

V. Thomas, deeded land by Nathanial Grey in 1707.

16. James Butler IV, son of Thomas III, son of Thomas II, son of Thomas I, is mentioned in the will of his sister-in-law, Katharine Price Butler in 1730, but there are no subsequent wills or inventories in Westmoreland which seem to identify him as then living or continuing to live in that county. It appears that he moved to Stafford about the time of the death of his father Thomas Butler in 1714. For on September 5, 1714, he was granted 800 acres in that county on the Long Branch of Acquia Run near the path to Brent Town (Northern Neck Grant Bk. 5, p. 208). It is important to remember the name "Acquia" for it identifies him and the connection of his family with William Mason and the Mason family. On the 31 of January 1727/8 he also patented 150 acres in Stafford in Overwharton Parish. He married Katharine,

last name unknown, and made his will the 24th of April 1732 as
James Butler of Acquia in the County of Stafford, "after payment
of debts the residue shall be reckoned in three equal parts; one
third equal part thereof I bequeath unto Katharine my beloved
wife, the other two parts to be equally divided among my three
sons, James, William and Thomas Butler. To my beloved wife
Katharine Butler all the tract of land lying on Acquia which is
now my dwelling plantation containing 202 acres more or less,
during her natural life, and after demise to my beloved son
James Butler. To my beloved son William Butler all that land
by me escheated containing 150 acres. To my beloved son
Thomas Butler all that parcel of land lying on the long branch of
the Acquia laid out for 400 acres; three sons executors." Teste
Benjamin Brent, William Wright, Daniel Connell. Probated
June 14, 1732. (Book m. 1729-1748).

The above patents and will show that all the lands patented and
willed by James Butler were on Acquia Creek. This should distinguish him from another James Butler who owned land on Potomac Run, next to William Downing. James Butler and wife
Katharine had issue:

    I.   James, m. Sarah. The St. Paul's Parish Register
           shows they had the following children baptized on the
           following dates:
           1.   Katharine, August 27, 1737.
           2.   Margaret, December 27, 1739.
           3.   John, December 27, 1740.
           4.   Sarah, January 17, 1742.
           5.   Thomas, August 30, 1747.
17. II.   William, m. Mary Mason. (See later).
     III.   Thomas, m. Mary Mason (Overwharton Register).
           His will was probated 1743; he left everything to his
           wife Mary.

17. William Butler, son of James Butler and wife Katharine of
Acquia, married Mary Mason, whose brother William Mason
made his will in Stafford, March 30, 1733. William Mason's will
was probated June 13, 1733, as follows: "To wife Mary 273 acres
for life, then to my daughter Margaret Mason; also land where I
now dwell 100 acres for life then to my daughter Margaret; to
daughter Margaret Mason 100 acres at Broad Run of Occoquan
where James Goggans lives. To my youngest daughter not yet
baptized (unnamed) 100 acres on Broad Run of Occoquan where
Richard Nelson lives, also 100 acres on north side of Broad Run.
If my daughter unbaptized die without issue then to my nephew
William Mason, son of my brother George Mason. Wife Mary,
executrix, and my well beloved friend William Butler, executor. "

The phrase, "well beloved friend" was then generally used to
designate relatives. (See will of Raleigh Travis in Hayden, pp.

300-301) in which Raleigh call his sister and nephew his "beloved friends". Many other examples can be given. This will connects with the South Carolina family whose records show that William Butler married Mary Mason.

William Mason seems to have been the son of Captain George Mason "Acquia" whose will was dated Oct., 18, 1710; recorded Mar. 11, 1711. He mentions wife, Margaret, and children, GEORGE, WILLIAM, Lyman, MARY, and Anne. (Rowland, "Life of George Mason", I-376). Capt. George Mason of "Acquia" was probably the son of Capt. William Mason who left a "last will and testament" about 1693 which has been lost. (45 V-174). The last named William Mason could have been a son of Col. George Mason I. Justice, Sheriff and Burgess of Stafford whose will or administration records are also lost.

William Butler's land fell in Prince William County which was cut off from Stafford about 1732. He was a justice of the County Court of Prince William November 4, 1742. (Minutes of the Council, p. 214). In June 1745, William Butler, Moses Linton, and others were members of the Vestry of Dettinger Parish. On June 8, 1747, he was elected Senior Church Warden and seems to have remained in that office until his death. (Dettinger Parish Vestry Book, 1745-1802, pp. 1, 2, 19, 147). In 1748 he bought 150 acres on Little River from Henry Caley. On 5th of August 1748, he sold to Joseph Butler of Washington Parish, Westmoreland County, 122 acres in Dettinger Parish (D. B. L., p. 72). Joseph Butler moved from Westmoreland to make his home on this land.

William Butler died in 1753 for at court June 25, 1753, "Mary Butler exhibited on oath an account of the estate of William Butler, deceased, which is admitted of record". (Minute Book, 1752-3, p. 161, the earliest remaining in the county.)

Known Children:

18.   I.   James, m. Mary Simpson, settled in South Carolina, was murdered in 1781 at the Cloud Creek Massacre by Bloody Bill Cunningham and his Tories. (See later 18).

       II.   Sarah, m. Jacob Smith, Jr., moved to South Carolina. (See Stone-Smallwood-Smith family).

      III.   Mary, m. Enoch Grigsby moved to South Carolina. (See Grigsby.)

      IV.   Elizabeth, m. Nathaniel Grigsby, who moved to South Carolina and died 1801. They had William Butler Grigsby born 1760, who married Jane King. (Family incomplete).

18. James Butler, son of Mary (Mason) and William Butler, born in Prince William County, Virginia about 1738, removed to Edgefield County, South Carolina about 1770 together with his three

sisters and other relatives. (See Stone-Smallwood-Smith family).

He settled near the Little Saluda River and together with his son, James, fell in the Cloud Creek Massacre November 7, 1781, as related in the account of the Stone-Smallwood-Smith family.

Children:

I. William b. 17th December 1759, d. 1821, m. Behetheland Foote Moore, b. in Virginia 28 December 1764, brother of William Moore who made his will in Edgefield 1814.

William Butler was a Lieutenant and Captain during the Revolution. (Book U. W. p. 35, No. 219); member of Congress and a Major General in charge of the Charleston District in the War of 1812. He was the father of Andrew Pickens Butler (1796-1857), Governor of South Carolina, 1836, and Colonel of the Palmetto Regiment in the Mexican War, killed while leading his regiment at the Battle of Churubusco. A grandson was Matthew C. Butler, (1836-1909) affectionately called "Peg Leg", Brigadier General C. S. A. at 27, who lost a leg at Brandy Station and was U. S. Senator, 1876-1894. (For this family see S. C. Gen. Register, Vol. 4, p. 297).

II. James, b. March 1761, killed at Cloud Creek.

III. Thomas, b. November 1763, m. Elizabeth Grigsby, his first cousin.

19. IV. Nancy, b. September 27, 1765, m. Elisha Brooks. (See later #19).

V. Elizabeth, b. December 17, 1766, m. Zachariah Smith Brooks. Lieutenant in the Revolution.

VI. Stanmore, m. Anne Patience Youngblood, had a daughter, Ann P. Butler, who married Nathan Lipscomb Griffin and had, among other children, Anne Patience Griffin who married Governor Milledge L. Bonham of South Carolina.

VII. Simpson, b. February 6, 1769.

VIII. Mason.

19. Nancy Butler born September 27, 1765, married Elisha Brooks who received 34/15/5 1/2 pay as a soldier in the Revolution (Stub Indents, Vol. U. W. p. 247). Their children were: Wesley; Matilda R.; Edna; Elizabeth; and Lavinia Brooks.

Lavinia Brooks, born August 1795, married November 4, 1812, Richard Watson, born July 22, 1787, died November 20, 1824.

Richard Watson was the son of William Watson, born January 6, 1755, died March 10, 1837, married January 1, 1784, Lucy, daughter of Ann (Clarke) and Richard Griffin, b. January 8, 1765. William Watson was the son of Margaret and Edward Watson, who emigrated from Virginia in 1771 and settled in the Mt. Moriah district in what is now Greenwood County. William Watson received 122/5/8 1/2 as pay as Commissary in General Williamson's Brigade in the Revolution (Stub Indents U-W).

After Richard Watson's death in 1824 his widow married a distinguished physician and naturalist, Dr. John Perkins Barrett, a native of England, and had two children, John Gould Barrett and Ann Barrett.

Children of Lavinia and Richard Watson:

20.   I.   Sarah Ann Mays Watson, b. September 1, 1813, m. (1) Dr. Samuel Perryman (See Perryman); (2) Captain Henry Hunter Creswell (For Creswell see later #20.).

      II.   Mary Elizabeth Watson, b. August 27, 1815, d. December 1, 1835, m. Colonel Zebulon Rudoulph, father of John Barratt Rudolph, one of the founders of the S. A. E. fraternity at the University of Alabama.

     III. William Watson

     IV. Richard Watson

     V.   Edward Watson

20. Sarah Ann Mays Watson, born September 1, 1813, married first, Dr. Samuel Perryman (See Perryman), secondly, October 7, 1840, Captain Henry Hunter Creswell. He bought "Scotch Cross" from the Perryman heirs and lived there until his death March 23, 1896. Mrs. Creswell died September 16, 1879.

Creswell children: (For Perryman children see Perryman).

     I.   Perryman Creswell, b. July 16, 1841, d. September 20, 1861, from typhoid fever while in Confederate Army.

     II.   Sarah Elizabeth Creswell, b. February 19, 1843, d. September 5, 1847.

     III. Mary Watts Creswell, b. June 4, 1845, m. January 12, 1869, Captain William Drayton Evins of Laurens, S. C. They moved to Evinston, Florida, where they both died. Three sons died without children. Two daughters: Anna Chapman Evins married Hal D. Wood and had seven children; Sarah August Evins born October 1875, died March 1944. Twice married, first to James Means of McIntosh, Florida. One son, James Means, Jr. Second husband was Mack Bateman.

     IV. Edward Watson Creswell, b. May 16, 1847, m. December 20, 1876, widow Amanda Hollister. No children, died 1926.

     V.   Montisco Creswell, b. August 5, 1849, d. 1850.

21. VI. Zemula Estelle Creswell, b. September 4, 1851, m. November 5, 1873, d. August 2, 1929. (See later #21)

VII.   Laura Creswell, b. December 24, 1854, d. August 31, 1855.

VIII.   Henry Garlington Creswell, b. June 12, 1856, m. November 1875, Emma Spriggs, d. 1937, left one son, William Elihu Creswell.

22.   Zemula Estelle Creswell and Robert Franklin Fleming were married at Scotch Cross November 5, 1873. Robert Franklin Fleming was born in Laurens, S. C., October 11, 1840, and died at Scotch Cross March 20, 1921. He was first Lieutenant, Company A, 3rd S. C. Regiment, Confederate States Army, and was wounded at Fredricksburg, Virginia, December 1861. He was educated at Laurens, S. C., and the University of S. C. Both he and his wife are buried at the family graveyard at Scotch Cross, four miles south of Greenwood. She was educated at St. Marys, Raleigh, N. C. They had three children:

23.   I.   Robert Franklin Fleming, Jr., b. August 16, 1874.

24.   II.   Henry Creswell Fleming, b. September 10, 1875.

       III.   Louise Catherine Fleming, b. July 27, 1877, at present she is County Home Demonstration Agent in Laurens.

23. Robert Franklin Fleming, Jr., married November 5, 1913, in Lancaster, S. C., Florence Phifer Brown, daughter of Ella Crawford and William Macdonald Brown. They live in Laurens, S. C. Robert Franklin Fleming, Jr., and Henry Creswell Fleming have had a jewelry store in Laurens since October 1901 to the present date 1945.

The children of Robert Franklin Fleming, Jr., and Florence are Robert Franklin Fleming, 3rd, born August 1, 1914. Educated at Laurens, Presbyterian College, Clinton, S. C., Cornell University, N. E. He was a chemist in the Corning Glass Works, Corning, N. Y., when he entered the U. S. Army, August 1942. He was first Lieutenant, Co. E., 542 Reg. Amphibian Engineer. He saw service in the Pacific Area.

Eleanor Crawford Fleming was born December 24, 1920. She was first honor graduate of Presbyterian College. She was Pvt. Eleanor C. Fleming, Co. B., S. M. D. E. T. (C. A. C.), Fitzsimmons General Hospital, Denver, Colorado.

Macdonald Brown Fleming, born June 8, 1923, was a member of the Junior Class of Presbyterian College when he entered service in World War II, June 1943, Naval Air Corp. Service was in the Pacific.

24. Henry Creswell Fleming, son of Estelle (Creswell) and Robert Franklin Fleming, married June 30, 1915, Laura Aylette Barksdale, Laurens, S. C. She was the daughter of Douglas C. Barksdale and his wife Laura Aylette Fair. They have two children:

      I.   Laura Aylette Fleming, b. November 5, 1917. She

was also a first honor graduate of Presbyterian College and received degree at Chapel Hill, North Carolina and is now Assistant Librarian at Wake Forest College, North Carolina.

II. Henry Creswell Fleming, Jr., b. October 4, 1919. Creswell, Jr., also finished at Presbyterian College, entered service in March 1942, second Lieutenant in the infantry and while training at Ft. Benning was promoted to First Lieutenant and while at Camp Carson, Colorado, was promoted Captain. While at Camp Carson he met Marjorie Nixon Bell from Colorado Springs, Colorado, and they were married, November 2, 1944. Marjorie Nixon Fleming was born at Columbus, Georgia. In Laurens, South Carolina, November 2, 1945, Henry Creswell Fleming III was born. The last information from Captain Creswell Fleming, Jr., is that he was at a port of embarkation. His wife and two children were in Colorado Springs, Colorado.

CLAIBORNE

of

England and Virginia

The arms of this family which appear on the seal of the
William Claiborne, Secretary for the Colony of Virginia and
founder of the Virginia family, is the same as that of the family
of Cliburne of Westmoreland, England, "Ar, three chevrons en-
terlaced in a base sa, a chief of the last" (Burke Gen. Armory;
56 V. 433).

The English connection of their family was long in doubt but
same was finally established by Dr. Clayton Torrence, Director
and Corresponding Secretary, of the Virginia Historical Society.
His interesting and exhaustive search is described in the Virginia
Historical Society Magazine (Vol. 56, pp. 328-343; 431-460).

Thomas Cleyborne, the elder, of the Parish of St. Margaret,
Borough of King's Lynn, Norfolk, merchant, was the grandfather
of Secretary William Claiborne. Thomas was admitted free of
King's Lynn in 1552/53. He was Mayor of the Borough of King's
Lynn in 1573; Justice of the Peace, 1574; Alderman, 1587. His
will was dated December 1, 1581, probated May 21, 1582. He
desired to be buried "in the parish church of St. Margarets' in
Kings Lynn near the Sepelture of my late wife". After many bequests to the church and charity he bequeather to "Dorothie Clayborn my daughter L. 300, of which L. 150 shall be paid to her on
marriage and the other L. 150 within one year immediately following, to her one of my best silver bowls; to Kathrine Clayborne
my daughter (the same); to my said daughters for their maintence
until their marriages L. 20 apiece yearly payable quarterly; to my
brother, George Revelye, clerk, I forgive him his debts to me;
to Johan, wife of William Lawrence, L. 10 equally divided amongst
them; to Anne Baxter, my daughter-in-law L. 50 which I have of
hers in my custody. I also give her L. 30 which I promised her
to be paid at day of marriage. To Michael Revett, notary public
the writer hereof 40/. The residue of my goods and chattels,
shipping adventures abroad I give my son and Thomas Clayborne
whom I make executor." Wits. Thomas Clayborn, Jr; Michal
Revett, notary (P. C. C. 24 Tirewhite) (For further evidence as
to identity of persons mentioned in will see discussion 56 V. 447).

Children:
I.   Thomas. (See later).
II.   Dorothy
III. Kathrine, probably the Kathery Claiborne who married June 15, 1587, William Lestrange.
IV. Johan, bapt. June 24, 1560; buried Sept. 29, 1575.

Thomas Cleyborne (c. 1557-1607) was executor of his father's will. He was admitted free of the Borough of Kings Lynn in 1578-9, his franchise being secured by birth. He was an Alderman in 1591 and Mayor of the Borough in 1592. He married on November 21, 1598, Sara James (nee Smyth), the widow of Roger James, of Bednal Green, Parish of Stebunheath, County Middlesex, citizen and brewer of London, who had died December 10, 1596. Soon thereafter Thomas moved to the Parish of Stepney, Middlesex, and then to the Parish of Crayford, Kent, where he died in 1607.

Children:
I.   Thomas, bapt. St. Dunstan, Stepney, Middlesex, July 1599, died 1633. Known children:
    1. Jane, bapt. 24 Aug. 1627 at St. Martins within Ludgate.
    2. Thomas, Bapt. 7 Jan. 1628/9 at St. Martins within Ludgate.
    3. George, Bapt. 12 Jan. 1629/30 at St. Martins within Ludgate, buried 11 Feb. following.
II.   William, bapt. in Parish of Crayford, Kent 10, Aug. 1600. (See later).
III. Sara, bapt. in Parish of Crayford, Kent 7, Mar. 1601/02.
IV. Katharine, bapt. in Parish of Crayford, Kent, 30 Mar. 1603.
V.   Blanche, bapt. in Parish of Crayford, Kent, 5 Sept. 1605, administered on estate of her mother, Sara, in June 1626.

William Claiborne, was baptized, as above shown in the Parish of Crayford, Kent, 10 August 1600. He was well educated for he entered Pembroke College, Cambridge, "Pensioner, age 16, May 31, 1617, son of Thomas of Crayford Kent. Matriculated 1617. (A. C. 1-350). In his twenty-first year he was appointed surveyor for the Virginia colony in June 1621 and arrived at Jamestown in October of that year. In March 1625-26 he was appointed Secretary of State for Virginia which office he held until 1637, and again from 1652 to 1660. This last period was during the time of the Commonwealth of the Cromwells.

Captain Claiborne returned to England about 1630 and became associated with Cloberry and Company, a firm of London merchants. While in England he obtained license to trade in furs from the Secretary of State for Scotland. This license, dated May 16, 1631, granted him the privilege to trade anywhere in America where there was not already a patent granted to others for sole trade. He then returned to Virginia and established a trading post at Kent Island in Chesapeake Bay, August 1631. He also purchased the Island from the Indians and sent a representative to the Virginia House of Burgesses.

Kent Island proved to be within the limits of a grant given the following year by Charles II to George Calvert, Lord Baltimore. When the Maryland colony arrived, Claiborne refused to recognize the overlordship of the Calverts to Kent Island and decided to cast his lot with Virginia. Petty warfare was conducted by both sides each of whom petitioned the King for recognition of their rights. Claiborne went to England in 1637 to present his cause and during his absence the Calverts attacked the Island and captured Captain John Butler, Claiborne's brother-in-law, who was in charge. In March 1637-38, the Maryland Assembly passed an act of attainder against Claiborne. In 1638 the Commissioners of Plantations, in England, decided the case wholly in favor of Lord Baltimore.

In October 1644, claiming authority from the Parliament of England, Claiborne invaded Maryland, drove out Governor Calvert and held the province until December 1646. Claiborne probably had influence in Parliament for in September 1651 he and Richard Bennett were appointed members of a Commission for the purpose of reducing Virginia and Maryland to obedience. These two colonies peacefully submitted. (17th Cent. pp. 61-65).

As "Colonel William Clayborne" he patented "5000 acres September 1, 1653, lying on north side Pamunkey River in the Narrowes, running * * * to a point of land where the said Colonel Clayborne landed the army under his command in 1644, * *) for the transportation of 100 persons." (C. P. 244).

Claiborne married Elizabeth, sister of John and Thomas Butler of Kent Island. The last named was the ancestor of the Butlers of Westmoreland county, Virginia. (See Butler).

Colonel Claiborne patented much land during his long career in the service of Virginia. He died about 1677. A painting of him hangs in the State Capitol at Richmond.

Children:

I. William, d. 1682, m. Elizabeth Wilks.

2. II. Thomas, b. August 17, 1647, d. October 7, 1683. (See later).

III. Jane, m. Thomas Brereton. On 10 February 1657, "Mistress Jane Claiborne, spinster", patented 1450 acres in Northumberland County, 750 of which had been granted to her father Colonel Claiborne (C. P.

359). Later, Thomas Brereton, as her husband, confirmed this grant to William Weldy. (C. P. 531).

IV. Leonard of Jamaica, died there 1694.

V. John of New Kent.

2. Lt. Col. Thomas Claiborne of "Ramancoke", King William County, was born August 17, 1647, and died October 7, 1683. He married Sarah Fenn. On October 20, 1665, he patented 500 acres in New Kent County (C. P. 541) and 1500 acres in same county in 1677. He was killed by an arrow while leading an expedition against the Indians in 1683. He had one son, Thomas (see later #3).

3. Captain Thomas Claiborne, born December 16, 1680, died August 16, 1732, built the mansion, "Sweethall", in King William County, long known as the home of the Claibornes. He married Anne, born May 20, 1684, died May 4, 1733, daughter of Henry Fox and Anne West, daughter of Colonel John West.

Henry Fox was son and heir of John Fox who settled in Glouster County. Henry patented lands in that county in the portion that was afterwards King & Queen. In 1693 he was a member of the Vestry of St. John Parish, K. & Q., and in 1699 he was a justice of that County. He represented King William in the House of Burgesses and died in 1714 while a member of the House. He had two sons, John and Thomas Fox, named in Council records and probably another Henry who was Sheriff of King William 1724-25. (B. J. M. C. G. C. 20 W (I) 263).

Colonel John West was a son of Captain John West, Governor of Virginia, 1635-37, who was a brother of Thomas West, 12th Lord Delaware, Governor of Virginia, 1610-18, who died enroute to Virginia in 1618. Capt. West was born Dec. 14, 1590, and died at his residence at West Point, (named for him) about 1660. He was a member of the Virginia Company in 1609, Burgess from York 1629-30, Justice 1634 and member of the Council from 1631 until his death.

Col. John West was born in 1632, being the first white child born on York River. He married Unity, daughter of Joseph Croshaw, Burgess for York who died in 1667 and mentioned his daughter Unity in his will.

The children of Col. John and Unity West were: Anne, who married Henry Fox; (2) Unity, m. Capt. Wm. Dandrige; (3) Thomas; (4) John; (5) Nathaniel. (Hening 6-321) (GT 116).

"The Descendants of Henry Fox and Anne West, his wife" have presented a chart to the Virginia Historical Society, showing Anne West's descent from 13 Magna Carta Barons. (See Lord Delaware chart attached and connecting Key chart under Norwood family).

Children of Captain Thomas and Anne (West) Claiborne:
- I. Thomas, b. January 9, 1704, d. December 1, 1735, dsp.
- II. William.
- III. Leonard, m. Martha, 1701-1720, daughter of Major Francis Burnell.
- IV. Nathaniel, 1716-1757, m. Jane, daughter of William Cole.
- 4. V. Augustine, 1720-1787, m. Mary Herbert (See later).
- VI. Daniel, d. 1790, m. Molly Maury
- VII. Bernard, m. Mrs. Poythess (Georgiana Ravenscroft).
- VIII. James, will in Amelia, probated June 26, 1755, dsp.
- IX. Thomas, will in Stafford, probated Jan. 13, 1735/36.
- X. Sarah (1713-1777) m. Joseph Thompson and moved to Albermarle County. Joseph was a Justice there in 1744-45; High Sheriff, 1745-46; Captain of Militia, June 27, 1745. His will was dated Oct. 23, 1763, probated April, 1765. He names wife Sarah; sons Roger, George, Leonard, and John Thompson; granddaughter, Sarah Claiborne Woodson. Executors, wife Sarah, brother George Thompson and sons Roger and George; Witnesses, Patrick Napier, William and Mary Paine. (U. B. 2, p. 177).
- XI. Martha, m. Patrick Napier, who made his will in Albermarle, Jan. 1773, probated, Mar. 1775. He names wife Martha; sons, Thomas, Richard, Patrick, Rene and Joseph Fox Claiborne Napier; daughters Mary Perrin Napier, Elizabeth Claiborne Napier, Ann Fox Napier; brother Rene Napier. (W. B. 2, p. 323) (58V. 238.).

4. Colonel Augustine Claiborne was born at "Sweethall", King William County, 1721, and died at "Windsor", Sussex, May 3, 1787. He married Mary HERBERT, daughter of Buller Herbert of Prince George County and his wife Mary Stith. Mary Stith was a daughter of Drury Stith of Charles City county (died 1741) who married Susanna, daughter of Launcelot Bathurst and granddaughter of Sir Edward Bathurst, Bart.

Soon after Colonel Claiborne married Mary Herbert, he built "Windsor", then in Surry county, but later fell in Sussex. Colonel Claiborne was a Burgess from Surry County 1748-54 and the first clerk of Sussex County when it was formed in 1754. He served as Clerk for twenty-two years, until 1776, when he became a Colonel of Virginia troops. He was also a member of the Committee of Safety for Sussex in 1775.

Children: (A. P. R.)
- I. Mary, b. Jan. 19, 1744.
- 5. II. Herbert, b. April 7, 1746.
- III. Thomas, ?

IV.   Augustine, b. February 2, 1747, d. 1796, m. Martha Jones.

V.   Anne, b. December 30, 1749, m. Richard COCKE.

VI.   William, b. November 3, 1753, m. Mary Leigh. They were the parents of William Charles Coles Claiborne, born in Sussex, 1775, died Nov. 23, 1817, Governor of Louisiana; and also of Nathaniel Herbert Claiborne.

6.   VII.   Susanna, b. November 29, 1751, m. Frederick Jones.

7.   VIII.   Buller, b. October 27, 1745, m. Patsy Ruffin.

IX.   Richard, b. 1757, d. 1818, m. daughter of Phillip Jones.

X.   Lucy (Herbert), b. August 22, 1760, m. Colonel John COCKE.

XI.   Elizabeth, b. 1761, m. Thomas Peterson.

XII.   John Herbert, b. May 30, 1763, m. Mary Gregory. He was a member of the Sussex volunteers in the Revolution at seventeen. (See D.A.R. Vol. 36, p. 14). His son the Reverend John Gregory Claiborne, m. Mary Elizabeth Weldon, his son John Herbert Claiborne, m. Sarah Joseph Alston; their daughter Sarah Alston Claiborne, m. William Baird McIlwaine.

XIII.   Sarah, m. Charles Anderson.

XIV.   Ferdinand, b. March 9, 1772.

XV.   Bathurst, b. April 6, 1774, m. (1) Miss Batts, (2) Mary Leigh Claiborne.

William Claiborne (1753-1809) a son of Col. Augustine Claiborne of Sussex, was born in Sussex Co., Nov. 3, 1753. He served as a private in the Sussex Militia, and was the father of several distinguished sons. His wife was Mary Leigh, daughter of John and Mary Leigh of Sussex. She was baptised Mar. 6, 1739. (APR).

Four of the sons of Mary (Leigh) and William Claiborne are shown in the A.P.R. as follows:

I.   Fernando, (Ferdinand) bapt. Mar. 9, 1772. Sponsors: Thomas West, John Ruffin, Jr., Mary Claiborne. Gen. Ferdinand Leigh Claiborne married a daughter of Col. Anthony Hutchens, a retired British officer who had settled on a large royal grant in what was West Florida. (D.A.B.) Their eldest son was John Francis Hamtrack Claiborne, born near Natchez, Miss., April 24, 1807, d. May 17, 1884, who was elected to Congress, 1835-39 from Miss. He was a voluminous writer on the history of his native state, and contributed largely to current magazines. His only son, Wilber Herbert fell in the war 1861-65.

II.   William Cole, bapt. Aug. 13, 1773. Sponsors: Fernando Leigh, Thomas Moore, Elizabeth West. He was educated at William and Mary. He moved to Sullivan Co., Tenn., where he became Judge of the Supreme Court, was elected to Congress in 1797 and re-elected in 1799. His vote as a member from Tenn. helped decide the presidential contest in favor of Jefferson over Aaron Burr. In 1801, President Jefferson appointed him Governor of Mississippi Territory and in 1803 he was appointed Governor of Louisiana; and when Louisiana was admitted as a state in 1812 he was elected by the people the first Governor. He was elected to the U.S. Senate, in 1816, but died before he could take his seat. (D. A. B.)

III. Nathaniel, bapt., Feb. 1, 1775. Sponsors: John Holmes, Butler Claiborne, Elizabeth Claiborne. (A. P. R.) He was educated at Richmond Academy and removed to Franklin County. He married Elizabeth Archer Benford of Coochland County, by whom he had eleven children; was member of House of Delegates (1810-12) and in the Senate (1821-25). From 1825 to 1837 he was a member of Congress from Virginia. He died Aug. 15, 1859.

IV. Thomas Augustine, bapt. Feb. 10, 1777; sponsors: Augustine Claiborne, William Leigh, Mary Claiborne. (A. P. R.)

V. Mary Leigh, b. 1781, d. 1812, m. 1796, Bathurst Claiborne, (1774-1808) son of Col. Augustine Claiborne. One of their children was Mary Leigh who married Abraham Cowper Shelton (1789-1840).

6. Susanna Claiborne, born November 29, 1751, married Frederick Jones of Dinwiddie. (A list of their children was not furnished). One daughter, Mary Herbert Jones, born March 12, 1777, married 1795, John Withers of Dinwiddie. He died in Huntsville, Madison County, Alabama, in 1848.

Children of Mary Herbert (Jones) and John Withers:
(Born in Dinwiddie Co., Va.)

I. John Wright Withers, b. 1796, m. Palmyra Jordan of Madison Co., Ala.

II. Susanna Claiborne Withers, b. July 23, 1798, m. Clement C. Clay, 1817, Huntsville, Alabama. He was afterwards Governor and Senator. She died Jan. 2, 1866.

III. William Frederick Withers, b. February 29, 1800, m. 1826 to Catherine Hawkins, 1846 to Harriet Carter.

IV. Priscilla Wright Withers, b. February 5, 1804, m. February 27, 1828, to William McDowell of Huntsville, Alabama.

V. Augustine Jones Withers, b. January 6, 1805, m.

October 8, 1834, to Mary Woodson, who died in 1861. He died in 1866.

15. VI.   Ann Eliza Withers, b. 1808, in Davidson County, Tenn., m. November 14, 1838, to F. J. Levert of Huntsville, Alabama.

    VII.   Mary Mitchell Withers, b. 1810, m. 1833 to Dr. R. W. Withers of Greene County, Alabama, who died September 19, 1854, and who is buried in Huntsville, Alabama.

    VIII.   Jones Mitchell Withers, b. January 12, 1814, in Madison County, Alabama, m. January 12, 1837, to Rebecca Eloise Forney of Alabama.

    IX.   Maria Herbert Withers, b. 1819, m. 1859 to Reverend Anastasius Meneaos of Epirus, Greece, Rector St. John's Church, Alabama, who died 1867. She died in 1866.

15. Ann Eliza Withers, daughter of John Withers, married Francis John LeVert, born 1790 in King William County, Va., died 1869 in Huntsville, Alabama. They had only one child, Mary Claud LeVert, born August 3, 1845, Huntsville, Alabama, died November 27, 1931 in Tampa, Florida. She married Daniel Coleman, born in Athens, Alabama, September 7, 1838, died in Huntsville, Alabama, June 1906.

Daniel Coleman was a Captain, C. S. A., States Attorney, Member of Alabama Legislature and U. S. Consul at St. Etienne, France,

Children:

    I.   LeVert Coleman, b. September 7, 1877, m. Katherine _____. He was a graduate of West Point and a Colonel on General Pershing's staff in World War I; was made companion of the Order of St. Michael and St. George and Commander of the Legion of Honor; has one son Daniel Coleman.

    II.   Claude Viedot Coleman, b. November 13, 1882; m. October 30, 1913, Edwin Russell Dickenson, b. October 9, 1873, at Gainesville. Mrs. Dickenson is a member of the National Society of Colonial Dames of America and resides at 305 South Boulevard, Tampa, Florida.

5. Herbert Claiborne, born April 7, 1746, married first Mary Ruffin, mother of his first child; married secondly, Mary Burnet Browne, daughter of Judith (Carter) and William Burnet Browne. His third wife was a Miss Scott. Children: Mary Herbert, William Burnet, Herbert Augustine, (see later #8), William C., Mary Carter, Judith Browne, Harriet Herbert, Lavinia Bathurst, Bettie Carter, Augusta.

8. Herbert Augustine Claiborne, born 1784 at "Chesnut Grove", New Kent County, Virginia, died 1841, married Delia Hayes,

daughter of Anne Dent (Black) and James Hayes; had following children who grew to maturity: Herbert Augustine (see later #9); Mary Burnet; John Hayes, (1823-1890) whose daughter Delia Claiborne married Lt. General Simon Bolivar Buckner, C.S.A., father of Lt. General Simon Bolivar Buckner killed in action on Okinawa in 1945; William James (1825-1906); Gilbert Burnet, Virginia Howard (1833-1897).

9. Herbert Augustine Claiborne, son of Delia (Hayes) and Herbert Augustine Claiborne, born 1819, died 1902; married Catherine Hamilton Cabell, (1855-1925), daughter of Colonel Henry Coalter Cabell, C.S.A. Children: Jane Alston (1833-1890); Herbert Augustine, b. February 20, 1886 (see later #10); Hamilton Cabell, (1888-1928), married Cornelia Ensign and had one daughter, Cornelia Claiborne.

10. Herbert A. Claiborne, son of Catherine (Cabell) and Herbert A. Claiborne, was born in Richmond, Virginia, February 20, 1886; married first, Eleanor Hazard Lindsey, (died April 21, 1915), daughter of Eliza (Wilson) and R. Hughes Lindsey; married secondly February 19, 1920, Virginia Watson Christian, daughter of Frances (Archer) and Andrew H. Christian.

Children of first marriage:
 I. Lindsey Cabell, b. April 18, 1915.

Children of second marriage:
 II. Frances Archer, b. March 4, 1921, m. John H. Guy,Jr.
 III. Herbert A. Claiborne, b. August 12, 1923.
 IV. Catharine Cabell Claiborne, b. November 12, 1927.

7. Buller Claiborne, son of Mary (Herbert) and Colonel Augustine Claiborne of Surry and Sussex, was born October 27, 1745. He married Patsy, daughter of Edmund RUFFIN. He served in the Revolution as 1st Lieutenant, 2nd Virginia, 24 October 1775; Captain, 31 January 1776, to 27 July 1777; served subsequently as a Brigade Major, and Aide de Camp to General Lincoln 1779-1780; commanded a squadron of Cavalry at Battle of Cowpens (Heitman). After the Revolution he was a Justice and Sheriff of Dinwiddie County.

His children were: Sterling (see later #11); James; Richard; Lucy, m. James Wright.

11. Stirling Claiborne, son of Buller Claiborne, married Jane Maria, daughter of Charles Rose.

Children:
12. I. William Stirling, b. 1809, m. Cornelia Roane. (See later #12).
 II. Charles Buller, m. Sallie Ann Coleman.
 III. Martha Ruffin, m. Joseph K. Irving.

12. William Stirling Claiborne, was born 1809 in Nelson County and died in Amherst County, Virginia. He married Cornelia .

Roane of Amherst; was a physician and served as a colonel in the Mexican War.

Children:

13.   I.   William Royall, b. May 7, 1836, m. Alice Clay.
     II.   Martha Ruffin, m. Thomas Wilcox.
     III.   Sterling Buller, b. April 1, 1846; m, (1) Anna Bolling, (2) Mary Haynes.
     IV.   Robert Roane, b. 1855, m. Jane W. Goss.

13. William Royall Claiborne, born May 7, 1836, in Amherst County, died 1899 in Lynchburg. He married Alice Watkins Clay of Bedford County, daughter of Mary (Watkins) and Paul Clay. He was a planter in Amherst County and Captain C. S. A.

Children:

14.   I.   William Sterling, b. December 11, 1872, m. Minnie Marlow.
     II.   Thomas Aurelius, b. December 2, 1875, m.
     III.   Charles Robert, b. March 2, 1878, m.
     IV.   Mary Roane, m. John Gaynos Claiborne.
     V.   James Alexander.

14. The Reverend William Stirling Claiborne, D. D., was born in Amherst County, Virginia, the son of William Royal and Alice Watkins (Clay) Claiborne. Attended Roanoke College, 1897, and the University of the South, 1897-01. Made a deacon in 1899 and ordained priest in 1901 by the Rt. Rev. Thomas F. Gailor, D. D., Bishop of Tennessee. Married Minnie M. Marlowe, of Chicago, Illinois, in 1902. Rector of Otey Memorial Church, Sewanee, from 1900 to 1914. Archdeacon of Sewanee and East Tennessee. Trustee of the University, 1910 until his death. Trustee of St. Katherine's School, Bolivar, 1914. Author: "Roy of the Mountains". Founded St. Andrew's School for Boys. Refounded St. Mary's-on-the-Mountain. Established Emerald-Hodgson Hospital. Captain Chaplain 167th Infantry, 42nd (Rainbow) Division, 1919. Founded the DuBose Memorial Training School. Died in Florida, January 7, 1933.

Children:

     I.   Alice Violita, b. May 1906.

LORD DELAWARE CHART

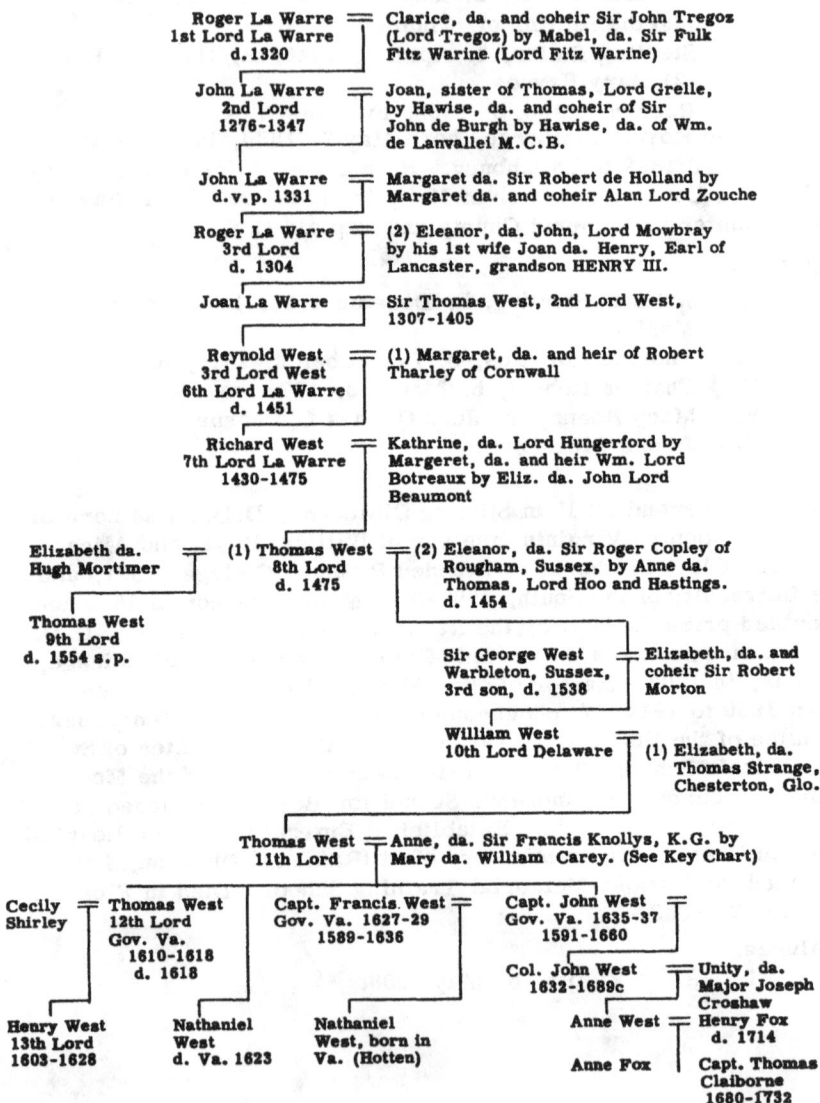

```
Roger La Warre    ══  Clarice, da. and coheir Sir John Tregoz
1st Lord La Warre     (Lord Tregoz) by Mabel, da. Sir Fulk
d. 1320               Fitz Warine (Lord Fitz Warine)

John La Warre     ══  Joan, sister of Thomas, Lord Grelle,
2nd Lord              by Hawise, da. and coheir of Sir
1276-1347             John de Burgh by Hawise, da. of Wm.
                      de Lanvallei M.C.B.

John La Warre     ══  Margaret da. Sir Robert de Holland by
d.v.p. 1331           Margaret da. and coheir Alan Lord Zouche

Roger La Warre    ══  (2) Eleanor, da. John, Lord Mowbray
3rd Lord              by his 1st wife Joan da. Henry, Earl of
d. 1304               Lancaster, grandson HENRY III.

Joan La Warre     ══  Sir Thomas West, 2nd Lord West,
                      1307-1405

Reynold West      ══  (1) Margaret, da. and heir of Robert
3rd Lord West         Tharley of Cornwall
6th Lord La Warre
d. 1451

Richard West      ══  Kathrine, da. Lord Hungerford by
7th Lord La Warre     Margeret, da. and heir Wm. Lord
1430-1475             Botreaux by Eliz. da. John Lord
                      Beaumont
```

```
Elizabeth da.   ══  (1) Thomas West  ══ (2) Eleanor, da. Sir Roger Copley of
Hugh Mortimer       8th Lord              Rougham, Sussex, by Anne da.
                    d. 1475               Thomas, Lord Hoo and Hastings.
Thomas West                               d. 1454
9th Lord
d. 1554 s.p.
                          Sir George West        ══  Elizabeth, da. and
                          Warbleton, Sussex,          coheir Sir Robert
                          3rd son, d. 1538            Morton

                          William West           ══
                          10th Lord Delaware         (1) Elizabeth, da.
                                                         Thomas Strange,
                                                         Chesterton, Glo.
```

```
        Thomas West  ══ Anne, da. Sir Francis West Knollys, K.G. by
        11th Lord        Mary da. William Carey. (See Key Chart)
```

| Cecily ══ Thomas West | Capt. Francis West ══ | Capt. John West ══ |
| Shirley Thomas West 12th Lord Gov. Va. 1610-1618 d. 1618 | Gov. Va. 1627-29 1589-1636 | Gov. Va. 1635-37 1591-1660 |

```
Cecily  ══ Thomas West     Capt. Francis West ══     Capt. John West  ══
Shirley    12th Lord        Gov. Va. 1627-29          Gov. Va. 1635-37
           Gov. Va.         1589-1636                 1591-1660
           1610-1618
           d. 1618                                    Col. John West    ══ Unity, da.
                                                      1632-1689c            Major Joseph
                                                                            Croshaw
Henry West   Nathaniel      Nathaniel                 Anne West        ══ Henry Fox
13th Lord    West           West, born in                                 d. 1714
1603-1628    d. Va. 1623    Va. (Hotten)              Anne Fox            Capt. Thomas
                                                                          Claiborne
                                                                          1680-1732
```

Known relationship of the Grigsbys and apparent relationship of the Doniphans to John Travis and his son William.

Alexander Doniphan = (1) Amy = (2) Margaret Mott
1659-1717 d. c1692
mentions grandson
GILES TRAVIS in
his will

Mott Doniphan = Rosanna Anderson
signed inv. of John Travis 1735
d. 1776

Alex Doniphan = Mary Waugh
wit. will of Wm. Travis 1765
dau Mary (Crosby) and Joseph Waugh I

dau. ? = John Gowry pat 300 acres 1719, d. 1730

dau. ? = GILES TRAVIS grandson of Alex Doniphan by marriage

Million Travis d. 1748 = Joseph Waugh II d. 1747

GOWRY WAUGH d. 1781 willed 300 acres pat. by John Gowry to his son George Lee Waugh

John Grigsby = Jane
signed inv. of John Travis 1735
d. 1750

John Grigsby d. 1730

James Grigsby signed inv. of John Travis 1735, d. 1752

Mary Grigsby d. 1747 = (1) Benj. Newton d. 1710 = (2) John Meese d. 1733

John Grigsby, Jr. wits. will of Wm. Travis 1765

William Heabard d. 1721 = (1) Margaret Newton = (2) John Travis d. 1735

Priscilla Heabard = Bayne Smallwood d. 1768

William Travis d. 1765 = Margaret dau Wm. Smallwood son of Pryor Smallwood

Barrick Travis of S.C. d. 1814 = Anne

Mumford Perryman d. 1820 = Elizabeth Travis c 1770-1835

Pryor Smallwood Travis

Alexander Doniphan Travis 1790-1852

Barrick Smallwood Perryman

Alexander Doniphan Perryman

TRAVIS

of
The Alamo

William B. Travis

John Travis or Travers (name spelled both ways in the records) may be a son of Giles Travers who probably married a granddaughter of Alexander Doniphan. Alexander Doniphan, sometime Justice of the County Court and Sheriff of Richmond County, made his will in Richmond, September 29, 1716, and twice mentions his "grandson" Giles Travers to whom he gave legacies (W. B. 1709-17, p. 297). Hayden in his "Virginia Genealogical" has erroneously interpreted this as "godson". (p. 300).

John Travers' grandson, Barrick Travis of Edgefield County, S. C. ("Berwick Traverse" according to his land grant) named one of his children "Alexander Doniphan". The name came into the Perryman family. Mumford Perryman who married Elizabeth Travis, daughter of Barrick, named one of his children "Alexander Doniphan Perryman".

The first record of John Travis was his marriage to Mrs. Margaret Heabard, June 22, 1722. (St. Paul's Reg. p. 19). John, the first of that given name in the Travers family was probably named for John Gowry (see later).

Margaret Heabard was the widow of William Heabard who died about 1720 in Stafford (Bk. K. 1721-30, missing, p. 61. See index). Their only child was Priscilla Heabard who married Bayne Smallwood of Charles County, Md. Priscilla was the mother of William Smallwood, General of the Revolution and Governor of Maryland. (See Stone, Smallwood, Smith Family.)

Margaret Heabard became involved in a law suit with Robert Beverley, an influential member of the Virginia Council, previous to her marriage with John Travis. The following record from Essex County Land Trials, 1711-1716, (p. 37) gives an account of the suit. "At Court Feb. 21, 1720, now at this day comes Margaret Heabard, mother and next friend of Priscilla

48

Heabard, appeared and entered herself defendant for 365 acres of land and pleads not guilty." On July 18, 1721, the case was tried by a jury who having received all the evidence, to wit, a patent granted to the said Robert Beverley for 4000 acres of land dated Oct. 9, 1719, found for the defendant Priscilla Heabard.

On October 6, 1721, Henry Hewett deeded 50 acres in King George to Margaret Heabard, widow, both of Stafford, for 500 lbs. tbco. The witnesses were David and Garrard Waugh (K. G. D. B. 1721-29, part 1, pg. 20). This property was sold "by John Travis of Overwharton Parish and Margaret, his wife, late Margaret Heabard, to Catesby Cocke" for 3000 lbs. tbco. on August 21, 1729. (K. G. Bk. "1A" 1729-34, p. 9).

Another transaction with Henry Hewett was shown by their deed of April 16, 1629, for 150 acres to Joseph Crouch which recites that same was "part of a dividend of 1600 acres brought of Captain William Heabard (uncle of Margaret's first husband patented 1633) by Francis Hooe, then by divers others sold to Stephen Hewett, decd. Henry Hewett, son of Stephen, sold to Margaret Heabard and now the said John Travers is married to the said Margaret Heabard," (K. G. D. B. 1, part 2, 1721-29, p. 639).

John Travis of Stafford lived ten miles from the King George court house, for on Feb. 10, 1729 the King George Court entered the following order: "John Travis of Stafford County being summoned as evidence by Thomas Monteith against Jeremiah Bronough and Rose, his wife, admrs. with the will annexed for John Dinwiddie decd., making oath that he had come six times and attended eight days on the suit and it appearing that he lived ten miles from the Court, it is ordered that the said Monteith pay the said Travis for attending same."(K. G. "OB" 1721-34, p. 484).

John Dinwiddie, brother of Governor Dinwiddie, had married Rose, daughter of Col. George Mason (D. 1716). John died in King George in 1726. His inventory was filed in that year but the record of his will has been lost. His widow, Rose, evidently married Colonel Jeremiah Bronaugh.

In 1722 in King George, Robert Doniphan deeded to John Dinwiddie part of a tract of land from 15650 acres of land granted to John and George Mott, 17 Oct. 1672. This deed was witnessed by John Travis who later testified in the law suit concerning same.

Margaret Heabard, widow, was the daughter of Mary Newton-Meese, widow of Benjamin Newton (1669-1710) of Stafford and also of John Meese who died in Stafford 1733. Inasmuch as Margaret was a widow by 1720, she was born before 1710 and must have been the daughter of Mary's first husband Benjamin Newton.

Mary Newton-Meese, her mother, was the daughter of John Grigsby of Stafford whose will was dated Mar. 17, 1728-29 and probated, Nov. 11, 1730. (See Grigsby). He gave his daughter "Mary Amees" (as spelled in the will) four negroes, Jemmy, Will, Tony and Bess. In her will she gave "Jemmy" to grandson William Travis; "Will" to grandson William Rogers and "Bess" to grandson Grigsby Rogers (W. B. "M", p. 813).

Mrs. Mary "Amees" was given a legacy in the will of Nathaniel Bryant proven in Stafford Mar. 23, 1732-3 as follows: "This day came Lew Cresey, John Grafford and William Grafford and made oaths that Nathaniel Bryant on his death bed the 21st day of their instant March gave unto Mary Amees all his whole estate to bury him excepting his horse, bridle and saddle which he gave to his godson, Nathaniel Jeffries 'Sworn before me, Thomas Grigsby, Justice'". (W. B. 1729-48, p. 100).

As shown later the names of John and William Grafford are spelled both "Grafford" and "Crafford", also "Craford and Graforth". Mrs. Meese's name varies also from "Ameese" to "Meese". The court clerks spelled by sound in those days.

The above John Crafford made his will in the April 13, 1733, and gave to his grandmother Mary "Meese" all my part of my grandfather's estate to her and the heirs of her body. He appoints "My grandmother Mary 'Amees' "my whole and sole executor." (W. B. "M" p. 184).

Mrs. Mary Newton's second husband was John Meese who may have been a son of Col. Henry Meese, Burgess, 166 and Member of Council, 1677-78. (Tyler Va. Biog: I p. 136) John Meese's estate was appraised by Charles Fowke, Mott Doniphan and John Puddyvat on July 12, 1733, who met at the home of Mary Meese the widow. (Do. p. 121)

That the first husband of Mrs. Mary Meese was Benjamin Newton, I, is evidently proven in the following way: On April 26, 1714, Phillip Crafford, or Grafford, mariner of St. Paul's Parish, Stafford, and LETITIA his wife sold land in Essex County which had been given to Letitia by HER FATHER BENJAMIN NEWTON in his WILL dated Jan. 3, 1709-10. (33 V. -393; 37 V. 180). (See Newton).

The above Letitia, wife of Phillip Crafford died June 18, 1725 (S. P. R.) and her husband Phillip married again Dec. 31, 1730, Mary Simmons (S. P. R.).

In 1732 Phillip Crafford was executor of the estate of Benjamin Newton, Jr., for 12 years. (37 V. -180).

Also in 1732 Phillip Crafford made a deed to John Travis (D. B. 1731-39, index only - book lost). This may have been a deed to John Travis because his wife was an heir of Benj. Newton. (Will lost).

John Crafford was evidently a son of Phillip by his first wife Letitia Newton. At the time John made his will in 1733 his father had remarried, so his father was passed by for his (John's) grandmother, Mary Newton-Meese. He was giving her husband's property back to her and her heirs.

Phillip Crafford had a daughter, Letitia, born May 4, 1718. She married Joseph Bowling, July 15, 1738. (S. P. R.).

Margaret (Newton) Heabard-Travis, wife of John Travis also had a daughter named "Letitia". Letitia Travis married James Grigsby, a cousin, Jan. 18, 1753. (S. P. R.).

That Benjamin Newton's wife was named "Mary" is proven by a deed that "Benj. Newton and wife Mary" made to William King, Oct. 29, 1699, for "150 acres in Stafford part of 400 acres given me by my father (John Newton) in Stafford in 1690". (Bk. Z, pp. 6-8). (37 V. -180)

Benjamin Newton, I, was assuredly deceased before April 26, 1714, as proven by the deed of his daughter Letitia and her husband Phillip Crafford on that date (ante). He was evidently dead by 1710 as Benjamin Newton, II (his son) and wife Elizabeth in that year deeded land in Richmond County to their son Benj. Newton, Jr. (III). (33 V. -393; 37 V. -180). Benjamin, II, married Elizabeth daughter of Thomas and Lucy Gregg (see Gregg). Benjamin, II, seems to have died in 1719 as his estate account was filed in Stafford in that year. (37 V. -180) (For authorities and full explanation, see Newton).

John Travis, on Nov. 9, 1724, was a witness to a deed from Howson Hooe, of St. Paul's Parish to Thomas Grigsby for 250 acres lying in countries of Stafford and King George. (D. B. 1622-28, p. 133). His lands and that of his wife appear to lay partly in both countries. He died before Sept. 9, 1735, for the inventory of his estate was recorded in Stafford, Sept. 9, 1735. Same was signed by Mott Doniphan and James and John Grigsby, his relatives. (W. B. "M", p. 184).

Mrs. Mary Meese's will was dated April 20, 1747, and probated June 9, 1747. (W. B. "M", p. 513). Her legatees were: "grandson, William Travis, one negro named James and one young bay mare; granddaughters Margaret and Letitia Travis. each an cow and calf-dishes and plates; grandson William Rogers one negro man named Will and cow and calf; Mary Rogers Coughclough the wife of William Cloughclough, personalty; grandson Grigsby Rogers, negro man named Andrew and negro wench named Bess, also all rest of my estate both real and personal to my grandson Grigsby Rogers, he to be executor". Witnesses, Ann Grigsby, Robert Sudduth, John Hobby.

An inventory of her estate, dated July 14, 1747, was filed by Grigsby Rogers. (W. B. "M", p. 518).

Her children were:

    I.   Margaret Newton, m. (1) William Heabard, and had Priscilla Heabard who married Bayne Smallwood of

Maryland; m. (2) John Travis and had following children:

1. William Travis, m. Margaret Smallwood. (See later).
2. Margaret Travis, fate unknown.
3. Letitia Travis, m. Jan. 18, 1753, James Grigsby. (S. P. R. - 211).

II. Letitia Newton, m. Phillip Crafford. She died June 18, 1725 (S. P. R.) and her husband Phillip m. (2) Dec. 31, 1730 Mary Simmons (S. P. R. 26).

Phillip Crafford's children, by 1st wife:

1. John Crafford, d. Dec. 20, 1733 (R. 232).
2. Letitia Crafford; bapt. May 4, 1718, m. Joseph Bowling, July 15, 1738. (S. P. R. 28-198). His inventory was filed in Fairfax, 1756.

Children of 2nd wife Mary Simmons whose will was dated Feb. 19, 1756. Children named in will were Peter, William and Mary, (Bk. 0-324)

3. Peter Crafford, b. Sept. 15, bapt. Oct. 20, 1731. (R. 41) He married Jane Gladstone, Aug. 7, 1755. (R. 212).
4. William Crafford, b. Nov. 2, bapt. Dec. 22, 1734. (R. 52).
5. Mary Crafford, b. Mar. 4, bapt. June 17, 1739. (R. 72)

III. (Daughter) m. John Rogers who made his will May 12, 1758; probated June 11, 1760 (0-379).

Children:

1. Grigsby Rogers, m. Mary _____ ; had a dau. Mary Rogers, b. Oct. 9, 1753. (R. 123).
2. William Rogers, m. Frances _____; had Robert Rogers, b. Oct. 9, 1753, and Sarah Rogers, b. Oct. 22, 1759. (R. 128).
3. Mary Rogers, m. Dec. 30, 1741, William Coulgh-clough, (R. 201) who bought land in Prince William from Benjamin Newton, III, Oct. 23, 1752. (37 V. -182)

IV. Benjamin Newton, II, m. Elizabeth Gregg. (See Newton).

William Travis, son of Margaret and John Travis lived in Overwharton Parish, Stafford County. Nothing is apparently shown concerning him in the remaining records between 1747, when he is mentioned in the will of his grandmother Mary Newton-Meese, and the year 1765 when he made his own will.

His will was dated May 1, 1765, and probated August 1765. He gave negroes, cattle, household goods, and other personal property to three daughters, Lucy, Mary and Eleanor Travis. Then he bequeathed "to my loving wife, Margaret Travis x x x two shares of tobacco, Indian corn and what other grain shall be made on my plantation this ensuing year. x x x Item. My intent and meaning is that if my loving wife Margaret Travis should hereafter marry, that then my said loving children with their estate left them by me shall be put in care and management of my loving friend, Mr. William Smallwood and further do appoint my loving wife Margaret and my loving friend Mr. William Smallwood my whole and sole executor and executrix". Witnesses, Alexander Doniphan, John Grigsby, Jr., James P. Garrett.

The will was presented by "Margaret Travis, one of the executors and proven by the oaths of Alexander Doniphan and John Grigsby, Jr." in August Court, 1765.

William Travis bequeathed only personalty and did not bequeath any realty in his will, although he does mention "My plantation". According to the law of primogeniture then prevailing in the Northern Neck, it appears that the first son inherited the realty. This is well illustrated by Jacob Smith, Sr., in the making of his nuncupative will in Fairfax in 1753. Jacob provided that all his realty be sold, converted into personalty and then divided among all his children. This was not done, as his real property, less widow's dower, was inherited and sold by Jacob Smith, Jr., his eldest son. Real property could not be conveyed by verbal wills. (See Stone-Smallwood-Smith family). So the fact that William Travis did not mention any son was no proof he did not have one - as it was not necessary to mention the son as he would inherit the real property. Very often the eldest sons were not mentioned in wills. Also, William Travis did not have a "remainder" clause in his will, for after the above legacies he did not bequeath the "rest of his estate and remainder" to anyone (for the example of a "remainder" clause, see Mrs. Mary Meese's will, ante).

William Smallwood was mentioned in the above will as a "loving friend". Often but not always, this designation meant some degree of relationship. As an illustration, Raleigh Travers, who made his will in Stafford in 1749 made his "loving friends", Sarah Cooke and Travers Cooke, his executors. Sarah was his sister and Travers his nephew. (See Hayden, p. 300).

William Smallwood is said to be the grandfather of the children. (Maryland Hist. Mag. 22, p. 168). It seems true otherwise why would William Travis provide that in the event of his wife's remarriage their children should be taken away from her and placed in the care of only a friend? Lucy Travis was under three years of age.

The designation "Father-in-Law" does not seem to have been used in those days. William Smallwood was a son of Pryor Smallwood of Charles County, Md., who died in 1734 (see Stone-Smallwood-Smith). He was given 200 acres, part of "Christian Temple Manor", in his father's will. In 1753, Bayne Smallwood, his brother, held 200 acres in the same manor. No deed from William to Bayne appears in the Charles County records in that intervening time. William was evidently not deceased as there is no record of his will or the administratives of his estate in Charles City County or in the Maryland Calendar Wills. William Smallwood was still living in King George County in 1782 for he furnished supplies to the army in that year (4 T. 55). He migrated from King George after the Revolution probably to the Carolinas or Kentucky.

Barrick Travis of Edgefield County, S.C., son of William Travis, had a son named "Pryor Smallwood Travis", who in turn had a son named "Smallwood". Mumford Perryman, who married a daughter of Barrick Travis had a son named "Barrick Smallwood Perryman".

Pryor Smallwood, father of William Smallwood owned land in Stafford for on April 3, 1724, he and his wife Elizabeth (McMillion) sold to George Mason of Stafford, 200 acres, known as "Cockpitt Point" on the Potomac River "part of an ancient patent". (Bk. 1722-28, p. 92).

The McMillions, Elizabeth Smallwood's family, also held land in Stafford. William Smallwood may have acquired some of these properties. He may have married one of the three daughters of David Barrick of Richmond which also would account for the name "Barrick" appearing in the family.

Children of Margaret Smallwood and William Travis:

    I.   Elenor Travis, oldest daughter, witnessed interlineations made on father's will.

    II. Mary Travis.

    III. Lucy Travis, b. December 16, 1762. (St. Paul Reg. p. 154).

3.   IV. Barrick Travis. (See later #3).

3. Barrick Travis, grandfather of Colonel William B. Travis of the Alamo, was living in Loudoun County, Virginia, in 1763. It seems that he had been indentured to one Robert Watson to learn a trade and on April 12, 1763, he unsuccessfully petitioned the orphans' court to release him from his indentures. The record recites "Upon the petition of Barrick Traverse against Robert Watson for ill usage and for the detaining of him, this day came the parties by their attorneys, who being fully heard it is considered by the court that the petition be dismissed".

The next day, April 13, 1763, the court further ordered "That whereas Sanford Gorham, an evidence for Barrick Traverse against Robert Watson, having attended court four days, it is ordered that the said Barrick pay him one hundred pounds of tobacco for his trouble".

A further order was made in this suit on December 13, 1763, that "Whereas the complaint of Barrick Traverse against Robert

Watson for ill usage was dismissed, it is ordered that the said Robert use the said Barrick better for the future". (Loudon O. B. B, pp. 93, 608, 269). Robert Watson died intestate. Inventory of his personal estate filed August 8, 1768. (W. B. 1, pp. 199-200.)

It will be noted that the name here is spelled "Barrick", by the clerks. It seems that his real name was "Berwick", pronounced "Barrick", just like "Warwick" is pronounced "Warrick". For when "Barrick", otherwise known as "Barrett", moved to South Carolina he obtained a grant of 100 acres of land on the Saluda River and in that grant his name is spelled, "Berwick". The grant was as follows:

"GEORGE THE THIRD, BY THE GRACE OF GOD, of Great Britain, France, and Ireland, KING, Defender of the Faith, etc., x x x Know ye, that we do give and grant to BERWICK TRAVERSE, his heirs and assigns, a plantation or tract of land containing one hundred acres situated in Berkley County on the north side of the Saludy River, bounded north east and east on land held by Donniphan, north west on land held by Weil, south east on land held by John Dooly and all other sides by vacant land.

"Witness his Excellency, the Rt. Hon. Lord Charles G. 1. Montagu, Captain General, etc., of our said Province of South Carolina, this 14th day of August, A. D. 1772, in the twelfth year of our reign." (Grant Book, 26, p. 437).

This change from "Berwick Traverse" to "Barrett Travis" illustrates the evolution and derivation of some of our American names. It is not known when he changed the spelling of his name, maybe he never did. Maybe the clerks, as they often did, copied the name wrong as "Barrett". However, among his grandchildren, for example, like Colonel William BARRETT Travis, the name may appear as "Barrett". "Berwick" is evidently derived from the family of that name living in the Northern Neck of Virginia where the Traverse family also resided. Both families settled there in the 17th Century. "Traverse" finally became "Travis" and "Berwick", "Barrick".

Barrick Travis's name is reported "illegible" in the census of 1790. See the first Census of the United States, Heads of Families, South Carolina, page 65, fourth name from the last one in the third column. Here he is shown with three sons, three daughters and three slaves. This agrees exactly with the number of sons and daughters he had at that time. Among his neighbors in the second and third columns of that page, most of whom will be mentioned later are: Jacob Smith, Captain William Butler, Arthur and William Watson, James Grigsby, Christopher Brooks, Sr., and Jr., Mumford Perryman, Fredric Sisson, Samuel Deloach.

Barrick Travis settled on Red Bank Creek, a branch of the Little Saluda River, near where Jacob and Smallwood Smith patented land, for Frederic Sisson who married Smallwood's

widow is shown as living near Barrick Travis in the census of
1790 and next to Mumford Perryman, son-in-law of Barrick.

Many fables have been written concerning the ancestry of his
famous grandson, Colonel Travis of the Alamo. Cyrus Townsend
Brady said in his "Conquest of the Southwest", (p. 101), that
"Travis was a foundling, discovered, tied to the bars of a gate on
the farm of Mr. Mark Travis, who took the babe and named him
'Bar' not 'Barrett'".

According to the Travis family bible, Mark Travis, born
September, 1783, married Jemima Stallworth, daughter of William Stallworth, Sr., January 1, 1808, at the Red Bank Church.
Their oldest child, William Barrick Travis, was born August 9,
1809.

However, it is not the influence of these long past stories
that prompts this writing, but a more recent one, which appeared
in the "Southern Historical Research Magazine" of February,
1937, published at Dallas, Texas. The article is entitled "Genealogy of Colonel William Barrett Travis". It connects Colonel
Travis with the distinguished Travis family of Jamestown, Virginia. It begins with Edward Travis I, member of the Virginia
House of Burgesses, 1644, who had a son Edward Travis II, who
as "son and heir of Edward Travis deceased , patented land near
Jamestown in 1663." (C. P. 503). This last Edward died at Jamestown, November 12, 1700.

The author of the article in the above magazine states (page
54), "From all available records it appears that Edward Travis,
II, and his wife, Elizabeth Champion, had at least two sons and
three daughters". Among these sons and daughters he shows a
Daniel Travis, whom he later places in Pasquotank far away on
the Eastern Coast of North Carolina. From this Daniel, he
traces a supposed line of descent down to Barrett Travis in South
Carolina, 125 years later.

All the records of James City County were burned in the
Civil War and there is no reason to conclude that Edward Travis,
II, ever had a son named "Daniel". However, it is very easy to
prove the antecedents of Daniel Travis of Pasquotank, North
Carolina. One of the earliest Quaker families in North Carolina
was the family of William Travis, who settled in Pasquotank,
and if one will turn to that estimable and accurate work, the
"Encyclopedia of American Quaker Genealogy", it will be found
that Daniel Travis, son of William Travis of the City of West-
minster, and Sary Travis, daughter of Robert West of New England, in Providence, married in the year 1666. (Vol. 1, 1. 120).

It is with regret that it must be said that the article on the
"Genealogy of Colonel William B. Travis", heretofore mentioned,
contains very many erroneous statements seemingly made without any check of authorities. The author says, page 61, "Barrett

Travis married Elizabeth DeLoach. How many children Barrett
Travis and his wife Elizabeth DeLoach had and their names are
unknown except as to two sons, Alexander and Mark, but the
compiler is confident that they were more than two, whose identity, up to this time remains unsolved.

"It is believed, but the belief may be wrong, that he had a
daughter, who married a Henderson, one a Lipscomb and one a
Lewis. "

Now Elizabeth was not the name of Barrick's wife at the time
of his death and none of his daughters married a Henderson, a
Lipscomb or a Lewis. Barrick's children are shown in the Probate Court records of Edgefield County, for a division of his
personal property was made between his heirs in 1814.

Contemporary court and bible records, written records, made
at the time people are living, are the only accurate sources of
information concerning persons dead for more than a hundred
years. Traditionary names that come down to descendents are
rarely accurate.

Barrick died intestate in 1812, and papers of administration
were taken out by his wife, Anne, and his son, the Reverend
Alexander Travis, on October 3, 1814. The papers show that
Anne Travis, widow, received from the sale of the personal
property the sum of $1,354.44. The balance of the money re-
ceived from the sale was paid out to the sons, and the legal representatives of the daughters shown below, each child receiving
$374.83.

At that time South Carolina laws prohibited married women
from holding property in their own name, so the husbands receipted for the daughter's share, which in one case (that of M.
Wilson) leaves the daughter's name unknown. (See children later
for daughter's names).

"Paid William Stallworth, Jr., for his legacy $374.83
"   Mumford Perryman,   "   "   "   "
"   Mark Travis,   "   "   "   "
"   Prior S. Travis,   "   "   "   "
"   M. Wilson,   "   "   "   "
"   Alexander Travis,   "   "   "   "
"   Anne Travis, widow,   "   "   " $1,354.05
"   Catherine Pope's legacy to Prior S. Travis,
      Administrator of the Estate of Catherine Pope,
                    $374.83"

The widow here is shown as "Anne" and not "Elizabeth". The
DeLoach's, an excellent family living near Red Bank, never lived
in Loudoun County, Virginia. Barrick Travis was evidently married before he came to South Carolina, for in census for Conecuh
County, Alabama, for 1830, Elizabeth Travis Perryman, his
daughter, is shown as over "sixty years of age", which would

make her born before 1770. Barrick Travis and the Smiths were living in Virginia in 1769.

Elizabeth Travis married Mumford Perryman, a soldier of the Revolution, who came from Henry County, Virginia, to Red Bank soon after the war. He was the son of Richard Perryman and his wife, Martha De Jarnette, of Prince Edward County, Virginia. Mumford had six children and it is easy to deduce for whom these children were named.

These children were: 1. Martha, named for Mumford's mother; 2. Anne, named for his wife's mother; 3. Barrick Smallwood, named for his wife's family, and the Smallwoods; 4. Milton Travis, named for the Travis's and Mumford's brother, Milton, who died in Anson County, North Carolina, September 1793. (Milton Travis Perryman, the writer's great grandfather, was born September 28, 1794, about a year after his Uncle Milton's death, Bible records); 5. Samuel, named for Mumford's brother, Samuel Perryman; 6. Alexander Doniphan, named for his wife's brother, Alexander D. Travis.

The derivation of the names of Barrick's own children can seemingly be traced. Among the purchasers at a sale of the personal effects of Catherine Travis Pope was Pryor Smallwood Travis and his son, Smallwood Travis. There is no reason for giving of names such as "Pryor Smallwood" and "Smallwood" to children unless they are family names. They are not names like "George Washington", "Benjamin Franklin" or "Abraham Lincoln".

Pryor Smallwood died in Maryland in 1734, long before Barrick and his wife Ann were born. Why should they give these names to their children unless they were related? "Alexander" the name of Barrick's youngest son was probably derived from Alexander Donniphan, grandfather of Giles Travis (Ante).

It will be recalled that a Mott Doniphan (together with John Grigsby), presented the inventory of John Travis in Stafford County, Virginia, September 9, 1735. (W. B. "M", p. 184). Mott was a son of Alexander Doniphan whose will was probated in Richmond County, Virginia, September 20, 1716. (W. B. 3, p. 297). Mott Doniphan in turn had a son named Alexander. The last Alexander witnessed the will of William Travis, son of John Travis, May 1, 1765, as heretofore shown. The executor of this will was William Smallwood, son of Pryor Smallwood. Here in South Carolina, years later, we find Barrick Travis's children bearing these names.

Mark Butler Travis lived within four miles of the Red Bank Church, and it was at Mark's place that his eldest child, Colonel William Barrick Travis, was born in 1809. Young William was about nine years old, when the family moved to Alabama for Mark and his wife Jemina Stallworth had their letter of dismission from the Red Bank Church, July 20, 1818.

Elizabeth Travis Perryman, Mark's sister, had her letter of dismission from the Red Bank Church, October 20, 1821, and also moved to Conecuh County, Alabama. Mumford Perryman, her husband died in South Carolina in 1820, and in his will provided for her departure to Alabama, saying, "In case my said wife should remove to the state of Alabama and purchase lands with the funds of my estate, it is my desire that said lands should become component parts of my estate and at the death or marriage of my said wife the whole of my estate both real and personal, with the exception of the sum allowed for the support of my son Barrick Smallwood Perryman, it is my desire that same may be equally divided amongst my children. "

William Barrick Travis grew to manhood in Alabama and moved to Texas before the outbreak of the Texas Revolution. While in Texas in 1835, he sent word to James Butler Bonham, then in Montgomery, that great events were in the making in Texas and urged him to come out and join him. (Milledge L. Bonham, Jr., S. W. Quart, 35, p. 128).

Bonham gave up his law practice and returned to South Carolina to bid farewell to his mother. This seems to indicate that he well knew the danger he would incur in Texas.

James Butler Bonham was born near Red Bank, February 20, 1807, the 5th child and third son of Sophia (Smith) and James Bonham. He was named for his great uncle, Captain James Butler, killed in the Cloud Creek Massacre, 1781. (See Butler). A younger brother, Milledge Luke Bonham, 1813-1890, commanded a regiment in the Mexican War, a brigade at first Bull Run, and was Governor of South Carolina, 1862-64.

Bonham grew up in the same neighborhood as William Barrick Travis. They attended the same schools, and the same church, the Red Bank Baptist Church. They were schoolmates until Travis's father, Mark Travis, moved to Alabama. (S. W. Hist. Quart. Vo. 35, p. 128). There was an extensive hegira from South Carolina to that state. Jackson's victory over the Creeks and Cherokees in the war of 1812 had opened Alabama for settlement.

Bonham arrived in Texas, December 12, 1835, but just when he joined Travis is in doubt. According to one authority, he joined him at San Felipe. Another investigator believes Bonham was at San Antonio before Travis, and on January 26, 1836, acted as chairman of a committee appointed by a mass meeting of the soldiers of garrison. (S. W. Hist. Quart. Vo. 36, p. 278).

But Bonham was not the only adventurer or soldier of fortune attracted to this post of danger. Such renowned fighters as James Bowie and David Crockett, probably scenting hard fighting hurried to the Alamo to meet the oncoming horde of Mexicans.

Travis was commissioned a Lieutenant Colonel in the "Regular" Army of Texas, December 24, 1835. He arrived at the

Alamo with 25 men on February 3, 1836, and assumed command of that garrison soon afterwards, when Colonel Neill, the Commander, was compelled to leave on account of illness.

Bonham held the rank of Lieutenant or Captain, and seems to have acted as an aid to Travis. He was sent out by Travis on February 16th to obtain reinforcements and went first to Fanning at Goliad, then to the town of Gonzales.

Several thousand Mexicans under Santa Anna appeared before the Alamo February 27, 1836. Two days later, in response to Bonham's appeal, 32 volunteers under Captain Albert Martin hurried to the Alamo and cut their way through the Mexicans on the morning of March 1st or 2nd.

"On the morning of March 3rd, Bonham arrived with two companions on the hill overlooking the fortress, the doom of whose noble defenders it was apparent was now inevitable. His two companions, Samuel A. Maverick and John W. Smith, men of undoubted courage urged Bonham to retire with them. His reply was, 'I will report the result of my mission to Travis or die in the attempt. Mounted upon a cream-colored horse, with a white handkerchief floating from his hat - a signal previously arranged with Travis - he dashed through the Mexican lines amid a shower of bullets and entered unharmed the gates which were thrown open to receive him. Unable to save his comrades he was determined to die with them." (Bonham, S. W. Hist. Quar. Vol. 35, p. 130).

The next day Travis sent out his last letter from the Alamo. It was addressed to the President of the Texas Convention and speaks of the return of Captain Bonham, his messenger. Travis said, "A blood red banner waves from the Church of Bejar, and in the camp above us, in token that the war is one of vengeance against rebels, they have demanded that we surrender at discretion or the garrison will be put to the sword. These threats have no influence on me or my men, but to make us fight with desperation and that high souled courage that characterizes the patriot, who is willing to die in defense of his country's liberty and his own honor... Victory or Death".

THE BARRICK TRAVIS FAMILY

Barrick Travis, grandfather of Colonel William Barrick Travis, as heretofore related, was residing in Loudoun County, Virginia, in 1763, when he was indentured to Robert Watson to learn a trade. Many Virginians of high and low degree indentured their sons to learn trades so this conveys nothing as to social status. Barrick lived near Jacob and Smallwood Smith, and the Grigsby brothers in Virginia, and probably moved with them to South Caro-

lina, where he settled on the Red Bank Creek in what is now Saluda County.

Children:

I.   Elizabeth Travis, m. Mumford Perryman. (See Perryman).

II.   Sarah Travis, m. William Stallworth, Jr., brother of
Jemima Stallworth who married Sarah's brother, Mark
Travis. William made his will in Abbeville in 1821,
and same probated in 1832. He named "Wife Sarah,
and all my children" without giving the names of the
children.

III. Catherine Travis, m. Elijah Pope, son of Jacob. She
died about 1814, as her brother, Pryor S. Travis,
administered on her estate in that year. Her children
were: 1. Harriett, who married John D. Williams;
2. Jane; 3. Maria Elizabeth.

     Maria Elizabeth Pope, born September 29, 1799;
died July 20, 1870; married December 20, 1821,
James C. Stallworth, son of Joseph Stallworth whose
will was probated in Abbeville, October 20, 1824.
James was born November 30, 1798, and died Octo-
ber 30, 1857. Children: 1. Catherine Anne; 2. Thomas
Travis; 3. Amon Alexander; 4. Elizabeth C.; 5. Sarah
Eugenia; 6. Martha Anne.

Thomas Travis Stallworth, oldest son of James C., was born
January 28, 1830, and died May 3, 1857, at Brazoria, Texas. He
married in Montgomery County, Alabama, October 11, 1849,
Martha Wyatt Gholston, daughter of Leonard Gholston and his
wife a Miss Howard; born March 26, 1852; died March 26, 1895,
in Meridian, Mississippi. Leonard was the son of Dabney Gholston. Children: 1. Groves Travis; 2. Viola; 3. Hugh Dabney.

Hugh Dabney Stallworth was born November 25, 1855, at
Brazoria, Texas, and died at Lucedale, Mississippi, October 19,
1929. He married January 29, 1880, Sarah Susan Moody, daughter of the Reverend Charles Wesley Moody and his wife, Sarah
Ann Blakeney, daughter of John Goodloe and Isabella (McLendon)
Blakeney. Their children were: 1. Charles Groves Stallworth;
2. Hugh Wagner Stallworth, born August 26, 1882; married June
29, 1915, Anita Bevil McMichael, daughter of Alonzo and Caroline (Bevil) McMichael. Mr. Stallworth is general manager of
the Purina Mills at Nashville, Tennessee.

IV.   Daughter, m. Mr. Wilson. The South Carolina laws
as to married women in 1814 seems to have been that
they could not hold property in their own name, so
their husbands receipted for the property, which in
this case leaves the daughter's name unknown.

V.   Pryor Smallwood Travis may have lived in Abbeville

or moved West. There is no record of his will in Edgefield. According to tradition, besides, Smallwood, the son, he had two daughters, who married Brooks; first cousins of Preston Smith Brooks.

VI.   Mark Travis, b. 6th September, 1783, at Cambridge, Edgefield County, S. C., died at Sparta, Alabama, 5th September, 1836; married Jemima Stallworth, January 1, 1808, daughter of William Stallworth, Sr. of Edgefield. Mark resided within four miles of the Red Bank Church.

William Stallworth, died in 1806 in Edgefield County, and his will was probated November 8, 1808. He married Jemima Tripp, daughter of Mrs. Jemima (McNamara) Tripp, a native of Ireland. Children named in will: Nicholas, Joseph, Sally, Nancy, Betsy, and children not named, Mary, Peggy, William, Jemima. He was a brother of Joseph Stallworth, whose will was probated in Abbeville County, South Carolina, November 7, 1796. Joseph appointed his brothers, William and Thomas, Executors.

Children of Mark Travis:

I.   William Barrick Travis, b. August 9, 1809, killed at the Alamo, March 6, 1836, m. Rosanna E. Cato, b. 3rd May 1812, daughter of William Cato of Alabama, who was born October 27, 1765. Mr. Cato married September 8, 1787, his wife Sarah, b. September 4, 1770.

Children: (1) Charles Edward Travis, b. 8th August 1829, a ranger in Texas, dsp. (2) Susan Isabella Travis, b. 4th August 1831; d. September 1, 1870, m. John D. Grisette of Buffalo, Leon County, Texas, who died 17th August 1896. Children: (a) William Barrett Travis Grisette, b. 28th April, 1846; (b) Mary Jane Grisette, b. 4th December, 1848, m. (1st) Thomas Green Davidson of Chapel Hill, Washington County, Texas, m. (2nd) C. R. DeCoussey.

Children of First Marriage:

(1)   Edward Travis Davidson, b. 4th April 1868.

(2)   John J. Davidson, b. 30 November 1870, m. at Plainview, Texas, 20th December 1891, Lelia Hamilton.

(3)   Mattie J. Davidson, b. 4th December 1873, m. 7 April 1890, J. H. Turbeville, Archer City, Texas.

Children of Second Marriage:

(4)   Charlie Travis De Coussey, b. 23rd May, 1886.

II.   Emalene Travis.

III.   Elizabeth Travis.

IV. Mark Butler Travis, b. 18th May, 1827, at Old Town, Alabama, joined famous Palmetto regiment under General Scott and was wounded in the head at Cherebusco. He was clerk of the Court for Conecuh County for four terms and was Colonel of Militia. He was Captain of Conecuh Guards in the 4th Alabama Regiment at first Bull Run, and when Colonel Jones was killed he rallied the regiment, but was severely wounded and retired from further service. He married Louise A. Bradley in 1850, and died in 1864 from his wound received at Bull Run.

Children: (1) Peirce Travis (2) Mason Travis, (3) Butler Travis, a graduate of West Point, served as a major in the Philippines.

V. Nicholas Travis, killed in duel 1860.

VI. Alexander Travis.

VII. James Calloway Travis, b. August 5, 1829, at Evergreen, Conecuh County, Alabama, died May 25, 1918; married May 1854, Sophronia A. Davis, daughter of William Davis, born 1839, died February 4, 1857. He was a planter and saw-mill owner, and County Surveyor for 15 years.

Children:

(1) Louis Travis, b. 10th February 1861, died in infancy.

(2) Mark Augustus Travis, b. November 29, 1864, m. December 4, 1882, Mary Hughes, born at Evergreen, April 19, 1864, daughter of Mary (Smith) and William T. Hughes. Mr. Travis is in the lumber business and resides at McKenzie, Alabama. He was County Surveyor for 12 years, County Commissioner for one term and Chairman of County Board of Equalization for four years.

Children:

a. William James Travis, b. March 18, 1884, m. Ida Alexander.

b. Mark Barrett Travis, b. January 25, 1887, m. Mamie Brown.

c. Henry Augustus Travis, b. March 17, 1890, m. Sallie Alexander.

d. Mary Sophraina Travis, b. October 1, 1896, m. George Coxwell.

e. Elizabeth August Travis, b. September 28, 1899, m. Grady Coxwell.

VII. Reverend Alexander D. Travis, b. August 23, 1790, Edgefield County, South Carolina, moved 1817 to Conecuh County, Alabama, where he died in 1852, and is buried at the Old Beulah Church under a plain marble slab.

Children:

(1) Martha Travis, m. Nicholas Stallworth, Jr., b. in Edgefield, February 21, 1810, died in Conecuh County, Alabama, 1853. He was Circuit Court Clerk of Conecuh County.

> Children: (1) Robert P. Stallworth, (2) Nicholas Stallworth, Major 23rd Battalion, Alabama Volunteers, C.S.A., moved to Falk County, Texas, (3) Daughter m. Hon. Samuel M. Brant, (4) Frank M. Stallworth of Falk County, Texas.

(2) John Duke Travis, m. Mary Ann Stallworth, sister of Nicholas Stallworth, Jr.

(3) James Monroe Travis, m. Mary Ann McCreary and had Phillip Alexander Travis of Montgomery, Alabama.

(4) Phillip Goode Travis, m. Adaline Calloway and moved to Texas.

NEWTON

of

Stafford

This short sketch of the Newtons of Stafford is given only to trace their connection with the Crafford or Grafford, Colclough, Gregg and Travis families and to correct some errors. For a more extensive account one should refer to the Virginia Magazines, 33 and 36.

The first one of this family in Virginia was John Newton of Westmoreland County. He was the eldest son of Thomas Newton of Kingston-upon-Hull, Yorkshire, England. It is probable that the family came to Hull from Northumberland, for the arms used by Thomas Newton were those of the Newtons of Newcastle-upon-Tyne , "Azure, two shinbones in saltire, the sinister surmounted of the dexter or, a crescent for difference". (36 V-293).

John Newton (1639-97) the emigrant, in 1669, aged 30, of Analby, married as his third wife, Elizabeth Laycocke, widow, aged 36, at Selby, Yorkshire. (do. 296).

Benjamin Newton (1669-1710), his third son, who was born in England, settled in Stafford County. Benjamin made a deposition on July 8, 1709, which is recorded in Westmoreland. He stated that he was "aged 40 or thereabouts" and that John Newton, the elder, his father, lived at a place called Anlaby, near Hull, and that he the deponent, knew Thomas Newton who lived in Hull and who always acknowledged the said John Newton (father of the deponent) to be his eldest son and heir, and the deponent also said that he (the deponent) came from the said Thomas Newton's (his grandfather's house) when he came to Virginia. (33V-300).

On Nov. 25, 1690, John Newton, his father, gave him 400 acres in Stafford adjoining his brother John Newton. Benjamin Newton and Mary his wife, Oct. 29, 1699, deeded to William King 150 acres of the above 400 acres. (Bk. Z-6). His wife, Mary, who signed the deed was a daughter of John Grigsby who made his will in Stafford Mar. 17, 1728/29, same probated Nov. 11, 1730. (W. B. "M" - 17) (see Grigsby). John Grigsby willed his daughter, "Mary Amees" four negroes. She had married John Ameese or Meese. (See full account under "Travis of the Alamo").

Benjamin Newton made a will in Stafford but the will has been lost. On April "26, 1714, Phillip Crafford of St. Paul's Parish, Stafford, and Letitia his wife sold to Lawrence Taliafero, gent., of St. Mary's Parish, Essex, one third of a tract in the Forest of Essex, part of a dividend granted Enoch Doughty by patent June 15, 1675, which tract was formerly in the possession of William Berry of Stafford by deed April 11, 1690, which Benj. Newton by his will dated 3 January 1709/10, gave to his daughter Letitia now wife of Phillip Crafford". (signed) Philip Craffort. Letitia Craffort. (Fleet's abs. 1711-14--W. D. Essex 1711-14, p. 240).

This deed proves that the names of Benj. Newton's children given in the Virginia Mag. (Vol. 37, p. 181) are incorrect for Letitia's name does not appear therein. In fact the names there shown are really the children of the second Benjamin, son of Benjamin I above. (See Benj. II post).

Elizabeth Newton, sister of Benjamin I, married Benjamin Berryman. Al Elizabeth Berryman she made a deposition on Feb. 10, 1755, in which she stated she was "aged 70 or thereabouts", and that "Benjamin Newton son of (of John) by the third wife married in Virginia and had issue one son Benjamin and three daughters. The last mentioned Benjamin, who married and had issue a son named Benjamin now living and is married to a daughter of Rachal Colclough of Stafford County." (33 V 300).

The "last named Benjamin" would seem to be the son "Benjamin II" who had issue a son named Benjamin III "now living" and is married to a daughter of "Rachael Colclough". In fact the St. Paul Parish Register shows that this marriage occurred Oct. 20, 1740. (P. 200).

The children of Benjamin I were:

I. Margaret, m. (1) William Heabard and had Priscilla Heabard who married Bayne Smallwood and was the mother of William Smallwood, famous General of the Revolution and Governor of Maryland. William Heabard died in 1721 and Margaret married, secondly, John Travis (d. 1733) and had William, Margaret and Letitia Travis. (See Travis of the Alamo).

II. Letitia, m. Phillip Crafford and had John Crafford, d. 1733, and Letitia Crafford, b. May 14, 1718 (R-128). The last named Letitia m. Joseph Bowling, July 15, 1718. (R-198).

III. (Daughter), m. John Rogers whose will was dated May 12, 1758, and probated June II, 1760. (Bk. O-379). They had Grigsby, William and Mary Rogers. The last named Mary Rogers married William Colclough, Dec. 31, 1741, (R). She is mentioned as "Mary Colclough" in the will of her grandmother, Mary (Newton) Meese.

IV.   Benjamin II, m. Elizabeth, daughter of Lucy and
Thomas Gregg. Lucy Gregg gave her granddaughter,
Sarah Newton, a legacy in her will dated Jan. 9, 1730.
(See Gregg). Benjamin and his wife Elizabeth made
a deed to Benjamin Newton, Jr., for land in Rich-
mond County in 1710 (33 V 393).

Benjamin Newton II made a deed May 1, 1718, as follows:
"Benj. Newton of St. Paul's Parish, Stafford to Robert
Richards of Westmoreland, Washington Parish, 175 acres lying
part in Westmoreland and part in Richmond being part of a tract
given in last will of Robert King unto Anne Hooe and after her
decease to her daughter Hannah Hooe and her heirs and the said
Hannah Hooe dying without issue the land became the inheritance
of her sister Elizabeth Hooe, now Elizabeth Guthrey, by her inter-
marriage with Samuel Guthrey which said Samuel Guthrey and
Eliz. his wife did by their deed 5 August 1710, sell unto Robert
King, son of the said Robert King, and the said Robert King did
sell same unto Benj. Newton, father to Benj. Newton, party to
these parts, by deed bearing date 4th day of Dec., 1710; land
granted to Robert King, 18 May 1669, father to the said Robert
King, for 850 acres, (signed) Ben. Newton. Teste, John Collyer,
Thos. Duncombe, E. Turberville". (Richmond Bk. June 1714,
Dec. 1720-301) (King's deed to Newton is in Bk. 1708 - II, p. 240).

Benjamin Newton II, probably died about 1719 as an account of
his estate was filed in that year. (37 V. - 180). That he left a
will which is now missing is shown by the fact that his brother in
law, Phillip Crafford, on Mar. 14, 1732, as "Executor of the
last will and testament of Benjamin Newton" filed in Stafford an
account of his administration. The account included the following
items, "to a mare delivered Ann Newton left her by will; paid to
Major Benj. Berryman for Elizabeth Newton's bill, paid to Phillip Atcheson for her coffin, paid for three gallons of rum expended
at her funeral, paid for ten pounds of sugar for same use; to 12
years maintenance of Benj. Newton and 4 negro children two of
which were appraised and the other two born since his father's
death; paid to Sarah Newton her legacy a horse colt; by 12 years
rent of the plantation I lived on".

Elizabeth, the wife of Benj. Newton II, seems to have died
during the period of Phillip Crafford's administration.

Children of Benj. Newton II:

I.   Ann. No further record.

II.   Sarah received above legacy of a horse colt. She also
received a legacy in the will of her grandmother
Lucy Gregg.

III. Benjamin evidently came of age in 1731/32. That his
uncle Phillip Crafford had maintained him for 12

years would carry the time back to 1719 when his father's estate account was first filed. Benjamin married Jane Colclough on Oct. 20, 1740, thereby proving the correctness of Mrs. Berryman's deposition of 1755, (R-200). Rachel Colclough made her will in Stafford, Dec. 9, 1748, and gave her daughter Jane Newton four negroes for life, then to go to her children at her death. Benjamin Newton moved to Prince William County. On Nov. 28, 1752, he acknowledged a deed of gift to his children and on July 23, 1753, he and his wife Jane deeded land to their cousin William Colcough. (P. W. "O B" 1752/53, pp 83, 180).

GRIGSBY

of

Stafford

John Grigsby, immigrant ancestor of this family, first appears in the records of Essex County, where, on June 9, 1671, he witnessed a deed for 600 acres conveyed by John Prosser to John Stephens. (Rap. 1668-72, p. 514). A deed dated 1778, in Stafford, refers to land leased by Howson Hooe to Thomas Grigg (Gregg), but not "Thomas Grigsby" as often quoted, said lease was dated September 1661, and was referred to as bounded by land formerly granted to Granger, Horton & Co. "purchased by John Grigsby of James Ashton by deed bearing date of September 26, 16_____, recorded in Stafford County and descended by will to his son Thomas Grigsby. "

John Grigsby removed to Stafford previous to August 18, 1686, for James Ashton of Stafford, in his will of that date, leaves Richard Elkin 100 acres adjoining upon John Grigsby of "the 1/4 dividend" (10 V. 292). James Ashton was a brother of John Ashton of Stafford whose will was made in 1675, sworn to 6 day, 7 month, 1682, and probated January 26, 1682-83. (Sweeney p. 88). John Ashton bequeathed legacies to his wife Elizabeth if she came to Virginia to live; to Thomas Bunbury L 5; to Captain John Ashton 20 sh., brother James Ashton to be exr. but after his death to my cousin John Ashton of Russell St. at the Adam and Eve in London.

On September 9, 1690, John Grigsby was one of the appraisers of the estate of Ralph Elkin, father of Richard Elkin, (45 V. 21). He may have been related to the Ashtons and Elkins for Richard Bryant in his will dated April 5, 1703, bequeathed to his son Nathaniel Bryant "all my land which I now enjoy in Virginia, his mother to live wholly upon the plantation where I now live;" to daughter Elizabeth Elkin 400 L. tbco., Richard Elkin to give my grandson Richard Elkin a mare, son-in-law William Redmond to live on plantation where his mother lives for 7 years; (probably step son) wife Ann, extrx. (partial abstract - Z. 227).

Nathaniel Bryant, above mentioned, in his nuncupatative will made March 21, 1732-3, gave unto Mrs. Mary Amees all of his whole estate (M-p. 100). Mary Amees (Meese) was the only daughter of John Grigsby.

John Grigsby, on April 3, 1699 patented 887 acres of land deeded him by Nicholas Battain (N. N. G. B. 2-234). The traditional wife of John Grigsby is Jane Rosser or Prosser, the name of a family associated with John Grigsby and the Ashtons but actual proof of this connection has not been found.

Captain Simon Miller, aged 37 years, in will in old Rappahannock County, dated February 16, 1679, proven May 22, 1684, gives "a mare foale to my wife's son Anthony Prosser; sons of Mr. Prosse to have every one of them a heifer after my decease." He made James Ashton, oversees of will, "he to dispose of children at 16 years of age" (Rap. Bk. 6 p. 10). Captain Miller's wife appears to have been the widow of John Prosser, whose will was probated in Rappahannock in 1677.

The Ashtons came from Lincolnshire, England. Colonel Peter Ashton of Lincolnshire owned lands in Stafford County. He patented 2550 acres there on March 27, 1665. (C. P. 434). Some of his land afterwards fell in Essex and was named "Chatterton" after an estate of that name in Lincoln owned by the Ashtons. Col. Ashton made his will in 1669, same probated 1671. He left his Virginia estate to his brothers, James Ashton of Kirby Underwood and John Ashton of Louth, in Lincolnshire who came to Virginia. (V. 25-165).

In Essex county on June 17, 1714, John Grigsby, Henry Fitzhugh and John Fitzhugh met and valued a plantation there called "Chatterton" as shown in the following document   (Essex Bk. 14, 1711-16, p. 401).

"We the subscribers, at the request of Lyonel Elton of Bristol, merchants, and John Taylor who intermarried with the relict of Stephen Lloyd, did meet on plantation called "Chatterton" in the above county June 7, 1714, and did value the estate that was in partnership between said James Lloyd, Issac Elton and Stephen Lloyd." (Rec. July 20, 1715).

St. Paul's Register (p. 37) for the year 1727 contains the following entry "John Grigsby, supposed to be one hundred and seven years old died October 11th." This could not refer to the John Grigs by of this sketch for his will was dated nov. 17. 1728/29 and probated November 11, 1730. (Bk. "M" p. 17).

This age seems improbable for the 18th century. If true it would place his date of birth in 1640. He could therefore have been the father of the above John Grigsby and of Thomas Grigsby who died about 1736. (See Gregg family).

John Grigsby, whose will was probated in 1730, had the following children named in his will:

I.   John was bequeathed the Nicholas Battain tract of
     land and three negroes, Sambo, Thorn and Dick. He
     signed the inventory of his nephew John Travis, in
     Stafford on September 9, 1735 (M-184). His inven-
     tory was filed in Stafford in 1750.

A Jane Grigsby, widow, made her will in Stafford, Dec. 5, 1755, proven April 13, 1756 (0-316). She was probably the widow of the above John. The witnesses to her will were William, John and Anne Grigsby.

Her children were:

1. John, m. Anne _____. They witnessed the will of John's Uncle James Grigsby in 1752 (0-220) and John witnessed the will of William Travis in 1763.

   Children from Overwharton Reg.
   (1) William, bapt. Nov. 11, 1744.
   (2) Susannah, bapt. Oct. 10, 1747.
   (3) Rachel, bapt. Aug. 12, 1750.

2. Moses, executor of his mother's will, m. (1) Kathrine Branson December, 1742 (0. Reg. 202); (2) Mary Mathews Aug. 20, 1753. John, son of Moses, bapt. March 1, 1758.

3. Thomas, Overwharton Par. m. Ann Dishman of Washington Par. November 25, 1729 (S. P. R. 25).

4. Aaron, m. Verlinda, daughter of James White of Westmoreland, mentioned in White's will 1763. Aaron, made his will in King George in 1764 and left all of his estate to his wife Verlinda.

   In Spottsylvania March 2, 1757, Aaron Grigsby of King George and Margaret his wife, daughter of John Proctor of Spottsylvania made a deed to William Mitchell (p. 204 printed bk.). Was Margaret a first wife?

II. Charles was mentioned secondly in his father's will. He was given a tract of land and two negroes, Roben and James. Charles' will was dated October 20, 1720, probated November 11, 1740. His wife Sarah, possibly "Wilkerson, " and children named were as follows.

1. James, m. Sarah Sudduth March 9, 1742. (S. P. R. 1). Elizabeth, daughter of James and Sarah, born Feb. 24, bapt. April 10, 1743 (R-90); (2) Charles (3) Wilkerson; (4) Elisha; (5) Margaret Smith; (6) Rose m. William Spicer. She and her husband of Hanover County made a deed April 11, 1786 to land in Stafford and recited that the land had been bequeathed by Thomas Grigsby to his brother Charles and that she was one of the legatees under the will; (23 W. -24); (7) Barbara Runnels; (8) Priscilla Grigsby;

        (9) Rachel m. Isacc Rose, December 9, 1751. (R-210).

III.   Mary, m. (1) Benjamin Newton (2) John Amees or Meese. She was given four negroes Jemmy, Will, Toney and Bess in her father's will. Three of these negroes are mentioned in her will dated April 20, 1747. (See Newton and Travers).

2. IV.   James was given a parcel of land and three negroes Jack, Ben, and Dall, in his father's will. Jack and Dall were mentioned in James' will 1752. (See later #2).

V.   William was given a parcel of land and three negroes, Allow, Jane and Grace in his father's will. There is no record of his death is Stafford. The inventory of a William Grigsby was filed in Faquier in 1782 but this may have been another William.

VI.   Thomas was given a parcel of land, three negroes, Nan, Germy and Mary, all hogs and half his cattle. Thomas patented 80 acres in Stafford in the branches of the Pasbytancy, adjoining Peter Ashton and John Grigsby, August 20, 1725 (A. p. 163).

        The St. Paul's register shows the bapt. of a large number of his slaves, from 1725 onward. He was sheriff of Stafford April 24, 1731. (37 V. -125) He married Rose, daughter of Gerrard Newton, for in 1729 Thomas Grigsby of Stafford and wife Rose, one of the daughters and co-heirs of Gerrard Newton, late of Richmond County, sold one-half of 500 acres divided between Rose and her sister Elizabeth, wife of Matthew Guibert of Maryland.

        Thomas made his will April 14, 1745, pro. Nov. 11, 1745. He mentioned wife Rose and all of his brothers except Charles, who had died in 1740. His widow, Rose, married Townsend Dade, December 12, 1745. (S. P. R. 205)

        He did not mention any children in his will. However, a Samuel Grigsby of Leeds Parish, Faquier County, mentions his mother, "Mrs. Dade of King George" in his will dated Oct. 22, 1781. (King's Faquier wills p. 29) Also a William Berryman of Westmoreland in his will, 1783, mentions a Mrs. Rose Grigsby of Stafford. (These entries are confusing.)

2.   James Grigsby, son of John Grigsby, made his will in Stafford, January 2, 1752, and same was probated April 14, 1752. (W. B. "O", p. 220). He gave his son, Redmond, a parcel of land

in Prince William and a negro girl named Mole; son, Nathaniel,
a negro girl named Alice; daughter, Elizabeth, a negro boy named
Jeremiah and household goods; son, James m. Letitia Travis
January 18, 1753 (S. P. R. 111), "parcel of land my father left
me and negro boy Daniel; son, Enoch, all remainder of property
in Prince William at my wife's decease and negro girl Jane; son,
Samuel, negro girl Nan; daughter, Susannah Grigsby, negro girl
Priss; wife to have 4 negroes and one servant man named Robert
Speckle; desires her to pay son Nathaniel 15 £ current money. "
Executor's wife and five sons, Redmond, Nathaniel, James, Enoch
and Samuel. Witnesses: John Grigsby, Anne Grigsby and Sarah
Fletcher. Susannah, the wife, and sons, Redmond and Nathaniel,
presented will for probate. His wife is said to have been Susannah
Redmond, probably daughter of William Redmond (ante).

Children:

I. Redmond was given land in Prince William. He was
    residing there in 1782.
II. Nathaniel, m. Elizabeth Butler, daughter of Mary
    (Mason) and William Butler (See Butler). He moved
    to South Carolina with his two brothers James and
    Enoch and died there in 1801. They had William
    Butler Grigsby who married Jane King. (Family
    records incomplete.)
III. Elizabeth was given a negro named Jeremiah.
IV. James, m. January 18, 1753, Letitia Travis, (S. P.
    R. 111) his cousin, daughter of John Travis and his
    wife Margaret Newton. Margaret was the daughter of
    Mrs. Mary (Grigsby) Newton-Meese and granddaughter
    of John Grigsby I. A James Grigsby made his will in
    Loudoun in 1797, but our James was probably the
    James Grigsby who moved to Edgfield County S. C.
    and was residing there in 1790.
V. Enoch, m. Mary Butler, sister of Elizabeth Butler
    who married his brother Nathaniel. (See later #3).
VI. Samuel, made his will in Faquier in 1781.

3.   Enoch Grigsby and his brother, Nathaniel, mentioned in
above will, later removed to Loudoun County, where Nathaniel,
on November 13, 1759, presented the inventory of the estate of
Edmund Linton. Linton was the second husband of Hester Smallwood Smith, mother of Jacob Smith, Jr. who married Sarah
Butler, sister-in-law of both Enoch and Nathaniel Grigsby.
(Loudoun Bk. A, p. 20).

On June 12, 1764, "Jacob Smith, orphan of Jacob Smith, deceased, came into court and made choice of Enoch Grigsby for
his guardian. " (Loudoun O. B. "B", p. 361).

Dr. Enoch Grigsby and his wife, Mary Butler (See Butler) sold land in Prince Williams in 1770 and soon afterwards moved to South Carolina. (W. M. 21 (2), p. 183). He was a Lieutenant in the Revolution and received 7/2/10 as pay. (Stub Indents Book U-W, p. 91, No. 632). He died in 1789.

Children: (See Mays' Family History for their descendants)
- I.   Colonel Rhydon Grigsby.
- II. Sarah Grigsby, m. Colonel Jonathan Weaver
- III. James Grigsby, killed in accident.
- IV. Susan Grigsby, m. Lodowick Hill, great-grandfather of the husband of Mrs. Susan B. Hill of Edgefield. Lodowick Hill served in the Revolution as "Late Sergeant in Rose" Troop, Middleton's Regiment, Sumpter's Brigade and received 115/5/10 pay due him for services from April, 1782 to October 1, 1784. (Stub Indents, Vol. L-N, p. 181).
- V.   Nancy Grigsby, b. 1775, m. General Samuel Mays (see later #13).
- VI. Elizabeth Grigsby, m. Thomas Butler, her cousin, brother of General William Butler.

13.   Nancy Grigsby, born 1775, died 1828, married 1793, General Samuel Mays of Edgefield and Greenwood Counties, born July 23, 1762, in Halifax County, Virginia, died January 25, 1816.

He fought in the Revolution, before he was 16 years old, at the Battles of Musgrove Mills, Blackstocks and Hanging Rocks in General Sumpter's Brigade. He moved to Newberry County after the Revolution and was a member of the Legislature. In the War of 1812 he was a Brigadier General of South Carolina Militia.

Children:
- I.   Sara Grigsby Mays, b. 1794, d. 1812, m. John Lispcomb.
- II.   William Anderson Mays, b. 1796, d. 1857, unmarried.
- III. James Butler Mays, b. 1798, d. 1836, m. Miriam Earle
- IV.   Dr. Rhydon Grigsby Mays, b. 1801, d. in Florida, m. Sara, daughter of Luke Smith. (See Smallwood Smith).
- V.   Richard Johnson Mays, b. 1808, d. in Florida, m. Anna Williams.
- VI.   Thomas Sumter Mays, b. 1805, d. Montgomery, Alabama, m. (1) Sallie Glasscock; (2) Eliza Glassock.
- VII. Samuel Warren Mays, b. 1805, twin of Thomas Sumter, d. Montgomery, Alabama, unmarried.
- VIII. Dannett Hill Mays, moved to Florida, died there, m. Jane Thomas.
- IX.   Caroline Elizabeth Mays, b. June, 1811, moved to

Tallahassee, m. Theodore Brenard.

    X.   Enoch Grigsby Mays, b. posthumously 1816, d. in Dallas, Texas, m. Chloe Linton.

14.   James Butler Mays, born June 27, 1798, in Greenwood County, S. C., died February 14, 1836, in Madison County, Florida, married 1834, Damaris Miriam Earle, born November 13, 1808, at Beaver Dam, Oconee County, S. C., died November 1881, at Riverview, Florida, daughter of Harriet (Harrison) and Captain Samuel Earle of Saluda River.

Mr. Mays graduated 1818 at South Carolina College. He served in the Seminole Indian War under Governor Call of Florida, was wounded in a battle at Lake Sampala, and died a few days later.

Children:
15.   I.   Samuel Elias Mays, b. November 12, 1834, m. Catharine Moseley
    II.   James Butler Mays, Jr., b. posthumously, September 13, 1836, m. Zadie Poe of Pendleton

15.   Captain Samuel Elias Mays, born November 12, 1834, in Pendleton County, South Carolina, died 1906, at River View, Florida, married 1857, at Washington, Wilkes Co., Georgia, Catharine E. Moseley, born March 9, 1838, died March 1894, daughter of Mary Ann (Brown) and the Reverend Mathew Francis Moseley, a Baptist Minister.

Captain Mays was educated at South Carolina College and served in the 2nd South Carolina Cavalry under General J. E. B. Stuart, 1861-65.

Children:
    I.   James Butler Mays, d. young.
16.   II.   James Francis Mays, b. October 11, 1860, m. Maud E. Walton.
    III.   James Butler Mays
    IV.   Samuel Edward Mays, b. 1864, m. Rowena Evers
    V.   Miriam Earle Mays, b. 1866, d. 1884, unmarried.
    VI.   Martha Dart Mays, b. 1868.
    VII.   Catherine Josepha Mays, b. 1873, d. 1897, unmarried.
    VIII.   Earle Walton Mays, b. 1876, m. Mary Wilming.

16.   James Francis Mays, born October 11, 1860, in Pendleton County, South Carolina, died December 29, 1938, in Lexington, North Carolina, married January 20, 1887, at Sunnyside, Georgia, Maud E. Walton, born May 26, 1866, at Sunnyside, daughter of Anne Thomas (Lewis) and Reverend Robert Hall Walton, Presbyterian Minister and graduate of Hampden-Sydney College.

Mr. Mays was educated at the Kingston, Georgia, Academy. He invented the original machine called the "Mays Calculator" which later developed into the "Burroughs Adding Machine."

Children:
17.   I.   Anne Moseley Mays, b. November 13, 1890, m. Glen E. Miller
     II.   Catherine Toombs Mays, b. September 1, 1893, unmarried.
    III. James Francis Mays, Jr., b. February 17, 1897, unmarried.
    IV. Maud Walton Mays, b. March 22, 1902, m. Major Don Halsey Griswold, U. S. Engrs.
     V.   Miriam Mildred Mays, b. March 22, 1902, m. Paul Hilliard Miller.

17.   Anne Moseley Mays, born November 13, 1890, married June 24, 1918, at Birmingham, Alabama, Glen Earle Miller, born July 9, 1887, at Kokomo, Indiana, son of Albertie Christine (Brobst) and Frank Jasper Miller.

Children:
     I.   Glen Earle Miller, Jr., b. September 21, 1920, 2nd Lt., U.S. Air Corps, Swarthmore College, A.B., 1941; University of Pennsylvania, M.A., 1942.
    II.   Anne Walton Miller, b. June 11, 1922, Swarthmore College, A.B. 1944.
    III. Frank A. Miller, b. July 14, 1924, Aviation Cadet, Army Air Corps, University of Pittsburg, as of 1944, Delta Upsilon Fraternity, Swarthmore, 1946.
    IV. John Anthony Miller III, b. March 3, 1930.

DONIPHAN OF NORTHERN NECK

The Doniphan family was prominent in Richmond, King George and Stafford. The founder of this family was Captain Alexander Doniphan. He evidently came from Plymouth, England, for on July 29, 1671, Thomas Yeabsley of Plymouth, Devon, England, gave a power of attorney to Alexander Doniphan of Plymouth, merchant, to collect debts due him, the said Yeabsley, in Maryland. (Md. Arch. LX, pp. 491-92.) Alexander is an ancestor of President Truman and of General Alexander Doniphan of Mexican War fame. (D. N. B.)

In 1674 Alexander made a deposition in Westmoreland in which he stated he was then 24 years of age. This would place his date of birth in 1650. (15 v 187.) Alexander was a Justice of the County Court, 1692-1714. He was a Captain of Horse in 1704, for in August of that year he made a claim for pay for his troop who guarded the captured Indians three days and nights. (Bk. I - 32). He was also High Sheriff of Richmond in 1716. (O. B.)

Alexander was married three times. His first wife was Amy, last name unknown, whom he married before 1677. (Westm. O. B. 1665-77, p. 311). His second wife, whom he married before 1692, was Margaret, daughter of George Mott of Rappahannock County, a large land owner. (Rich. D. B. I - 34). His third wife, mentioned in his will, was Susanna. Alexander made his will Sept. 20, 1716, and same was probated February 6, 1716/17, in Richmond. (W. B. 1709-17 - 297). His will is quoted hereafter with reference to the properties bequeathed his children.

Children of first wife Amy.
 I. Alexander, Jr., m. (1) Elizabeth, (2) Sarah Sallis and died without issue in Stafford about 1725. (Will in lost book "K", 1721-30 - 106). On May 1, 1692, Alexander, Jr. and his father witnessed a deed from John Fosaker and Elizabeth, his wife, to William Bronaugh for 135 acres in Richmond adjacent to David Bronaugh and Heabard's land. (D. B. I, p. 10. Fleet 16 - 3).

   Elizabeth Barnard, widow, of Stafford, deeded him 150 acres in that county on July 28, 1701, on the condition that if he died without heirs, the land would revert to her. (Bk. "Z" - 87.) On March 5,

1704, his father deeded him one-half of the land
bought from George Jones on March 5, 1683. (D. B.
4-5). His father also bequeathed him in 1716, "250
acres bought of George Jones." This land was part
of a grant of 1300 acres to George Jones and Henry
Clarke March 16, 1674, and recorded Oct. 12, 1678.
(Bk. 1677-82 - 18). Henry Clark's daughter, Ann,
married Francis Gowre. Francis died in 1691 and
on May 13, 1709, Stanley Gowre, son and heir of
Francis, and the four daughters of Angell Jacobus
who (Angell) had married Elizabeth Clarke (sister
to Ann) sold 210 acres of this land to John Gowre.
(See Jacobus)

This association of the Doniphan and Gowre families, evidently neighbors on adjoining lands, would
tend to show that the name "Gowry" (Gowre) came
into the Waugh and Doniphan families through the
Giles Travis family with whom they intermarried.
Giles was a grandson of Alexander Doniphan I. Million Travis, daughter of Giles, married Joseph Waugh,
Jr., and they had sons named "Gowry" and "Travers".

Alexander, Jr., and his wife Elizabeth sold the
land bequeathed by his father the next year. (D. B.
4-7). His second wife, Sarah (Sallis) Doniphan,
married secondly, February 25/26, William Hansford of Spotsylvania. (S. P. R.) She and her second
husband on July 13, 1726, sold the above-mentioned
150 acres to Anthony Thornton. Sarah conveyed her
dower rights. (Staff. D. B. 1722-28, pp. 276, 78.)

II. Anne, evidently deceased before 1716, the date of
Alexander, Sr.'s will, married, probably John Gowre
(Gowry) of Stafford. John Gowry's daughter seemingly married Giles Travers. Alexander Doniphan
twice mentions his "Grandson Giles Travers" in his
will. Anne Doniphan, together with her father,
Alexander, Sr., witnessed a deed in Richmond, July
3, 1693. (D. B. 2 - 47). Maybe Anne was an elder
daughter who was deceased before his youngest daughter Anne was born. (See later.) It will be noted that
in many families younger children were named for
deceased sisters and brothers.

Children of second wife Margaret Mott
III. Robert, in a deed recorded in Stafford, stated that
he was the "eldest son of Margaret Mott and Alexander Doniphan." (K. G. D. B. 1 - 145.) His father
gave him "all I have in this world", evidently mean-

ing the remainder of his estate not bequeathed. On October 1, 1722, Mott and Robert Doniphan deeded to John Dinwiddie part of a tract of land from 15650 acres granted John and George Mott October 17, 1670. This deed was witnessed by John Travis, who later testified in a law suit against John Dinwiddie. (16W (I) - 290-91) (17W (I) - 78.) Robert is said to have married Mary Wilton and died in King George, intestate, about 1735. Apparently he left an only child:

> (1) Robert, Jr. is said to have married Ellen Hackley, a cousin, daughter of James Hackley (d. 1748) of King George and Elizabeth, his wife, daughter of Ellen (Mott) and Richard Shippey of Richmond. Ellen, Sr. was one of the daughters of George Mott. Robert Jr. died in 1743/44 for his will was proven by James Hackley and Ellen Doniphan, March 2, 1742/44. (K.G. Bonds I - 30.) His will was recorded in lost will book I.

IV. Mott, m. Rosanna, daughter of Capt. George and Mary (Mathews) Anderson of Stafford. Mott received two tracts of land in his father's will. In the fourth clause of his will he gave "to son Mott Doniphan 180 acres out of a tract I bought of Joshua Davis, being 330 acres lying back of my river lands and to his next son that should be born. In case my son Mott should die before another son, then to fall to MY GRANDSON GILES TRAVERS. "

In the fifth clause of his will his father gave "to son Mott Doniphan that parcel of land I bought of William Griffin xxx to him and his second son, then to my son Robert Doniphan. "

It appears from these two clauses that Alexander was trying to bequeath land to Mott's second son, because Mott's first son, as his son and heir, under the rule of primogeniture, would inherit all of his extensive land holdings in case Mott died intestate.

On September 9, 1735, Mott presented the inventory of John Travers (Travis), probably a son of the above-mentioned Giles Travers, to the court of Stafford County. (W.B. "M" - 184.) On May 1, 1747, Mott purchased from Thomas Stubblefield and Ellen, his wife, all of Ellen's dower rights in the estate of her former husband, Robert Doniphan, Jr. (K.G.D.B. 3 - 180.)

Mott was a vestryman of Acquia Church, Overwharton Parish, in 1757, the year the church was built. He died about 1776, for his will was filed about that time in lost will book "N" (1767-83 - 333) and is missing.

Children:

> (1) Alexander, m. June 17, 1740, Mary, daughter of the
> Reverend Joseph Waugh and Mary (Crosby) Waugh.
> Mary Waugh inherited 1176 acres on Potomac Creek
> (D. B. 5 - 307.) On April 4, 1757, his father Mott
> deeded him "a plantation in Fairfax County on Dogue
> Run . . ."being part of a patent granted to John
> Mathews October 13, 1694, for 2466 acres. On
> October 8, 1751, Alexander was appointed guardian
> for his wife's nephews John and Travers Waugh.
> (O. - 205.)

On May 1, 1765, Alexander Doniphan and John Grigsby Jr. witnessed the death bed will of William Travis of Stafford. John
Grigsby, Jr. was a second cousin of William Travis (See Grigsby
and Travis). His father Mott Doniphan had, in 1735, presented
the inventory of John Travis, father of William Travis, to the
court (ante). It seems from this and other circumstances that the
Doniphans were related to this branch of the Travis family.

On March 2, 1761, Thomas, Lord Fairfax, granted a patent of
177 acres in Stafford to Capt. Alexander Doniphan on Potomac Run,
being part of 246 acres deeded by said Fairfax to Capt. Edward
Mountjoy, late of Stafford, decd., II, August, 1704. (G. B. I - 58.)

Alexander made his will in Stafford March 29, 1766, and same
was probated July 1768. (T26 - 276.) This will had been destroyed
in the county records, but Mr. George Harrison Sandford King of
Fredericksburg, an able and accurate genealogical writer, discovered the will in the Superior Court of Chancery in Fredericksburg.

Alexander Doniphan had several children. He gave to "loving
son, George Anderson Gowry Doniphan, and my loving son Anderson Doniphan" several negroes. (do. 275). It is stated that the
first wife of the Reverend Joseph Waugh, father of Mary (Waugh)
Doniphan, was "Rachel, daughter of John Gowry." (15W (I) - 190).

This statement is followed by a question mark, showing that
same was doubtful. Mary Waugh, wife of Alexander Doniphan,
was a daughter of Mary (Crosby) Waugh, the second wife of the
Reverend Joseph Waugh and not of Racheal, the first one. Therefore, it would seem that George Anderson GOWRY Waugh must
have derived his "Gowry" name in some other way than by descent
through Racheal Waugh.

Children of Alexander and Mary (Waugh) Doniphan:

> (1) William, b. March 21, 1742 (Overwharton Parish
> Register).
> (2) Elizabeth, b. April 18, 1744. Reg. m. 1773, William
> Smith.

(3) Anne, b. February 28, 1747, not mentioned in father's will.

(4) Alexander, b. March 12, 1750, m. Mary Davis, dau. of James Davis (1735-1808) of King George County. Alexander died intestate about 1817 in K. G.

(5) Mott, b. June 10, 1752, dsp Sept. 8, 1783, in K. G. (D. B. 6-394).

(6) Mary, was mentioned in father's will in 1768 as unmarried.

(7) Joseph, born about 1757, married in 1783 Ann Smith, sister of William Smith, who married Elizabeth Doniphan (above) and moved to Mason County, Ky., where Joseph died in 1813. They were the parents of General William Alexander Doniphan (1808-87) of Missouri, famous in the Mexican War. (D. N. B.)

(8) George Anderson Gowry, born about 1759, died several years before November 18, 1785, intestate and under age in Stafford (D. B. "S" - 307).

(9) Anderson, b. 1764, d. 1841, m. 1793, Susan Smith, sister of William and Anne Smith.

Children of Mott and Rosanna (Anderson) Doniphan (cont'd.)

(2) Anderson married Magdelene, widow of Thomas Monteith. Anderson died 1761 in King George. His children were: (1) Gerrard; (2) Rosanna; (3) Mary, married Travers Cooke, Feb. 26, 1754; (4) Lucretia; (5) Elizabeth.

(3) Anne, m. Aug. 4, 1743, George White. (See Children Overwharton Reg.)

Children of Margaret (Mott) and Alexander Doniphan I. (cont'd.)

V. Margaret was bequeathed by her father "75 acres of land bought of Joshua Davis, being 300 acres, and to her male heirs." If no male heirs, then to son Robert Doniphan. She was called "Margaret Doniphan" in his will, and was evidently unmarried.

VI. Elizabeth was given by her father "the remaining part of that tract (Joshua Davis') which is 80 acres. Also to Elizabeth her mother's wedding ring, if my daughter Elizabeth should die and her heirs, then that 80 acres to my son Robert." She married Stephen Hansford of King George County, for on May 4, 1758, Stephen Hansford and Elizabeth, his wife, deeded to Alexander Doniphan 80 acres in King George, being the land given to Elizabeth by her father Alexander Doniphan, decd. (D. B. 4 - 317).

VII. Ann was given one feather bed and a young mare in

her father's will. She was mentioned last and was
seemingly the youngest daughter. She was evidently
unmarried, as she was called "Ann Doniphan" in the
will.

For more information on the Doniphan family, one should read
Mr. King's excellent article in Tyler's Magazine, Volume 26.
What little is shown here is the result of trying to find some further
connection with "grandson Giles Travis" mentioned in Alexander
Doniphan's will, but there were too many lost wills, and several
of the Doniphans died intestate.

GREGG OF STAFFORD

Thomas Gregg patented 400 acres in Westmoreland on the branches of the Pasbatancy Creek, March 18, 1662, adjacent to John and William Heaberd and Henry Meese for the transportation of nine persons (C. P. 566). This land afterwards fell in Stafford and later in King George.

June 7, 1666, Colonel Henry Meese patented an additional 100 acres adjacent to his own land and that of Thomas Gregg (C. P. 560).

In 1669/70 Thomas Gregg brought suit against William Storke in Charles County, Md. (9W (2) 182). He was a Justice of the Stafford Court in 1680 (R. 1680 fo. 1-26). In 1691, Thomas Gregg, Sr. refused to take the oath of allegiance to William and Mary. He evidently adhered to King James II as his rightful sovereign (4, 7 V. 248). On April 14, 1698, Thomas Gregg patented 795 acres on Nipiscoe Run (N. N. G. 2, p. 89).

William Heabard, son of John Heabard, on March 8, 1692, chose Thomas Gregg, Sr. as his guardian. (47 V. 248).

By inference from this and the following records, Thomas Gregg, Sr. seems to have married Lucy Heabard, sister of John Heabard.

John Heabard's wife was Anne Freake, daughter of William and Anne Freake of Westmoreland. Mr. Freake was a large land owner and also a vestryman of Appomattox Church in Westmoreland, along with John Washington and Andrew Monroe, ancestors of two presidents of the United States. In a law suit in Richmond County, June 15, 1700, it was shown that "William Heabard and his mother Anne" were respectively grandson and daughter of William Freake (17 V. 76).

William Heabard died about 1721 (Inventory in Stafford) and his wife, formerly Margaret Newton, married John Travis in 1722 (S. P. R.)

The first name of the wife of Thomas Gregg, Sr. was "Lucy", who signed as "Lucy Gregg, Sr." in 1700, as a witness to a deed of Thomas Gregg, evidently her son (Z. 357). A "Lucy Heabard" was brought over by Robert Moseley who patented 520 acres in Stafford in 1661 (44 V. 164). Moseley was decd. by May 24, 1664, when Robert Fosaker was in possession of his estate (44 V. 193). Inasmuch as John Heabard and his son William Heabard did not marry a "Gregg", it is evident that "Gregg" married "a Heabard".

Children of Lucy and Thomas Gregg, Sr.

> I. Thomas, Jr. appears in the records of Stafford July 19, 1690, when Charles Baldridge was summoned to give added sceurity to the estate Capt. William Heabard gave unto William Heabard, the son of John Heabard, decd., one of the bondsmen being dead and the other, Mr. Francis Dade, petitioned the court to discharge him. Thomas Gregg, Jr., was ordered to receive the estate from Charles Baldridge. (45 V. - 15)

On June 14, 1690, the securities for John Heabard's estate were John Mathews and Charles Baldridge. Charles was a son of William Baldridge and Elizabeth, his wife. Elizabeth, the widow of William Baldridge married, secondly, Captain William Heabard of Stafford, apparently uncle of William Heabard II.

Thomas Gregg, Jr. was probably born before 1670, as he appears to be 21 years old in 1690. He received a grant on January 25, 1694/5 of 200 acres on Potomac Creek next to Col. Henry Meese. (G. B. 2-109). The grant was bequeathed to him by a nuncupative will, but as it was not written and signed, it was insufficient to pass a legal title, so Thomas had to compromise and pay something before he could obtain a patent. The grant reads as follows: "Whereas Nicholas Bullbrooke of Stafford died seized of 200 acres in Stafford on Potomac Creek about 20 years since which Bullbrooke upon his death bed, did verbally give the same unto Thomas Gregg, Jr. But in regard to the said verbal will it is not good in law to devise land, composition is made with him." (G. B. 2-109).

On March 20, 1701, Thomas Watts deeded to Thomas Gregg a parcel of land on S. side of the Potomac Creek bought by his father Thomas Watts, late of Stafford, from William Norgrove (Z. 77).

Thomas Gregg, in 1692, was a lieutenant in the militia (2W (2) 182), a Justice in 1702, (1. V. 371) and a surveyor in 1703. (1. V. 372).

In 1699 Thomas Gregg and Thomas Elzey returned the inventory of Thomas Elzey, Sr., and on April 1, 1700, a division of the estate was made between Thomas Gregg and Thomas Elzey, Jr. The wife of Thomas Elzey was named "Margaret." (Bk. Z., pp. 10, 30). In 1700, also, he rendered his account of his part of the estate of Elizabeth Wood (Z, p. 39). On December 5, 1706, he sold 50 acres, bought of Sampson Darrell, to John Gowry. One of the witnesses to the deed was Lucy Gregg, Sr., which indicates there was a "Lucy Gregg, Jr." (Z 357).

William Wood, in his will dated June 6, 1706, mentions land that he sold to Thomas Gregg (Z. 347). In 1707, Joseph Waugh (eldest son of Parson John Waugh) and Rachel, his wife, deeded land to Thomas Gregg (34 V. 274; 37 V. 162). The land was patented by Col. Henry Meese October 20, 1665, and "by divers conveyances came to John Waugh, my father. " (Z. 375). On May 13, 1707, Thomas Gregg sold 300 acres to William Harwood, part of a patent of 795 acres granted April 14, 1698. (Z. 381).

In 1706, he deeded to William Wood, 300 acres next to "brother James Gregg, " part of the same above patent. (Z. 381). On account of the loss of records, the date of his death is unknown. His wife Lucy made her will January 9, 1730, and gave legacies to Edward Humston, grandson, and Sarah Newton, granddaughter. From this it is inferred that Thomas Gregg died without male heirs, as his grandson, Edward Humston, was "heir at law" of Thomas Grigsby, as shown later. His wife therefore seems to have been Lucy Grigsby, daughter of Thomas Grigsby.

Children:

I. Daughter (unknown), m. Edward Humston, who patented 200 acres in Stafford December 11, 1704. (G. B. 3-61). He was dead before April 10, 1728, for on that date his son, Edward Humston, as "son and heir" of Edward Humston, late of the county, decd., deeded to brother Thomas Humston, 211 acres, part of a tract of 330 acres granted to Edward Humston, grandfather of said Edward, April 15, 1667. (G. B. 6, p. 26). (Bk. 1722-28, p. 515). In the index of lost book "K" (1721-1730), it is shown that Edward Humston inventory was recorded on page 291.

Children:

1. Edmund Humston, the "grandson" mentioned by Lucy Gregg on September 8, 1731, was appointed guardian of Priscilla, daughter of William Heabard (Bk. O., p. 50). This apparently confirms the inference, as before stated, that Lucy Gregg Sr. was a Heabard. William Heabard was the last of his family.

On April 1, 1722, Edward Humston and Edward Humston, Jr. witnessed a deed of John and Rachel Colclough to Benjamin Colclough. (Bk. 1722-28, p. 86). On November 5, 1736, Edward Humston and Sarah, his wife, acknowledged deed "to all tracts which Thomas Grigsby, late of Stafford, bequeathed, by his last will, to Edward Humston, the younger, being heir at law. "

2. Thomas Humston, dsp, December 1, 1730, (S. P. R.). He was deeded land, as above mentioned, and an inventory of his estate was filed in 1731.

II. James Gregg was mentioned as "brother" in deed of Thomas Gregg, 1706 (Z. 381). The will of a "James"

or "Jones" Gregg is in missing book "K", page 58
(1721-30). His inventory was filed on page 218 of
same book (See General Index). His children were
evidently of age in 1734, for his estate was divided,
by his brother John, among the following children,
May 29, 1734 (M-161).

1. Mathew, m. Cathrine _____. They had
   the following children in Overwharton Register:
   (1) James, b. May 18, 1740; (2) John, b. Dec.
   19, 1744. Mathew's will was made in 1749 and probated Aug. 9, 1757. "Sick and weak," to sons
   James and John Gregg, land; to sister Lucy £ 5;
   to cousins (nephews) William and John Peake, sons
   of Lucy, £ 5. Wits: Wm. and John Peake.
2. John, inventory filed 1756.
3. Sarah, m. William Brown, December 11, 1756
   (S. P. R).
4. Lettice (Letitia)
5. Jeremiah.

III. John Gregg was a bondsman for George Mason in re
estate of George's stepmother, Ann Mason, May 21,
1735. He was also a Justice in Stafford, 1730. (Mason
49) (W. B. 1729-48, p. 21). An inventory of a John
Gregg was filed in Stafford, 1736.

IV. Elizabeth Gregg, m. Benjamin Newton II. (See Newton)
It is regretted loss of records prevents a connected narrative
of this family. A Mathew Gregg m. _____ Chinn, Aug. 15,
1751. Mathew, son of Mathew, was baptized September 15, 1752.

A John Gregg married Elizabeth Waugh in Spottsylvania Oct.
6, 1737.

COLCLOUGH OF STAFFORD

John Colclough was the first of this family in Stafford. He patented 200 acres in Stafford November 10, 1665, "On S. W. side of Quantico Creek with back line of Richard Heabard. " (C. P. 544) He is said to be a brother of Major George Colclough of Northumberland County, Va. (38 V 234). George Colclough, son of Sir Caesar Colclough of Staffordshire, Eng., died in Virginia according to the Visitations of Staffordshire 1664-1700. (Tyler II, eleven, p. 40). In 1654 John Colclough was the master or owner of a vessel which traded regularly with Virginia. (18 V. 47-48). In Jan. 1654/55, Thomas Colclough, one of the owners of a ship "Charles", petitioned the Council to grant a commission to the master of that vessel, which for divers years past had traded in Virginia to surprise such vessels as he found trading there contrary to the Act of Parliament 1650. (do. p. 49-50.)

Mrs. Martha W. Hiden says (58 V 234), "Before the county court of Northumberland in 1657, Ursula, then the wife of Major George Colclough and widow of (2) Colonel John Mottrom and of (1) Mr. Richard Thompson, deposed as follows: 'all the money I had when I married was £ 158-2S-8d which my brother John paid my brother Thomas Colclough's man for my husband's use. ' (Va. Col. Abstracts 19, p. 25.) From the fact Major George Colclough had a brother Thomas, it is likely that he is the same person who was part owner of the ship 'Charles.' It is also likely that John Colclough, part owner of other vessels in the Virginia Trade, was a third brother. "

John Colclough and Jasper Bennett of Stafford, on January 1677, deeded land in Stafford to Samuel Hayward. (Rec. 1680, folio 26, no. 25).

The date of John Colclough's death is not known. Owing to loss of records it is difficult to obtain correct data on this family.

His children appear to be:
    I.   John II, whose inventory was filed in Stafford in 1702. (This, however, could be the inventory of John I.) Hannah Colclough, evidently a widow, made her will November 10, 1700; same probated 1701. (W. B. 1699-1709-56). She was possibly the widow of the above

John II. She mentions her son (1) Charles Colclough
and her daughter (2) Ann Colclough. (No other child-
ren named.) She bequeathed legacies to her brother
Arthur Chapman, to her cousins (nephews) Arthur and
Thomas Walker, and her brother, Benjamin Colclough.
David Barrick of Richmond County sold land to
Thomas Walker, son of Thomas Walker, in 1715.
(D. B. 7 - 74, 76.)

II.   Benjamin, m. Rachel _____. He patented 150
acres on New Dodson Creek Oct. 20, 1694. Benjamin
died about 1723 for an account of his estate was filed
in that year in Stafford. Racheal died Dec. 25, 1749.
(R. -237). Her will was dated Dec. 9, 1748, and
same was probated in 1750. She died at the age of
71, for on November 13, 1739, she made a deposition in which she stated she was 61 years of age.
(37 V 181). The dates of birth of three of Benjamin
and Racheal's children are shown in the St. Paul's
Register as follows: (1) William, born July 2, 1716,
bapt. Sept. 22, 1716. He married Mary Rogers,
daughter of John Rogers and his wife Mary Newton,
granddaughter of Mrs. Mary Newton Meese. (See
Travis of Alamo). (2) Alexander, (twin), born July
2, 1716, bapt. Sept. 22, 1716. (R. 2). He died Nov.
10, 1716. (R. -233). (3) Sarah, born Mar. 1720,
m. _____ Kidwell. (R. - 30).

William Colclough, who married Mary Rogers, either moved
to Prince William, or his land fell in that county when it was cut
off from Stafford, for he bought land from his cousin, Benjamin
Newton III in Prince William on July 23, 1753. (O - 1752-53 - 180).

Other children of Racheal Colclough are shown in her will,
which was as follows: "Land in Fairfax equally to son John and
William; to daughter Elizabeth Bowling a negro to her for life,
then to her son John Bowling, his brother Alexander Bowling and
brother Sim Bowling; to daughter Mary Thornbury a feather bed;
to daughter Sarah Kidwell, that which was her grandfather's; to
daughter Jane Newton, four negroes for life, then to go to her
children; to daughter Mary Durham, negroes. The land I have
given Alexander Colclough, the son of Robert Colclough, I give
unto William Colclough, the land where I now live." The crop of
tobacco to daughter Mary Thornbury, Rachael Bowling, Elias Bowling, Jane Newton and Margaret Durham. Granddaughter Jane De
Bolling not of age, personalty to be held for her. (Dec. 9, 1748.)
(O. 1748 - 68-133.)

READE OF ELIZABETH CITY AND BEDFORD

A Thomas Reade was residing in Elizabeth City about 1710. It is certain that he was a member of the Reade family of York, for the family of his son John Reade in Henrico was evidently related to that family.

John Reade married first, Mary Mallory; secondly, Elizabeth, who married secondly, Evan Owen. John Reade died in Henrico in 1739 and Elizabeth Reade was appointed administratrix with Col. John Bolling and Richard Randolph as her sureties. (Bk. 1737-46, p. 98).

Mary Reade, daughter of John Reade, was under age in 1745, for a chancery suit on her behalf was brought by her guardian, Francis Mallory, against Evan Owen and wife Elizabeth in that year. Richard Randolph was ordered to arbitrate the difference. (Do. pp. 262, 280, 338-357.)

Francis Mallory died and at an April court, 1753, Mary Reade, orphan of John Reade, then made choice of Col. John Bolling as her guardian. (Chesterfield, O.B. #1-319.) At a May court in 1753, a chancery suit brought by Hannah Reade, an infant, by Archibald Cary, her next friend, against William Reade (her brother) was dismissed (Do. 341). Previously in 1742, Elizabeth Reade, daughter of John Reade, deceased, had also made choice of Francis Mallory as her guardian. (Elizabeth City O.B. 1731-47, p. 306). Francis Mallory was her uncle, for in his will probated July 18, 1744, he gave his "cousin" (niece) £15, providing she comes to age of 21 or marries (D.W. 1737-49).

If Francis Mallory, an uncle, was chosen guardian by Mary and Hannah Reade, what kin were the other guardians, arbitrators and "next friends?"

Col. John Bolling (1700-1757), the first guardian of Mary Reade, was related by marriage. His first wife, Elizabeth Lewis, was a granddaughter of Mildred Reade, sister of Francis Reade and daughter of Colonel George Reade of York.

Archibald Cary, "next friend" for Hannah Reade, was a grandson of Henry Cary and his wife Judith Lockey, to whom Benjamin Reade gave a legacy. Archibald Cary's mother was Sarah Schlater, aunt of Mary Schlater who married Samuel Reade of

York. Samuel Reade's daughter Mary married John Cary. Archibald's wife was Mary Randolph, daughter of Jane Bolling and Richard Randolph. Richard Randolph was surety for Mrs. Elizabeth Reade and arbitrator of the differences between her and the Reade children. His wife, Jane Bolling, was a sister of Col. John Bolling.

While this may prove relationship, it does not exactly prove who were the parents of Thomas Reade of Elizabeth City.

He was probably not Thomas, son of Thomas Reade of Warwick, for the Warwick family was not related to any of the above guardians and "next friends" which phrase usually meant "next of kin". (See Beale.)

He appears to have been about the right age to be Thomas Reade, son of Francis Reade, of King and Queen. That Thomas was given a legacy in the will of his great grandmother, Alice Beale, probated February 24, 1703. In the will of her son-in-law, William Colston, he is mentioned as being under 18 in 1701. (See Beale.)

That Thomas appears to be the only available "Thomas" unaccounted for in the Reade family.

In 1704, one Riddle was holding 700 acres in King and Queen for a Thomas Reade. This was about one-half the size of the 1600 acre grant next to "Tower Hill," patented, January 28, 1662, by Edward Lockey. (C. P. 421, compare with C. P. 385) (Also compare C. P. 466, 515, 565, grants to John Madison.)

Benjamin Reade, after giving "Tower Hill" in the third paragraph of his will to two of his "nephews" (half of Tower Hill, or 744 acres, ultimately came to John Reade, the contingent beneficiary) bequeathed "all the rest of my land in King and Queen to my two Kinsmen, Mr. Robert and Mr. Francis Reade, to be equally divided between them." (See will.)

The 700 acres held by Riddle for Thomas Reade was about one-half of the 1600 acres bequeathed to Francis and Robert Reade. (Quit Rents 1704).

Thomas Reade married Ann Allen. The Allen family owned land adjacent to the Riddle family in Elizabeth City in 1663. It may be that Riddle might have been holding this land for Thomas Reade of Elizabeth City, for the families appear to be related. (See Allen.)

In 1714 Thomas Reade, together with Robert Armistead and William Williams, witnessed the will of Edward Penny (c. 193) On July 25, 1718, he, with Robert Armistead, Thomas Allen and Francis Rogers, appraised the estate of Dunn Armistead. (c. 87)

On February 13, 1717, Francis Rogers made his will. Same was probated May 17, 1719, and therein Francis Rogers bequeaths his son Francis "the plantation bought of Thomas Reade." The will was witnessed by Robert Armistead, and Thomas Reade was one of the appraisers of Roger's estate. (B. 1715-21, pp. 195, 201, 204, 255.)

In 1718, John Ballie patented 69 acres adjoining the land of Thomas Reade, George Walker and Eaton's School land. (c. 47)

From the above patent it appears that Thomas Reade held land next to Eaton's School land which was in possession of the Williams family.

On June 19, 1697, land belonging to Eaton's Free School was leased to William Williams for 20 years dating from Dec. 26, 1697 (B. 1684-99, p. 176). Thomas Reade in his will, 1721, provided that "my negro Tony be sold at outcry to pay off the Williams." From this it appears that either he inherited land which was subjected to be a legacy due to the Williams', or he owed them for land which he had purchased.

On June 22, 1721, Thomas Reade, with William Armistead and John Cooke, appraised the estate of Giles Duberry. Hugh Ross qualified as executor and Francis Mallory was his security (C-133)

Thomas Reade married Ann Allen, sister of William Allen of Elizabeth City, for in Thomas' will dated Oct. 18, 1721, probated December 20, 1721, he provided that his sons Thomas and William be placed in the "care of their uncle William Allen and to enjoy their estate at 13." He bequeathed his land to be equally divided between his three sons, John, Thomas and William. His daughter Hannah and wife Anne were to divide his personal property - wife Anne and son John were to be executrix and executor. (B. 1721-23, pp. 25, 31, 42) (B 1704-30, p. 12) (See Allen.)

Children:

5   I.   John, m. (1) Mary Mallory, (2) Elizabeth - (See later).

       II.   Thomas, m. Elizabeth, daughter of Richard Hawkins, who made his will in Elizabeth City in 1737. Hawkins' wife, Hannah, then married Charles Jennings. (B. 1737-49, p. 15).

           Richard Hawkins was the son of Thomas Hawkins, who made his will in Elizabeth City January 2, 1725/26, probated June 21, 1727.

           Thomas Hawkins married Elizabeth, daughter of Thomas Hart of James City, as proven by his following deed dated May 18, 1696; to John Scaley, "tract on north side of James River in James City, 75 acres, at head of line of Rice Hooe's pat. ye N. W. part of 500 acres purchased of Maj. Samuel Swan by Thomas Wombell and appears to be due said Swann as heir to his father Col. Thomas Swan by his pat. December 18, 1668, and sold by Thomas Wombell to Thomas Hart, given unto Elizabeth Hart, now wife to ye said Thomas

Hawkins - 150 acres by said Hart's will (Bk. 1684-99, p. 399.)

On September 18, 1734, Thomas Reade came into court and acknowledged his bill of sale to John Reade (O. B. 1735-47, p. 83) (Original is missing.)

On May 16, 1737, Edward Parrish sold Thomas Reade 28 acres "beginning at a myrtle tree by the side of the dam, adjoining Eastward on the land of the said Thomas Reade and is one-half of the dividend lately belonging to William Reade, decd, with buildings thereon belonging." (1737-49, p. 49)

Thomas Reade deeded Robert Armistead of Elizabeth City, on September 19, 1739, "all of that Island of land situated and being in county of Elizabeth City lying westerly from the new mill dam of the said Armistead and all the low ground adjacent thereto separated southerly by a thoroughfare that parts that from the highlands of said land together with an acre of land lying southerly of said thoroughfare. xxx The said two parcels of land being part of a greater tract or dividend of land formerly belonging to THOMAS READ, decd., FATHER to the said party to these presents and by him devised to the said Thomas in fee as by the will of the said Thomas of record in the county of Elizabeth City." (1737-49, pp. 88, 89.)

Samuel Butts and Hannah, his wife, of Norfolk County, formerly Hannah Reade, sold 50 acres to Thomas Reade and Edward Parrish, December 2, 1742. Thomas Reade and Elizabeth his wife, on November 5, 1744 sold to William Westwood "25 acres adjoining the land the said William Westwood lately purchased of Thomas Williams, late of the aforesaid county, the said 25 acres being a moiety of 50 acres lately purchased by Thomas Read and Edward Parish of Samuel Butts or Hannah his wife by deed bearing date of Dec. 2, 1742."

This appears to be the last transaction of Thomas Reade in Elizabeth City. He may have moved out of the county, as his will is not on file in the county. His children are known because of the will of his son, John Reade.

Children:

1. Hawkins, m. (1) Rachel Curtis, whose death is shown in the Charles Parish register of York County in Oct. 1735. The birth of her four children are shown in that register. He married secondly Elizabeth Pescud (14 W. (1) 116)

   Children of first wife:
   a. Elizabeth, b. October 19, 1782.
   b. John, b. March 15, 1784.

   Children of second wife:
   a. Mary

b. Richard Hawkins

2. William, m. Anne Armistead, b. 1745, died October 1780, (Reg.) daughter of Edward Armistead (7 W. (1)-18). William's will was dated Feb. 5, 1778 and probated Sept. 15, 1783 in York. (Bk. 23, p. 23) His daughter Elizabeth married William Smith (See Allen and Armistead).

3. John, m. Anne Sandifur. John made his will in Elizabeth City, Dec. 9, 1773, as follows: "To my wife Anne Reade, cattle, hogs, etc., during her natural life and widow hood, also one-fourth part of my mill, son Robert Sandifur Reade land in Elizabeth City bought of Clausell. Son John to have use of timber. To son John Reade tract bought of Thomas Skinner, also 3/4 part of mill and half my property in the miller, wife Anne to have other half for life.

"If my wife is deceased or marries, all I have given her I give to my son John. To my brother Hawkins Reade personalty. If Robert S. Reade or John Reade die without lawful heirs, same is to be equally divided between my brother William and Hawkins Reade and the three children of my sister Mary Hurst, to Elizabeth, Mary, and Richard Hawkins Hurst. Wife Anne and brother William and Hawkins, exrs. teste: John Brodie, Edward Hurst, George Jarves, Peter Sandifur, Edward Armistead." (W. 1701-1904, part 1, p. 265.)

4. 4. Mary, m. Edward Hurst

III. William died in infancy. His property was divided between his two brothers and his sister Hannah.

IV. Hannah m. Samuel Butts of Norfolk County. See deed of Edward Parish to William Westwood May 16, 1743, mentioning land bought Hannah Butts, late Hannah Read (John Reade, post).

5 John Reade, son of Anne (Allen) and Thomas Reade was executor of his father's will in 1720, together with his mother, although under 13 when his father died. He married (1) Mary Mallory, sister of Francis Mallory of Elizabeth City. (See Mallory.) As stated before, in 1742, in Elizabeth City County "Elizabeth Reade, daughter of John Reade, decd., made choice of Francis Mallory as her guardian." (O. B. 1731-47, p. 306.) Francis Mallory, in his will dated January 7, 1743 and probated July 18, 1744, gave his cousin (niece) Elizabeth Reade £15 "providing she comes to age of 21 years or marries." (D. W. 1737-49).

In Henrico, Mary Reade, sister of Elizabeth Reade, after the death of their father, the above John Reade, in 1739, upon coming to the age of fourteen in 1744, also chose Francis Mallory as her guardian. Francis Mallory on behalf of his nieces and nephews brought suit for an account against their stepmother, Elizabeth, who had remarried Evan Owens. (Hen. Rec. 1737-46, pp. 262, 280, 338, 357).

John Reade, while living in Elizabeth City, on May 15, 1734, brought suit against Henry Walker, evidently a neighbor, who owned land nearby. Walker confessed judgement to Reade for £ 5. (Bk. 1731-47, p. 77.)

On September 18, 1734, Thomas Reade, his brother, came into court and acknowledged his bill of sale to John Reade (Do., p. 83.)

John Reade evidently sold his land to Edward Parrish and moved to Henrico, as he does not again appear in the Elizabeth City records. Edward Parrish and Rachel, his wife, sold to William Westwood on May 16, 1743 "All that plantation whereon the said Edward Parrish now lives, which he purchased of JOHN READE containing 85 acres and all that piece or parcel of land containing 25 acres, being the moiety or half of the 50 acres of land lately purchased by the said Edward Parrish and THOMAS READE of Samuel Butt and Hannah his wife, LATE HANNAH READE, by deed dated 22 December 1742."(Bk. 1737-49, pp. 176, 477.) Wits: Dunn Armistead, John Jennings, Robert Armistead.

John Reade evidently moved to Henrico about 1733 or 1734, for his first transaction there was on April 2, 1733, when he purchased of THOMAS JONES for the sum of 15 pounds current money of Virginia, a tract of land containing 500 acres which DANIEL JONES, father of the said THOMAS JONES purchased of Richard Grills, adjoining the land whereon the said READ liveth. Witnesses: John Hancock, William Ferguson (Records 1725-37, p. 387.)

May 5, 1735 John Reade purchased of John Grills, both of Henrico, a tract of land containing 200 acres lying on Winterpock Swamp at line of said Reade which was formerly THOMAS JONES'S, to Cheathem's line, that of Cashens, and of Grills. Delivered by turf and twigg. Witnessed by Thomas Stratton, Lodowick Elam and John Allfriend (Records 1725-1737, p. 478).

October 30, 1735, Martha Goode conveyed to JOHN READE of Dale Parish, Henrico Co. for the sum of 35 pounds current money of Virginia, a tract of land containing 300 acres on Middle Creek which belonged to Samuel Goode, late husband of the said Martha, lying on the north side of Appamattox River adjoining Richard Womack. Witnesses: John J. Flournoy, Robert Lorton, Philip Prescot (1725-37, p. 508).

John Reade died in 1739, for at the March Court, 1739. Certificate was granted to Elizabeth READ for administration of the estate of JOHN READ, deceased. Her sureties were Richard Randolph and John Bolling. The estate was ordered to be appraised by William Branch, Samuel Goode, William Moore and John Elam. (Records 1737-46, p. 98). His widow, and second wife Elizabeth, married Evan Owen about February 1741/42, for at the February Court, 1741/42, EVAN OWEN and ELIZABETH his wife were administrators of the estate of JOHN READ deceased in a suit against William Goode. Judgement rendered with interest from 12 February 1738. (Records 1737-46, page 167.)

As stated above, Mary Reade, daughter of John Reade, deceased, chose Francis Mallory for her guardian. In her behalf, he brought a suit in Chancery against Evan Owen and Elizabeth his wife (her stepmother), administratrix of John Reade, deceased. Richard Randolph was ordered by the Court to arbitrate the difference. He made his report at the December Court 1745. The balance of the estate amounted to the sum of 180 pounds, 13S, 1d. This balance was ordered to be divided among the relict and the five children of John Reade, decd. (1737-46, pp. 262, 280, 338, 357.)

The names of the children were not given, but from other records they were William, Mary, Hannah, and Elizabeth. The fifth one appears to be Francis Reade, who settled in Bedford County near William Reade.

When Chesterfield County was formed, the land of John Reade fell in that county, and on the 6th of October, 1749, in Chesterfield, the account of the estate of JOHN READ deceased was returned. Account with EVAN OWEN. Richard Eppes and John Royall were ordered to examine and settle the same (Chesterfield Order Book #1, p. 15.)

29 November 1749, Evan Owen of Chesterfield County and Alexander Spears of Glasgow (Scotland) conveyed to William Harris land lying on North side of Appamattox River adjoining William Read near the Main Road, Robert Goode and Richard Eppes (Deeds #1, p. 60.)

December Court 1752, MARY READE, one of the witnesses to the will of Joseph Wilkinson, certified to his signature (Order Book #1, p. 295.) John Bolling witnessed this will also.

April Court 1753, Mary Reade, orphan of John Reade, decd., made choice of John Bolling as her guardian (Order Book #1, p. 319).

May Court 1753, Chancery suit brought by Hannah Reade, an infant, by Archibald Cary, her next friend, against Thomas Jones and William Reade was dismissed (Order #1, 341). Archibald Cary of Ampthill, Chesterfield (1720-1787), married Mary Randolph, daughter of Jane Bolling and Richard Randolph. She was the sister of John Bolling (Hardy, p. 72 and 129.)

Children of Mary (Mallory) and John Reade:
    I.   William, m. Joanna Jones (See later).
    II.   Mary chose Francis Mallory, her uncle, as her
          guardian and after his death chose Col. John Bolling

as her guardian, as previously stated.   No further
record.

III.   Hannah was under age in 1753, for a chancery suit
in that year was brought for her, an infant, by
Archibald Cary, as previously stated.   No subsequent
record.

IV.   Elizabeth made choice of Francis Mallory as her
guardian in Elizabeth City in 1742, as previously
stated.   She may have been living with him at that
time.   No further record.

V.   Francis (?), m. Margaret Boyd, 1762.   She was the
daughter of William Boyd, who made his will in Bedford, January 29, 1791. (W. B. 2-124).   He mentioned
the children of his daughter, Margaret Reade, decd.
Some of the children were not of age at that time.
His executor was Francis Reade.

Francis made his will July 2, 1819, same pro-
bated October 25, 1819. (E-120).   He named wife,
Florence, and children, John; Thomas, decd.;
William; Francis; Andrew B.; Alexander W.; grand-
son James Read, son of Thomas; (daughter) Jane
Block, decd.; Ann Sharp; Margaret Saunders; Nancy
Boyd; Issabella P. Read; Mary Read.   Executors:
Charles C. Patterson, Andrew B. Read.   Witnesses:
Matthew O'Bryan, Isaac Thomas, William Champion.

VI.   William Reade, m. Johanna Jones, daughter of
Thomas and Sarah (Hancock) Jones.   On April 7,
1753, William Reade of Chesterfield conveyed unto
Thomas Jones a tract of land containing 200 acres
lying on Winterpock Creek, adjoining William
Robertson, John Cashon and Henry Turpin, formerly purchased by John Reade from Thomas Jones,
Richard Grills and John Grills in consideration of
£ 50. (Deeds #1, p. 543.)   This property had been
bought by his father John Reade on May 5, 1735 (Bk.
1725-37, p. 478.)

On April 20, 1754, William Reade of Chesterfield conveyed to
Thomas Rudd of the same, for £ 300, 511 acres lying on Appomattox River at line of Richard Wormack, part of said tract had
been conveyed to the said Reade by Thomas Jones July 25, 1746.
(Deeds 11 (II), p. 154).   June Court, 1754, the wife of William
Reade relinquished her dower rights (O. B. I, p. 488).   This
seems to be the 500 acres purchased by John Reade from Thomas
Jones April 2, 1733, (supra) with a few additional acres purchased
by William Reade from Thomas Jones in 1746.

No further record of William Reade is found in Chesterfield
County.   He moved from there to Bedford, where he is found soon

thereafter. (For further record of William Reade in Bedford, and his descendants, see "Ligon Family", pp. 557-562).

Four Reade sisters, his daughters, married four Rucker brothers and a fifth one, Elizabeth, married Simon Miller, a relative of the Ruckers. (See Boddie and Allied Families, p. 171 for their descendants.)

ALLEN OF ELIZABETH CITY

Thomas Allen is said to have patented 550 acres in the above county September 16, 1636 "beginning at the first branch that extends southerly out of Long Creek upon the east side of the Chesapeake River towards the great Indian field" for the transportations of eleven persons (C. P. 47). This land, however, from a regrant of the patent made May 6, 1637, was across the James River in Lower Norfolk County. (C. P. 57).

Richard Allen, evidently the founder of the Elizabeth City family, patented 85 acres in that county March 10, 1652, next to the land of William Houlder, for the transportation of two persons (C. P. 275). On February 5, 1663, Richard Jones patented 100 acres in Elizabeth City, bounded easterly on land purchased of Thomas Ceeley, northerly on land of EDWARD RIDDLE, westerly on land of RICHARD ALLEN for the transportation of himself and Jane Allen (C. P. 493). Also Jones, on May 30, 1673, patented 240 acres adjoining the land of RICHARD ALLEN and RICHARD THOMAS (L. B. 6-467).

There was evidently some relationship between the RIDDLE and ALLEN families, because both families seem to be related to the Powell and Thomas families. Jane Allen may have been Richard Allen's wife. Edward Riddle may have been married more than once. He married Elizabeth, widow of Moses Baker, who died about 1693, for on September 29, 1693, Moses Baker, Jr. brought suit against Edward Riddle, his father-in-law (step father), for the estate left him by the last will of his father, Moses Baker (O. B. 1688-99, p. 19). Both Edward Riddle and his wife Elizabeth died a few months later, for on February 29, 1693/94, at a court held that day, administration, with will (cum testemento) of the estate of Elizabeth Riddle was granted Samuel Rallyson in right of his wife Hannah, and it was ordered that Samuel Rallyson produce an inventory of the goods and effects of Elizabeth Riddle, relict of Edward Riddle (Do., p. 26). On March 19, 1693/94, an attachment was awarded Moses Baker against Samuel Rallyson for three silver spoons, a silver tankard and many other valuable articles (Do., p. 32-34.) Young Moses Baker's differences with his step-father lasted a long time, for in one of his declarations, he stated he was a godson of Col. John Powell and sued for property left him in the last will of Col. John Powell (Do., p. 245).

In those days godparents were sometimes grandparents, but more often uncles and aunts.

Edward Riddle on May 25, 1689, had appraised the estate of one Spink whose widow, Rebecca, married William Robinson. On September 22, 1690, he also appraised the estate of Henry Ricketts (Do. 79, 106). He seems to have left a son, Edward, who moved to King and Queen and was probably the ancestor of a family of that name who resided there until the Revolution. Hannah, daughter of Elizabeth Baker Riddle, was formerly the wife of John Rivers, who died before September 18, 1692, for on or before that date she had married Samuel Rallyson. (Do., pp. 17, 42). (Book 1688-99 is sometimes numbered both at the top and bottom of the pages with different numbers (see microfilm, F. Va E 3j, Part 1, Gen. Soc. of Utah). In Chapmans, p. 211, Elizabeth Riddle's name is shown as "Mary", instead of "Elizabeth", but her real name was "Elizabeth, as shown by many court orders.)

Richard Allen appears to have had two sons: (1) Thomas, and (2) John Allen (See later).

On October 18, 1691, Robert Holmes leased to Thomas Allen, Elinor, his wife, and Richard, their son, half of 100 acres of land on Dogwood Ridge, to be paid for yearly in a certain sum of tobacco for ten years. (Do., p. 105). Probation of Robert Holmes' estate was granted March 18, 1697/98 to Ann Carrell and Ellynor Allen. It is probable therefore that the two women were daughters of Robert Holmes (Do., p. 128). In 1718, Thomas Allen and Thomas Reade appraised the estate of John Pitts (C. 194). He also appraised the estate of John Carver in that year, and in 1727 he witnessed the will of Zachariah Chappell, who bequeathed to his cousin, (Zachariah's nephew) William Allen, land in Warwick County. (C. 119). Thomas Allen held 227 acres in the Quit Rents of 1704 and patented 328 acres more in 1714 (C. 46). The date of his death is not known.

The will of Ellynor Allen was probated in 1754. Her sole legatee was her daughter-in-law, Elizabeth Allen, widow of her son Thomas (C. 82).

2.   John Allen of Elizabeth City appears to have married Ann, daughter of John Williams. Williams' will was dated April 9, 1692 and probated May 8, 1692. He left a son Robert, and to daughter Ann Williams, cattle in the possession of John Parsons, Sr., and John Parsons, Jr. To daughter Mary Williams, a legacy when 17; Loving friend William Browne and John Herron, executors. Witnesses: Robert Crooke and John Allen. Estate appraised by John Cotton and John Allen June 5, 1692 (Bk. 1689-99-116-117, 270: C. 251). On December 18, 1695, Ann Allen was ordered to return an account John

Allen's estate (C. 82). On August 8, 1698, Ann Allen
married Martin Bean. (C. 82) Bean was appointed
Constable for the Back River Precincts December 11,
1715. (1715-21, p. 83).

John Allen's children are not positively known, but they appear to be William Allen and Ann Allen, who married Thomas
Reade.

Children:

1. Ann, m. Thomas Reade, who made his will in 1721.
He provided that his sons, Thomas and William, be
placed in care of their "Uncle William Allen" and to
enjoy their estates at 13.

2. William, in 1724, sued John King for a money debt.
(O. B. 1723-29, p. 75). Giles Duberry died in 1721
and Hugh Ross qualified as executor with Francis
Mallory as security. Estate was appraised by
Thomas Reade, William Armistead and John Cook
(C-133). Thomas Morgan was appointed guardian
of Thomas Duberry, orphan of Giles. William Allen
was on his bond. John Thomas was security. (Do.
321). In 1723, William Allen patented 150 acres adjacent Anthony and William Armistead. (G. B. XI 235)

On August 17, 1715, Thomas Howard and Elizabeth, his wife, of Elizabeth City, deeded William
Allen 50 acres on north side of Back River x x x
"patent granted unto William Morgan, Alias Brooke,
22 May, 1637, being land where Thomas Williams
and Rebecca, his wife, lately lived." (1715-21, p.
1, pp. 4-8).

On July 17, 1717, William Allen and Ermen, his wife, sold
John Roberts "half of my lot in Hampton". (Do. 82.) On February
12, 1718, Francis Rogers and Phillip Williams were securities
for him in the administration of John Stringer's estate "his loving
friend". (Do. 121.) Thomas Williams of Pasquotank, N. C.,
March 10, 1718/19 appoints William Allen his attorney. (Do. 203.)
On June 20, 1719, Thomas Williams cancels this p. a. and appoints
his wife, Rebecca Williams, in his place. (Do. 213.) April 13,
1719, Thomas Williams and Rebecca, his wife, sell to William
Allen, "ship carpenter", 50 acres in Back River for Spanish
money, said 50 acres being part of a patent granted William Morgan, alias Brookes, May 22, 1637, "which said land came to me
as the only surviving heir of my father William Morgan, deceased",
the other part of said patent being in possession of the heirs of
Daniel Preedy, decd. (Do. 178-79.) Thomas Hooper leased William Allen some lots in Town of Hampton September 19, 1716.

(1715-21, Part 2-46.) In 1717 William Allen brought suit for trespass against Anthony Armstead and Hannah, his wife. Verdict: Judgement for plaintiff £ 10. (Do., pp. 84-93.)

William Allen also came into possession of the other half of this patent then owned in 1719 by the heirs of Daniel Preedy in the following manner:

On June 19, 1721, Thomas Curle and Ann, his wife, and Judith Preedy, daughters of Daniel Preedy, decd., sold to Joseph Otterson of Elizabeth City 50 acres of land joining on the land Thomas Williams "now the land of William Allen" and the land late belonging to Thomas Lewis—now Samuel Watts' on Back River. Said land was sold by William Morgan, alias Brooks, unto Ralph Mourton by deed dated March 16, 1639 and by said Mourton given to Robert Preedy and the said Robert Preedy devised the said land by will dated March 1, 1667, unto his son Daniel Preedy and the said Daniel devised the said land by will to his two daughters, Judith and Ann. Witnesses: Charles Jennings, Francis Mallory. (Do. 299.)

On June 21, 1721, Joseph Otterson and Mary, his wife, sold the land to William Allen, carpenter. (Do. 302.)

There seems to have been some relationship between William Allen and the Powell-Roberts family, for in 1723 the County Court ordered that William Allen should have the guardianship of John Roberts. (O.B., Part 2, 1723-29, p. 8.)

Children of William and Ermin Allen:
1. William, m. Jane, daughter of Mark and Elizabeth (Westwood) Johnson. Jane was formerly the wife of Michael King. Her mother married, secondly, Anthony Armistead and was the mother of Hannah Armistead, who married John Allen, brother of William. William Allen's will was dated June 11, 1752; mentions wife Jane; children: 1. John; 2. William; 3. Henry; 4. Johnson; 5. Mary. (Children not of age.) (C-84.)

   In 1759 Jane Allen made a deed of gift to her son Henry Allen of a plantation of 140 acres lying on north side of Back River, "being the plantation given me by will of my father Mark Johnson." (Bk. E. 1758-64, p. 55.) Henry Allen, her son, was deceased before 1771, for John Allen, evidently his nephew, made his will in 1771; same probated 1773. His legatees were "John Bayley and James Bayley, sons of James Wallace Bayley, I gave their mother in her lifetime by deed of gift, all I ever intended she should have of my estate; to nephew John Allen, son of my brother, Henry Allen, decd., the plantation given me by my

father William Allen, decd., reversion of bequest to
nephew John Allen's brother Henry Allen with reversion to John Allen's next eldest brother; to William
Smith, son of Elizabeth Smith; brother Abraham Allen
a plantation bought of Martha _____, to Elizabeth
Smith as long as she remains single. William Smith's
guardians are to be Captains John Tabb and Henry
King. Executors: nephew John Allen and William Mallory." (C. 89.)

John Allen, the above-mentioned nephew, evidently
died unmarried, for he made his will July 8, 1776,
same recorded February 27, 1777. He gave brother
Henry "a tract of land adjoining the land given me by
my uncle John Allen bought by my father of Francis
Mallory, reversion of the bequest to brother Edward,
to William Smith, son of Elizabeth Smith, when he
comes of age, brothers Thomas and William, two
youngest sisters, Ann and Dianah Allen." (C. 83.)

2. John Allen, m. Hannah Armistead. He had two daughters, Elizabeth and Mary, mentioned in their grandmother's will. He may have had other children. His
will does not appear. The will of John Allen, dated
December 4, 1771, probated January 28, 1773, was
probably that of his nephew, John, son of his brother
William. (C. 82-83.)

MALLORY
OF
HUTTON AND STUDLEY, YORKSHIRE,
AND OF VIRGINIA

The Mallory family is a very ancient one in Yorkshire. The arms of this family were: "Or, a lion rampant gules, collared. " The pedigrees shown in Foster's "Yorkshire" and the Virginia Magazine (13) begin with a Sir Thomas Mallory, who married a daughter of Lord Zouche. So far this marriage is not confirmed by published records. The Mallory family seem to have been located in Yorkshire previous to the time of this Sir Thomas Mallory, who was born about 1315. In 1240, Sir Anketin Mallory, Lord of Wigganttorpe, and Sarah, his wife, were holding lands in Mowthorpe. Their son was Nicholas Mallory. Mowthorpe went to Nicholas Mallory's eldest daughter, Margery, wife of Robert Salvin, whose son Anketin received a grant of free warren there in 1309. Part of Mowthorpe may have been settled on a younger branch, for in 1299 William Mallory was holding lands there which he quit claimed. (Vic. Hist. York, Vol. 11, p. 204).

The Mallory family can be clearly traced through the descent of the manors of Hutton Conyers and Studley. Sir Christopher Mallory married Joan, daughter and heir of Robert Conyers, who brought the manor of Hutton Conyers to her husband.

In 1133, Roger de Conyers held this manor, having been enfeoffed by Bishop Ralph Flambard. About 1200, a division of the Conyers' estate was made between Roger, son of Robert De Conyers, the right heir, and his uncle Roger. Hutton was allotted to the elder branch.

Roger was succeeded by his son Robert, who died in 1259, succeeded by Roger, his son. Another Robert followed and held Norton Conyers in 1284. It was either he or a son of the same name who returned as Lord of Hutton in 1316.

In 1334, Robert de Conyers settled the manor on himself with remainder to grandson Robert, son of Thomas de Conyers. This younger Robert succeeded him in the manor and died without male heirs. His daughter and heiress, Joan Conyers, married Sir Christopher Mallory, as before stated. In 1347, Sir Christopher confirmed the grant which had been made by Robert de Conyers.

2. Sir William Mallory, son of Sir Christopher, succeeded him. He married Catharine, daughter and co-heir of

Ralph Nunwich of Nunwich. The date of his death is not known.
It was probably his son William who succeeded to the manor of
Hutton before 1398. (Cal. Pat Rolls 1396-9, p. 465).

    3. This William Mallory, Esq. married Joan, daughter
of Sir William Plumpton of Plumpton near Knaresborough. A
second Christopher followed him and Christopher's widow, Isabel,
married William Vincent, who claimed a third of the manor as a
dower against William Mallory, the son of Christopher. This
dispute lasted four years and was finally settled by a quit claim
made in 1438 of the third part in question by William Vincent and
Isabel to William Mallory. (Vic. His. York, Vol. 1, pp. 403-405).

    4. Christopher Mallory, who married Isabel, later the
wife of William Vincent, does not appear in the existing pedigree.
He evidently died young and seems to have been succeeded by a
son, William.

    5. William Mallory, Esq., son of Christopher, married
Dionisia Tempest, daughter of William Tempest, Esq., of Studley,
son of Sir William. The manor of Studley was held by Richard de
Aleman in 1180 and continued in that family for several generations
until by an heiress it came to the family of Le Gros and from them
in the same way to Isabel, wife of Sir Richard Tempest, second
son of Richard Tempest of Bracewell. Isabel died in 1421, and the
manor came to her son, Sir William Tempest of Studley, upwards
of 30 at his mother's death.

Sir William Tempest was knighted before 1409 and married
Eleanor, only daughter and heiress of Sir William Washington of
Washington County, Durham, by Margaret his wife, daughter and
heiress of John Morvil. They were cousins. (Test. Ebor. III,
319). She died January 2, 1451, and was found seized of half of
the manor of Washington. (Inq. P. M. 24, Jan. 14, Neville 1451).

William Tempest, Esq., of Studley, son of Sir William, died
January 1444. (Inq. P. M. 1446, 30 Col. 4, p. 169). His son,
John, died at two years of age. His two daughters and co-heirs
were (1) Isabel, who married Richard Norton of Norton Conyers;
and (2) Dionisia, who married William Mallory, Esq., of Hutton
Conyers and brought him the manor of Studley. Dionisia was aged
36 at the time of the inquisition, October 24, 1451. (See 12 V.
218 for a description of Studley.)

William Mallory died in 1475 (will in Latin 13 V-324) and was
succeeded by his grandson William, son and heir of John Mallory,
who had predeceased his father.

    6. John Mallory, son of William, who died in 1475,
married Isabel, daughter of Lawrence Hamerton of Hamerton in
Craven, Yorkshire, and widow of Radcliffe. Their eldest son was
Sir William Mallory.

All of the early pedigrees seem erroneous in stating that Sir
William Mallory married Joan Constable, a granddaughter of

Henry, fifth Lord Fitzhugh, b. 1429, d. 1473. Instead, she was a granddaughter of William, the fourth Lord, who died in 1452. According to the "Complete Peerage", by G. E. Cocayne (Vol. V, pp. 427-33), Lora Fitzhugh, daughter of William, the fourth Lord, married Sir John Constable, who died in 1473 and her daughter Joan married Sir William Mallory, who died in 1475. Joan Mallory's son, John Mallory, was aged 26 at the time of the inquisition taken upon the death of his father, Sir William Mallory, in 1499. This would place his date of birth in 1473, or 44 years after the birth of Henry, the fifth lord. Forty-four years for three generations would average less than 15 years to a generation.

The will of Henry, fifth Lord Fitzhugh, could not be located, so the following authorities are given to show that Lora, Joan Constable's mother, may have been the daughter of this Henry:

"Sir William Mallory of Studley and Hutton married Joan, the daughter of Sir John Constable of Halsham by Lora his wife, daughter of Henry, Lord Fitzhugh, to whom Lord Fitzhugh left by his will in 1473 500 marks towards her marriage. (Teste Ebor., Vol. III, Surtees Soc., Vol. I, 1864, pp. 278-79).

"The will of Sir John Constable of Halsam, Kt., dated Dec. 20, 1472, was probated March 1472/73. He desired to be buried in Halsam Church near the body of Lora, his late wife (daughter of Henry, Lord Fitzhugh). Sir John appointed as feoffees for the settlement of his estate Richard, son of Henry, Lord Fitzhugh; Robert, son and heir of Ralph, Lord Greystoke; and Sir William Skipwith. He gave 200 marks each to daughters Joan and Elizabeth for their marriages." (Do.)

In Glover's Visitation of York (Surtees Soc., Vol. 63, 1675) the pedigree of Constable of Burton Constable and Halsham shows that Sir John Constable married Lora, daughter of Henry, Lord Fitzhugh. However, the authority accepted in this case is Mr. Cocayne in the "Complete Peerage."

Alice Neville, wife of Henry, fifth Lord Fitzhugh, was a daughter of Richard Neville, Earl of Salisbury. She was a sister of Richard Neville, Earl of Warwick (1428-1471), the Kingmaker, and descended from the kings of England in many lines. (See Key Chart.)

The Mallorys lived close to the border of Scotland and the families with whom they intermarried were descended from the early Scottish kings. (See Charts.)

7. Sir William Mallory died July 2, 1498. Inquisition P. M. was held on November 4, 1499, found that his son and heir, John, was 26 years of age.

8. Sir John Mallory, his son, succeeded him and inherited Studley and Hutton. He was born in 1473, according to the inquisition P. M. taken at his father's death. He was married three times. His first wife was Margaret, daughter of Edmund

THE SCOTTISH SUCCESSION

(Marks in chart.
b - beheaded
d - died
k - killed.)

See Aston Chart
for decent from Charlemagne
and Alfred the Great.

DUNCAN
King of Scots
murdered by
Macbeth 1040
== Margaret da
Edward the Etheling

MALCOM III
d 1093
== Maud of Huntington
d 1131

DAVID I
1124-1153
== Ada de Warren
d 1178

Henry
Prince of Scots
d.v.p. 1152
== Maud de Chester
d 1233

David, Earl
of Huntington
1149-1219

Ada == Sir Henry
Hastings d 1250

Sir Henry
Hastings
d 1269

Sir John
Hastings
the
Claimant

Robert Bruce
Lord of
Annandale

Isabella

Isabel da
Gilbert de
Clare
d 1230
== Robert Bruce
the
Claimant
d 1295

Marjorie
heiress
Carrick
== Robert
Bruce

ROBERT BRUCE
1306-1329 → B

MALCOM IV
1153-1165

WILLIAM
THE LION
1165-1214

ALEXANDER II
1214-1249

ALEXANDER III
1249-1285

Margaret
eldest da
== Alan
McDonald
Earl of
Galloway
d 1234

Helen
McDonald
== Roger de
Quincy, 2nd
Earl
Winchester
d
→ A

John Comyn
the Black

Devorguilla
McDonald
== John
Balliol

Margaret
Balliol

John Comyn
The Red

JOHN BALLIOL
1292-1296

EDWARD
King 1332

John Comyn
k 1314

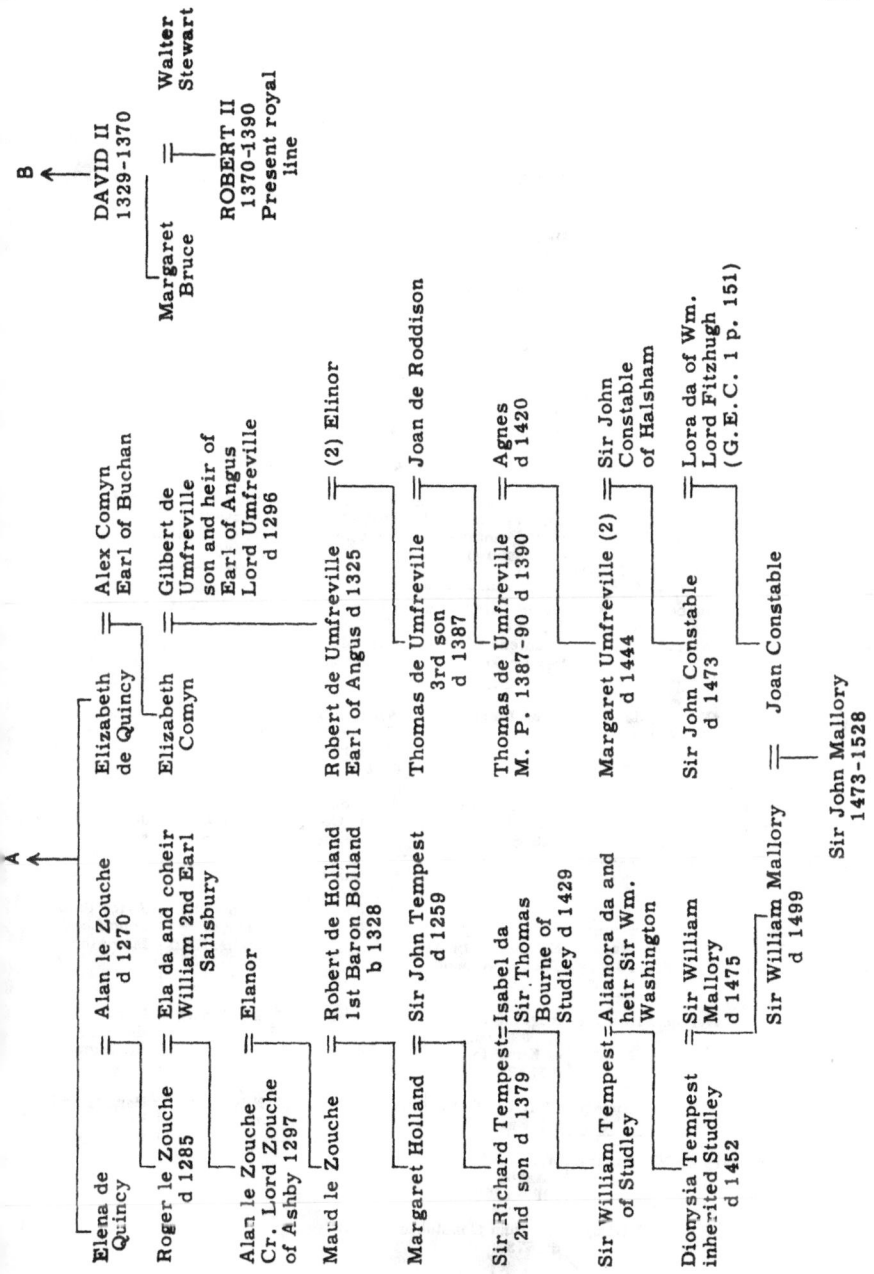

B →

DAVID II 1329-1370 === Alex Comyn Earl of Buchan

Walter Stewart

Margaret Bruce === ROBERT II 1370-1390 Present royal line

A →

Elena de Quincy === Alan le Zouche d 1270

Elizabeth de Quincy === Gilbert de Umfreville son and heir of Earl of Angus Lord Umfreville d 1296

Roger le Zouche d 1285 === Ela da and coheir William 2nd Earl Salisbury

Elizabeth Comyn

Alan le Zouche Cr. Lord Zouche of Ashby 1297 === Elanor

Elanor

Maud le Zouche === Robert de Holland 1st Baron Bolland b 1328

Robert de Umfreville Earl of Angus d 1325 === (2) Elinor

Margaret Holland === Sir John Tempest d 1259

Thomas de Umfreville 3rd son d 1387 === Joan de Roddison

Sir Richard Tempest 2nd son d 1379 === Isabel da Sir Thomas Bourne of Studley d 1429

Thomas de Umfreville M. P. 1387-90 d 1390 === Agnes d 1420

Sir William Tempest of Studley === Alianora da and heir Sir Wm. Washington

Margaret Umfreville (2) d 1444 === Sir John Constable of Halsham

Dionysia Tempest inherited Studley d 1452 === Sir William Mallory d 1475

Sir John Constable d 1473 === Lora da of Wm. Lord Fitzhugh (G.E.C. 1 p. 151)

Sir William Mallory d 1499

Joan Constable === Sir John Mallory 1473-1528

DESCENT FROM MAGNA CARTA BARONS
AND HENRY I OF FRANCE

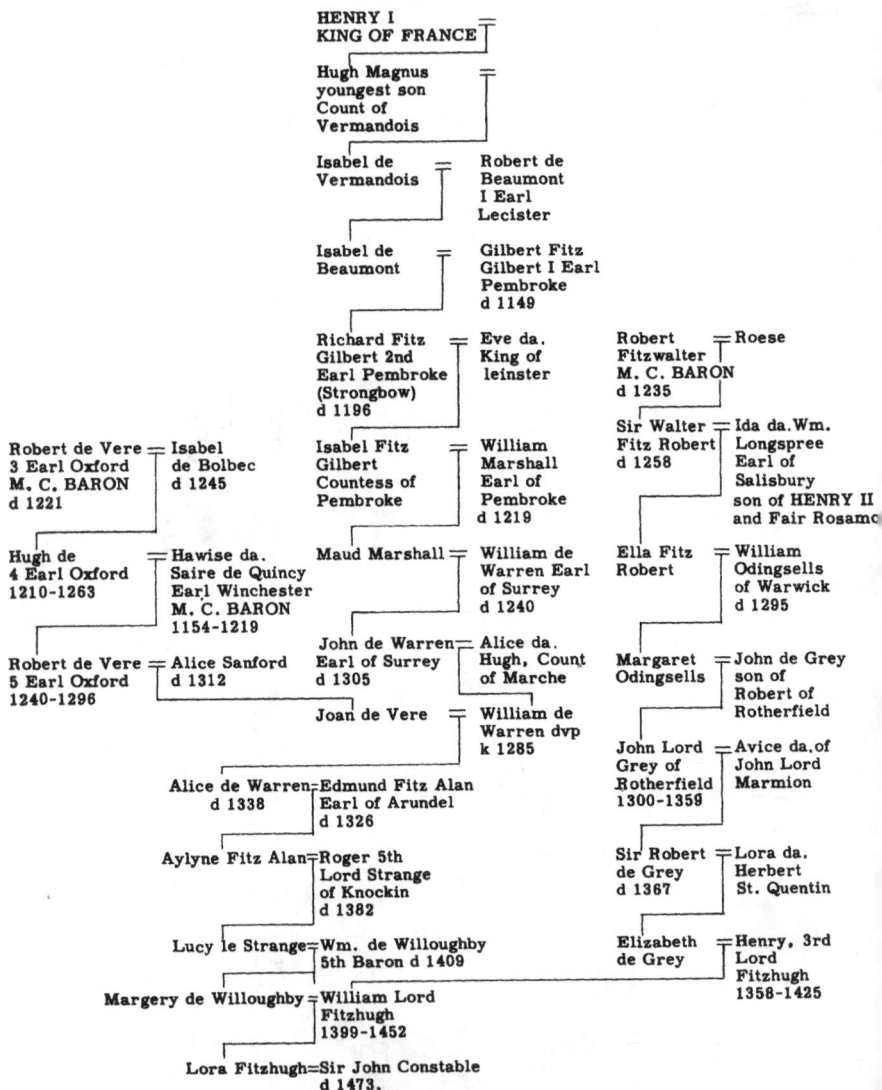

HENRY I =
KING OF FRANCE

Hugh Magnus =
youngest son
Count of
Vermandois

Isabel de = Robert de
Vermandois   Beaumont
           I Earl
           Lecister

Isabel de = Gilbert Fitz
Beaumont   Gilbert I Earl
           Pembroke
           d 1149

Richard Fitz = Eve da.   Robert = Roese
Gilbert 2nd   King of   Fitzwalter
Earl Pembroke   leinster   M. C. BARON
(Strongbow)   d 1235
d 1196

                                  Sir Walter = Ida da.Wm.
                                  Fitz Robert| Longspree
                                  d 1258   Earl of

Robert de Vere = Isabel   Isabel Fitz = William   Salisbury
3 Earl Oxford   de Bolbec   Gilbert   Marshall   son of HENRY II
M. C. BARON   d 1245   Countess of   Earl of   and Fair Rosamo
d 1221   Pembroke   Pembroke
                                   d 1219

Hugh de = Hawise da.   Maud Marshall = William de   Ella Fitz = William
4 Earl Oxford   Saire de Quincy   Warren Earl   Robert   Odingsells
1210-1263   Earl Winchester   of Surrey   of Warwick
          M. C. BARON   d 1240   d 1295
          1154-1219

Robert de Vere = Alice Sanford   John de Warren = Alice da.   Margaret = John de Grey
5 Earl Oxford   d 1312   Earl of Surrey   Hugh, Count   Odingsells   son of
1240-1296   d 1305   of Marche   Robert of
                Joan de Vere = William de   Rotherfield
                          Warren dvp
                          k 1285   John Lord = Avice da.of
                                    Grey of   John Lord
Alice de Warren = Edmund Fitz Alan   Rotherfield   Marmion
      d 1338   Earl of Arundel   1300-1359
                d 1326

Aylyne Fitz Alan = Roger 5th   Sir Robert = Lora da.
             Lord Strange   de Grey   Herbert
             of Knockin   d 1367   St. Quentin
             d 1382

Lucy le Strange = Wm. de Willoughby   Elizabeth = Henry, 3rd
            5th Baron d 1409   de Grey   Lord
                                     Fitzhugh
Margery de Willoughby = William Lord   1358-1425
               Fitzhugh
               1399-1452

Lora Fitzhugh = Sir John Constable
               d 1473.

Thwaites of Lund on the Wold, who died in 1501, and mentioned Margaret in his will. (Test. Ebor. IV, 177). Sir John paid a subsidy for his lands in Hutton Conyers in 1524 and settled some lands there on his son William, who was his heir and succeeded him in 1528. He died March 23, 1527/28. His inquisition P. M. found that his son was 30 years of age. (Foster Vis. York, pp. 93-175.)

9. Sir William Mallory of Studley and Hutton was a son of his father's first wife. He married Joan, daughter of Sir John Norton of Norton Conyers by Margaret, daughter of Sir Roger Ward of Givendale. (For Conyers, see Glovers Vis. of York, p. 244). Sir William died April 27, 1547, and Inq. P. M. was held September 21, 1547. His eldest son and heir was Christopher Mallory, who survived him only eight years. At time of his death Christopher had no children and his lands were inherited under a settlement by his brother William Mallory and wife Ursula. A posthumous son, John, was subsequently born to Christopher. In 1578, John had a writ Amoveas Manus for a third part of the manors of Studley and Nunwich, late of his father Christopher. (Vic. His. York, I, 404.)

10. Sir William Mallory of Studley and Hutton succeeded his elder brother Christopher, who died March 23, 1553/54. William Mallory, Esq., was found by the Inquest P. M. to be his next of kin, then being 23 years of age and more. During the Rising of the North in 1569, he was on the side of the Queen, giving news and advice to the Earl of Sussex. In 1570 he was appointed High Steward of Ripon, which he held for life. (C. S. P.) In 1585 Sir William was M. P. for Yorkshire and was High Sheriff of the county in 1592. He was exceedingly zealous in suppression of the Catholics. In 1575 the Commissioners at York for Ecclesiastical Causes requested him to pull down the golden tabernacle at Ripon, Brest Lowe, and to use the same in repairing the Chancel. Sir William is said to have been very keen in advancing the Reformation. (Troubles of Our Catholic Forefathers, Sec. 3, pp. 46, 69, 83, 92) (13 V. 328). He married Ursula, daughter of Sir George Gale of York, Master of the Mint and sometime Lord Mayor there. George Gale, in his will, 1536, gave his daughter Ursula and her husband £ 20.

In the following year "Dame Mary Gale" bequeathed to her daughter Mallory her "Tabette of golds" and to her goddaughter, Jane Mallory, her "flower of gold." (Wills York Register) (13 V. 328).

Sir William was buried at Ripon March 22 1602/03. His will was dated June 15, 1586 and probated April 5, 1603. William Mallory of Hutton Conyers, knight. "To George Mallory my son, one annuity of £18 out of my manor of Washington; to Thomas Mallory my son, one annuity of £ 19 out of the same; to Charles

my son, one annuity of £ 17 out of my lands at Hutton Conyers;
to Robert Mallory my son, one annuity of £ 17 out of the same;
to Francis Mallory my son, one annuity of £ 17 out of my lands
at Great Studley; to Anne my daughter, £ 300; to Dorothy Mallory
my daughter twelve score pounds; to Julian Mallory my daughter,
£ 300 where of she hath already paid unto her. £ 50, to remain
with her mother until she be so, if she marries without her consent she to have but 200 markes, and the other 100 markes to be
paid to Elizabeth Mallory my youngest daughter. To John Mallory
my son and heir my lease of the Tythe of Raynton, etc., he paying to Elizabeth my youngest daughter for ten years £ 10 a year,
and for her further advancement I rest in the mercy of God and
her mother's goodness. My wife to have all my plate and after
her death to John my son if he be living, if not to William Mallory his son. The residue to Dame Ursula my wife and John my
son exrs." (13 V. 328- 29).

His heir was Sir John Mallory of Studley and Hutton whose
eldest son and heir was Sir William Mallory, Esq., of Studley
and Hutton. Sir William was five years old at the time of the
Herald's Visitation to York, 1585. (13 V. 442). Therefore the
statement in the Virginia Magazine (14 V. 101) that Thomas
Mallory, ancestor of the Virginia Mallorys, was a sixth son of
Sir John Mallory of Studley (above) was in error. This probably
arose from the fact that pages 442-443 of the magazine were
transposed (See 14 V. 101). Thomas Mallory was born about
1566. Therefore, he could not be a younger brother of William
Mallory, Esq., who was born in 1580.

11. Thomas Mallory (1566-1644) was a son of Sir William
Mallory and Anne his wife, daughter of Sir George Gale of York.
This is confirmed by Alumni Cambrensis (Vol. III, p. 1301),
which states he was son of Sir William Mallory of Studley, York.
He matriculted at Cambridge, Michelmas 1582, from Trinity.
He later received the degree of B. D. and was presented with the
living of Ronaldskirk in the North Riding of York June 27, 1599.
In addition to Ronaldskirk, he also held livings at Mobberley
Archdeacon of Richmond, November 16, 1603. On July 25, 1607,
he was made Dean of Chester. Later, on October 11, 1619, he
purchased the advowson of Mobberley Church and became its
parson in 1621. During the Civil War, Dean Mallory and his sons
were active royalists in support of King Charles I. In 1642 Dean
Mallory was forced to flee from his rectory at Mobberley and
took refuge in Chester. He died at Chester April 3, 1644 and is
buried in the Quire of the Cathedral.

Dean Mallory married Elizabeth, daughter of Richard Vaughan,
Bishop of London (A. C. III, p. 130). Richard Vaughan matriculated at Cambridge Nov. 16, 1569; B. A. St. Johns 1573/4; M. A.
1577 (A. C.), according to D. N. B. (Vol. LVIII, p. 170). Richard

Vaughan (1550-1607) was successively Bishop of Bangor, Chester, and London. He was born about 1550 at Nyffryn in Llyn, Carnarvonshire, and was second son of Thomas ap Robert Vychan, or Vaughan, of that place, by his wife a member of the Griffen family (Dwnn Heraldic Visitations, II, 183). He was related to John Aylmer, Bishop of London, and it was probably through his influence that Vaughan was sent to Cambridge. He was successively Canon of St. Paul's Cathedral 1583-4, Bishop of Bangor, 1596, and of Chester in 1597. In 1604, James I promoted Vaughan to the Bishopric of London as successor to Bancroft and he was enthroned December 26, 1607. He died of apoplexy March 30, 1607-08 and was buried in Bishop Kemp's Chapel at St. Paul's. An inscription to his memory was destroyed in the great fire of 1666. A portrait of Vaughan is in the University Galleries at Oxford (Cat. Pict. 1796, p. 12) and another by Cornelius Janssen is in the library at Fulham Palace.

Children of Elizabeth (Vaughn) and Thomas Mallory:
1. Richard was the eldest son of Dean Thomas Mallory. The line of this eldest son is represented by a long line of clergymen. The present representative (1939) is the Reverend Herbert Leigh-Mallory of Mobberly, Rector of Mobberly 1885-1904, Canon of Chester, 1922 (Burke L. G. 1939, p. 53).
2. William, bapt. 1606, was knighted 1642, died sp.
3. Thomas, bapt. at Davenham Aug. 27, 1605. (See later #12.)
4. George, Curate of Mobberly, settled in Ireland.
5. John, bapt. at Davenham, 1612.
6. Avery
7. Edward
8. Philip, came to Virginia and for many years was rector of Charles Parish in York County (See Swem Index). He returned to England and died in London in 1661. His will was dated 23 July, 1661; pro. 27 July, 1661 (12 V. 598). His will stated that he was "late of Virginia now resident in London; to nephew Roger Mallory all my plantations in Virginia; to mother, Mrs. Elizabeth Mallory, £ 10; to brother Thomas Mallory, £ 10; to nephew Thomas Halford, £ 10; to sister TUCKER £ 5; to sister Lepington, £ 5; niece Frances Pidgeon, 10 head of cattle to be delivered in Virginia; nephew Richard Mallory, rest of goods in England and Virginia; cozen William Mallory £ 20; wits: Benjamin Shepard, Warham Horsmanden. "
9. Jane, m. John Halford of Davenham and had a daughter, Elizabeth, who married her first cousin, Richard Halford. Thomas Halford, mentioned in Phillip Mallory's will, came to Virginia and had a grant of land in 1668.
10. Elizabeth, m. Thomas Glover.

11. Mary, m. Edward Wryley

12. Katherine, m. John Batte. He was a grandson of Henry Batte of Okewell near Birstall in Yorkshire, who lived in the reign of Henry VIII. Henry witnessed the will of Sir Henry Savile in Thornhill and had 40s yearly annuity for life given him out of his lands for the keeping of his courts. Henry purchased the manors of Birstall, HecKmondwyke and Heaton in Bradford dale.

Robert Batte, son and heir of Henry, was a fellow and vice master of University College, Oxford. He had several children, among whom was Cathrine, who married Phillip Mallory and a son and heir, John Batte, who succeeded him and married Kathrine Mallory (above).

John was a captain of foot in the Royalist regiment of Agbrigg and Morley at the battle of Adwalton, also a Justice of Peace in West Riding (Waters 105). His children were: John, drowned in the Irish Sea while coming from Virginia with his father, and William, Thomas, Henry and Martha, who were in Virginia. Thomas and Henry Batte, sons of John Batte, deceased, patented 5878 acres on the south side of the James and Appomattox Rivers, April 29, 1668 for transporting themselves and John Batte, Jr. Among the head rights were Phillip Mallory, Nathaniel Mallory, Sr. and Jr., William Mallory, Thomas Mallory, Elizabeth Mallory and another Thomas Mallory.

Thomas Batte went on an expedition to the Appalachian Mountains in 1671 with Abraham Wood and others (15 W. 234). August 20, 1690, the Henrico Court ordered Thomas Batte to deliver to Essex Bevil two cows and the likewise to Mary Bevil. "Mrs. Amy Batte on behalf of her daughter Mary Batte and ye Essex Bevil acknowledged receipt of same." (O. B.) Thomas Batte was residing in Henrico in 1679. He had only one son, Thomas, who died unmarried, and one daughter, Mary. (24 W (1) 217).

John Batte, the father of Thomas and Henry, seems to have returned to England. He may have been the John Batts who, together with John Davis, patented 300 acres at the head of Charles City (York) County April 2, 1639. This patent was renewed in the name of John Davis for 450 acres and Stephen Gill for 300. (C. P. 107). On November 7, 1643, John Batt patented 526 acres in James City County lying at head of Eastermont Branch of Back River (C. P. 151).

It seems that William Batt was also a son of Captain John Batte, for on June 8, 1639, Thomas Symons patented land in James City County for the transportation of William Batts and his brother Henry Batts. (C. P. 155). On July 18, 1648, William Batts surrendered his right to a patent of 1100 acres of land in James City (now Surry) to William Ewen to be renewed for 1400 acres at the head of Upper Chippokes Creek (C. P. 147).

On April 11, 1649 he patented 128 acres upon "Lower Chippokes Creek" adjacent land of George Powell. He purchased 800 acres from William Powell on July 1, 1656. As "William Batts of Lower Chippoakes", he sold "Rich Neck", later the ancient home of the Ruffins, to Ralph Jones in 1658. In 1658 he represented Elizabeth City in the House.

In 1673 Henry Batte, son of Captain John, patented 3528 acres on south side of Appomattox River and second branch of the Black water. As "Captain Henry Batte" he was a member of the House of Burgesses 1685-86. (Stanard Col. Reg. 85) He married Mary Lounds, daughter of Henry Lounds and his wife Ann, who gave 258 acres in Henrico to their granddaughter Elizabeth, wife of Henry Ligon who had married Elizabeth Batte before 1704. (Ligon Book 364). Captain Henry Batte died some time before September 4, 1720, for on that day his five daughters agreed to divide 1200 acres of land lying on both sides second swamp bequeathed them by the "last will and testament" of their father, Henry Batte (P. G. D. B. 1713-28, Part 2, p. 471). These five daughters and their husbands were: (1) Mary, wife of John Poythress, Sr.; (2) Elizabeth and William Ligon; (3) Anne and William Stratton; (4) Rachell and James Parham; (5) Sarah and Abraham Jones. William Ligon and Elizabeth, his wife, deeded their 240 acres portion of the above 1200 acres to Moses Beck of Prince George, September 11, 1721. The witnesses to the deed were Henry and William Batte (Do., p. 485). This Henry Batte made his will in Prince George, July 5, 1727, pro. October 7, 1727 and mentions "Mother Mary Batte" and his five sisters. (29 V. 100).

It is said that this Batte family became extinct in the male line. On December 13, 1736, Peter Jones and Dorothy, his wife, Henry Batte and Elizabeth, his wife, patented 1600 acres in Henrico on North side of Appomattox (Do. 381-82). Who was this Henry Batte? Was he the son of a William Batte who held 750 acres in Prince George in 1704? Captain Henry Batte also held 790 acres in 1704.

12. Thomas Mallory (1605-1671) was son of Thomas Mallory, dean of Chester (D. N. B. says he was the fourth son and the Virginia Magazine says he was the third son (D. N. B. XXXV, p. 431; 12 V. 400).

He was baptized at Davenham August 27, 1605; matriculated at New College, Oxford, October 15, 1624; B. A. May 7, 1628; N. A. January 17, 1631/32. He was appointed rector of Easington, Oxford, 1632. On May 14, 1634 he was presented by Richard Mallory and Bishop Forster of Sodor and Man, to the family living at Northernden, Cheshire. He was ejected as a Royalist by the Cromwellians, but after the restoration, because of his loyalty to the crown, he was appointed by Charles II to his father's old place of Dean of Chester December 1, 1660 (D. N. B. 35-431).

He married firstly Jane, who died February 12, 1638 (registers), and secondly, Mary. His son Francis was a legatee under the will of William Forster, Bishop of Sodor and Man. Dean Mallory died at Brindle, near Eccleston, in 1671.

He was the father of the emigrants to Virginia and mentioned them as being in Virginia in his will dated at Eccleston in Lancashire, July 10, 1671. He gave his wife, Frances, £ 400 for life, same to be divided among children alive at her death, except son Thomas, in Virginia, was to receive £ 100. Children, with their legacies, were as follows (12 V. 401):

13. I. Thomas, son in Virginia, 20 s.to buy him a ring (See later).

4. II. Roger, son in Virginia, 20 s. to buy him a ring (See later).

   III. John, son, druggist of London, 20 s. to buy him a ring.

   IV. Mary Forde, daughter, 20 s. to buy her a ring. She may have married John Ford of King and Queen.

   V. Jane Stamp, daughter, £ 100.

   VI. Susanna, daughter, £ 20.

13. Thomas Mallory, mentioned first in the will of his father, was in Virginia at the time of his father's death. In a deposition made in Charles City County in 1676, he gave his age as "about 40" (3 V. - 344).

He had previously deposed in 1665 that he was aged 30 years (13 Fleet 75). This would make his date of birth about 1635. In 1657, Thomas and Phillip Mallory witnessed a deed of Henry and William Batte in Charles City (10 Fleet 76). In 1656 he married Mary, the relict and administrator of Robert Longman (Do., 32, 36). In 1672-74 he was High Sheriff of Charles City County (13 Fleet 80-83).

Francis Mallory, his son, held 100 acres of land in Prince George 1704 and was Sheriff of that county in 1705. On August 17, 1713, he sold to John Williamson 240 acres in "Sussex" on S. S. of Nottoway River (D. B., 1709-15, p. 211). September 14, 1714 he gave a power of attorney to Edward Goodrich and John Hamlin. (B. 1713-28, p. 31). His will was dated last day of February 1718-19, pro. 1719, "very sick and weak," estate to be divided into two parts, child wife now goes with to have one part to remain together until all are 21. John Hamlin, John Woodleif and Edward Goodrich to be overseers. To wife Elizabeth, lands and plantations I now live on for life, then to son John. Rent of lands in Prince George and Surry to son Francis. Extrs: Wife, Edward Goodrich, John Hamlin. Teste: John Robertson, John Irby, John Denis.

He probably has many descendants. In the Brunswick Census of 1782 appears the names of Clement P., Francis, Roger and William Mallory.

14.   Roger Mallory, mentioned second in the will of his father, Thomas Mallory (1605-1671), was living in Virginia at date of the will, July 10, 1671. Also Roger's uncle, Phillip Mallory, in his will dated 1661, gave "to my nephew Roger Mallory, all my plantations in Virginia" (ante).

Roger patented 2514 acres in New Kent in 1660, for a second patent was issued for this land in 1688 because the original record was lost. (G. B. 7, p. 660). This patent was issued to "Captain Roger Mallory", so he must have been a captain in the militia. The county records of New Kent have been lost. In 1693 Roger Mallory patented 300 acres of land escheated by George Nelson (G. B. 9-131). At that time he was living in King and Queen, which had been cut off from New Kent. He was a Justice in King and Queen 1693. (Fleet 5-102).

Also, in 1660 Roger Mallory patented 750 acres of land in York, "For the use of Phillip Mallory," for the transportation of 15 persons. (Yk. 1657-62, p. 244). In January 1679, Peter Perry, aged 28, in court at York County, testified about being in New Kent at the house of Captain Mallory where he was asked to accept a bill due from Captain Mallory to Mr. Robert Spring. (1675-84, Folio 214.)

Roger Mallory died shortly after December 22, 1695, for that was the date of deed made to him for 6160 acres of land by the Chickahomony Indians on Pamunkey Neck.

In 1697 John Buckner petitioned for a patent to this land, "he having purchased right from Roger, Charles and Thomas Mallory, sons of the decedent." Later, in 1699, "The General Assembly having taken into consideration settlement of land on Pamunkey Neck gave preference to the above three sons of Roger Mallory, bounded as by deed and computed at 2000 acres because the said Mallory had been given other lands in exchange." (H. B. 1695-1702, pp. 286-317). The maiden name of Roger Mallory's wife is unknown.

Children:
15.   I.   William, m. Anne Wythe (See later #15.)
           II.   Roger held 100 acres in King William in 1704. (W. T. p. 224). He was a Justice in that county in 1702-1714. (1 V-368). In 1711 and 1718, the Chickahomony Indians made a complaint against Roger Mallory, Thomas Mallory and John Quarles of King William for occupying their land. (Ex. Jour Council III, pp. 272, 466, 487.) It is not known when Roger Mallory died or who were his children. A Roger Mallory made his will in Orange County, Parish of St. Thomas, September 6, 1743, as follows: "I give to Taverner Beale land bought of Nicholas Christopher he paying

to my executrix £ 45. Whole estate to beloved wife to be equally divided among my children, she, Sarah Mallory to have same for life." (W. B. I - 290.)

III. Thomas held 150 acres in King William in 1704. He was living in 1718.

IV. Charles of K. G. is not shown in Quit Rents for 1704 and was probably deceased at that time. His children were given legacies in the will of their Uncle John Mallory in 1747. On November 19, 1699, Michael Bartlets of New Poquoson in York gave power of attorney to Charles Mallory of King and Queen to make sale of 506 acres of land in King and Queen lying on north side of Mattapony. (Elizabeth City Bk. 1684-99, p. 461).

V. (Daughter), m. John Quarles who held 100 acres in King William in 1704. He was living in 1718.

VI. Elizabeth, m. Martin Palmer (?), who held 1200 acres in King William in 1704.

VII. John, merchant of London (said to be a son of John Mallory, druggist of London, 12 V.-402) was undoubtedly a son of the above Roger Mallory. The said John Mallory, citizen and leather seller of London, made his will in London as follows:

Abstract of the will of JOHN MALLORY, Citizen and Leather seller of LONDON.
Dated 23rd May, 1747

To my wife and her heirs my estate of STRATFORD LANG-THORN CO. ESSEX. Also I give to her lease of my house in the STRAND.

To Treasurer of Saint GEORGES Hospital £ 100 - for use of sick & lame there.

To Treasurer of the New Foundling Hospital for use of that charity, £ 100.

To Mr. GALFIDUS MANN and Mr. RICHARD COOKE, 20 guineas each for mourning.

I make my wife sole executrix and give her residue of my estate on condition that she pays to said Mr. MANN and Mr. COOKE £ 4000 within 3 years, to be held by them in trust as follows --

To pay interest to my wife for her life and after her death to pay to children of my brother WILLIAM near JAMESTOWN in VIRGINIA £ 400; in King Williams County, to the children of my sister ELIZABETH PALMER (Sic) £ 300 -- to children of my brother ROGER £ 1200 -- To children of my brother THOMAS £ 1200 -- To children of my sister QUARLES £ 300 -- To children of my brother CHARLES £ 400 --

To children of my cousin (nephew) FRANCIS MALLORY of

James River in VIRGINIA £ 200 --
   If any of said children die their shares shall go to their law-
ful representatives.
Witnesses: CHAS. WARING
            JNO. VICKEREY
            JOHN LOCKER
   Proved 6th December, 1752 by MARY MALLORY, widow,
relict and executrix.
                         Prerogative Court of Canterbury
                         Registered 303 BETTESWORTH

15.   William Mallory (1660(?)-1720) was probably the eldest
son of Roger Mallory, as he is mentioned first in the will of his
brother John Mallory of London and also he seems to appear in
the records earlier than his brothers. His wife was Anne, daughter of Thomas Wythe, Sr., Burgess of Elizabeth City, 1680. (B.
J. 1659-93, p. 120).
   On December 18, 1696, William Mallory made a deed of gift
of one negro and a gray mare to his son Francis in lieu of £ 40
due from his grandmother, Ann Wythe (Elizabeth City, 1684-99,
p. 119).
   William Mallory bought land in Elizabeth City in 1680, for on
November 27, 1690, Diana Moore, wife of John Moore of Gloucester, quit claimed a tract of land in that county which her husband and his former wife Susannah had sold to William Mallory
August 16, 1680 (D. W. 1684-99, p. 115).
   On May 2, 1693, Ann Mallory, daughter of Thomas Wythe, Sr.,
and wife of William Mallory, appointed her father-in-law, "Captain Roger Mallory of King and Queen", her attorney to relinquish
her dower rights in certain lands in that county. (W. 1-197)
(Elizabeth City 1684-99, p. 115). This was probably some of the
"3740 acres in Pamunkey Neck formerly surveyed by Col. William
Claiborne, decd., for Captain Roger Mallory", which had been
patented by William Mallory November 21, 1687. (G. B. 7-572).
Anne Mallory also relinquished her dower rights in a deed to John
Ford of King and Queen (E. C. 1684-99-115). Was John Ford the
husband of "Mary Ford", daughter of Thomas Mallory of London,
mentioned in his will 1671 (ante)?
   William Mallory was a lawyer. His name appeared on many
pages of the early order books as a representative of litigants.
He was probably the most active attorney in Elizabeth City in his
time.
   He also had personal controversies with several individuals.
On January 18, 1697/98, he complained in the county court against
Captain William Armistead, "that while sheriff 1695-96, he con-
cealed 26 taxable persons from the tax lists and prays the benefit
of the Act of October 1677 entitled, 'An Act imposing fines on

Sheriff for concealing taxables'". (1684-99, p. 144). He held 200 acres in Elizabeth City in 1704 and patented 274 acres there May 2, 1706 (C. 45).

Sometimes one facetiously refers to an ancestor as a "horse thief" or a "hog stealer", but here is an actual example.

The following is the account of a trial held in court at Elizabeth City February 19, 1699/1700 (Bk. 1684-99, p. 202).

"William Mallory, plaintiff, brought his action upon the case for slander against Martin Bean and Ann, his wife, defendants, for ye said Ann publickly declared ye plaintiff was a 'Hog stealer' and had stolen Nelson's hogs. Ye defendants appears in court and plead not guilty and puts ye cause upon the country, whereas a jury was sworn; went forth in trial thereof, William Hudson, Marke Parrish, Francis Rogers, Richard Hursbly, Daniel Preedy, and return a verdict, 'We, ye Jury find for ye plaintiff five shillings and ye defendants ordered to pay costs'".

In 1715, William Mallory complained against Hugh Ross "that he went in danger of his life." This case was later dismissed on motion of William Mallory. (1715-2, part 2, p. 34).

The Beans and Ross' were related to William Mallory. They appear not to be as well off in this world's goods as Mallory, and probably had some unknown controversy with him. Yet in many other ways they appear to have been amicable. John Bean married Anne Ross, daughter of Elizabeth Ross. Both John and Anne Ross witnessed William Mallory's death bed will in 1719 (post). William Bean, their son, witnessed the will of Francis Mallory, son of William, in 1744 (post).

The above Elizabeth Ross was a niece of John Mallory, merchant of London, brother of William Mallory, for in her will in 1756 (p. 209) she mentions a legacy left her by her "Uncle John Mallory."

Elizabeth Ross was the widow of Francis Ross, who died in 1731. Her maiden name is unknown, but it may have been "Bean."

Anne Bean, who accused William Mallory of hog stealing, was the widow of John Allen, who died in 1695. She married Martin Bean August 18, 1698, and seems to have been Anne, the daughter of John Williams, who died in 1692. (Chapman, pp. 72, 171, 209, 251).

In 1689, William Mallory was security for Thomas Gray on his bond as guardian for the children of Thomas Morgan (C-183). In 1693, William Mallory, Pasco Dunn and Captain Anthony Armistead appraised the estate of John Powers. The estate was divided by Edward Myhill and William Mallory on behalf of the widow, Hannah Powers, who married Pasco Dunn in 1695. Mr. Dunn and Robert Crooke represented the orphan, Elizabeth Hinde, daughter of Hannah and Thomas Hinde, by a previous marriage. Elizabeth Hinde married Thomas Cary of Warwick (Ch. 148, 149, 198).

On September 17, 1718, William and Anne Mallory deeded their son Francis a plantation in Elizabeth City "whereon he now dwells. " (1715-21, p. 160.)

William Mallory made his will August 17, 1719, probated February 15, 1720: "To son Francis Mallory the plantation whereon I now dwell bounded by a line marked from Mr. Thomas Wythe to Mr. Anthony Armistead; to son William Mallory residue of my lands to be enjoyed by him at age of 16 years; I give my personal estate (except my copper kettle) to be equally divided between my son William and my daughters Mary and Anne; I give the kettle to joint executors of this will, Mr. Thomas Wythe to be overseer. Teste: John Bean, Ann Bean, (Bk. 1715-21, Part I.)

Children:
6.   1.   Francis, m. Anne Johnson (See later #16).
7.   2.   William, m. Mary Allen (?) (See lager #16a)
       3.   Mary, m. John Reade (See Reade of Elizabeth City).
       4.   Anne, probably dsp.
16.   Francis Mallory, m. Anne Johnson, the widow of Edward Myhill. She was the daughter of Winifred (Proby) and Phillip Johnson (d. 1699). Winifred Proby was the daughter of Peter Proby and his wife Jane, daughter of Bertrand Servant (Bk. 72, 158, 200). Francis and Anne were married in 1719 or 1720 (Chapman, p. 73).

On May 28, 1720, Francis Mallory filed the inventory of his father's estate (1715-21, p. 265). On May 17, 1721, Francis and Anne Mallory deeded a plantation to their son Johnson Mallory, "If he dies without heirs then to William Mallory, our brother, and our sisters Ann and Mary to be equally divided. " (Do., p. 318). On the same day Hugh Ross signed as surity on the bond of Francis Mallory, executor of his father, William Mallory. Francis and Hugh posted bond as administrators of Giles Du Berry's estate. (Do., pp. 319, 320.) In 1719, Francis Mallory, William Marshall, and other prominent citizens were presented to the Grand Jury for not attending church (Do., Part 2, p. 141). On July 21, 1720, Francis Mallory returned the inventory of the estate of William Williams and same was ordered recorded. (Do., Part 2, p. 198).

In 1732 the will of Lockey Myhill was proven in court by William and Ann Mallory (Do., 2-186). In 1735 William and Francis Mallory appraised the estate of John Williams. Administration was granted to Ann and William Jones (Do., Part 1, p. 173).

At a court held November 17, 1742, "Elizabeth Reade, orphan of John Reade, deceased, made choice of Francis Mallory as her guardian. " (Elizabeth City O.B. 1731-47, p. 306). She was a niece of Francis Mallory and so named in his will. Francis bequeathed her a legacy of £ 15 upon marriage or at 21.

Elizabeth Reade was the daughter of Mary Mallory, sister of Francis and first wife of John Reade of Elizabeth City and Henrico. John Reade died in Henrico in 1739. (Hen. Rec. 1737-46, p. 98.) Mary Reade, sister of the said Elizabeth, had also chosen Francis Mallory as her guardian. Francis, on behalf of Mary Reade, had brought suit against Elizabeth (Reade) Owen, stepmother of Mary Reade, and Evan Owen, her second husband. (Do., pp. 262, 280, 338.) This suit was decided at the December Court, 1745, when Richard Randolph, who had been ordered to arbitrate the differences found that the balance of the personal estate amounted to £ 180, 13 s., 1 d. This balance was ordered divided among the relict and five children of said John Reade deceased. (See Reade.) (Do., p. 352.)

Francis Mallory made his will January 7, 1742, and same was probated July 18, 1744, as follows: "To granddaughter Ann Mallory 5 negroes, if she dies before coming of age, to son Johnson Mallory; to cousin (niece) Elizabeth Reade £ 15, providing she comes to age of 21 years or marries, if not to Johnson Mallory; friend Captain Tabb a gold ring; son Johnson Mallory land in Warwick and this also the reversion of land in King William now in possession of Indians, he to be sole executor." Teste: John Tabb, Margaret Tabb, William Bean. (D. and W. 1737-49, p. 187.) Francis had an only child, Johnson Mallory. (See later #18.)

16a.   William Mallory, second son of Anne (Wythe) and William Mallory, according to his father's will, was not sixteen when his father died in 1720.

William's wife was named "Mary", last name unknown. On February 6, 1748, he and his wife Mary deeded four and one-half acres for £ 12 to Johnson Mallory, part of nine and one-half acres purchased from Westwood Armistead.

William Mallory was deceased before July 20, 1753, and his wife seems to have married Thomas Roberts of York, for on that day Thomas Roberts made a deed of gift to her children, as follows: "To William Mallory, Fanny Mallory and Mary Mallory, children of William Mallory, decd., of Elizabeth City; whereas certain articles of agreement were made July 20, 1753, between Mary Mallory and Thomas Roberts, that until William Mallory the son of William Mallory came of age, Mary should hold three parts of the estate of William Mallory for their maintenance. Now Thomas Roberts, for love and affection and for 5 sh., they to have premises for their natural lives, December 20, 1759. Teste, Francis Mallory, Eliz. Morgan." (1759 (?), p. 142.)

William Mallory, the son, moved to York County where he made his will May 19, 1801, probated July 20, 1801. He gave his daughter Mary Craig the plantation "I now live on"; and to son William S. Mallory the plantation called "Back River. " (York wills.)

17.   Johnson, m. Diana _____. His will was dated May 9, 1760, pro. May 5, 1762. He gave to daughter Margaret Mallory" £ 400 current money, six large silver spoons, six tea spoons and four negroes; the same to my daughter Mary Mallory; to daughter Ann King cattle; to son Francis land in Back River and all land in Warwick being 200 acres; to son Edward land and plantation at Hanes Creek, this county, all lands and plantations in York and four negroes; to son Francis, silver set of buckles, my troopers and militia arm; wife to have dower; to Henry King one mourning ring 20 s.; remainder of estate to sons Edward and Francis; Henry King to be trustee for Francis. Extrix, wife Diana with sons Francis and Edward. " (15 V. 99.)

His children were: (1) Margaret; (2) Mary; (3) Ann, m. _____ King; (4) Edward; (5) Francis (See later #18.)

18.   Francis, son of Johnson and Diana Mallory, was married three times, twice before twenty-one years of age, and once thereafter. His last wife was Mary, sister of Miles King. Francis was Colonel of Militia in Elizabeth City County during the Revolutionary War. He was killed March 8, 1781 while commanding a small force of Militia opposing a far superior force of British Regulars under Lt. Colonel Dundas. (See 14 V., p. 431-437 for a description of the Battle.)

Mrs. Mary Mallory's will was dated January 20, 1789, pro. April 24, 1789. (C. 172.)

Her legatees were: Son (1) Charles King Mallory (See later #19); daughters (2) Elizabeth King Mallory; (3) Mary King Mallory; (4) Diana Mallory, who married George Wray.

19.   Charles King Mallory married Frances Lowry Stevenson, daughter of William Stevenson, an officer in the Revolutionary War. Charles entered William and Mary College in 1795, graduating in 1800. He became a member of the Virginia Legislature and was Lt. Governor of Virginia during the war of 1812. He later became Collector of the Port of Norfolk, where he died April 15, 1820. One of his children was (20) Francis, Member of Congress, 1837-43, who married first, Mary Elizabeth Shields. His second wife was Mary Frances Wright, daughter of Colonel Stephen Wright of Norfolk. They had eleven children, five dying in infancy, including the eldest son.

20.   Francis Mallory, their second son, born May 28, 1833, commanded the 55th Regiment of Virginia Infantry and was killed while leading his regiment at the battle of Chancellorsville and is buried in Elmwood Cemetery, Norfolk. (15 V. 99.)

WYTHE OF ELIZABETH CITY

There was a Wythe family in York which does not seem to be connected with the Elizabeth City family. The Wythes of Elizabeth City became extinct with the death of George Wythe, signer of the Declaration of Independence, but the York family seems to have survived.

Thomas Wythe of York married Rebecca _____ and had a daughter, Rebecca, who married Captain John Tiplady of York. John Tiplady's will was probated in York in 1689. By this first wife Rebecca, he had a daughter who died young, named Susanna.

Thomas and Rebecca Wythe also had a son, Dr. John Wythe of York, who married a daughter of Henry Heyward of York. Dr. Wythe's inventory was recorded there in 1712. He had a son, Henry of Warwick who left children. (13 W (I) - 175) (See Minute Book). Rebecca Wythe married, secondly, Thomas Hethersole, whose will was probated in York in 1679.

The Wythes of Elizabeth City begin with a Thomas Wythe, who was a member of the House of Burgesses from Elizabeth City, June 9, 1680. Mr. Edward Myhill was the other Burgess. (B. J. 1659/60-93, p. 120) (15 v 320). In the session of 1680-82 Thomas Wythe appears as a member only in the first session. (Do. - 10.) He was paid 200 lbs. tobacco November 10, 1682, and was a Justice in 1688. (Do. 150-179).

On March 20, 1691, Edward Sweeney sold to Thomas Wythe 204 acres, formerly part of a patent of 500 acres granted to John Laydon Oct. 3, 1638 (C. P. 102), and purchased of John Hewett according to his patent for 204 acres dated June 1, 1648 (C. P. 175) and by him sold to Humphrey Lee and by his nephews, John Lee and John Owen, assigned "to Me." (1688-99, p. 221.)

Thomas Wythe married Anne Smith, a widow. William Smith, her son, made his nuncupative will in Elizabeth City October 18, 1693. The will was proven by the oaths of Thomas Wythe, Jr., aged 23 and Mary Felts, aged 22. They stated that after all debts were paid, he left his entire estate to his mother, Mrs. Ann Wythe. Probation of this will was granted by Thomas Wythe, Sr. His bondsmen were Thomas Wythe, Jr. and William Mallory. (Bk. 1689-99, pp. 138, 154; O. B. 24.)

Thomas Wythe, Sr. made his will December 14, 1693; same probated March 19, 1693/94. He gave to grandson Thomas Wythe land that he had bought from Mr. Sweeney; legacies to son, John Tomer; granddaughter Anne Wythe; son Thomas Wythe; Mr. Crook, G. House, and loving wife. Exrs: Son Thomas and grandson, Thomas Wythe. Overseers: Armiger Wade and John Tomer. Wits: John Bean, Jr. (Bk. 1689-99 - 165). It seems probable that John Tomer was a son-in-law. Thomas Wythe, Jr. calls him "loving brother" in his will and gave a legacy to his "Godson, John Tomer." Mrs. Ann Wythe married, thirdly, Thomas Harwood, September 7, 1695. (C-71.)

Children:

I.   Ann, m. William Mallory. (See Mallory.)
II. Thomas, b. 1670, m. Anne, daughter of John Shepard and widow of Quintillian Gutherick. Anne married thirdly, July 11, 1695, the Rev. James Wallace. (C-71.)

Thomas Wythe, Jr. made his will March 10, 1693/94: to son Thomas, not 16; loving brother, John Tomer; daughter Anne; to wife Anne "after decease of my mother"; godson, John Tomer; godson, Francis Mallory (son of William Mallory); godson William Wilson. Wife, Anne, Extrx. Overseers: Armiger Wade and John Tomer. Wits: Robert Crooke, Hugh Ross, John Allen. Security for Ann Wythe, Capt. Anthony and Capt. William Armistead. (1689-99, pp. 155-163; O.B. 45.)

Quintillian Gutherick, first husband of Mrs. Ann Wythe-Wallace, made his will November 18, 1689, and same was recorded April 21, 1689. (1689-99, pp. 84-103, O.B. 1689-99, pp. 15-59.) His widow, Anne, now wife of Thomas Wythe, Jr. was appointed administratrix. Elizabeth Gutherick, her daughter, and niece of Baldwin Shepard, married Nicholas Curle, June 14, 1770. (C.-72) Baldwin Shepard, uncle of Elizabeth Gutherick, mentioned her in his will dated February 27, 1696/97 (1689-99, 231). His other legatees were: daughter Elizabeth Coffield, son John and wife, Elizabeth Shepard. His wife married, secondly, John Poole, October 1699. (C. 72) Baldwin Shepard was Burgess for Elizabeth City, 1683 (B.J.). As an "orphan" of John Shepard, he patented 1,000 acres in Northumberland June 9, 1665, due as son and heir of John Shepard to whom it was granted May 6, 1652. (C.P. 456).

The grant to John Shepard in 1652 was for 20 persons, among whom were Capt. Leonard Yeo, Mrs. Clare Yeo, Mrs. Thomas Shepard, Sr., Thomas Shepard, Jr. and John Shepard (C.P. 257, 58.).

John Shepard was Burgess for Elizabeth City 1653-54. (B.J.) He was probably the son of Thomas Shepard who was Burgess from Elizabeth City 1632-33. (B.J.) John also patented 179 acres in York June 5, 1645. (C.P. 156.) Thomas Shepard patented 66 acres in Northumberland July 5, 1653, "due by virtue of the rights of part of a patent to Capt. Yeo for 850 acres, which being surveyed was found to be wanting 107 acres of the quantity granted. (C. P. 234) (See also C. P. 29.)

Capt. Leonard Yeo was Burgess for Elizabeth City 1644-45 and patented much land. From the patents in C. P. it is possible that the Yeo, Shepard and Thompson families were related.

Anne Gutherick Wythe-Wallace made her will as "Ann Wallace" March 14, 1739; probated February 18, 1740. She mentioned her granddaughter, Mary Westwood; grandson James Westwood, children of her daughter Ann Westwood; grandson Matthew Ballard; grandson George Wythe (later signer of the Declaration of Independence); granddaughter Mary Wallace; daughter-in-law Martha Wallace; son James Wallace. Wits: John Selden, Lucy Ballard. (Bk. 1737-49, 99.)

The Reverend James Wallace was from Errol, in Perthshire, Scotland. His home place in Elizabeth City was named "Errol." His tomb bears arms, "A lion rampant." Crest, "Argent an ostrich head, necked, holding a horse shoe." (8 V-63; 7 V 285.) He died Nov. 3, 1712, aged 45 years, and was a minister in Elizabeth City for 21 years.

The children of Ann and James Wallace were:
I. Euphan, b. 1697, m. (1) William Roscoe; (2) William Dandridge. (No children.) (32 V-328)
II. Anne, m. Robert Armistead. They had a daughter, Ann, who married William Reade, son of Thomas Reade II of Elizabeth City.
III. James, m. Martha, died in 1775. (Will C. 41.) His wife Martha made her will Dec. 10, 1768. (C. 241.)

The children of Ann (Shepard) and Thomas Wythe, Jr. :
I. Anne married Robert Ballard, inventory York, 1735.
II. Thomas, m. 1720, Margaret, daughter of George Walker. Thomas made his will Nov. 3, 1728, pro. Oct. 15, 1729. Legatees were: wife Margaret, negroes, except those hired to Robert Ballard of York County; sons Thomas and George and daughter Ann (children under 18). Nephew, Matthew Ballard; brother James Wallace; mother Ann Wallace. (1704-30 - 188.)

Children:
I. Anne, m. Charles Sweny, grandfather of Charles Wythe Sweny.
II. Thomas made his will May 2, 1754, pro. 1755. He gave brother George "the land I bought of George Pickett and Francis to repay the debt I owe him." Slaves to be divided between his wife and Fanny

Sweny; wife to have use of Uphan Sweny's part during her natural life. George Wythe, brother and heir at law, qualified as Executor. (C. 255)

III.　George (See later).

George Wythe, signer of the Declaration of Independence, was born on his father's plantation on Back River, Elizabeth City County. His elder brother, Thomas, was heir at law of their father. Upon his death in 1755, without heirs, George inherited his property.

George's mother was the daughter of George Walker of Elizabeth City, Quaker, and his wife Ann Keith. Ann was the daughter of George Keith (1638-1716), an eminent Quaker Divine, Headmaster of William Penn's Charter School in Philadelphia, 1689. (DAB.)

George Wythe represented Williamsburg in the House of Burgesses, 1754-55, and built a house there which has been restored and is one of the celebrated show places of present day Williamsburg. He represented William and Mary College in the House 1758-61, Elizabeth City County, 1761-68. Was Mayor of Williamsburg in 1768 and Clerk of the House 1769-75. He was sent to the Continental Congress in Philadelphia in 1776, where he signed the Declaration of Independence. In 1777 he was Speaker of the House of Delegates of Virginia, and in 1778 became one of the three Judges of Virginia's High Court of Chancery, and henceforth was known as Chancellor Wythe.

He was opposed to slavery and wrote his will emancipating his negroes. He was married twice, but had no children. Emancipating the negroes seems to have displeased his principal beneficiary, George Wythe Sweny, his grandnephew, who is said to have poisoned his coffee with arsenic. Sweny was charged and tried for murder, but was acquitted. Slaves who were witnesses could not testify under the prevailing law. George Wythe is buried in the churchyard of historic St. John's Church in Richmond, Va.

MUMFORD - DE JARNETTE - PERRYMAN FAMILIES
of Virginia and South Carolina

The writer's maternal grandfather was Mumford De Jarnette Perryman (1821-96) of Alabama. His name was derived from these three families.

The first of the Mumford name in Virginia was Thomas Mumford, gentleman, who came on the First Supply. In June 1608, Captain John Smith left the fort at Jamestown to discover Chesapeake Bay. He made a complete circle of the bay, accompanied by fourteen men, among whom was "Thomas Mumford, gent.". (Tyler's Narratives, p. 141.) Thomas Mumford also accompanied Captain Smith in his second voyage made with twelve men, leaving Jamestown July 20th and returning September 7, 1608. Thomas is mentioned frequently in Smith's Narratives, but his fate is unknown. He was a member of the Second Virginia Company of London and may have returned to England.

A Thomas Mounford patented 200 acres in New Norfolk County (Nansemond) March 5, 1646, "Upon Western Br. of Nansemond River adjacent William Stories land. Formerly granted to Richard Heynes * * * and sold to said Mounford." (C. P. 168.)

His next patent was dated October 24, 1650, for 700 acres "lying near head S. W. Branch of the Nansemond River." His name was erroneously shown as "Thomas Mullford." (C. P. 201.) On February 28, 1664, he again patented 300 acres in the same locality. (C. P. 450.)

This Thomas Mumford was very probably the ancestor of the Mumfords and Munfords of Virginia. The Nansemond records are destroyed, so the disposition of his land is not known.

On account of the similarity of names in their families, it is possible that his sons were Thomas and Edward Mumford, who later appear in the records of York and Gloucester.

Children: (?)
      I.   Thomas Mumford of York was born in 1650, as he made a deposition January 24, 1692/93 in the suit of Myhill V. Reade (See Benjamin Reade) in which he stated he was "aged 42 or thereabouts." He is said to have married Jane, widow of John Duke, who patented land on the Chickahominy in 1673. Jane was

the daughter of Mayor John Scarsbrook, Burgess of
York, and his wife Jane, daughter of Captain Nicholas
Martiau, also Burgess of York. In 1683 William
Cary and Martha, his wife, one of the daughters of
Col. John Scarsbrook, decd., sued Thomas Mount-
ford, who married the surviving executrix of Col.
Scarsbrook, who made his will April 10, 1679. (Bk.
1675-84, p. 539.) The "surviving executrix" was
probably Col. Scarsbrook's daughter Jane, wife of
Thomas Mumford. (T. 1-279; T. 4. 7-214.)

Thomas Mumford married again, for on June 29, 1705, Thomas
Moumfordt and Rebecca, his wife, of the Parish and County of York
sold 470 acres on Mulberry Island, Warwick, to John Martin, merchant of the same county, "same belonging to the inheritance of
William Stephens, cooper, of Mulberry Island, decd.," who by last
will dated April 5, 1656, bequeathed to his son William Stephens,
who died before he attained age of 21, then land was held to be enjoyed by Margaret, wife of said William Stephens, who married
one Daniel Wyld by whom she had one daughter, Margaret (Wyld)
who married Captain John Martin, who had a daughter Margaret
Martin who sold to Thomas Mountfort by deed December 20, 1702.
(York 1701-13, p. 166.)

On January 29, 1706, John Martin sold to Richard Oliver the
land bought from Thomas Mountfort. (Do., p. 212.)

In 1713, Joseph Mountford and John Wills, possibly his brother-
in-law, sued John Dozewell and Rebecca, his wife, late wife of
Captain Thomas Mountfort, for a property settlement. (p. 414.)

Daniel Wyld was a Burgess from York. He made his will in
1676 as "of Brewton Parish, York, now resident in Stepney,
Middlesex; to daughter Margaret, wife of John Martin of Middlesex, mariner, two plantations situated at the head of Queens Creek;
my loving Kinsman (also cousin), Mr. Nicholas Harrison of London, tinman; to sister Mrs. Margaret Okickley of London, widow;
to Captain Richard Martin of Wapping; to poor of ST. ANDREWS,
WORCHESTER." (Waters 1050.)

Thomas Mumford was a Justice in York 1691-92. He appears
often in the records. His son was Joseph Mumford who, in
December 1703, as "son of Captain Thomas Mumford of Martins
Hundred's, James City, and administrator of Eliz. Paine, decd.,"
filed the inventory of her estate. (Tyler 6-276.) He is probably
the Joseph Mumford who married Lucy, daughter of Randall and
Elizabeth Holt of Surry.

Joseph Mountford of York Hampton Parish made his will in
York, 1736. He gave his son Thomas a plantation called "Scarsbrook," daughter Elizabeth James and granddaughter Lucy James,
a negro apiece; son Zakariah Mountfort "plantation where I now
live and half of the mills. If he dies, to son Robert; also to

Robert, plantation called Ballards. (Sons under age.) To Robert, my sword and belt; daughter Jean, three negroes; wife, Rose Mountfort." (Wills 1736, p. 430.)

The register of Charles Parish, York, shows that Elizabeth Mumford, daughter of Joseph and Elizabeth Mumford, was born February 2, 1700.

On account of the similarity of names in the two families, and the differences in the names mentioned in their wills, the records are confusing. A Joseph Mountford held 307 acres in York and 558 acres in Warwick 1704. A Thomas Mountfort held 890 acres in Warwick and 600 in James City in 1704.

II. Edward Mumford on September 25, 1679 patented 80 acres in Gloucester, "Mary his wife being the daughter of Joseph Watkins, bought of John Fleet of the Island this day measured and taken up by Mrs. Elizabeth Banister, the widow of Mr. John Banister, decd. by her sold and passed away immediately upon surveying thereof to the said Mumford." (P.B. 7, p. 4.)

Edward Mumford formerly resided in York County for on October 26, 1668, a certificate was granted him as Edward "Mumford" for 150 acres of land for the importation of Jeremiah Darnell, Mathew Collins and Mary Walker (Bk. 4, 1665-1672, p. 282.)

He was probably the Edward Mountfort to whom Henry Clarke of York gave a power of attorney January 3, 1655 (Surry Bk. 1).

Mary Mumford was the daughter of Joseph Watkins, whose wife was Elizabeth, widow of William Purnell. She was the widow of Christopher Stafford previous to her marriage to William Purnell.

This is shown in a bill of sale of Joseph Watkins dated Feb. 2, 1657, as follows: "I Joseph Watkins being possessed (by virtue of my marriage with Elizabeth, relict and late wife of William Purnell, decd., upon an order of court from Governor and Council of State at James City) of ye person and estate of Humphrey Stafford, son and heir of Christopher Stafford, decd., by ye said Elizabeth, his then wife, do sell to Thomas Allen one bay mare." (Bk. 1657-62, p. 50.)

In 1672 Humphrey Stafford was granted the right to resurvey a parcel of land formerly granted him by patent. (M.C.)

The Stafford Family

Christopher Stafford was probably a son of William Stafford, who came over in the Furtherance in 1622 and was aged 17 in 1624/25 when he appears in the muster of Captain Nicholas Martiau in Elizabeth City (Hotten). He also seems to have been in the muster of Francis Mason as aged 16 (Hotten).

William Stafford of Kethes Creek, Warwick River County, planter, patented 100 acres on west side of said creek about a mile upwards from the mouth over against plantation of William Rabnett, Aug. 23, 1634. (C. P. 20.) On November 12, 1635 he patented 300 acres in the same vicinity, for transportation of six persons, among whom was his wife, Rebecca, and Christopher Stafford. (C. P. 33.) His plantation is mentioned in patents issued to William Wells of Elizabeth City, 1636, and to John Hayward of James City in 1639. (C. P. 41, 114.) Captain Richard Barnhouse patented 33 acres in James City near head of Kethes Creek in Martins Hundred, "bounded west upon Mr. Stafford's land" in 1653. His land is also mentioned in 1663. (C. P. 283, 499.)

In 1672 Humphrey Stafford was granted an order to resurvey a parcel of land formerly granted him by patent and what surplus is within his bounds, he is to name according to custom. (M. C. G. C. 1672.)

The Watkins Family

Joseph Watkins, whose daughter, Mary, married Edward Mumford, was a son of Richard Watkins. (G. B. 8, p. 33.) This is shown in a grant to Joseph Mumford, son of Edward, which will be quoted later.

A Richard Watkins, aged 20, came over in the Abraham of London, Mr. John Barker, master, in 1635. (Hotten 138.)

In 1642 Captain Richard Popeley sold land adjacent to the Middle House Plantation, Richard Watkins', and upon the Palisades. (C. P. 161.)

In 1646, Richard Watkins appears in various transactions in the York records and in that year witnessed the will of Christopher Stoakes. He may have married Elizabeth, daughter of Stoakes.

Inventory of Richard Watkins' estate was returned in York December 20, 1669, by John Tiplady. Same was signed by George Johnson and Charles Dunn. The estate was divided according to testator's will (now lost). (B 4, p. 453.)

Professor Alexander Bruce says that Watkins had one of the largest libraries in Virginia. Richard Watkins was survived by his wife, for on May 24, 1669, the probate of the last will or testaments of Mr. Richard Watkins, decd., is granted relict and executrix being this day proved in court by the oaths of John Tiplady, Jr. and Judith Dunston (Bk. 1665-72, p. 341.).

The inventory of Richard Watkins contained the following books: "Guilds Exposition upon Samuel Robotham precionses of Christ; Roberts Evidences; The Variety of Worldly Pleasures; David's Devotion, two small Plasm's (?) Books; Matthew's Legacy; two old bibles; St. Georges History." The estate was divided according to testator's will (now lost) on January 10, 1670. (Bk. 4-1665-72, p. 453.)

Edward Mumford, after his patent of 80 acres heretofore mentioned, also patented 25 acres in Gloucester in 1682. (P.B. 7-230.) On April 20, 1685, he patented 148 acres at head of Poquoson dam in Warwick County. (Poquson) The date of his death is not known, as the records are destroyed. The Abingdon Parish register shows the dates of birth of two of his children.

His children were:

      I.   Mary, b. 1683. (deposition), d. 1765, m. John De Jarnette (See later).

      II. Edward, bapt. July 15, 1685.

      III. Daniel, bapt. October 22, 1687.

      IV. Joseph, eldest son and heir, is placed last here for narrative purposes. As Joseph Mumford of "Gloster" on April 21, 1690, he received a grant of 410 acres in Warwick. The patent was for land located as follows: (P.B. 8, p. 33.)

"On line of John Brown, Sam. Chappell, Mr. Ranshaw and James Russell, 350 acres part of a patent to Robert Heisman March 20, 1638, after several assignments came to Richard Watkins and from him descended to Joseph, his son and from him to Mary his daughter and sole heir and now wife of Edward Mumford at whose request this land was surveyed, being now a widow, desires that a patent for the same be made to her son Joseph Mumford, her son and heir apparent. The other 70 being for transportation of 2 persons." (P.B. 8-33.)

There appears to be no further record of Joseph, as he lived in Gloucester. He should not be confused with a contemporary Joseph who lived in York.

Joseph of Gloucester had a child, whose baptism is shown in the Abingdon Parish register as follows:

      I.   Thomas, bapt. January 13, 1719/20.

Thomas Mumford, son of Joseph, lived some years in King and Queen, then moved to Amelia. This move was probably about 1757, for in that year Richard and Hansford Anderson of King and Queen sold to Thomas Mumford of King and Queen 520 acres in Raleigh Parish, Amelia, part of a grant of 1030 acres to Mathew Talbot, June 10, 1737. (Tyler 3, p. 67.) He married Sarah, daughter of George Booker of Gloucester December 22, 1744. His will was probated in Amelia March 5, 1785. His children were: 1. Anne; 2. Thomas, will in Amelia, 1787; 3. Martha, m. Samuel Booker; 4. Edward, soldier in Revolution; 5. Sarah Wiley.

Edward Mumford, soldier in the Revolution, married Sally Mosby, daughter of Captain Littleberry Mosby, who served three years in the Continental Line. Captain Mosby made his will in Powhatan May 21, 1821. He mentions his daughter, Sally Mumford, and her husband, Edward Mumford. They were among Captain Mosby's heirs who received a warrant for 1000 acres of land for his services in the Revolution. (Burgess III, p. 1203.)

DeJarnette

2. John DeJarnette, first of his family in Virginia, lived in Gloucester County. The Gloucester county records were entirely destroyed during the Civil War, and there remains not one trace by which we can tell anything about this family except from the Abingdon Parish records, and that gives the children of John and Mary DeJarnette shown below.

Mary Mumford DeJarnette, wife of John DeJarnette, made her will in Prince Edward County April 4, 1765, and same was probated August 19, 1765. She willed everything to her son-in-law, Jacob McGehhe, who married her daughter, Ellenor. Evidently she was living with them at the time of her death. It is not known when her husband died.

Children: (from Abingdon Parish Register)

1.
    I.   Elias, son of John and Mary Dejurner, baptized Aug. 20, 1704.

    II.   John, son of John and Mary Dejurner, baptized Nov. 4, 1706.

    III. Mary, daughter of John and Mary Dejurer, baptized February 5, 1708.

2.
    IV. Daniel, son of John and Mary Dejurer, baptized Jan. 24, 1713. (Evidently named for his uncle, Daniel Mumford.)

    V.   Joseph, son of John and Mary Dejernat, baptized January 3, 1716. (Evidently named for Joseph Mumford.)

    VI. Ellenor, daughter of John and Mary Dejernat, baptized September 5, 1720.

1.   Elias DeJarnette, baptized August 20, 1704, moved to Prince Edward County, probably about 1740, with his brother Daniel.

He made his will August 9, 1768, and same was probated July 1769. Wife's name mentioned in will was Elizabeth.

Children:

I. Rebecca

II. Elias, made his will April 23, 1783, in Halifax. He mentions his wife, Sarah; mother, Elizabeth; and following children: Frances, Hannah, Elizabeth, Sarah, Nancy and Reuben.

III. Marrymah, m. James Hinds.

IV. Thomas, was living in Halifax County, 1785.

V. John Thomas, made his will April 11, 1788. Same probated April 20, 1789. Children: Reuben, John Bowler, Stephen, Elias, Elizabeth, Nancy, Milly, Dicey and Polly.

2. Daniel DeJarnette, son of John and Mary DeJarnette, baptized in Gloucester, January 24, 1713, was living in what is now Prince Edward County as early as 1743, for in that year his land was surveyed in Amelia County. Prince Edward was formed from Amelia.

He made his will September 11, 1754, and his personal estate was appraised December 1755, amounting to £ 313, 10 s., 6 d. His executors were his wife, Martha (Ford) DeJarnette, Richard Perryman and James Davenport.

His wife made her will January 3, 1780, and same was probated March 16, 1782. Her executors were her brother, Christopher Ford of Amelia, and her son Christopher. She mentions also the children of her two deceased daughters, Martha Perryman and Lydia Taylor.

Children:

I. Mary.

II. Elizabeth Ford, m. _____ Crenshaw.

III. Daniel.

IV. Mumford.

V. John, made a deed in Prince Edward which shows him to be a resident of Anson County, N.C. He represented Anson County in the House of Commons 1784 (N.C. Col. Rec., Vol. 19) and died 1785, leaving three minor children, Mumford, William and John. A Deed in Book H. 2, p. 397, dated May 31, 1802, shows that the two last-named died minors and that their share of their father's property was deeded to Mumford, then 21. Mumford DeJarnette married Frankey Haines Pickett, daughter of Samuel Pickett. He made his will August 1823, and mentions four children, but only one - John - by name.

VI. Christopher.

VII. Lydia, m. _____ Taylor.

3. VIII. Martha, m. Richard Perryman. (See Perryman.)

Perryman
of
Skimino, York

Robert Perryman, first of his family in Virginia, left the Port of Bristol, England, in 1666 or 1667 (exact date not shown) "destination Virginia" and landed in York County. (Bristol & America, 1663-1679, p. 105.) There he married Mary, daughter of John Scott, one of the early settlers on Skimino Creek in York County.

Mathew Hubbard of Middleton Parish, York, on October 1, 1666, sold John Scott 100 acres of land lying upon Skimino Swamp, part of 500 acres patented October 6, 1658. (B-1665-72, p. 161, fo. 135.) Mathew made his will in April, 1667, and gave his son, John Hubbard, "my dividend of land at Skimino, only the 200 acres excepted that is sold to Abraham Venckler and John Scott." (Do., p. 163.)

Mary Hubbard, a daughter of Mathew, married William Harrison (1648-1713) and inherited some of her father's land. The Harrisons were prominent Quakers and their story is well told by Francis Burton Harrison in his book "Harrison of Skimino."

The Bates family were also neighbors of the Perrymans. The two families were possibly related, as they were often associated in such transactions as witnessing deeds and wills and in going security on one another's bonds. Edward Bates of this family was Lincoln's attorney-general during the War between the States, and George Bates was Governor of Missouri. The Bates family were probably more active in the Society of Friends than the Harrisons. The history of the Quakers of Skimino and Queens Creek, York, is well related in their family history, "Bates of Skimino."

John Scott of Skimino, heretofore mentioned, made his will March 29, 1673; same probated in that year. "Sick and weak," he gave his son William Scott "all my land," if he not live "then to my daughter Mary Scott and her heirs forever," wife, Judith, was executrix. Teste: Rice Jones, Will Eaton. (B 1672-76, p. 45.)

William Scott died young and Mary Scott, his sister, inherited the land. Her marriage to Robert Perryman was evidently a few years later - exact date unknown.

The first record of Robert Perryman in York seems to be his appointment as Constable for the upper precinct of Bruton Parish by the County Court of York on February 27, 1678/79. (B 5, fo. 76.) This was considered a post of some importance in those days. On May 8, 1682, he and Christopher Pierson appraised the estate of James Bullock. (B. 1675-82, Fo. 397.) Robert Perryman, on Jan. 24, 1682/83, and also Thomas Mountfort, John Myhill and Edward Brewer, were jurors in the case of James Atkinson v. Robert Reade. (B. 1675-84, Fo. 448.) On August 24, 1683, Mr. Robert Perryman and Mr. William Pinketheman were security for

Robert Martin, who was ordered to possess the estate belonging to the orphan of Thomas Reynolds, decd. (Do., Fo. 514.) On January 24, 1683/84, Robert Perryman, Edward Brewer and Robert Bee were ordered to meet at house of Morris Hurd, decd., and appraise his estate.

Robert Perryman died in 1704 intestate and his widow, Mary, married Edward Young, for on August 24, 1704, "Edward Young and Mary his wife, late widow of Robert Perryman, decd." were granted administration on decedent's estate. Their sureties were John Bates, Thomas Pinketheman and John Layton. Edward Wigg and William Pinketheman were appointed appraisers. (D. B., 1702-06, p. 243.) On February 24, 1704/05, inventory of Robert Perryman was returned by the above four appraisers. (Do., p. 305.

In 1708 Robert Perryman, Jr. sued Edward Young for his portion of his father's personal estate as yet undistributed. The following is the order of court entered on February 24, 1708.

"Upon petition of Robert Perryman setting forth that his father Robert Perryman died leaving behind him a small personal estate of which there remains undistributed, upon appraisement an amount of £ 22, 13 s., 3 d., besides some hogs and cattle not appraised, and there being left the petitioner's mother and FOUR children and praying order for his part thereof. Judgement is granted him against Edward Young, in whose custody the said estate was lodged, for £ 4, 4 s., 8 d., and ordered that he pay the same to the said Perryman." (Film 13, 1706-10, p. 197.)

On November 15, 1709, Robert Perryman, Jr. sold his plantation, and with his brother Richard evidently moved out of York to King and Queen, where the family is later found. They do not appear further in the York records.

Robert, in deeding his land, incorporated in the deed a very instructive chain of title as follows: "Robert Perryman, son and heir of Robert Perryman, late of the parish of Bruton in York, to John Bates of York for £ 20, plantation and tract of land containing 100 acres, part of a greater tract taken up by Mathew Hubbard and by him deserted and afterwards granted to Mr. Thomas Ballard by order of the General Court, and by him conveyed again to Mathew Hubbard and by him again patented March 28, 1662, which said patent contained 590 acres and the said 100 acres was sold by him to John Scott, formerly of this county, and after his death the said 100 acres became due to Mary Perryman, daughter of the said John Scott and wife of Robert Perryman who are both decd., and plantation falls to said Robert Perryman who is eldest son and lawful heir of the said Mary, which said survey or plat thereof is under the hand of John Soane dated November 4, 1689." (Film 1701-13, p. 340.)

A division of the Bates land according to the will of George Bates, father of John Bates, who purchased the above plantation, shows who were the neighbors and friends of the Perrymans. (Nov. 11, 1697, Folio 158, 159, 161, Bk. 1698, 1702.) "Division of land made according to the will of George Bates of York in the year 1676, between Edmund Brewer and Mary his wife and her two sons, John and James Bates. From Robert Perryman's line, near his old field then up the line dividing the land of John Bates and James Bates - to George Tindalls, then southwardly to Edmund Brewer line and Mary, his wife, thence to Thomas Wades."

Richard Perryman is the only other known child out of the four children of Robert and Mary Perryman. Richard appears in the court several times in connection with a law suit against John Thornton. In court January 18, 1713, "In the action on the case between Richard Perryman and John Thornton for 40 sh. the case being proved by the oaths of the plaintiff and William Batten, judgement is granted the plaintiff." (Film 13, 1709-16, pp. 288, 299, 314.)

Robert and Richard Perryman moved to King and Queen County where the records have been entirely destroyed.

The Arms of the Perrymans were: "Or, on a pile vert, a chevron engraved between three leopards' heads of the field." (Burke.)

The Perryman family in the Southern States descends from Richard Perryman, who bought 150 acres of land on the Nottoway River in Amelia County from Anthony Griffin, 14th day of February, 1751. (D. B. 4, p. 99.) As will be shown later, he formerly lived in King and Queen County, and the records of that county are entirely destroyed.

This Richard Perryman was either the son of Richard[2] of York (who brought suit in York County in 1713 against John Thornton), or he was the son of Richard's elder brother Robert[2] Perryman. This Richard[3] Perryman died about March 1769 and he would have been too old to have been the Richard[2] Perryman of 1713 who was a grown man at that time.

He received a patent for 110 acres of land on the head of Nottoway River in Amelia County, May 12, 1759. (Bk. 34, p. 202.) This land afterwards fell in Prince Edward County. He bought 100 acres from Thomas Owen, March 9, 1762. (D. B. 2, p. 93.) May 20, 1762, he and his wife, Mary, deeded land in Prince Edward "On the south side of Nottoway" to Thomas Hudson.

He died about March 1769, and it is not known when his wife died. She and Robert Perryman, evidently her son, gave a power of attorney to Mumford DeJarnette March 6, 1769, as follows:

"Whereas the Will of Richard Perryman duly intimated that the former land and plantation whereof he lived, being in the County of King and Queen, was to be sold for the benefit of the legatees; therefore, we have thought it proper by and with advice to em-Mumford DeJarnette a party effective to make sale of the above land and tenements and convey deed, likewise to collect the years rent for the same plantation." (D. B. 3, p. 302.)

The will of Richard Perryman has not been found. It was probably recorded in King and Queen and the record destroyed. Phillip Perryman, who was a soldier in the Revolution, was living in King and Queen in 1782. Also a Daniel Perryman is shown in the Census of 1782. (Fothergill's Census.) Daniel was a soldier in the Revolution. A Daniel Perryman made a deed in Henry County July 25, 1783. The deed recites that the property was an inheritance of his wife, a daughter of Daniel Lovell, and a Lovell-Markham pedigree is given in the deed. (See also Paxton's "Marshall Family.")

A Benoni Perryman married Morrin Haynie in Bedford, Nov. 25, 1782. (Bk. G, p. 343.) He was a soldier in the Revolution and received a grant of 100 acres in Kentucky. (McAllister.)

Children of Richard Perryman:

2.   I.   Richard, b. 1729, m. Martha DeJarnette.

     II.   Robert, was living in Halifax County in 1764, where he had a suit against Jonathan Woodson. (Pleas. 4, p. 407.) He was a tithable in Pittsylvania 1767. He took the oath of allegiance to the State of Virginia August 30, 1777. He furnished a rifle to Captain Thomas Dillard's company of militia in the Revolution. (V. M. 4, p. 183.) He made a deed to Richard Stone in Franklin County, Virginia, January 8, 1791.

     III.   David, was a private in Lunenburg County Colonial Militia 1758. (Hening, Vol. 7.) He was also an Ensign in Captain James Coleman Company, Halifax Militia, during the Revolution. (W. M. Q. (2 Ser.), Vol. 7, p. 60.) July 18, 1765, as "David Perryman of St. Patrick Parish, Prince Edward County," he sold 50 acres to Elisha Boudre. (D. B. 2, p. 7.) He sold 100 acres to Mumford DeJarnette August 18, 1767. (D. B. 3, p. 174.) He was added to the list of Tithables in Halifax in 1769. (Pleas Book 6, p. 427.) He bought 260 acres on forks of Winns Creek from Samuel Downs, February 16, 1769. (Bk. 7, p. 302.) July 1774 he sold 110 acres on both sides of Winns Creek to Moses Farley. (D. B. 9-352.) He moved to Columbia County, Georgia, after the Revolution, where he died about 1803. (Estate Distributed Book K, p. 213-18.)

October 3, 1792, as David Perryman of Columbia County, Georgia, he sold 18 acres on Winns Creek in Halifax to James Brooks.

He married a daughter of William and Joyce Dixon
of Halifax. (See William Dixon Will, Book 6, p. 421-
1797.)

Children:
1. Dixon, made will in Columbia County 1806 (children
were minors.) He was Tax Collector, 1804;
2. James; 3. Elisha; 4. Jeremiah, d. 1806;
5. Robert, of Warren Co., Ga.; 6. John; 7. Flora.

2.   Richard Perryman, son of Richard and Mary Perryman,
was born in 1729, as he gave his age as 48 when he took the oath
of Allegiance to the State of Virginia in 1777. (V. M. 9, p. 140.)
He married Martha DeJarnette, daughter of Daniel and Martha
(Ford) DeJarnette of Prince Edward County.

He moved to Halifax County shortly after his marriage, for
Daniel DeJarnette of Dale Parish, Chesterfield County, sold 300
acres in Prince Edward County to Richard Perryman of Halifax
County March 31, 1764. (D. B. 2, p. 209, Amelia.) Thomas
Townsend sold him 125 acres on both sides Mill Creek in Halifax
April 18, 1764. (D. B. 5, p. 98, Halifax.) He bought 150 acres in
Halifax June 17, 1765, (D. B. 3, p. 3.) and as Richard Perryman
of Antrim Parish he sold the same on July 15, 1765 to Christopher
Billups. He sold 125 acres on both sides Mill Creek February 20,
1767. (D. B. 6, p. 385.) He bought another 125 acres on both
sides of Mill Creek in Pittsylvania (cut off from Halifax) Dec. 12,
1767, (B. 1, p. 107), from Wilborn Hawkins, and as Richard
Perryman of Parish of Russell, County of Bedford, he sold the
same April 11, 1773.

He was residing in Henry County (cut off from Pittsylvania) in
1777 when he took the oath of Allegiance to the State of Virginia.

According to the tax lists, he was residing in Henry County
in 1784. No further record of him has been found.

Children:
3.   I.   Mumford, m. Elizabeth Travis; II. John; III. Samuel;
IV. Mary.
V.   Milton, made his will in Anson County, N. C. Sept.
4, 1793. He mentions his three brothers: Mumford,
John and Samuel, and his sister Mary in his will.

3.   Mumford Perryman was born in Prince Edward County,
Virginia, about 1762, died in Edgefield County, S. C., 1820.

Mumford Perryman was a soldier in Captain John Cunningham's
Company, Colonel Abraham Penn's Regiment of Henry County
militia (D. A. R. Mag., 45, p. 206), General Steven's Brigade, and
fought at the Battle of Guilford C. H. March 17, 1781. This regiment was ordered to march to Hillsboro, N. C. March 11, 1781
to report to General Stevens. (V. M. 17, p. 190.) The Pension

Petition of John Smith of the Henry County Militia shows he was
at the Battle of Guilford, C. H. under General Stevens. (V. M. 17,
p. 73.) Hill, in his "History of Henry County, Va.", says that
the Henry County Militia Regiment fought at the Battles of Guilford C. H. Eutaw Springs and was at the surrender of Lord Cornwallis at Yorktown 1781. (Page 94.)

Mumford Perryman moved to Edgefield County, S. C. shortly
after the Revolution and married soon after his arrival there,
Elizabeth Travis, daughter of Barrick Travis and aunt of Colonel
William B. Travis of the Alamo.

Mumford Perryman bought 200 acres of land from James Tom-
lin in 1793, located on Red Bank Creek not far from Saluda, S. C.
(Edgefield D. B. "K", p. 251.)

Chapman, in his History of Edgefield County (p. 306) in speak-
ing of the Red Bank Baptist Church, says:

"Mumford Perryman, who had been clerk, died in 1820. He
was the grandfather of General Perryman of Texas, who was distinguished in the War between the States and was in 1891 one of
the judges of that state. Col. Wm. Barrick Travis of the Alamo
once attended the Red Bank Church. The Perrymans and Travis'
were related."

Mumford Perryman was also a Justice of the Peace in Edgefield, as shown by many deeds attested to before him. He made
his will the 15th day of September, 1820, and same was probated
on the 12th day of October, 1820. (W. B. "C", p. 47.) It provided
that if his widow, Elizabeth, desired to remove to the State of
Alabama, that she have full power to sell his lands and buy land
in Alabama with the proceeds and expressed the desire that his
two minor children be educated the same as his others had been
and made special provision for one son, Barrick Smallwood Perryman, who was an invalid. This is the only child mentioned by
name in the will.

Elizabeth Perryman, as administratrix, sold the land of Mumford Perryman's estate in 1821. She had her letter of dismission
from the Red Bank Church October 20, 1821. Mark Travis and
his wife, Jemima Stallworth, had their letter of dismission from
this church July 20, 1818, and had previously moved to Conecuh
County, Alabama.

The census for 1830, Conecuh County, shows Elizabeth Perryman over 60 residing there with two sons in household and 19
slaves.

The Conecuh County records have been destroyed and no further information concerning her is found.

The children of Elizabeth (Travis) and Mumford Perryman now
known, were:

4.   I.   Milton Travis, b. September 28, 1794, m. Mrs.
           Johanna (Haines) Saunders. (See later.)

5.   II.   Samuel, b. February 17, 1797, m. September 1, 1813, Sarah Ann Mayes Watson. (See later.)

      III.   Alexander, was in Conecuh in 1830 and 1840.

      IV.   Barrick Smallwood. (No further record.)

      V.   Nancy, m. _____ Medlock.

      VI.   Martha, m. _____ Gallaugher.

4.   Milton Travis Perryman, son of Elizabeth (Travis) and Mumford Perryman, was born in Edgefield County, S.C., Sept. 28, 1794, and died in Mobile, Alabama, September 26, 1871. He married about 1820, Mrs. Johanna (Haines) Saunders of Edgefield County, widow of William Saunders. She was born in 1787 in New Bern, N.C. and died in Mobile, November 3, 1874. (Tombstone.)

The land of William Saunders was divided between his widow, Johanna Perryman, and her infant son, William Saunders, Jr. in 1820. Milton T. Perryman was appointed guardian for his stepson, William Saunders, Jr.

He, Samuel De Loach and Joseph Stallworth, signed his mother's bond for $30,000 as executrix of his father's estate in 1820.

Milton T. Perryman moved to Conecuh about 1821 and then about 1835 to Mobile, where he was a cotton factor and merchant. He also owned a line of steamboats running on the Alabama and Tombigbee Rivers and managed plantations in Monroe and Wilcox Counties.

Mr. Perryman resided on Ann Street between Dauphin and Government. The Mobile Daily Register of September 28, 1871 says:

> "Death of an Old Citizen
> "Mr. Milton T. Perryman, for forty years a highly esteemed citizen of Mobile, died on Tuesday and was buried yesterday in the Magnolia Cemetery, his remains being followed to the grave by a large concourse of friends and acquaintances."

Children:

      I.   Mary S., b. 1820, d. February 16, 1854 in Mobile, m. Dr. T. C. DeLoach.

6.   II.   Mumford DeJarnette, b. 1821, m. Elizabeth T. Stover.

      III.   Erastus S., b. October 1827, d. April 20, 1889, m. Elizabeth A. Bondurant. He volunteered and served in the Mexican War and was in General Scott's March from Vera Cruz to Mexico City. He also served in the Civil War as a Lieutenant of Cavalry. In 1880 he was a member of the Board of Review of the City of Mobile, and was President of the Mobile Insurance Company. He left one son, Erastus S., Jr.

      IV.   Martha, b. 1832, m. M. A. Thomas of New Orleans.

      V.   Josephine, b. 1834, dsp.

6.   Mumford DeJarnette Perryman, son of Johanna and Milton Travis Perryman, was born in Edgefield County, S.C., 1821, and died at Woodlawn, Jefferson County, Alabama in 1895. He married December 26, 1850, Elizabeth Tirzah Stover, born in South Carolina January 24, 1826, died at Woodlawn, Alabama, June 6, 1891. She was the daughter of Sarah (McWillie) and William Bradford Stover. Sarah McWillie Stover was the sister of Governor William McWillie of Mississippi and the daughter of Colonel Adam McWillie, who commanded the 2nd Regiment of South Carolina Volunteers in 1812. His regiment was stationed at Haddrell's Point and was in service from October 6, 1814 to February 28, 1815.

Colonel Adam McWillie, second son of John McWillie, came to South Carolina shortly after the Revolution and settled near Camden in Kershaw County. He married Ann McCullough, daughter of James McCullough and Annie Beall. James McCullough was a Royalist, or rather, Loyalist. Ann McCullough was born December 18, 1768, married 1787, and died October 6, 1844.

John McWillie, pronounced at present in the Kershaw country, South Carolina, "Macquillie", married Margaret Davidson, an orphan, ward of General Churchill, who was then Governor of Edinburgh Castle, in which John and Margaret were married. He is said to have been Donald Macdonell, a captain in the regiment of the Kippoch branch of the Clan McDonald at the siege of Carlisle, 1745, where he was captured and later sentenced to death for treason. He was for some time held in a prison ship at Plymouth, expecting daily to be executed, but was at length pardoned through an intercession of an English friend of his family, who interested himself in his behalf on certain conditions, one of these being the changing of his name and taking service in the British Army, and another was to refrain from returning to his home in the highlands. Both obligations were observed, his subsequent military service extending to nearly every quarter of the globe. ("McWillie-Cunningham Families," R. B. Johnson, p. 8.)

His descendants in Mississippi have preserved his sword and several of his commissions. He was in the British Regular Army in America during the Revolution, a Major of the "Royal Irish Battalion of Foot", and after the War he returned to Ireland and died there. His monument is at Frogdoo, County Armaugh, Ireland, showing that he died January 18, 1808, aged 88 years.

Mumford D. Perryman was engaged in the cotton brokerage business with his father in Mobile in 1850 and was in the same business in Buena Vista, Monroe County, Alabama in 1860. Later, according to the census of 1860, his personal property was listed at $140,000. After the war he managed his plantations in Southern Alabama until he retired in 1888 and moved to Woodlawn, Alabama, now a part of Birmingham.

Children:
- I. William, died in infancy.
- II. Sarah Johanna, m. John C. Cunningham of Evergreen, Alabama. Children: Claude; Arthur; William; John Ann; Sidney; Stover; Herndon; Gilbert; and Perryman.
- III. Milton Stover, b. January 4, 1857, m. _____. Children: William C. Perryman, died young.
- IV. Annie Henrietta, b. July 21, 1859, m. John Bennett Boddie.
- V. Thomas, died in infancy.

7.   VI. William Erastus, b. June 3, 1865, m. Fannie Jones

8.   VII. Travis McWillie Perryman, b. January 21, 1868, m. January 15, Margarita Fitzgerald.

    7. William Erastus Perryman was born June 3, 1865, at Buena Vista, Monroe County, Alabama; died at Birmingham, Alabama, May 5, 1914. He married, June 1892, Fannie Moore Jones, born April 8, 1875, at Furman, Wilcox County, Alabama, daughter of Frances Delphine Moore and Dr. Capers Capehart Jones of Birmingham, Ala. Dr. Jones was an active and renowed Confederate Veteran. He attended the Blue and Grey Reunion held at Gettysburg on the 75th anniversary of Battle, July 3-5, 1938.

    Mr. Perryman attended the University of Alabama. He resided at Woodlawn, Jefferson County, Alabama, and was for many years Mayor of Woodlawn, serving in that capacity until Woodlawn was annexed to the City of Birmingham. He invented and manufactured cotton seed crushing machinery which was shipped throughout the world.

Children:
- I. Mumford DeJarnette, b. March 4, 1894, d. June 20, 1929. Dsp.
- II. Capers Jones, b. August 9, 1896, m. February 1, 1939, Will Aileen Moore, born March 10, 1903, at Montgomery, Alabama, daughter of Lulu (Tanner) and William Henry Moore. Mr. Perryman was an honor graduate in electrical engineering at the Alabama Polytechnic Institute in 1919 and also attended Union College, Schenectady, N. Y. He later served as a Division Superintendent of the Alabama Power Company. He is now engaged in the investment banking business in Montgomery and is a member of the Country and Sportsman's Club. During World War I he served in the U. S. Army Engineering Corps.
- III. Elizabeth, b. June 25, 1906; died young.
- IV. William Erastus, Jr., b. December 30, 1903, m. Eva Hayes. He graduated from the Alabama Polytechnic Institute in 1926 and has been connected with

the Alabama Power Company since graduation. He
is now District Superintendent of the Jasper Alabama
District. He is a member of the Rotary and Country
Club and has two children: Martha Ann and Elizabeth.

V.   Frances, b. September 15, 1908.

8.   Travis McWillie Perryman, born January 21, 1868,
married January 15, 1900, Margaret Fitzgerald, born September
4, 1874, at Allenton, Alabama; died July 19, 1931, daughter of
Alice (Carter) and William Madison Fitzgerald.

Mr. Perryman was educated at Howard College, Marion, Ala.
He died on his plantation near Allenton, Alabama in 1946.

Children:

I.   William Stover, b. December 18, 1900, at Allenton,
Wilcox County; m. December 24, 1927, Alma Lois
Dale, daughter of Cora (Mayo) and Frank M. Dale
Mr. Perryman attended Moore Academy at Pine
Apple, Alabama, then the University of Alabama,
A. B., 1922. He is a plantation operator, cattle
raiser, saw mill owner; belongs to the Sigma Nu
fraternity and resides at Oak Hill.

Children:

I.   Dorothy Dale, b. June 1, 1930.
II.   William Stover, Jr., b. March 4, 1935.

5.   Dr. Samuel Perryman, second son of Elizabeth (Travis)
and Mumford Perryman, was born in Edgefield County, S.C., Feb.
17, 1797, and died June 17, 1838. He married January 21, 1830,
Sarah Ann Watson, daughter of Lavinia (Brooks) and Richard Watson. Sarah Ann Watson was born September 1, 1813. Her mother,
Lavinia Brooks, born August 1795, was a daughter of Nancy Butler,
born September 27, 1765 and her husband, Elisha Brooks. Elisha
Brooks was a Revolutionary soldier. (Stub Indents, Vol. U-W, p.
247.)

Nancy Butler was a daughter of Captain James Butler, killed
in the Cloud Creek Massacre November 7, 1781 along with his
young son, James Jr.

The Butler family is distinguished in the annals of South Carolina. Captain William Butler (1759-1821), son of Captain James,
was a member of Congress and a Major General in charge of the
Charleston District in the War of 1812. He was the father of Andrew Pickens Butler (1796-1857), U. S. Senator from South Carolina, 1846-1857. Another son of his was Pierce Mason Butler
(1798-1847), Governor of South Carolina, 1836, and Colonel of
the Palmetto Regiment in the Mexican War, killed while leading

his regiment at the Battle of Churubusco. A grandson was Matthew C. Butler (1836-1909), Brigadier General C.S.A. at 27, who lost a leg at Brandy Station, and was U.S. Senator, 1876-1894. Well might this family be called the "Fighting Butlers." (See Butler.)

Dr. Perryman sold his plantation in Edgefield County, moved to Abbeville County, and settled on a plantation called "Scotch Cross." Scotch Cross had been built by Captain John Wesley Brooks, the uncle of his wife. This place had been settled by some Scots about the time of the Revolution. In front of his house, two main roads of upper Carolina Cross - one from Columbia and 96 going towards Barksdale Ferry on the Savannah River into Georgia. The other was from Augusta, Georgia, and Hamburg, going north to Greenville and on into North Carolina.

At the time of his death he owned plantations in South Carolina and Alabama which are mentioned in his will. As for Scotch Cross, he says, "The plantation whereon I now live called 'Scotch Cross' is to remain in possession of my wife, Sarah W. Perryman, and is to be used for the support of my wife and the education of my children until they arrive at age."

Mrs. Sarah Watson Perryman married, secondly, October 7, 1840, Captain Henry Hunter Creswell. Captain Creswell bought Scotch Cross from Dr. Perryman's heirs and lived there until his death March 23, 1896. Mrs. Creswell died September 16, 1879. She had four Perryman and eight Creswell children. Five of her sons were Confederate soldiers. (See Butler.)

Children of Sarah Ann (Watson) and Samuel Perryman:

9.   I.   William Watson, b. February 6, 1831, m. Susan Elizabeth Partlow. (See later #9.)

      II.   Elizabeth, b. December 2, 1832; died young.

      III. Samuel, b. December 25, 1834, m. 1855 Josephine Chatham. He was educated at Cedar Springs under Dr. Leslie and then went to South Carolina College. He married in 1855 and moved to his plantation near Mt. Moriah Church in Greenwood County, S.C. In 1859 he moved to Goliad, Texas, where he died Feb. 14, 1867. He fought throughout the Civil War, 1861-1865 in Hoods Texas Division, and participated in many battles, but his record was not furnished. His widow married, secondly, Mr. Jackson; no children.

            His children were: Edward, Samuel, and a daughter, all of whom died young. His youngest child, Lucy Perryman, married Jacob Jubal Cockerell of Eutaw, Alabama. A grandson, Perryman Cockerell, married a Miss Blanch and lived in Birmingham, Ala.

10.   IV.   Richard Mumford, b. December 16, 1836, m. Emma

Eliza Hart Partlow. (See later.)

9. General William Watson Perryman, born at Barrats-
ville February 6, 1831, received his early schooling at Barrats-
ville and graduated from Due West College, S. C. He studied law
under James L. Pettigrew at Charleston, S. C. He married Susan
Elizabeth Partlow on February 13, 1851. They built and settled
a home at New Market, S. C. He formed the first company to
leave the county of Abbeville, now Greenwood. It was called
Secession Guards - Company "F", 2nd Regiment, Kershaw's
Brigade, of which he was Captain, leading them upon many battle-
fields where they fought gallantly. Partial paralysis from typhoid
fever caused him to leave his command and he was commissioned
General of the enrolling forces of South Carolina in 1863.

He removed to Texas after the war and died at Liberty, 1890.
His wife died in 1909.

Children:
- I.   James Samuel, b. October 8, 1852, was killed by
       being thrown from a wagon October 20, 1869.
- II. William Richard, died in childhood.
- III. Mary Elizabeth, b. February 6, 1856. She married
       Samuel R. Perryman April 21, 1885 at St. Charles
       Hotel, New Orleans, La.; d. October 3, 1885.
- IV. Sarah Isabel, b. March 21, 1858, married Dr. J. P.
       Cook of Liberty, Texas, February 20, 1879; d. March
       26, 1885, leaving an infant daughter, Sallie Perry-
       man Cook, who married Mr. Teague. They have one
       child, Emma Teague, now married.
- V.   Emma Dover, b. 1860, m. in Liberty, Texas, Walter
       Christian Moore of Houston, Texas. They lived a
       while at San Antonio, Texas, and then moved back
       to Houston. Walter Christian Moore died July 3, 1943
       in Houston, Texas, and his wife, Emma Perryman
       Moore, died March, 1941.

Children:
1. Perryman Moore, m. June 24, 1918; had two children.
2. Annie Bess Moore, m. Douglas McGregor.
3. Lydia Beard Moore, m. September 16, 1915, Henry
   Harrison Bryant of San Antonio, Texas. They had
   two daughters, Emily Ann and Lydia. Emily Ann
   Bryant married Captain John Whitelow Browning of
   World War II. Their daughter is Joan Whitelow
   Browning, born in 1941.
4. Louise Moore, died in infancy.
5. Ruth Moore, died in infancy.

6. Christie Moore, m. Mr. Garwood. Her husband and son were officers in World War II.

10. Richard Mumford Perryman, third son of Sarah N. Watson and Dr. Samuel Perryman, was born December 10, 1836, and died July 4, 1915, buried at Liberty, Texas. He was educated at Barratville, S.C. and Asheville, N.C. After reaching maturity, he made his home with his brother, W.W. Perryman, at New Market. In 1860, he married Emma Eliza Hart Partlow, sister to Susan Partlow who married his brother William, and moved to Texas. He served throughout the Civil War in Hood's Division. His wife died December 11, 1909.

Children:

I. Mary Sue, b. July 14, 1861, m. Rev. J.A. Smith and lived in San Antonio, Texas and had four children: 1. Emma Virginia Smith, who married August 11, 1910, Robert Craig Dunlap of Dallas, Texas. They have two children: Robert Craig, Jr. and Emma Virginia Dunlap; 2. Mary Lucile Smith, second daughter, married Fred Stevens of Liberty. Children: Bessie Grey and Mary Lucille Stevens; 3. John Allen Smith married July 4, 1918 to Helen Huppertz, was captain in World War I, and after the Armistice he joined the regular army, where he remained until World War II. He was a Lieutenant Colonel in Patton's 3rd Army. He had a daughter, Helen, and a son who was also in the service; 4. Richard Perryman Smith is an M.D. practicing in Dallas, Texas.

II. William Samuel, m. Zema West of Liberty, Texas. They had two children: Ina May and Zema West Perryman.

III. Richard Marshall, m. Effie McWhorter. They have seven children and live at Liberty, Texas. Children: Lorena; Mary, m. Mr. LaCore; Walter William; Ruth; Lillie; Buster; Louise Estelle.

IV. Lena Bell, m. Simeon DeBlanch in 1911.

V. James Richardson, m. December 19, 1908, Lottie Shepherd.

BARKER, BRADFORD, TAYLOR
OF FLOWERDIEU HUNDRED

"Flowerdieu Hundred" was named for Temperance Flowerdieu, wife of Sir George Yeardley, Governor of Virginia. When the colonists arrived in Virginia this land was owned by the Weyanoke Indians. Their chief town was at the head of a creek later known as Powell's Creek. In 1617 Sir George Yeardley received from the Indian King a tract of land called "Tanks Weyanoke" (Little Weyanoke) and the next year he patented 1000 acres on the south side of the James, west of a creek. He named both the creek and the place "Flowerdieu Hundred."

On October 5, 1624, Sir George Yeardley sold Flowerdieu to Captain Abraham Piersey, a leading merchant of Virginia and a member of the Council. Captain Piersey died in 1627. He left two daughters: Elizabeth, who married, first, Captain Richard Stephens, and, secondly, Sir John Harvey. Mary, his other daughter, married Captain Thomas Hill, and later Thomas Bushrod.

Mistress Elizabeth Stephens, on October 15, 1636, patented this place, "1000 acres in Charles City Co., known and called by the name of 'Flowerdieu Hundred', being bounded from the creek of the same name . . . lying along the south side of the main river over against Weyanoke. Due in right decent from my father, Abraham Piercey, late of Va. and is a part of my share and portion of inheritance as co-heir from my father, to whom the said land was due by purchase from Sir George Yeardley, by deed dated Oct. 5, 1624." (C. P. 50.)

Soon afterwards, Mrs. Elizabeth Stephens sold part of this grant to William Barker, mariner, who received a patent for 1300 acres for the transportation of 26 persons May 11, 1639. The patent was for "500 acres bounding on land lately purchased of Mrs. Elizabeth Stephens, now Lady Harvey, lying at the head of the creek and 800 acres on the same creek, adjacent to land belonging to Capt. Francis Hooke." (C. P. 108.)

Capt. Francis Hooke had patented his land on October 26, 1637; "2000 acres bounded on Flowerdieu Hundred side by a creek, and on Martin's Brandon side by Asheley's or Capt. Ward's Creek."

William Barker, mariner, master of the ship "America", sailed from Gravesend July 23, 1635 with 88 persons. (Hotten, p. 95.) On November 26, 1635, William Barker, mariner, John

146

Sadler and Richard Quiney, merchants, patented 1250 acres in Charles City Co., "Extending in the woods from a tract of land called 'Merchants Hope', formerly granted to said Barker and his associates." (C. P. 35.)

William Barker, mariner, was also in possession of land formerly owned by Capt. Nathaniel Powell, for James Smallwood, in his patent dated March 5, 1634 for 500 acres, stated that said land, formerly Capt. Nathaniel Powell's, was now in the occupation of William Barker, Mariner.

William Barker, always with the title of "Mariner", patented much land for the transportation of many persons. He patented "400 acres on Chappell's Creek, adjacent 'Merchants Hope' Nov. 26, 1635." (C. P. 35.) He, John Sadler and Richard Quiny, merchants, patented 1250 acres adjacent "Merchants Hope" formerly granted to said Barker on the above date. (C. P. 35.)

On August 29, 1637 he patented 600 acres, being a point of land called "Baker's" which was formerly bounded in Capt. Nathaniel Powell's dividend. (C. P. 70.)

William Barker, mariner, and "his Associates & Co.", as Sadler and Quiny are called in the patent, obtained a grant in Charles City Co. on February 12, 1638 "600 acres of said land being heretofore called by the name of Powlebrooke, now known as Merchants Hope . . . and 600 acres conveyed and assigned to said Barker & acknowledged by him equally to belong to his said associates by John Taylor, Citizen and Girdler of London, being purchased by him of Thomas Powell of Howlton, in the county of Suffolk, yeoman, brother and lawful heir of Capt. Nathaniel Powell, late of Va., deceased, as by deed now upon record from said Taylor more at large appeareth." (Records destroyed.) The other 1250 acres being due for the transportation of 25 persons. (G. P. 100)

John Sadler, Richard Quiney and Symon Sturges of London, merchants, also patented 4550 acres in Charles City Co. Aug. 5, 1634, said land "commonly called 'Martin's Brandon', lying between Chippokes Creek (upper) and Ward's Creek. Due by purchase from the heirs of Capt. John Martin, late of Va., and 4050 acres conferred to the said purchasers by order of the Grand Assembly March 1643." (C. P. 147.)

John Sadler and Richard Quiney also patented 1140 acres in the same vicinity January 11, 1649 "lying from the head of Ward's Creek up the easternmost branch of same four miles, called by the name of 'The Ponds'". (C. P. 188.)

Richard Quiney and John Sadler were brothers-in-law. Richard was married to John's sister, Ellen Sadler, daughter of John Sadler of Stratford on Avon. The pedigree of Richard Quiney entered by him in the Visitation of London 1634 shows the marriage. Shakespeare's daughter, Judith, married his brother, Thomas Quiney, a wine merchant living in Stratford on Avon February 10, 1615/16. (Waters-198.)

Richard Quiney, citizen and grocer of London, made his will Aug. 16, 1655; same probated Jan. 3, 1656. (Ruthen 6.) He gave all his lands in Virginia to his son, Thomas Quiney. (Waters-198.)

John Sadler of St. Stephens, Wallbrook, London, grocer, made his will December 11, 1658, proved Jan. 3, 1658. He gave to his son, John Sadler, "all my moiety of certain plantations in Virginia called Martin's Brandon and Merchants Hope. My female cattle I give to the lawful minister of the said place or parish and twenty pounds in goods shall be delivered to Master Charles Sparrow of Martin's Brandon for repairing the church and parsonage house there." (Waters-621.)

His son, John Sadler, "late of London, now of Hunsdon, Herts., made his will January 2, 1698; proved, November 16, 1718. He gave in trust to Sir Charles Ingleby for his daughter, Elizabeth Sadler, all that moiety of a plantation in Virginia called "Martin's Brandon" containing by estimation 6400 acres of land and also another plantation known by the name of "Merchants Hope", containing 1900 acres, she and her mother to receive the income for life. (Waters 622.)

Thomas Quiney of London, son of Richard Quiney, made his will May 20, 1701; proven June 13, 1701. He "gave and bequeathed all my moiety of two plantations in Virginia, the one called Martin's Brandon, the other Merchants Hope (the other moiety whereof equally divided belongs to Mr. John Sadler, late of London, druggist) unto my niece Elinor Richardson, until her youngest son, the said Robert Richardson, shall attain the age of one and twenty years when I give the same to him and his male issue." (Waters 799.)

On August 19, 1720, Robert Richardson, gent., and Mary, his wife, deeded their moiety or half of these two tracts known as Merchants Hope and Martin's Brandon, left by the will of Thomas Quiney to Nathaniel Harrison of Prince George. Nathaniel Harrison later bought the other moiety, or half of the two tracts, from the Sadler heirs. Combined, the two so-called moietys formed the large Brandon estate long held by the Harrisons.

In the land grant of August 5, 1634 to Sturges, Sadler and Quiney, it was stated that Martin's Brandon was due by purchase from the heirs of Capt. John Martin. (C.P. 147.) However, in a grant dated March 16, 1636, it was stated that the site or tract of land commonly called by the name of Martin's Brandon was due by purchase from Captain Robert Bargrave. (C.P. 55.)

Among the Bargrave family of Kent were several bold sea captains who brought many servants and traded or sold them to settlers for their transportation. Captain Robert Bargrave was a grandson of Captain John Martin, who settled on the tract which he called "Martin's Brandon" in 1617. Captain John Martin, son of Sir

Richard Martin, had a daughter Dorcus, who married Captain George Bargrave, who also sailed the seas to Virginia, as likewise did his brother, Captain John Bargrave. Martin's Brandon was inherited by George's son, Robert Bargrave, who sold the same to Sturges and Quiney.

In the great Indian massacre of 1622, Captain Nathaniel Powell and his wife, the daughter of Mr. Tracey (Rec. L. C. 3, p. 569) were killed at Powell's plantation "Powlebrooke." When this land came into the possession of William Barker, mariner, and his associates, the name was changed to "Merchants Hope" for William Barker's good ship of that name.

It is thought that the story of the descent of these lands and the history of their owners might be of interest.

William Barker, mariner, represented Charles City in the House of Burgesses in 1645. (H. B. 1619-1659, p. xviii.) He was deceased before March 3, 1655, for at the County Court on that day the widow of Capt. Frome was ordered to pay a debt of 5/22/6 to Robert Netherland, who married the administratrix of William Barker.

William Barker had three children who quarrelled about the division of "Flowerdieu Hundred." His wife was Frances, daughter of James Ward, who secondly married Robert Netherland and thirdly, Lt. Col. Thomas Drew. (See later.)

Children of William and Frances (Ward) Barker:
I. John Barker married the widow Pitt on Nov. 24, 1662. Following out the conditions of his brother-in-law, Richard Taylor, he gave to Thomas Drew, his "father--law," 30000 lbs. of good tobacco to guarantee him from all trouble for maintaining Hannah Pitt or Pett, daughter of his wife. The deed of gift was witnessed by Richard Pace and Richard Taylor. (1661-64, p. 94.)

John died without children, for at a court in 1677 it was stated "That whereas after the death of John Barker, late of Flowerdieu Hundred did own all that tract of land known by the name of Flowerdieu Hundred, containing 1000 acres . . . did lawfully descend to Sarah, the wife of Richard Taylor, decd., and now the wife of Robert Lucy, and to Elizabeth, the wife of Philip Limbry, sister and co-heir of the said John Barker have held same jointly since April 24, 1673 . . ." (O. B. 1677-79, p. 235.) This land was surveyed by James Minge. Robert Lucy and Sarah, his wife received the upper part on the James River and Philip Limbry and Elizabeth, his wife the lower part.

2. II. Sarah Barker, m. (1) Richard Taylor; (2) Robert Lucy; (3) Capt. James Bisse. (See later.)

III. Elizabeth Barker, m. Phillip Limbrey. She died before her husband, and he married, secondly, Jane
_____, who upon his death married Elias Osborne.
   Frances Drew, on June 4, 1677, petitioned the
court for the custody of two children of her daughter,
Elizabeth, stating that she (her youngest daughter) did
leave at her death four motherless children; two are
now dead and two fell into the hands of Jane, Phillip
Limbrey's second wife. She asked that Elias Osborne
be required to bring in Limbrey's will, advising that
"His temper and demeanor is well known to the court."
It was ordered John and Elizabeth Limbrey be given
into the custody of their grandmother, Mrs. Drew.
(O. B. 1677-79, pp. 181-4.)

2.   Sarah Barker, daughter of Frances (Ward) and William
Barker m. (1) Richard Taylor; (2) Robert Lucy; (3) Capt. James
Bisse. On March 1, 1661/2, Richard Taylor of Flowerdieu Hundred made a bond to Mrs. Frances Netherland of the same, widow,
to protect her from any claim of inheritance to be had or made by
Sarah, John or Elizabeth Barker, children of her first husband,
William Barker, decd. (1661-64, p. 69.) "... Further, if John
Barker at his lawful age, did manage his own estate and deliver to
said Frances and her husband certain properties for life at Flowerdieu Hundred, from his particular own plantations, excepting the
said John Barker's and the said Taylor's own plantations and the
plantations already let by lease. The said Frances and the said
Colonel Drew, her intended husband, is meant to whom only the ci-
vility of John Barker is proposed." (1661-64, p. 95.) Wits.:
Howell Pryce, John Barker. On June 10, 1664, Frances Netherland acquitted her son, Richard Taylor, from "a bond writ by
Howell Pryce concerning land for my life in Flowerdieu Hundred."
(1661-64, p. 99.)
   On April 14, 1678, Robert Lucy and Sarah, his wife, for natural love and affection for John and Richard Taylor, sons of said
Sarah, did sell their moiety unto Benjamin Harrison. (O. 1677-79,
p. 286.)
   In October 1684, Captain Edward Hill, as guardian for John
Taylor, orphan of Richard Taylor, decd., did obtain administration on the estate of Katherine and Sarah Taylor, decd., sisters
of said John. Captain John Hamblin, as marrying Elizabeth, one
of the daughters of Richard, decd., and Richard Bradford, as
marrying the other daughter, Frances, of said Richard, claim a
child's share of said deceased sister's estates. They, with John
Taylor, who is now of lawful age (Aug. 9, 1684) jointly acquit Sarah
Lucy as administratrix of estate of Robert Lucy from all claims
either under the estate of Richard Taylor, decd., or of James Ward

decd. (O. 1687-95, p. 149.) Sarah Lucy married for the third time Capt. James Bisse. (O. 1689-95, p. 272.)

Children of Sarah (Barker) and Richard Taylor:
3.   1.   Frances Taylor, m. Richard Bradford (See later #3.)
        2.   Richard Taylor, dsp. In court in 1691, Richard Taylor entered his claim for land in possession of his brother, John Taylor, in Flowerdieu Hundred by virtue of a deed dated April 14, 1678 by Sarah and Robert Lucy. He desired a division of their land and of 521 acres at Blackwater surveyed by Mr. Richard Ligon. (O. 1687-95, p. 365.)

            In John Taylor's will, probated Nov. 9, 1709 in Prince George, he leaves to daughter Elizabeth Duke 1000 acres at Blackwater "formerly the land of his brother Richard Taylor." Evidently Richard Taylor died without issue.

        3.   John Taylor, m. Henrietta Maria _____. (Last name unknown.) He was captain of Militia, Justice and Burgess from Charles City in the sessions of 1692-93.

            In 1673, Sarah Lucy and her husband, Robert Lucy, received the upper part of Flowerdieu containing the residence. In a later division between her sons, Richard and John Taylor, the site of the present house was included in John's portion.

            John Taylor made his will in Prince George County (formerly Charles City) April 5, 1707; same probated November 9, 1709. He gave his daughter, Elizabeth Duke, two negroes and a horse named "Trooper", "besides what I have already given her;" to daughter Henrietta Maria Taylor, four negroes, etc.; to daughter Sarah Taylor, four negroes; residue of estate to his wife, Henrietta Maria Taylor; to daughter Frances Taylor, certain property. Test: Michael Talbott, Sarah Bradford, Sarah Proudlove.

            These daughters married as follows: (1) Elizabeth, m. Henry Duke of Prince George; (2) Frances, m. Mr. Greenhill; (3) Henrietta Maria and (4) Sarah married brothers, John and Francis Hardyman, sons of Lt. Col. John Hardyman. (For descendants, see Duke-Symmes family history.)

            Flowerdieu was sold by Capt. John Taylor to Joshua Poythress (Duke-Symmes, pp. 65-69). Flowerdieu is still in the possession of Joshua Poythress' descendants. The present owners are Dr. and Mrs. Willcord Dunn, of Richmond, Virginia.

4. Elizabeth Taylor, m. Capt. John Hamblin

3. Richard Bradford, who married Frances Taylor, daughter of Sarah (Barker) and Richard Taylor, first appears in the records February 12, 1655, when Abraham Wood acknowledged that he had received full payment from him "of all debts due and demands from the beginning of the world" to that date. (Fleet, 10, p. 35.)

On July 21, 1656, Thomas Stegge received 1656 pounds of tobacco "in full payment of Bradford's debts." (p. 46.) September 3, Howell Pryce assigns to Richard Bradford "half of 1200 acres lying at the head of Queens Creek." (p. 89.) On August 4, 1662, Howell Pryce sold him "1197 acres and 11 poles of land bounded according to patent already delivered." (Fleet 11, p. 24.) Also in 1662 he was appointed Administrator of James Phelps, decd., and in 1664 the probate of the will of John Robinson was given to him.

On November 27, 1671, Richard Bradford patented the above 1197 acres bounded on two sides by Old Tree Run and Fishing Run. (P. B. 6-385.) In 1710 Richard Bradford and Richard Bradford, Jr., then in Charles City, later Prince George, signed a petition to add part of James City to Charles City County. (18 V 399.) He was Sheriff of Charles City in 1705, and held 1397 acres in the Quit Rents of 1704. (17 V 155; 8 W 277.)

Richard Bradford and Richard Bradford, Jr. witnessed a deed of Ralph Bradford, another son of Richard Bradford, Sr., on July 14, 1716. (See below.) This seems to be the last appearance of these two in Prince George. They evidently lived in Charles City where the records are destroyed.

The children of Richard and Frances (Taylor) Bradford were: (1) Richard Bradford, Jr.; (2) John Bradford, (See later); (3) Ralph Bradford, who, on July 14, 1716, as Ralph Bradford of Prince George, deeded Edward Goodrich, David Goodgame and Joshua Goodgame of said county, for £ 10 current money, 400 acres in the parish of Westover which was in part given by the last will of James Ward, decd., to Frances, the mother of said Bradford, and the other part given by the will of Richard Taylor, decd., which land was "sold by my father, Richard Bradford, to James Tucker" and by the said Tucker to Edward Goodrich and the Goodgames. Teste: William Wynne, Richard Bradford, Richard Bradford, Jr. (P. G. Bk. 1715, p. 136.)

John Bradford (son of Richard and Frances Bradford) had 191 acres surveyed for him on the lower side of the Great Creek of the Meherrin River November 14, 1721. (1715-30, p. 759.) The main reason he is assigned as a son of Richard and Frances Bradford is because his oldest son was named "Richard" and his oldest daughter "Frances" (so named in his will). His second daughter was named "Rebecca", which was his wife's name, and his youngest daughter was named "Sarah", probably for her grandmother, Sarah Barker. (See will later.)

John Moore, "son of Richard Moore", had 204 acres surveyed adjacent to John Bradford's 191 acres. John Bradford willed Margaret Moore 200 acres on Beaver Pond Creek, after her death to go to her son, Tobias Moore.

John Moore's wife was Tabitha Pace, daughter of Richard Pace, whose will was probated in Bertie, N.C., March 12, 1736. Richard Pace mentions seven married daughters, among whom were Tabitha Moore, and Rebecca Bradford. (See Pace.)

To further show a connection between Richard Pace and John Bradford, Richard Pace patented 285 acres in Prince George July 12, 1718. He afterwards assigned or gave this land to John Bradford. (Duke-Symmes, p. 71.) (See Pace.)

Rebecca Pace has previously been assigned as the wife of William Bradford, who died in Northampton Co., N.C. in 1763. (3 Tyler - 167.) He was a son of a Thomas Bradford whose will was dated May 1761; probated November Court, 1762. (Northampton Wills 1762-1791, Part I, p. 35.)

The examination of these facts makes it appear that inasmuch as John Moore was contemporary with John Bradford, and inasmuch as he married Tabitha Pace, John Bradford married her sister, Rebecca Pace.

William Bradford, son of Thomas, was of a much later generation. (See later relationship shown by the Moores, Paces and Bradfords in South Carolina.)

This article (3 Tyler 167) says, "Jesse Lane, born July 3, 1733, died October 28, 1806; married December 16, 1755. Winifred Aycock, daughter of William Aycock, who took out a grant of land in Northampton Co., N.C., 500 acres, August 26, 1746 (N.C. G.H. 1900) and August, 1779, was one of the grand jury in the first court held in Wilkes County, Georgia, (G.G. Smith's "Story of Georgia") and his wife, Rebecca Pace, the widow of William Bradford. Winifred Aycock was born April 11, 1741 and died in 1794."

Inasmuch as the William Bradford we are concerned with died in 1764 in Northampton, his widow could not have been the mother of Winifred Aycock, born in 1741.

John Bradford died in Brunswick County, Virginia, in 1735. His will was as follows:

Will of John Bradford, Brunswick County, Virginia

November 3, 1732 — Probated November 6, 1735 (29 V 507)
To eldest son, Richard: a survey of land on the south side of Fountain Creek, surveyed by the late Col. Thomas Cocke in 1732 —also 400 acres on north side of river called "Pamplico" when he is of age. He shall allow his mother, my wife, half the profits of the Mill.

To son Nathaniel: Land lying on north side of Pea Hill, also tract of 150 acres in N.C., being land I bought of Francis Ellidge on south side of Beaver Pond Creek; also land in N.C. on north side of Tarr River, called "Pamplico" 640 acres.

To son John: 200 acres on south side of Fountain Creek; and survey of land surveyed by Arthur Williams on South side of Jelks Swamp.

To eldest daughter Frances, negroes and land.

To 2nd daughter Rebecca, negroes and land.

To youngest daughter Sarah, negroes and land.

To Gabriell Pickrell: 300 acres.

To Thomas Powell: land

To Margaret Moore: 200 acres on Beaver Pond Creek, and after her death to her son Tobias Moore.

To Francis Ellidge: land.

Wife, remainder of estate for life and appointed her executrix.

Witnesses: Richard Bradford, Margaret Moore, Phillip Prescott.

Children of John and Rebecca (Pace) Bradford:

1. Richard, eldest son, was bequeathed by his father land on Fountain Creek, also 400 acres called "Pamplico". Fountain Creek was in Northampton Co., N.C., as shown by grant to his brother Nathaniel, and "Pamplico" seems to be in Edgecombe Co., N.C. He may have been the father of Thomas Bradford of Northampton. (Will 1761.) (See later.)

2. John was bequeathed 200 acres on south side of Fountain Creek. A captain John Bradford was executor of Hugh Hardy's estate in Halifax, N.C. 1761, also of Jennings Hackney in 1765. He may have been the Colonel John Bradford who was very prominent in Halifax during the Revolution. Colonel John Bradford died in 1787, leaving a large family. He is said to have been born in 1708. (D.A.R., Vol. 137, p. 42.) He would hardly have been a colonel in active service at the age of 70. (N.C. Col. Rec. 12-509.) On Jan. 1, 1760, John Bradford and Patience, his wife, sold Jesse Pope 185 acres. (B. 7-264.)

3. Nathaniel, bequeathed 150 acres on the south side of Beaver Pond Creek in N.C.; also patented 300 acres near Fountain Creek in Northampton County, N.C., April 11, 1745. (G.B. 5-338.) On April 28, 1750, he sold these 300 acres to Robert Jones, Jr. of Surry (BI-421). He evidently moved to Edgecombe County where he had been willed 640 acres on the Tarr River. In 1747, Nathaniel Bradford of Edgecombe sold 100 acres to Benjamin Lane, part of a patent granted to

Thomas Brown March 2, 1774, and sold to Nathaniel
Bradford. (Halifax 3-280.) Nathaniel Bradford sold
to John Bradford 185 acres granted March 20, 1749
for £ 25 on November 11, 1751. (Halifax 4, 167.)
Captain Nathaniel Bradford of Edgecombe and wife
Sarah sold land to Hugh Hardy, November 20, 1756.
(BK, Part 14, 1756-61, p. 231.)

In 1745, Joseph Lane sold to John Bradford 200 acres on Hardy
Branch, granted to Joseph in 1745. (Halifax 4-471.)

Joseph Lane (1710-1774) was the father of Jesse Lane, who
married Winifred Aycock December 16, 1755, the daughter of
William Aycock.

It is evident that this is the Bradford family which was related
to the Aycocks, for John and Nathaniel Bradford, Jr. and the Aycocks, Lanes and Popes moved to Wilkes County, Georgia.

Nathaniel Bradford Sr. of Edgecombe made his will October,
1756; same probated 1757. He mentions wife Sarah and children:
(1) John; (2) Nathaniel; (3) Mary; (4) Patience.

Inventory of William Aycock's estate was filed in Wilkes Co.,
Georgia, January 4, 1778. Among the debtors to the estate were:
"John Bradford, to William Aycock dr, about the year 1745 for
horse lent in Virginia. Henry Pope to William Aycock 1757 for a
mare in Virginia." (History of Wilkes, Vol. I, p. 31.)

In 1802, Nathaniel Bradford had 200 acres in Wilkes, 287 in
Washington, 287 in Franklin. (Do., Vol II, p. 40.) Nathaniel
Bradford and wife Tamar sold land next to Burwell Pope and Tho-
mas Wooten in 1790. (Do., 107.)

William Bradford of Virginia, on December 5, 1789, sold to
John De Priest of Georgia 200 acres on north fork of Dover Creek,
granted July 20, 1782. This deed was recorded in Elbert County,
Georgia, and William Bradford seemed to be living there in 1792.
(Habersham, Vol 3, 151.)

A Thomas Bradford appears early in the records of Bertie and
Northampton Counties in North Carolina. He seems to be a son or
grandson of John and Rebecca (Pace) Bradford because of the relationship shown later between his children and the Pace and Moore
families.

Thomas Bradford was residing in Bertie Precinct, N.C. in
1732, for on April 5, 1732 he and his wife Elizabeth of that precinct (later Northampton County) for £ 10 sold to Phillip Mulkey
of Edgecombe Precinct 180 acres on the south side of Moratuck
River (later Roanoke) near Thomas Whitmel's corner. (Edge. 1732-
41, p. 15.)

There were but three counties in North Carolina at that time,
and the territorial divisions of these counties were called "precincts." The designation of these precincts was changed to that
of "county" in 1738. (Wheeler Hist. N.C.)

The above deed was signed by Elizabeth, first wife of Thomas Bradford, for when he made his will in Northampton on May 23, 1761, the wife mentioned was Mary.

Thomas Bradford and Samuel Norwood in 1734 sold to Barnaby Melton for £ 20, 150 acres granted William Reeves March 30, 1721. (Nor. BK. E, p. 182.) It is probable that Thomas Bradford married Elizabeth, daughter of Samuel Norwood, for James Smith, in his undated will, probated in 1762 in Halifax, leaves a legacy to his daughter, Mary Norwood, wife of Samuel Norwood, and to her daughters, Mary Norwood and Elizabeth Bradford. It seems that Thomas was the only Bradford in Northampton with a wife named "Elizabeth". (Halifax Wills 1-70.)

Thomas Bradford made his will in Northampton as follows: Thomas Bradford, 23rd day of May, 1761. To my loving wife, Mary Bradford, my plantation (where I now live) and my Mills and a Negro fellow named Ned, wench named Judy, six cows and calves, one black mare, furniture & 4 iron pots, one kettle—so long as she shall live a Widdow and after her death or marriage to be divided between my two sons William and Henry Bradford. To my son William Bradford, my Plantation where I now live beginning at a Spanish red oak on the River and running along my Son Nathl Bradford's line to a Corner pine, then along a line of marked trees to a corner Red Oak on Richard Span's line—also one Negro Boy named Peter, my mill, bed & furniture, one horse colt & my smith's tools.
To my son, Henry Bradford, Parcel of land containing 200 acres beginning on Richard Spann's line and a new line made between Wm Bradford & the sd Henry Bradford; also one Negro girl named Joan. To my dau. Edith Bradford, negro girl Beck; bed & furn. Dau Sarah Bradford, negro boy Ned. To Elizabeth Bradford, 5 Shil. Proc. Money. To son Nathaniel Bradford, 100 acres of land joyning his own & ye county road where John Richardson now lives; also my close bodied white coat; negro fellow Ton. To my son Richard Bradford, parcel of land containing 440 acres in Orange County on Lick Creek; negro Boy named Gibb; negro boy Gim. To my son Thomas Bradford, Junr. — all my Island land.
Appoint wife and my son Nathl. Bradford Exrs. Teste: John Avent, Wm. Brooks. Probated, November Court, 1762. (Wills 1762-1791, Part I, p. 35.)
His children were:
1. William, died young. His property was inherited by William and John Bradford.
2. Henry, moved to South Carolina. On Sept. 16, 1778, as Henry Bradford of "Northampton" he sold 200 acres to Henry Macon of Halifax for £ 230 "next to Eaton Haynes' line which was formerly Nathaniel Bradford's (B. 6-267.)

On August 11, 1779, Henry Bradford and John Bradford of St. Mark's Parish, Craven Co., S.C. deeded to Eaton Haynes of Northampton, N.C. 300 acres for £ 300 "beginning at Roanoke River, dividing line between William Bradford and said Henry Bradford to a line that was formerly Nathaniel Bradford's, now Eaton Haynes', which said land was devised to William Bradford and inherited by the said Henry and John Bradford as heirs at law of the said William." (B. 6-355.)

3. Nathaniel. In November 1761, Thomas Bradford, Sr. deeded to Nathaniel Bradford for £ 200, 120 acres. (B. 3-49.) On November 3, 1772, Nathaniel Bradford and Frances, his wife, for £ 139 deeded Samuel Lockhart 120 acres formerly deeded by Thomas Bradford, decd., to Nathaniel Bradford beginning at Thomas Bradford's corner by the Roanoke River; and 100 acres given by will of his father, Thomas Bradford, decd. (BK 5-227.) Nathaniel Bradford's will appears in Will Book A of Sumter Co., S.C.; abstracted as follows: "Nathaniel Bradford's will, August 3, 1807, legacies to sons Nathaniel, John and Richard Bradford; daus., Mary Drake and Sarah Ream. Exrs: Wife and Absalom Williams." (BK. H-260.)

A Thomas Britten made his will Jan. 10, 1807 and mentions "half brother" Richard Bradford, son of Nathaniel Bradford... cousins Jared and David Neilson... exr. David Neilson (BK A-3). A Robert Singleton made his will in Sumter Co., S.C. Nov. 8, 1798. He mentions daughter Elizabeth Bradford and his executors were Richard Bradford and son John Bradford.

4. Richard was willed 440 acres in Orange County, on Lick Creek, by his father. In 1770, Richard Bradford deeded land to Louis Williamson. (B5-25.)

5. Thomas was willed all of his father's Island land. On November 25, 1770, as "Thomas Bradford of Craven County, S.C." he deeded to Nathaniel Moore of Northampton a survey of land taken up by Captain Thomas Bradford by patent 3 November 1753, being an island in the Roanoke River, near Capt. Richard Spann, containing 80 acres. Wits: John Bradford. (B5 - 118.)

It will be noted that these three sons, Henry, Nathaniel and Thomas Bradford, Jr., moved to Craven County, S.C. (Later divided into Chester and Lancaster Counties.) They were accompanied by the Moores and Paces, their relatives. (See Moore and Pace.)

Descendants of Thomas Bradford are still residing in Lancaster County. They say he had a wife named Mary and a daughter named Mary. The daughter Mary married John Stover and had two sons, one named William Bradford Stover and the other, Thomas Bradford Stover. (See Stover.)

The will books of Lancaster were burned in the War of 1861-65, and only the deeds remain. It seems that Thomas Bradford was deceased before 1780, the year of William Moore's will, and there is no further record of him.

Thomas and Mary Bradford seem to have had these children:

(1) Isham is mentioned in the will of his relative, William Moore:

William Moore, son of John and Tabitha (Pace) Moore, in his will in South Carolina, dated Aug. 9, 1780, gave land and household goods to ISHAM BRADFORD, son of MARY BRADFORD. (Charleston Wills, See Index.) Isham Bradford of Claremont County, S. C., (later Sumter) on Mar. 1, 1791, deeded Thomas Pace and Nathaniel Pace, Jr. of the county and state aforesaid, for 10 shillings, a tract containing 225 acres on Swift Creek and 175 acres on the road from Charleston to Camden, granted Thomas Stater Aug. 72, 1751. (Lancaster BK. 80-81.) (See Moore.)

Thomas Bradford does not appear further in the records and Mary Bradford, mother of Isham, seems to be the widow of Thomas. The name "Isham" came from the Moore family, who were related to the Bradfords. (See Moore.)

The above deed of Isham Bradford was recorded in LANCASTER County, where part of the land in question was situated. This was in 1791 after the Census of 1790, the first in the United States, was taken.

(2) Mary, m. John Stover. John Stover died in Lancaster County between 1788 and 1790, as he does not appear in the Census of 1790, although according to a deed he was living in 1788. This deed was from William Johnston and Jean, his wife, of Lancaster County to John Stover of Lancaster, dated Dec. 17, 1788. Same was in consideration of 4000 lbs. of tobacco for 100 acres of land "where the said John Stover now lives." Wits: THOMAS BRADFORD and SAMUEL BRADFORD. (Bk. B-212.)

The "widow Stover" was head of a family of four males under 16 and four females, including herself, in the Lancaster Census of 1790. She moved to Liberty Hill in Kershaw County, where as "Mary Stober" in 1800 she had one son between 10 and 16, one between 16 and 26, one daughter between 10 and 16, one between 16 and 26, and herself, between 26 and 45, in her household. (See Stover.)

These two sons were William Bradford Stover, born June 24, 1782, and Thomas Bradford Stover, born Oct. 7, 1788. These dates from their family Bible agree with the ages shown in the above Census of 1800.

(3) Thomas, who with his brother Samuel witnessed the above deed to John Stover in 1788, appears in the Census of 1790 for Lancaster as head of a family consisting of himself, wife, one son over 16, five under 16, one daughter and four slaves. In Kershaw in 1800, where he evidently moved along with the Stovers, he was head of a family of four males under 10 and three females 10 to 16, also his wife and himself between 26 and 45. He does not appear in 1810 and evidently migrated to the southwest, probably to Alabama, where the Stovers afterwards moved. (Neither Thomas nor Samuel Bradford appear in the Lancaster Census of 1810.)

(4) Samuel, who also witnessed the deed of 1788, also appears in the Lancaster Census of 1790 as head of a family consisting of himself, wife, one son over 16 and four slaves. He does not appear either in Lancaster of Kershaw in 1800, and evidently migrated.

STOVER OF LANCASTER AND KERSHAW, S.C.

This family of Stover is descended from John Stover, who died in Lancaster County, South Carolina, between 1788 and 1790. His wife is said to have been Mary, daughter of Thomas Bradford. From records hereafter shown, this tradition seems substantially correct.

The records of the Stover family of the Valley in Virginia have been carefully checked, and there does not appear to be any connection between that family and the above John Stover. His family may have originated in South Carolina and underwent a change in name. Mary Stover's name in the Census was sometimes spelled "Stober".

On February 11, 1775/76, John Martain Strober of Craven in South Carolina and Sarah, his wife, sold to Benjamin Hall of Craven, for £ 130, 25 acres in Parish of St. Marks in Craven on both sides of Flat Creek, a branch of Lynch's Creek, bounded by Robert Harper. Surveyed October 5, 1758 for John Baker. Wits: Jonas Guffen. (Before William Welch, J.P.) (C. and E. 52 recorded April 20, 1790.)

(From Charleston Wills Book II, 1767-71, p. 176.) Will of Jacob Strobar, Parish of Peter, County of Granville, dated July 29, 1767; probated September 19, 1767. To wife Catharine "one-third of my estate except the cash and money due that I desire may be laid out for negroes to put them on plantation; to sons John Strobar and Jacob Strobar my plantation to be equally divided between them and two lots in Perrysburgh Town, one that is building to John and the other to Jacob, to son Henry £ 1000 current money out of plantation, rest of personal and real estate to be divided between them as they come of age—younger children to be schooled. Jacob Hartstrom and son John to be executors, likewise my brother George Strobar. Wits: Henry Dunn, Lewis M. Morgan, Nicholas Westuby."

John Strobber paid for 115 days militia duty 1781-82.

John Slover, or Stover, paid £ 2 - 17/4 June 28, 1785 for furnishing Gen. Morgan's Brigade with munitions and pork in 1780. (S.C. Rev. Indents, Bk. R-T.)

The only Stovers shown in the Census of 1790, besides the "widow Stover", (see later) were John and Charles Stover of

Clarendon County, Camden District. John Stover was head of
a family of three males under 16, five females, and eight slaves.
Charles had himself and one son over 16, three males under 16,
six females and 18 slaves.

John Stover, the direct ancestor of this family, on December
17, 1788, bought from William Johnston and Jean, his wife, of
Lancaster County, for 4000 lbs. tobacco, 100 acres on Bever
Creek in Lancaster "where the said John Stover now lives". (B-
212.) This deed was witnessed by Thomas Bradford and Samuel
B. Bradford. They were probably his wife's brothers, as John
Stover married Mary Bradford, daughter of Thomas Bradford,
and one of her sons was named "Thomas Bradford Stover".

The above record is the first and only one so far found of John
Stover. He does not appear in the Census of 1790 for Lancaster,
but his wife appears in that census as the "widow Stover", head
of a family of four males under 16 and four females including herself.

She moved to Liberty Hill in Kershaw County and appears as
"Mary Stober" in the 1800 Census for that county. She had one
son between 10 and 16, one between 16 and 26, one daughter under
10, one between 16 and 26, and herself between 26 and 45, in her
household.

These two sons were William Bradford Stover, born June 24,
1782, and Thomas Bradford Stover, born October 7, 1788. (Family
Bible.) These dates agree with the ages shown in the above Census
of 1790.

Thomas Bradford, who witnessed the above deed of 1788, appears in the Census of 1790 for Lancaster as head of a family and
so does Samuel Bradford.

In Kershaw in 1800, Thomas Bradford was head of a family of
four males under 10 and three females 10 to 16, also his wife and
himself between 26 and 45. (Neither Thomas nor Samuel Bradford
appears in Lancaster in 1800.)

Mary Stober appears in the Census for Kershaw in 1810 as
head of a family of one son between 16 and 26, one daughter between 16 and 26, and herself, over 45. (Born before 1765.)

Her son William Stover appears by himself in the Census of
1810 for Kershaw as head of a family consisting of himself and
wife.

On October 22, 1808, John Hood and Elizabeth, his wife,
deeded to Mary Stover and Thomas Stover of KERSHAW 150 acres
in Lancaster on Rocky Creek, originally granted to William Mattox. (G. 208-9.)

On May 16, 1818, Mary Stover deeded to Thomas Stover 141
acres on both sides of Rocky Creek in Lancaster. Witnesses:
James Clancy, Jean Douglas, before James Dougles, J. P. (M.
208.) This deed was recorded in 1831 after Mary Stover's death.

Mary Stover died before January 15, 1827, for on that date
Robert Cunningham, William B. Stover, William B. Gardner,
and William McCain, heirs of Mary Stover, deceased, deeded to
Thomas Stover the southwest one-half of 150 acres deeded to
Mary Stover and Thomas Stover by John Hood. (M. 299.)

Women did not have any property rights in South Carolina in
those days. Inasmuch as their husbands signed the deed for their
property, their names remain unknown.

Children of John and Mary Bradford Stover:

1. William Bradford Stover, born June 24, 1782, m.
   Sarah McWillie of Kershaw County, South Carolina,
   daughter of Colonel Adam McWillie. (See "McWillie-
   Cunningham Families" by Robert B. Johnson.)

   William Bradford Stover moved to Alabama about
   1825, where he appears in the Census for Conecuh
   County in 1850 (p. 182) as follows:

   William B. Stover, age 69, born in South Carolina
   Sarah Stover, age 60, born in Ireland
   Elizabeth Stover, age 22, born in Alabama

   Their family Bible shows that he was born June
   24, 1782; his wife, June 6, 1790; his daughter Elizabeth Tirzah, June 24, 1826. m. Mumford D. Perryman.

2. Daughter, m. Robert Cunningham.
3. Daughter, m. William B. Gardner
4. Daughter, m. William McCain
5. Thomas Bradford Stover, b. October 7, 1788, died
   January 18, 1854, m. Mary Elizabeth Russell, born
   October 12, 1799, died May 29, 1880. She was the
   daughter of William and Mary (Ballard) Russell.
   Mary Ballard was a daughter of Thomas Ballard,
   a captain in the Revolution, and his wife, Mary
   Parks.

(Notes from an article published in the Kershaw News-Era, by
Mrs. E. C. Croxton, Health Springs, S. C., "THE STOVER FA-
MILY", 1946. Furnished by Mrs. Ben C. Hough, Jr.):

"Nearly a century and a quarter have passed since there was
solemnized a marriage between THOMAS STOVER and MARY
ELIZABETH RUSSELL near Liberty Hill, South Carolina. They
became members of the Presbyterian Church there. (It may not
be amiss to say here that natives of that cultured community used
to tell that even the dogs of Liberty Hill were Presbyterian.)

"The Russells, said to be from Warren County, North Caro-
lina, were people of means and culture and what is now known as
Stoneboro was their home place—then known as Russell Place.
Mary Elizabeth had two sisters—one became Mrs. Ruben (Millie)

Bailey. (Elmer Bailey is a grandson of this couple.) The other sister, Martha, became Mrs. Sigmon Gillum.

"Thomas Stover died at the age of 56 and is buried at Liberty Hill. Mary Elizabeth lived to be 81 years old and is buried in Bethel Church yard. They were the parents of ten children. All reached maturity except first son, William, who, when quite a young man, was killed by a horse."

Children:
1. JOHN CUNNINGHAM STOVER m. REBECCA TRUESDALE (See later.)
2. JAMES LEVEAL STOVER m. (1) _____ BASKINS; (2) AMELIA CREIGHTON.
   Children by first wife:
   a. Thomas Charles Stover m. _____ Jones.
   b. Jimmie W. Stover m. _____ Drakeford.
   c. David Bertram Stover m. Minnie Cherry.
   d. Henrietta Stover m. Martin Cauthen.
   Children by second wife:
   a. Robert Lee Stover m. _____ Tennant
   b. Edward B. Stover m. _____
   c. Janie Stover m. _____ White.
3. THOMAS BRADFORD STOVER m. (1850-51) MARY VAN-LANDINGHAM. Thomas was killed in the Civil War.
   Children:
   a. JOHN STOVER m. "TEENIE" ROLLINGS.
   b. SION STOVER m. EMMA HILLIARD.
   c. SARAH STOVER m. Alista Cauthen.
   d. MINNIE STOVER never married
4. DAVID STOVER, (was killed in the Civil War.)
5. WILLIAM STOVER m. POLLY TRUESDALE
   Children:
   a. Elizabeth Stover m. Thomas Barton.
   b. Mattie Stover—unmarried, died at 78, buried at Salem.
   c. Nannie Stover m. S. N. Hammond. 3 children.
   d. David Stover m. Alice Stover.
   e. William Stover m. (1) Nancy Cauthen; (2) Eunice Cauthen.
   f. Andrew Stover m. (1) Lila Carter; (2) Bessie McKnight.
   g. Truesdale Stover m. Sallie Cauthen.
   h. Essie Stover m. Andrew Moseley.
   i. Dora Stover m. J. M. Moseley.
   j. Sarah Stover m. Ruffin Mackey
6. MARY STOVER m. JOSHUA HENDRIX.
   Children:
   a. John Hendrix m. Sallie Crenshaw
   b. William (Billie) Hendrix
   c. Thomas Hendrix m. Ella Bell

      d. Elizabeth Hendrix m. Joe Caskey (She died young.)

      e. Sarah Hendrix m. Joe Caskey. 4 children.

      f. David Hendrix m. Matilda Hunter. 6 children.

7. SARAH STOVER m. JOHN GAY

  Children:

      a. Alice Gay m. Hollis Horton

      b. Laura Gay m. Burrell Jones

      c. Sue Gay m. James Robertson

      d. Millie Gay m. Thomas Horton

      e. Rebecca Gay m. John Gaskins

      f. Lou Gay m. John Gaile

      g. Simmie Gay m. Butler Gay

      h. Vergie Gay m. John Estridge.

8 & 9. MARTHA STOVER and JANE STOVER never married. They made their home with brother, William Stover. The house in which William Stover and Polly Truesdale Stover reared all their children is standing about three miles west of Health Springs, South Carolina. William was born about 1828.

John Cunningham Stover, son of Thomas B. and Mary (Russell) Stover, was born March 13, 1822 in Kershaw County and died June 22, 1904. He married February, 1846, at Kershaw, Kershaw County, North Carolina, Sarah Rebecca Truesdale, born Sept. 27, 1827; died April 11, 1907; daughter of Camilla (Cauthen) and John Truesdale. He was a planter and served during the War Between the States as a soldier in Co. I, 12th Infantry, commanded by Col. T. F. Clyburn, Confederate Army.

Children:

    1. Camilla, b. February 3, 1847.

    2. Laura Cornelia, b. September 23, 1848, m. B. M. Jones (See later).

    3. Sarah, b. July 9, 1850, m. Mr. Gray.

    4. John, b. October 30, 1852.

    5. Matilda, b. 1853, m. Mr. Robinson.

    6. Alice, b. August 11, 1854, m. Mr. Horton

    7. James, b. May 28, 1858, m. Miss Orvens.

    8. Rebecca Nancy, b. April 15, 1860.

    9. Susan, b. March 15, 1862.

   10. Martha Louisa, b. January 24, 1866

   11. Samuel, b. September 23, 1867, m. Mrs. Gay

   12. Virgia Viola, b. 1869, m. Mr. Estridge

   13. Henry, b. September 16, 1870, m. Mrs. Gay

Laura Cornelia Stover, born September 23, 1848, died Feb. 27, 1920 at Kershaw; married November 18, 1869 Burrell Marion Jones, born August 24, 1847, died August 31, 1934 at Kershaw.

He was a son of Harriet (Horton) and Col. Burrell Jones of Kershaw. Col. Jones was born September 29, 1809 and died May 16, 1896 and his wife was born August 30, 1830, died October 12, 1906. Col. Jones' father, Samuel Jones, b. 1756, d. January 20, 1847, was the last Revolutionary War veteran of Kershaw County. He came to South Carolina with his father William Jones and wife Elizabeth King from Virginia.

Burrell M. Jones served in a South Carolina regiment during the War Between the States.

Children:

1. James Samuel Jones, b. September 15, 1870, unmarried.
2. Lemuch Cunningham, b. October 4, 1873, m. _____ Crow.
3. Wade Hampton, b. September 22, 1876.
4. Rebecca Stover, b. June 11, (?), unmarried.
5. Harnett Susan, b. July 1, 1881, died young.
6. Laura Amelia, b. December 16, 1882, unmarried.
7. Marion Burrell, b. June 30, 1884, unmarried.
8. Ida Louise, b. June 19, 1886, m. _____ Mathis.
9. Edward John, b. March 6, 1888, m. Turluck.
10. Dora Lyllie, b. May 6, 1890, m. B. M. Ellison, Sr. (See later.)

Dora Lyllie Jones, born May 6, 1890 at Kershaw, married February 12, 1920, at Charlotte, Mecklenburg Co., North Carolina, Burrell Marion Ellison, born March 12, 1884 at Easley, Pickens Co., South Carolina. They reside at Easley, South Carolina.

Children:

Burrell Marion Ellison, Jr., born November 15, 1920 at Easley, South Carolina, married August 7, 1944, at York, S. C., Carolyn Cloud Holland, born July 30, 1925, at Monroe, Union Co., South Carolina, daughter of Lila Christine (Duke) and Charles W. Holland.

Mr. Burrell M. Ellison, Jr. was educated at the Citadel and the University of South Carolina. He served as a pilot during World War II and was awarded the Distinguished Flying Cross, the Air Medal with three clusters and has several theater ribbons. He lives in Lancaster, South Carolina.

Children:

1. Burrell M. Ellison III, b. February 28, 1946.
2. Laura Carolyn Ellison, b. August 8, 1948.

PACE

This is the family of Richard Pace, the man who saved Jamestown in 1622 by warning its inhabitants of the impending Indian massacre. His story is told in Chapter IV of "Colonial Surry", so it will not be necessary to repeat it here.

1. Richard Pace's plantation was called "Pace's Paines," which he patented in 1620. He died before Sept. 1, 1628, when his son George repatented Pace's Paines. (C. P. 10.) His widow, Isabella, married Captain William Perry. An account of Captain Perry has heretofore been given in Chapter VI. (do.)

2. George Pace, son of Richard, married Sarah Maycock, daughter of the Reverend Samuel Maycock, member of the Council in the first Virginia General Assembly in 1619. He was killed in the Massacre of 1622, leaving his young daughter Sarah as his heiress. She was granted a patent for 200 acres in Surry in 1626. (See Chapter IX, do.)

The Governor of Virginia, on May 20, 1617, had asked "orders for Mr. Maycock, a Cambridge scholar, on account of the lack of ministers."

Samuel Macocke was admitted sizar at Jesus May 28, 1611, son of Roger, husbandman, of Yelvetoft, Northants. School Shadwell, Leciester. Migrated to Caius May 15, 1612, matriculated 1612, scholar 1613-14, went to Virginia 1618, added to Council 1619, K. 1622. (A. C.)

Upon his arrival in Virginia Samuel Maycock was made a member of the Council by Sir George Yeardley and continued in office under Sir Francis Wyatt until he was killed. He also bore the title of "Captain."

Among the killed at Captain Maycock's plantation of 200 acres adjoining Flowerdieu Hundred was Edward Lister, who came over in the "Mayflower" to Plymouth, Mass. and was a signer of the "Compact."

There is a deed in the Charles City County records by which "Richard Pace, son and heire as the first issue of my mother, Mrs. Sarah Maycock, wife unto my aforesaid father, both deced", confirms a sale of 800 or 900 acres "lying near unto Pierce's Hundred als Flowerdieu Hundred" to Mr. Thomas Drew as per bill of his father October 12, 1650.

In addition to the grant of "Pace's Paines" received from his
father in 1628, George Pace patented 1700 acres August 1, 1650
in Charles City County, "lying on s. side of James River, commonly called 'Maycock's', beg. at mouth of a little swamp by the
river where Pierce, his hundred, takes ending, running w. to a
swamp which leads to Powell's Cr. and along the cr. to the river"
for the transportation of 34 persons. (C. P. 199.) He also patented 507 acres "on S. side of James River and E. side of
Powell's Cr. Dec. 6, 1652." (C. P. 273.)

Thomas Drew, Gent., patented 490 acres in Charles City June
4, 1657, "on N. side of Flowerdieu hundred Cr., n. upon land
purchased by Mr. Pace." (C. P. 347.)

George Pace probably died about 1657, for in 1659 Richard
Pace "as son and heir of George Pace, decd.", sold land in
Charles City. (P. G.) (O. B. 1655.) In 1677 Richard Pace was
paid 200 lbs. of tobacco for wolves' heads. He died in that year,
for in 1677 Mary Pace was granted administration on the estate
of Richard Pace. (O. B. 1677-79, pp. 249, 270.) On April 19,
1679, Thomas Douglas and Capt. Jordan were appointed to appraise the estate of Richard Pace on behalf of the orphan. (Do.,
p. 279.) It seems that Mary Pace married, secondly, Nicholas
Whitmore, and that her first husband, Richard Pace, was formerly the executor of Hugh Kirkland. This is shown in a Court
order entered at Westover August 3, 1692 as follows: "The mat-
ter of the account between Thomas Kirkland v. Nicholas Whitmore
and Mary, his wife, admix. of Richard Pace, one of the executors of Hugh Kirkland, is referred to Capt. Taylor and Capt.
Perry for audit." (Charles City Orders, 1687-1695, p. 409.)
(This book was recently returned from the North, where it was
taken after or during the Civil War.)

4. George Pace, undoubtedly the orphan son of the above
Richard Pace, was holding 1000 acres in Prince George (cut off
from Charles City) in 1704. George married a daughter of Edward WOODLIEF, son of John Woodlief and his wife, a daughter
of Colonel Robert WYNNE, speaker of the House of Burgesses.
Edward Woodlief in his will probated in P. G. February 1719,
mentions his "daughter Pace."

The date of George Pace's death is not known, but he evidently
had two sons, John and Richard, who moved to Bertie Precinct,
N. C.

Children:

      I.   John, Sr. made his will in Bertie Precinct, N. C.
              March 25, 1726-27 and same was probated August
              1727. His children were: sons, John, William and
              George; daus., Frances, Ann, Eliz. Pace and Mary
              Melton. (Grimes abs.) His wife was not named.

A William Lowe who held 1584 acres in Prince George in 1704 moved to N. C.; where he made his will in Chowan (later Bertie Precinct and Northampton County) in 1720. He willed land in Prince George, Va., to his sons, John and William Lowe; mentions his son-in-law, Robert Dixon, and also his daughter, "Elizabeth Pace". This "Elizabeth" may have been the wife of John Pace.

5. II. Richard (see later).

5. Richard Pace, whose daughter Tabitha married Richard Moore's son, John, evidently moved to nearby Surry County and held land near the Moore family. This is shown by a grant of 1200 acres to one Thomas Avent March 1729, given by the Va. Council. (V. M. 34, p. 203.) This grant was in Surry County, "beginning at <u>Richard Moore's</u> line to Stewart's line and over Otterdam Swamp to include all land between John Davis and <u>Richard Pace.</u>"

John Barlow, who lived on Otterdam Swamp in Surry, died in 1728. He gave his son, William, a plantation "extending down the branch to Richard Pace's corner." The men named to divide his land among his three sons were "Richard Pace, Richard Moore and Thos. Avent." These three men also witnessed the will. (Bk. 7, p. 864.)

Previous to his removal to Surry, Richard Pace patented 285 acres in Prince George, July 12, 1718. This land afterwards fell in Brunswick County and was situated in the Parish of Lawne's Creek, Brunswick, on the north side of Three Creeks. This land was conveyed by him to John Bradford "beginning on said creek side from a corner of Capt. John Sadler's, then by Sadler's line to George Hambleton's." Three Creeks arose in Brunswick about seven miles west of the Greensville Brunswick county line. The remaining distance to its mouth on the Nottaway River is in Greensville. (Duke-Symmes Hist., p. 71.)

Richard Pace removed to Bertie Precinct (later Northampton County), N. C., where he made his will March 12, 1736; same probated 1738. (Grimes' Abstracts.) He names sons, William, Thomas and Richard Pace; daus., Ann Stewart, Amy Green, Frances Green, Tabitha Moore, Mary Johnson, Sarah House, and Rebecca Bradford who was the wife of John Bradford of Brunswick. (Impression of a lion rampant on seal.)

Thomas Pace, son of the above Richard, made his will in Northampton July 4, 1764; probated February 1765. He gave wife Amy use of manor plantation "where I now live during her widowhood if she should marry again I give her plantation on Stone Hill; daughter Cecilia, £ 50 and negro girl; daughter Frances two negroes; son THOMAS plantation where I now live;

son NATHANIEL PACE old plantation where I formerly lived and 13 negroes. Son NATHANIEL, exr. Friend Blake Bates, Overseer. " (Bk. A, Part I, p. 125.)

In 1792 in Kershaw County, S.C., JOHN MOORE, probably son of John and Tabitha (Pace) Moore "In consideration for the love and affection for his 'Cousin' THOMAS PACE," deeded him cattle and household goods. This may have been Thomas Pace (Jr.) mentioned above. (D.B. 1792, See Index.)

WILLIAM MOORE, son of John and Tabitha (Pace) Moore, in his will in S.C., dated 1780, gave land to ISHAM BRADFORD, son of MARY BRADFORD. (See Moore and Bradford.)

ISHAM BRADFORD of Claremont Co., S.C. on March 1, 1791 deeded THOMAS PACE and NATHANIEL PACE, Jr., of the county and state aforesaid, 225 acres in aforesaid county on Swift Creek, and 175 acres on the road from Charleston to Camden, granted Thomas Stater (?), August 27, 1751. (Deed recorded in Lancaster.) (Lancaster Bk. B, 80-81.)

Nathaniel Pace was head of a family in Camden District, Claremont County (now Sumter) in 1790.

MOORE
of
Prince George and North Carolina

This family is connected with the Pace family of Surry and is descended from Richard Pace who saved Jamestown. It is also the family of my old friend Rittenhouse Moore Smith of Mobile, Ala., whom I have not seen for about forty years.

1.   The first one of the Moore family from whom the family is clearly descended was Richard Moore who held 472 acres in Prince George in 1704. He seems to have patented much land in Prince George in that part of Prince George which is now Brunswick.

His will was dated in Prince George February 13, 1726, and probated August 2, 1726 as follows: "of Bristol Parish.: son John lower part of plantation whereon I now live, place called Spring Grove to be his upper boundary, also 50 a. purchased from Wm. Whittington; son Benjamin, upper part of this land; son William parcel of land purchased of Wm. Whittington called Spring Garden and joining Wm. Grigg; grandson Thomas Moore; son of my son Thomas Moore dec'd.; dau. Mary Lewis, (wife of Edward—ch. Ann and Edward, p. 822); dau. Elizabeth Baugh; sons Samuel and Roger, 1 shilling; grandson George Rives; wife Elizabeth; son Roger, exec. Witnesses, John Fitzgerald, Thomas Sturdivant, John Lewis, Jr." (Deed 1713-28, Part 3, p. 1030.)

2.   John Moore, the first son mentioned in the above and probably eldest son, because he is later mentioned as "heir at law", moved to Bertie Precint, N.C., part of which later became Northampton County. While there he made two deeds to lands formerly belonging to Richard Moore as follows:

"John Moore of Bertie Precint in N.C. to Wm. Johnson of same for 10 pounds 140 a. part of patent of 500 a. granted to Richard Moore, descended to said John Moore as being heir-at-law, on Bever Pond Creek; witnesses: James Parrish, John Nance Jr. 3/3/1739." (Deeds 2, p. 25.)

"John and Tabitha Moore of Northampton Co., N.C. to Wm. Walker of Va. for 22 pounds 100 a. in Brunswick on county line, part of patent to Richard Moore dated 1720. Witnesses: Wm. Allen, Edward Reves, Thomas Clanton. " (Deeds 3, p. 320.)

The 100 acres deeded above was probably part of a patent of 204 acres granted November 11, 1721 to "John Moore, son of Richard Moore" on the lower side of Great Creek of the Meherrin River. This was adjacent to John Bradford's survey of 191 acres.

Tabitha, wife of John Moore, who signed the above deed, was a daughter of Richard PACE (see Pace) who made.his will in Bertie Precint, March 13, 1736, and therein mentioned his daughter, Tabitha Moore. John Moore was made executor of his will.

John Moore's will was dated September 1, 1753, and probated Nov. 1753 in Northampton. Children mention in the will were: Mark (see later #3), Sarah, John, Isham, William, Nathaniel and Richard Moore. Wife was Tabitha; extrs., Richard Moore and Thomas Pace. Wits: George Harper, John Mardesly. (Grimes absts. p. 393).

3. Mark Moore was living in Northampton Co. N. C. in 1758 where his son, John (see later #4) was born. His wife was Sarah Mason and he is said to have been an Episcopal Minister.

4. The Reverend John Moore was born Jan. 1, 1758, and died Apr. 28, 1832. He married Rebecca Fletcher, the widow Leslie who had one son, Capt. William Leslie. He was licensed to preach by John Pope in 1784 and ordained by Bishop Ashbury in the Methodist Church. He removed to Davidson County, Tenn., in 1807 and in 1818 to Limestone County, Ala. His children were: John Fletcher, d. 1850, m. Nancy Fletcher; Nancy, m. Thomas Hart Harris, M. C. from White County, Tenn.; David; Richard; Dr. Alfred (see later #5).

5. Dr. Alfred Moore, married Elizabeth, dau. of Rev. Edmund Jones, of Jackson, Tenn.

Children:

I. Judge John Edmund, Judge 4th Judicial District, Col. C. S. A., died in service 1865.

6.   II. Sydneham, m. Eliza Hobson of Greensboro, Ala. (see later).

III. Olivia, m. Gov. Edward A. O'Neal of Ala. April 12, 1838. He was born in Madison Co., Ala., when the state was a territory and died Nov. 7, 1890. His father, Edward O'Neal was a native of Ireland.

Gov. O'Neal was major of the 9th Ala. Infantry, C. S. A. in 1861; Colonel of the 26th Ala. in 1862. He led his regiment in the Peninsular campaign, was wounded at battle of Seven Pines and again at Boonsboro; commanded Rode's Division at Chancellorsville and Gettysburg. Later was sent south to join forces opposed to Sherman and was at the battle of Peach

Tree Creek before Atlanta. He acted as a brigade and division commander in the field but did not reserve a commission as General. He was a member of the Constitutional Convention of 1875, was elected Governor of Ala., in 1882 and 84. (D. A. B.)

6. Sydneham Moore married Eliza Hobson of Greensboro, Ala. He was a captain in the Mexican War, and upon his return was elected a member of Congress. He served as a regimental commander under General Lee in Virginia and was killed at the Battle of Seven Pines.

Children:
I. Captain Alfred, C. S. A., killed at Missionary Ridge.
II. Rittenhouse lived in Mobile, Ala.
III. Sydneham moved to Birmingham, Ala., about 1890. The writer well remembers his three beautiful daughters.
IV. Alice, m. Robert Smith. Their children were Robert and Rittenhouse Smith of Mobile, Sydneham Smith of Birmingham, Ala.

John and Tabith Moore's other children mentioned in John's will in 1753 in Northampton were as follows:

2. John in Kershaw County S. C., 1792 "in consideration of love and regard for my cousin THOMAS PACE" deeded him land, cattle and household goods. (D. B. 1792)

3. Isham, who had 145 slaves in the Census of 1790 for South Carolina died in Sumpter Co., S. C., will 1803; children: Richard, John, Mathew S., daus. Tabitha Polk; Ann, m. J. Butler; Alice and Sarah Moore; grandchildren Mathew S. J., Harriet and Hannah Moore. (Vol. I Sec. A p. 260).

4. William made his will in S. C. Aug. 9, 1780, probated May 28, 1784; wife Barbara, sons: John, Leonard and William Harrison Moore, a minor; land to ISHAM BRADFORD, son of MARY BRADFORD. Executors were wife and friends: John Moore, James Moore, Sr., and ISHAM MOORE. Wits.: Nathaniel Moore, Susanna Fabre, Nancey Moore. The property devised was in Sumpter and Lancaster Counties. (Charleston Wills IV, p. 14.) Barbara Moore was living in Sumpter County in 1790. She was evidently a widow, with one son under 16, and four females including herself, in her family, with 17 slaves.

5. Nathaniel was living in York Co., S. C. in 1800. In 1770 he was deeded land by Thomas Bradford of Craven Co., S. C. (later Lancaster) Nathaniel was then living in Northampton, N. C. (See Bradford) In Lancaster Co., S. C. in 1800, Nathaniel Moore and wife Mary, of York District, deeded 200 acres to Robert Thornton. (D. B. 1800)

6. Richard made his will in Northampton, N.C., 1787 and mentioned children: James, Charles, Anne, Judith, Sarah and Tabitha. (Old's Abstracts).

7. Sarah. (No further record).

York County South Carolina adjoins Chester County on the north, while Lancaster is just east of Chester with Kershaw on the south; Sumpter is next to Kershaw on the south west. The Bradfords, Moores and Paces from Northampton, N.C. settled in these Counties.

WYNNE

The Wynne family seems to have resided in and about Canterbury, England, for three or more centuries before coming to Virginia. The first mention of the name found in the records is that of "John Wynne" member of Parliament from Canterbury, 29th of Edward III (1356). (Hasted History of Canterbury, Vol. 1, p. 49). From that time on down to Robert Wynne, Mayor of Canterbury, 1599 the name appears often in the records. (Ibid, Vol. 2, p. 607).

Robert Wynne, the mayor, was the grandfather of Colonel Robert Wynne, Speaker of the House of Burgesses in Virginia during the Long Parliament, 1661-74. Colonel Robert Wynne was Speaker longer than any other one man in Virginia's history.

The Wynnes were members of Woolendrapers Guild. Robert Wynne, woolendraper, apprenticed to John Rose, Alderman, was released from his indentures and became a Freeman of the City in 1590. (Cowper, Roll of Freeman of Canterbury, p. 243). Nine years later, 1599, he was mayor of the ancient city of Canterbury. His sons became freemen by right of birth. Thomas Wynne, gentleman, son of Robert Wynne, became Free in 1612, and Peter Wynne, son of Robert Wynne, became Free in 1626. (Ibid, p. 95).

Robert Wynne, the Speaker, dying in Virginia 1675, gave his youngest son a house "lying without St. Georges in Canterbury" and an inspection of the parish records of St. George finds this family shown therein.

At St. Georges on September 6th 1609, "Mr. Robert Wynne", evidently the Mayor, was buried, and his wife (not named) was buried on the 8th of the same month. (Parish Register of St. Georges, p. 180).

Thomas Wynne of Canterbury, grocer, and Mary Wickham of Faversham were married at Ospringe, July 20, 1613. (Canterbury Marriage Licenses, 1st Series, 1568-1618, p. 458)

At St. George, May 9, 1625, "Mr. Thomas Wynne's child" was buried (St. George's Register, p. 183). On July 20, 1629, the wife of Mr. Thomas Wynne was buried. Thomas Wynne took upon himself a second wife soon afterwards for "Thomas Wynne

174

of Canterbury, grocer, widower, and Ann Nichols of the Almony of St. Augustine, Canterbury, widow of James Nichols, late deceased" were married at St. Martins, October 26, 1629. (Canterbury Marriage License, 2nd Series, p. 1107)

No further record is shown of Thomas, but Peter Wynne, his younger brother, as "Peter Wynne of Canterbury, gentleman", and Martha Coppin of St. Margarets, Canterbury, were married at St. Martins, August 12, 1620. William Coppin, father of Martha, signed the marriage bond.

Robert Wynne, son of Peter Wynne, gentleman, was christened at St. Dunstans Canterbury, 28 December 1622. (Printed Register, p. 12) He was evidently the Speaker of Virginia's Long Parliament.

At St. Georges on January 25, 1630, Sarah, daughter of Peter Wynne, gentleman, was buried; August 20, 1631, Mr. Wynne's sister, the wife of Paul May, was buried; and May 30, 1638, Peter Wynne, gentleman, was buried. (Register, p. 183-85)

Peter Wynne's father in law, William Coppin, gentleman, was buried at St. Georges March 18, 1633. A memorial tablet erected to him in St. Georges is mentioned in Hasted's History. (Hasted Kent. Vol. IV, p. 470, 466). St. Margaret Parish where William Coppin lived was adjacent to St. Georges and the two parishes were later combined.

William Coppin was probably a grandson of John Coppin, member of Parliament from Canterbury, 1553-54. This family is also shown in St. George's register. At St. Georges March 25, 1645, "Thomas, son of John Coppin" was christened. Mary Coppin, wife of this John, was buried in St. Alphages in 1685, and the Coppins Arms, shown on her tomb are "Per pale, azure and gules, 3 boars heads, couped, a chief or, a mullet for difference". (Hasted Kent Vol. IV, p. 470, 466)

It is not known exactly when the above Robert Wynne, Christened at St. Dunstan 1622, came to Virginia, but he first appears in the Virginia records along with Captain Abraham Wood who will be further mentioned. Robert Wynne was a Justice in Charles City County Court, October 3rd, 1656. (W & M 4 (1), p. 167) He was also evidently a Captain of Militia as he is shown as "Captain Robert Wynne".

He represented Charles City in the House of Burgesses, March 1657-8, and March 1659-60, and was Speaker of House, 1661-74. In 1673 Colonel Wynne was a member of a Court Martial sitting at James City (V. M. 20, p. 28).

Colonel Wynne died in 1675. His widow, Mary, is referred to in a suit in the General Court as his executrix the 8th of October 1675. (Mins of Council, p. 424)

On account of owning property in England his will was probated there. If it was not for this the place of his old home in England would not be known as the Charles City records for that period have perished. He appears to have married a Mrs. Poythress, a widow, as he mentioned his "son-in-law Captain Francis Poythress". "Son-in-Law" in those days meant "step-son". His will was as follows:

"Robert Wynne of Jordan's Parish, Charles City County in Virginia, Gent., dated July 1st 1675, probated August 15th, 1678.

"To be buried in Jordan's Church as near as possible to my son Robert.

"My estate in England to be divided as follows:
To my eldest son Thomas Wynne one farm in Whitestaple Parish in Kent near Canterbury commonly called Limbet Banckes; if he die to my son Joshua, and if he die, to my daughter Woodlief.

"To my son Thomas two houses in Canterbury in St. Mildred's Parish in the same form as the said farm.

"To my youngest son Joshua Wynne one house and Oatmeal mill lying in Dover Lane without St. Georges in Canterbury, commonly called the Lilly Pot; and two houses adjoining where a Ropemaker and one Rawlins were formerly tenants.

"Touching my estate in Virginia, to my son Thomas all the cattle of his own mark except one cow called Moll which is to be killed for provisions.

"To my son Joshua my plantation called Georges with all the Tobacco houses.

"To my daughter Woodlief one servant of four years to serve the next shipping after my decease.

"To my grandchild and godson young George Woodlief one filly foal.

"All the rest of my estate in Virginia and England to my wife and executrix Mary Wynne.

"Overseers: Thomas Grendon, Merchant, and my son in law Captain Francis Poythress.

"Teste: Thomas Brome, John Burge."

Children:
    I. Thomas was mentioned as "eldest son" in his father's will. He was born in 1657 for in a deposition given in a suit in Prince George in 1707 he gave his age as 50 years. (V. M. 14, p. 174). In 1701 he patented 200 acres on the south side of the Blackwater in Charles City (afterwards Prince George). In the 1704 Quit Rents "Captain" Thomas Wynne held 400 acres in the Prince George. In 1707 he and his wife Agnes deeded land in Surry to his son, Robert, and his daughter, Mary Malone.

On April 24, 1703 the Council upon reading "a petition of the King and Great men of the Nottoway and Meherrin Indians praying that Thomas Wynne be appointed their interpreter in the place of Thomas Blunt with whom they have experienced dissatisfaction, he was accordingly appointed Interpreter to those two tribes and also the Nansemonds. " (C. J. 2.315)

He promptly acted to prevent certain colonists from settling on Indian lands around Bear Swamp and other places belonging to them and for a time pacified their "dissatisfactions and uneasiness", but after a time they petitioned for another interpreter on the grounds that he was "remiss and negligent". (Ibid 3-104).

On November 30, 1707, he entered 500 acres on Cabin Shick Swamp on the south side of the Nottoway and prayed the Council that it be surveyed as it was uncertain whether it was in Prince George or Surry.

Thomas Wynne made his will in Surry, February 18, 1716-17 and same was probated May 21, 1718.

Children:

1. Thomas
2. Lucy
3. Mary, m. Nathaniel MALONE.
4. Robert Wynne was Justice, Coroner, Sheriff 1716; and Major of Militia in Surry. (V. M. 48, p. 151). He died in Sussex July 23, 1754 (Register) and his will was probated August 12, 1754. He mentioned wife, Mary; granddaughter, Mary Butler; grandson, Joel Tucker; son in law, William Raines and Angelica, his wife; son in law, Jefferson Raines; granddaughter, Elizabeth Parham; grandson, Robert Parham; brother, Thomas Wynne; granddaughter, Martha Bell; grandson, Joel Tucker; daughter, Cornelia Raines.

Children:

(1) Lucretia, m. Joseph Tucker and had the following children:
   a. Lucretia Tucker
   b. Mary Tucker, b. May 26, 1745. (Bristol Parish).
   c. Joel Tucker, m. Judith_____ . He died in 1772.

Children shown in Albermarle Register:
1. Patty, b. February 8, 1756.
2. Joseph, b. October 26, 1760.
3. Elizabeth, b. April 16, 1764.

(2) Martha, m. Matthew PARHAM.
(3) Angelica, m. William Raines.
Children shown in Register:
a. Robert Wynne Raines, b. June 25, 1739, m. Jane.
Children:
1. Peter Green Raines, b. Feb. 28, 1760.
2. William Raines, b. Feb. 10, 1762.
3. Littleton Raines, b. Jan. 26, 1766.
b. Richard Raines, b. March 2, 1740.
c. Jean Raines, b. November 20, 1744.
d. Jefferson Raines, b. November 20, 1744.
e. Nathaniel Raines, b. March 21, 1748.
f. Ann Raines, b. July 22, 1746.
g. Theodosia Raines, b. December 1749.
(4) Cornelia, m. Jefferson Raines.
(5) Martha, m. Benjamin Bell.
Children:
a. Martha Jefferson Bell, b. Nov. 16, 1751.
b. Hannah Bell, b. Dec. 3, 1753.
c. Jefferson Davis Bell, July 27, 1755.
(6) Anne, m. Thomas Butler.
Children:
a. Martha, b. November 18, 1745, d. Oct. 19, 1742.
b. Mary, b. Mar. 21, 1742, m. Thomas Vines.
Children.
1. William Vines, b. May 20, 1760.
2. Thomas Vines, b. Oct. 5, 1761.
3. Isaac Willis Vines, b. Jan. 12, 1766.
4. John Vines, b. Apr. 19, 1768.
5. Elizabeth Vines, b. Apr. 19, 1770.
6. Mary Vines, b. Jan. 26, 1773.
7. Martha Vines, b. Jan. 19, 1775.

Mary Butler may have been the second wife of Thomas Vines, or may have been the wife of Thomas Vines, Jr.

Thomas Vines and wife Elizabeth had following children shown in the Albermarle Register:
1. John, bapt. May 10, 1748; godparents, Lawrence Gibbons, Geo. Robertson,

Dorothy Vaughn (wife of Thomas).

2. Isaac Willis, bapt. Mar. 19, 1745, none given.
3. Lucas, bapt. Jan. 22, 1749, godparents, Thomas Vaughn, John Mitchell, Anne Hill.
4. Herbert, bapt. July 7, 1758.

There is no indication in the register that the Thomas Vines who married Mary Butler was Thomas Vines, Jr. Thomas and Mary Vines' children begin in the register in 1760. There are no more children shown after the baptism of Herbert in 1758, so Mary Butler could have been his second wife.

Thomas Vines came from York County as he is shown as "Thomas Vines of York" in a deed from Robert Mitchell in 1740 (See Mitchell).

Thomas Butler (above) also may have had a second wife, for a Thomas Butler with wife Elizabeth had the following children in the register:

1. Thomas, bapt. Nov. 1, 1752; godparents, Thomas Vaughn, Robert Mitchell, Dorothy Vaughn.
2. Amy, bapt. May 17, 1757, godparents, Thomas Vines, Jr., Mary Jones, Mary Butler.
3. Anne, bapt. Apr. 20, 1760.
4. Willie, bapt. Feb. 7, 1762, godparents, David Tucker, Eliz. Butler.

Thomas Butler, Jr., and wife Mary had a son "Vines", baptized May 30, 1767.

A Thomas Butler was mentioned as a "grandson" in the will of William Mitchell in 1778 (see Mitchell). William Mitchell's will was witnessed by Thomas Vaughn and John Mitchell. He appears to be the Thomas Butler baptized Nov. 1, 1752, for his godparent, Thomas Vaughn witnessed William Mitchell's will.

II. Joshua Wynne, youngest son. (See later).
III. Robert Wynne, dead before 1675.
IV. Mary Wynne, m. John Woodlieff, son of Captain John Woodlieff, Burgess, Charles City, 1652, and grandson of Captain John Woodlieff who came to Virginia in 1608. The second Captain John Woodlieff was

granted land in 1683, "near a place called 'Jordans' and bounded westerly upon Francis Poythress." One will recognize similar names in Robert Wynne's will.

II. Joshua Wynne, youngest son of Colonel Robert Wynne was a Justice in Charles City, February 23, 1698; member of the House of Burgess, 1702-1704: and after Prince George was cut off from that County he was Sheriff of Prince George 1705 and 1711. (Burgess Journal Vo. 1702-12, p. 50, Executive Journals of Council 1-408; 3-28, 272,159.) In 1708 Major Joshua Wynne and Mary, his wife, deeded a tract of land in Surry. (V. M. 14, p. 174).

Joshua married Mary, a daughter of Captain Peter Jones of Charles City. In 1661 Peter Jones was Captain of a company of Train Bands from City Creek to the Falls of the Appamattox on the south side and from Powells Creek to the said Falls on the north side. In 1674 he was Major in command of the Fort built at the Falls. The City of Petersburg founded at the site of the Falls is named for his grandson.

Peter Jones' wife was Margaret, daughter of Major General Abraham Wood who held this commission from Berkeley during Bacon's Rebellion. General Wood was also a Justice in Charles City, 1655; Colonel of a regiment from Charles City and Henrico in 1656, Burgess 1652-56. He entered the Governor's Council in 1657 and remained a member until 1671.

Mrs. Margaret Wood-Jones afterwards married Thomas Cocke of Malvern Hills. As Margaret Cocke of the County and Parish of Henrico she made her will, August 12, 1718, same probated May 4, 1719, as follows:

"to grandaughter Margaret wife of Edward Goodrich
to grandaughter Mary wife of John Worsham
to grandson Peter Wynne one Mullato man named John Henry being appointed to be given by will of my deceased husband Thomas Cocke. I also confirm gift of boy named Thomas I made to Major Joshua Wynne in his life time.
to daughter Margaret Jones - 2 silver spoons
to daughter Mrs. Mary Randolph - 1 negro boy
to son Peter Jones - son of my son Abraham Jones decd., 10 shillings to buy him a ring.
to grandson Joshua Wynne 2 steers, grandsons Robert Wynne, William Wynne and Francis Wynne a cow each when they arrive at lawful age.

to godson William, son of William Randolph, - 1 Mulatto boy
to son Peter Jones - rest of estate.
Executors: son and William Randolph. "

Joshua like his brother, Thomas, was an Indian Interpreter. In 1704 the Nottoway, Meherrin, Nansemond, Pamunkey and Chickahominy Indians petitioned the governor to allow some of their chief men to go north to conclude a peace with the Senecas, and ransom the Nottoway king taken prisoner last summer. The desired leave to take with them Captain Joshua Wynne and Captain Thomas Wynne "without whose consent and approbation they were to conclude nothing". (C. J. 2-380) These brothers seem to have been fearless adventurers for this was a far away, difficult and dangerous journey.

In 1707, Major Joshua Wynne was one of a commission of 6 persons appointed to examine upon oath "such ancient inhabitants of Prince George (and other border counties between this Colony and North Carolina) and discover the truth as to the said bounds be-the said colonies. "

Joshua Wynne died in 1715 as an account of his estate was filed in that year (Orders) and on March 30, 1715, a suit was brought against Peter Wynne as administrator of the estate of his father, Joshua Wynne. (V. M. 20, 86).

Children:
1. Peter Wynne, m. Frances, daughter of John Anderson and the widow of John Herbert. She was the executrix of Herbert's will in 1716. (V. M. 18, p. 190. Her will was probated in 1725. She mentioned her Herbert children, but no Wynne children. (Wm. 8, (1), p. 147)

In 1731 Peter Wynne was granted 1000 acres on north side of Butterwood Creek in Prince George and in 1732 he assigned 100 acres of same to Henry Wyatt.
2. Joshua Wynne, m. Mary. In 1724 he was residing near Stony Creek Bridge in Prince George and in 1738 he was militia officer in Prince George.

Children:
(1) Robert, m. Frances_____and had (1) Margaret, b. October 25, 1741; (2) Mason, b.

May 29, 1745. (Bristol Parish).
(2) Martha, b. April 6, 1720.
(3) Joshua, b. November 26, 1722, m. Lucretia
_____ and had (1) Sloman, b. October 13, 1745;
(2) Joshua, living in Dinwiddie 1782; (3) Robert,
b. 1749, died December 21, 1824, aged 75.
(4) Thomas, b. April 6, 1726.
(5) Sloman lived in Sussex where his will was probated in 1760.

Children named in will:
(a) Matthew married Sarah_____ and had
following children shown in Albermarle
Register:
1. Martha, b. January 11, 1743.
2. Anne, b. February 20, 1747.
3. Sloman, b. May 24, 1750.
4. Mathew, b. May 7, 1754.
5. Bolling, b. October 23, 1757.
6. Salley, b. December 8, 1758.
7. John, b. December 25, 1760.
(b) Sloman Jr., m. Mary.
Children in Register:
1. Stith, b. June 12, 1741, He married
Sarah Children from Register: John,
b. October 4, 1762; Gray, b. June 23,
1767; Hamlin, b. October 12, 1770;
Elizabeth, b. February 12, 1774.
2. John, b. June 6, 1746.
(c) Lucretia
(d) Anne
(e) Robert m. Lucy_____. The following
children are shown in the Albermarle
Register. This Robert may not be Robert,
son of Sloman.
1. Buckner, b. January 21, 1760.
2. Betty, February 26, 1761.
3. Lucy, December 12, 1762.
4. Robert, May 20, 1764.
5. Mathew, July 3, 1765.
6. Peter, October 11, 1769.
7. Threewits, January 8, 1771.
8. Stith, April 25, 1773.
9. Nancy, May 7, 1775.
(f) William married Mary.
Children from Register
1. Thomas, b. February 19, 1741.

2. Mary, b. February 22, 1743.

3. William Richardson, b. Sept. 28, 1746.

(g) Elizabeth.

(h) Stith.

3. Robert Wynne m. Frances. On May 13, 1718 he sold lands in Prince George to William Cotten and Martha, his wife. In 1728 he received a grant of 369 acres on the south side of Nottoway River in St. Andrews Parish, Brunswick and on January 6, 1742 he conveyed same to Lewellyn Jones of Brunswick.

4. Frances Wynne made a deed in Prince George 1717.

5. William Wynne. (See later)

William Wynne, a younger son of Major Joshua Wynne, was born in 1705, for he made a deposition in Prince George in 1727 in which he gave his age as 22. (V. M. 38, p. 243). His land fell in Brunswick County when same was formed from Prince George. He was a Justice in Brunswick in 1732 and Sheriff of the County in 1736. (Ex. Journals of Council 4-266, 368).

He soon moved to the far western frontiers of the country for in 1738 he patented 200 acres on the south side of the Dan River in what is now Pittsylvania County. In 1745 he together with Clement Reade and Robert Jones had leave of the council to patent 36000 acres in the western country. In 1752, when the new County of Pittsylvania was formed he was a member of the first County Court. He was granted a patent of 2000 acres joining upon his former survey on the Dan River. This was at "Wynnes Creeks and Wynne's Falls", two places which were named in his honor. This land is now the site of the present city of Danville.

William Wynne's son, Thomas, and Richard Echols were among the first vestrymen of Antrim Parish and served the Parish in this capacity for many years. William Wynne made his will October 8, 1777, same probated March 26, 1778, as follows: (D&W 5, p. 444).

"Grandson, William Wynne, son of my daughter, Mary Wynne, to inherit the home place 295 acres on Sandy Creek after the death of Frances, my wife. The residue of the estate consisting of several negroes to be equally divided amongst all my children, William, Thomas, John and Robert Wynne, Margaret Hendricks, Elizabeth Echols, Mary Wynne and Martha Dixon. Esecutors: sons, William and Thomas. Witnesses: William Collie, Charles Collie, Stephen Velita, Phebe Worsham, and Mary Collie."

Children:

I. William. In 1774 William Wynne of Pittsylvania sold to John Worsham 200 acres on both sides of Dan River at mouth of Rutledges Creek to Jackson. Said land was given him by his father, William Wynne. Deed was recorded in Halifax. He was head of a family of three persons in Pittsylvania in Census of 1782 but was out of the county when Census of 1785 was taken.

II. Thomas. On September 27, 1770, William Wynne, Sr., made a deed of gift to grandchildren, Mary, John, Patty and Francis Wynne of a negro each, and to John a boy named George. (D. B. 2, p. 7).

In 1784, John Wynne, Jr., of Lincoln county, North Carolina gave power of attorney to George Humphrys of Caswell County, North Carolina to recover a negro boy, George, given to John Wynne by his grandfather, William. (D. B. 7, p. 221)

On November 1764, 295 acres were surveyed on lower Sandy Creek of the Dan River for George Musick. This land was transferred to William Wynne, Jr., son of Thomas Wynne, by George Musick in 1769, 1773 and 1780. William and his grandmother, Frances Wynne, sold 295 acres to Humphrey Hendrick for £ 2000, February 15, 1780. This was the home place mentioned in William Wynne's will.

Thomas Wynne was head of a family of ten persons in 1782 but was out of the county in 1785.

III. John, on September 27, 1775, was an Ensign of Halifax Militia (V. M. 19, p. 307). In 1870 Captain John Wynne's company of Halifax Militia fought at the Battle of Guilford. C. H. (McAllister). In 1782 he was head of a family of eight persons. He sold 208 acres to Thomas Fearn in 1783, next to Robert and Charles Wynne, same being land he now occupies. He was out of the county in 1785.

IV. Robert was head of a family of twelve persons in 1782 and of eleven in 1785. On November 13, 1788, he sold 300 acres to his brother in law, Humphrey Hendricks, and evidently moved out of the county. His son, Robert, was probably the person of the same name who later moved to Sumner County, Tennessee, with his cousins, the Echols and Dixons. (see later).

V. Margaret, m. Humphrey Hendricks who was head of a family of eight persons in 1785.

VI. Elizabeth, m. Joseph Echols who was head of a family of nine persons in 1785.

VII. Martha, married September 15, 1763, Colonel Henry
Dixon of Caswell County, North Carolina. Caswell
is just across the border from Pittsylvania.

Colonel Henry Dixon was a son of Henry Dixon,
Sr. of Caswell County. Colonel Dixon, affectionately
known as "Hal" to his soldiers, had a long and distinguished record of service in the Revolution. He
was Captain, 1st North Carolina, 1 September 1775;
transferred to 8th North Carolina, January 1777;
Major 3rd North Carolina 4 October 1777; Lieutenant
Colonel 12 May 1778; wounded at Stono Ferry 20 June
1779; transferred to 2nd North Carolina, 6th February
1782; died in service 17 July 1782. (Heitman).

In Captain Henry Dixon's company of Continentals
were the following Wynnes:

> Jones Wynne, Pvt. enlisted 1777, in service
> 60 months, received grant of 457 acres.
> William Wynne, Pvt., Dixon's Company.
> Knibb Wynne, Sgt., Dixon's Company.
> Williamson Wynne (1760-1828), son of Major
> Joshua Wynne of the Georgia Continental line,
> born in Virginia, served as a private in Captain
> Dixon's company   (DAR, Vol. 104, p. 38).

Colonel Dixon's will was probated in September
1782. He named wife, Martha, and children, Roger,
Robert, Henry, Frances, Elizabeth and Wynne Dixon.

Wynne Dixon, his son was Ensign 10 North Carolina, 1st March, 1781; 2nd Lieutenant, 5th July 1781,
transferred to 1st North Carolina, February 1782;
served to close of war. Died 24 November 1829.

Wynne Dixon (1764-1832) married first Keturah
Payne January 8, 1786; and secondly Rebecca, daugh-
ter of David Hart. He was a charter member of the
North Carolina Society of the Cincinnatti. In 1796-97
he represented Caswell County in the North Carolina
Senate. He removed to Tennessee and then to Kentucky.

Wynn Dixon was the father of the Honorable Archibald Dixon of Henderson, Kentucky, who married Elizabeth Cabell. Their son, Dr. Archibald Dixon m. Margaret Herndon and was the father of Margaret Dixon
who married Edward A. Jones.

Henry Dixon (1777-1852) son of Colonel Hal Dixon,
and the brother of Wynne, married 1798, Mary Johnston (1772-1850) and had several children among whom
were:

1. Henry, m. Anna Mariea Ashby and had Mary H.
Dixon who married George W McClure.

2. Cornelius, (1813-85) m. 1836, Isabella Clay (1817-1911) and had Robert F. Dixon, b. 1853, who married Rosa R. Green, b. 1859. Their daughter, Susan Dixon married L. B. Curd.
3. Judith, (1821-71), m. 1838, Thomas T. Towles and had Elizabeth Towles, b. 1849, who married William Meade Alvin.

Henry Dixon, Sr., father of this distinguished Revolutionary family made his will in Caswell County as follows:

"Henry Dixon, of Caswell County, North Carolina, being old and infirm but of sound Sense & Memory - -

"4th August 1795, Wife, Elizabeth, to have a good sufficient & Genteel maintenance out of my Estate suring her Life to be afforded her by my Two Sons Charles Dixon & Tilman Dixon; to my son, Charles Dixon, the tract of land whereon I now live containing 630 acres, which was granted to me by the State of North Carolina; one negro man named Jeff; to my granddaughter, Frances Dixon, daughter of Henry Dixon, deceased, negro girl named Cloe; feather bed and fur. Rest of estate both real and personal to my Two sons, Charles Dixon and Tilman Dixon. Appoint Sons, Charles and Tilman Dixon, Executors." (Caswell Wills, Vol.1, p. 21)

Charles Dixon, son of Henry, Sr., was Ensign 6th North Carolina, 2nd April 1777; transferred to 3rd North Carolina, 1st July 1778; Lieutenant, 8th February 1779; wounded at Eutaw Springs, 8th September 1781, transferred to 4th North Carolina 6th February 1782; retired 1st January 1783. (Heitman)

Tilghman Dixon, son of Henry Sr., was 1st. Lieutenant, 1st North Carolina, 20 October 1775; Captain 5th February 1777; taken prisoner at Charleston, 12 May 1780; exchanged 14th June 1781; retired 1st January 1783. (Heitman).

He married Maria Don Carlos 1789. She was born 1767. They both died at Dixon Springs, Tennessee, and are the ancestors of Mr. Charles W. Dixon of Gould, Arkansas. Eliza Henry Dixon, a daughter of Captain Tilghman Dixon, born 1802, died 1871, married Dr. James Waller Overton (1785-1865). Their daughter, Elizabeth Overton (1830-80), married James L. Calcott (1824-59) of Natchez, Mississippi.

Major Thomas Donoho of Caswell served in the Revolution in the 6th North Carolina and other regiments with the Dixons. He was 1st Lieutenant 6th North Carolina, 16th April 1776; Captain 10th September 1776; Major, 13th October 1781; in 4th North Carolina 6th February 1782. Served to close of war; died 1825. (Heitman)

Major Donoho married Keziah Saunders and died in Caswell County in 1825. He is the ancestor of the Donohos of Sumner and Trousdale counties in Tennessee.

Soon after 1790 these families began their migration to blue grass fields of Sumner County, Tennessee. In Caswell County in 1790 were Henry, Charles, Martha, Tillman, Wynne and Roger Dixon. Also Patrick, William and Major Thomas Donoho. Accompanied by some of their Wynne, Hendrick and Echols relatives of Pittsylvania, Virginia, they started on their long trek through the Indian Country.

Patrick, Charles, Edward and Thomas Donoho bought land in Sumner County. Deeds to them show that they came from Caswell County, North Carolina. (Sumner Bk. A, pp. 14, 24, 129, 130, 171.)

Sumner County, Book 1, 1793-97, shows that Wynne Dixon sold land to Thomas Bradley; Tighlman Dixon to Catherine Bledsoe; Charles & Wynne Dixon to Tighlman Dixon; Elkahanah Echols bought land from James Montgomery. (pp. 359, 212, 443, 456, 128).

In 1787 Joel Echols, ancestor of the Echols family of Sumner, and Joseph Hendricks were soldiers in Captain Hunter's company, Evans Batallion of Sumner County Militia.

Young Robert Wynne, probably the son of Robert Wynne of Pittsylvania, Virginia, heretofore mentioned, married Cynthia Harrison, January 6, 1800. They were the parents of Colonel Alfred Robert Wynne of Castalian Springs, Tennessee, and of Cynthia Wynne who married Albert Gallatin Donoho of Trousedale County.

Robert Wynne died a few years after his marriage for on July 31, 1805, his widow, Cynthia, married Samuel Kerr of Wilson County.

Alfred R. Wynne, his son, lived at Hickory Ridge in Wilson County until he was sixteen when he returned to Sumner. He was a Colonel of Militia in 1860 and served one term in the State Senate in 1866.

In Colonel Wynne's lifetime the Echols, Wynnes and Dixons of Dixon's Springs were said to be related, but no one knew exactly how. It is interesting to find that this is true.

Colonel Wynne, born Dec. 1800, died Dec. 16, 1893; married Almira Winchester Feb. 15, 1825. She was born March 30, 1805, and died June 24, 1884. She was the daughter of General James Winchester of "Cragfont", Sumner County. Colonel Wynne lived at Castalian Springs about a mile from "Cragfont". The Colonel's home which was built for them by General Winchester about 1825, is a splendid example of early Tennessee architecture; it is now occupied by the Colonel's grandson, George Winchester Wynne.

Children of Almira and Alfred R. Wynne:
   I.   James Wynne, b. December 8, 1825,
   II. Robert Bruce Wynne, b. Feb. 17, 1827.
   III. Selima Wynne, b. Sept. 9, 1828.
   IV. Caroline A. E. Wynne, b. Jan. 4, 1830; d. Dec. 2,

Home of Colonel Alfred R. Wynne

1854; unmarried.

V. Ida Wynne, b. 17, Jan. 1832.

VI. Maria Louise Wynne, b. 18 July, 1834; d. 28 March, 1927; unmarried.

VII. Lucilius William Wynne, b. 6 May, 1836; m. Rebecca Frye; (no issue) d. 18 Dec., 1860.

VIII. Valerius P. Wynne, b. 3 Feb., 1838.

IX. Andrew Jackson Wynne, b. 8 Dec. 1839.

X. Susan Winchester Wynne b. 25 Sept. 1841; d. 18 Aug. 1923.

XI. William Hall Wynne, b. 18 Nov. 1849; d. 14 June 1862. He was a Confederate Soldier at thirteen and a half years of age. Co. K, 2nd. Tenn.

XII. Joseph Guild Wynne, b. Nov. 1845; d. Aug. 1887 unmarried. Co. K, 2nd. Tenn.

XIII. Mary Meriwether Wynne, b. 6. April 1847; d. April 6, 1906; unmarried.

XIV. Winchester Wynne, b. 12 July, 1850.

Winchester Wynne, youngest son and child of the Colonel, b. July 12, 1850, died June 23, 1926, resided in the old home. He married, Dec. 8, 1886, Dora Schamberger, born Evansville, Ind., Jan. 23, 1862.

Front View of Cragfont

Rear View of Cragfont

Bledsoe's Lick

Children:

George Winchester Wynne, born Oct. 25, 1887, married Oct. 16, 1912, Eula Woolf Westbrook of Marengo County, Alabama. They reside in the old ancestral home at Castalian Springs, Tenn; and have one child, George Winchester Wynne, Jr. born May 3, 1914, who is married and has children.

Adele Wynne, born 14 Feb., 1878, lives in Fayetteville, Tenn. She is a daughter of Andrew Jackson Wynne, son of Colonel Wynne. Andrew Wynne was a physician in Marengo County, and served in the Second Tennessee Regiment in the Confederate Army. He married Caroline Adele Prowell, b. March 2, 1843, d. 13 Dec. 1911. He died Jan. 27, 1906. Adele Wynne married 19 April 1905, David C. Barry. Their children were: (1) David Sidney Barry, b. Jan. 16, 1906, d. June 5, 1929; (2) Hall Wynne Barry, b. May 14, 1909; (3) Benjamin Barry b. Aug. 3, 1911.

WOODLIFFE of BUCKINGHAM, ENGLAND
and
PRINCE GEORGE, VIRGINIA

ROBERT[2] WOODLIFFE of Peterley, Buckingham, was the son of NICHOLAS[1] WOODLIFFE (Vis. Bucks 1566, Harleian, Vol. 58, p. 228). He married first Jane, daughter of Roger Smith, who died without issue. He married secondly, Anne, daughter of Sir Robert Drury of Edgerley Bucks, a younger son of Sir Robert Drury of Hawsted, Suffolk, Speaker of the House of Commons (Burke's Extinct Baronetcies, p. 169) (Coppinger's Manors of Suffolk, Vol. 7, p. 35) (Dict. Nat. Biography, Vol. 6, p. 57).

In 1552 the manor of Stonors in Bucks was sold by Dorothy Verney to Robert "Woodlast" and William Howse (Vict. Hist. Bucks, Vol. 2, p. 332). In 1551 Geoffrey Dormer conveyed the manor of Peterley to Robert Woodliffe, but probably for a term of years only, as Robert Dormer, his grandson, held it in 1580. In 1557 Robert Woodliffe settled Peterley upon himself and Anne Drury whom he was about to marry. He died in 1593 and was succeeded by his son Drew who in 1596 joined with his mother in conveying their interest in the manor to Sir Robert Dormer (Do. Vol. 2, p. 350).

Children:[(1)]

I. ANNE.
II. MARGARET.
III. EDMUND, b. 1565, matriculated at Oriel College, Oxford, 23 Nov. 1581, aged 16 (Foster's Alumni).
IV. GRIFFIN, b. 1566 (First four children are shown in Visitation of 1566 for Bucks).
V. THOMAS, b. 1570, matriculated at Oriel College, Oxford, 2 July 1585, aged 15 (Foster).
VI. DREW was son and heir in 1596.
VII. JOHN came to Virginia in 1608. (Last three from Oxford Alumni, and Victorian History of Bucks).

JOHN[3] WOODLIFFE came to Virginia in 1608, for Alexander Brown in his "First Republic" (p. 345) says that in 1619 "Capt. John Woodliffe, who had been in Virginia 11 years, was to have the command of Berkeley Hundred".

John Woodliffe had evidently returned to England for on the 4th of September 1619, while in England, he signed an agreement with four

other persons to settle a plantation in Virginia to be known as Berke
ley Hundred, and he was to act as Captain and Governor over the
Hundred.

This agreement was as follows (N.Y. Public Library Bulletin,
Vol. 3, p. 167):

"Covenants and agreements made between Sir. Wm. Throcl
morton of Clowerwall in Gloster, Kt. and Baronet of the
first part.
Richard Berkeley of Stoke Gifford of the second part.
George Thorpe of Waneswell of the third part.
John Smith of North Nibley of the fourth part and
John Woodleife of Prestwood in County of Buckingham, Esq
of the fifth part.
4 day of Sept. 1619.
Whereas a voyage is intended unto the land of Virginia with
shippe called the 'Margaret' of Bristol of the burden of 47
tun within 10 days furnished with 32 men.
Commission of said date to be Captain and Governor. Plac
to be called Berkeley and land and territory thereabout to b
called Berkeley Hundred

****

"5 - Item - Whereas the said John Woodleife hath at his owne
charges about Aprill last transported four men into Virgir
beinge in his family there abydinge with his wife and childr
who are by several agreements by severall Indentures to
serve him fower yeares the peece or nere thereabouts, and
hath also furnished at his like charges with apparell and ar
It is agreed the charges sustained by him about the same
shall be allowed unto him, etc. the men to become joint ser
vants of the company".

John Smith of Nibley, one of the parties above mentioned, was a
well-known antiquarian of his time and wrote a History of Berkeley
Hundred in three volumes. The above papers were preserved by hi
and his descendants and were published by the Public Library of Nev
York in 1899.

John Woodliefe is shown to be of Prestwood in Buckingham.
Prestwood is a village adjacent to the manor of Peterley (Vict.
Hist. Bucks, Vol. 3, p. 350). Prestwood and Peterley are in
the Parish of Great Missenden, whose registers do not begin until 1678.

The proprietors of Berkeley Hundred became dissatisfied with
Capt. Woodliffe's administration, and on the 28th day of August,
1620 revoked his commission as Captain and Governor. They
probably, like all speculators, expected too much in the way of
profit, and were dissatisfied when confronted with failure. Nearly
all of the 32 men died the first year. The New York Library Bulletin (Vol. 3, p. 290) contains a long list of the names of the dead.

Only three or four men were left alive. An early death seems to have been the fate of most of the first adventurers to Virginia. John Woodliffe, who was there with his family, was seasoned to the country.

George Thorpe and William Tracy were appointed to govern over Berkeley Hundred in the place of Capt. John Woodliffe. They were also made members of the Council. Tracy, who was related to Richard Berkeley, was slain by the Indians the 6th of April, 1621. Mrs. Tracy was also killed. Joyce Tracy, their daughter, who married Capt. Nathaniell Powell, was killed in the Indian massacre of February 22, 1622. George Thorpe also perished on that day. Thomas Tracy, son of Capt. William Tracy, survived and returned to England.

Capt. John Woodliffe does not show in the muster roll of settlers taken in Virginia, 24th February 1624-25, so he must have been in England on that date.

The census of February 24, 1624-25 shows that Thomas Harris and his wife Adrai had with them "Ann Woodlast, 7 years old, their kinswoman" (Hotten's Emigrants, Vol. 1, P. 203). The spelling "Woodlast" or "Woodlest" often appears for this family of "Woodliffe", as shown in the Victoria History of Bucks, Vol. 2, p. 322, and Burke's Extinct Baronetcies (1838), p. 169. This probably results from some confusion in interpreting the old English "f" for "s" in the records. Anyway, since "Woodlast" is used interchangeably for "Woodliffe", it is all the more proof that "Ann Woodlast, aged 7" was the young daughter of Capt. John Woodliffe who was left behind with her kinspeople in Virginia when he returned to England, or was killed in the Indian massacres. It will be noted that the Articles of Agreement state his wife and children were there in 1619.

The problem therefore arises how were they kin. If Thomas Harris was the third son of Sir William Harris of Cricksey, Essex, his pedigree could be easily traced in England. The expressions "Kinswoman" and "Kinsman" in those days were used to describe distant cousins. "Cozen" then was used more often to describe nephews and nieces. The chart pedigree at the end of this article shows the probable relationship of Anne Woodlast and Thomas Harris. Their degree of relationship was that of third or fourth cousin, and their common ancestor was Sir Robert Drury, one time Speaker of the House of Commons. This idea of their relationship is not so far fetched for those families who in those days recorded their pedigrees in the Visitations. They probably knew their pedigrees much better then than pedigrees are known today. An example of a similar recognized relationship is shown in "Waters Gleanings" (p. 391), wherein it appears that Lawrence Washington of Gardsens, Wilts., in his will made 1661, left property to John Washington, his third cousin.

It is not shown whether Capt. John[3] Woodliffe returned to Virginia or not. He owned 550 acres in the Territory of Great Weyanoke in Charles City County, which were unplanted in 1626 (Hotten, Vol. 2, p. 269).

His son, John[4] Woodliffe, had a regrant of this land in 1637, as follows:

> John Woodliffe, 550 acres in Chas. City Co., Aug. 24, 1637, Page 467. Part of said tract in the territory of Great Weyanoake near headland called Beggars Bush, Near land formerly belonging to William Parrott, E. upon Samuel Jordan; remainder, 200 acs. at Charles hundred, S. upon Samuell Jordan & N. upon William Julian. Due in right of his father Capt. John Woodlife, granted by Sir George Yeardly in 1620. (C. P. 68).

John[4] Woodliffe came from England as he was granted land for his own transportation. It is probable that he was in Virginia with his father in 1619 (See ante) but returned to England with him and later came back to Virginia. This grant was as follows:

> John Woodliffe, 200 acs., Chas. City, July 25, 1638, Page 580. Near a place called Jordans, towards place called Beggars Bush & W. upon Francis Poythers. For his per. adv. & trans. of: John Smith, Henry Stephens, Elizabeth Wills. (C. P. 93.)

This land bordered on the south side of the James River, for on July 9, 1635, Jenkins Osborne patented 400 A. in Charles City, lying between the land of Capt. Woodliffe and William Bayly, north upon James River and south into the woods.... (C. P. 25). Francis Poytheress, July 13, 1637, patented 400 A. in Charles City, E. upon land of Capt. Woodliffe & W. on Bailey's Creek... (C. P. 60) Edward Hill, gent., patented 450 A. there July 25, 1638, north upon a head of land called Jordans, W. upon land of John Woodliffe... (C. P. 93.)

John Woodliffe, on Aug. 18, 1642, obtained a regrant of the above three patents, 350 acres at a place called "Jordans", W. upon land of Wm. Jarret, 200 acres at a place called "Bermuda Hundred".....the other 200 adjacent to the above, 550 acres by patent dated Dec. 10, 1620, and the remainder by patent July 25, 1638.... (C. P. 130).

At the time Capt. John Woodliffe received his patent, Dec. 10, 1620 a patent was also granted to Samuel Jordan, an ancient planter "who hath abode ten years complete in this colony," for 50 acres in Charles Hundred, on the great river, S. upon John Rolfe, N. upon land of Capt. John Woodliffe, 388 acres upon Sandy's Hundred, towards Temperance Bailey, W. upon Capt. Woodliffe..... (C. P. 226.).

John[4] Woodliffe was likewise called "Captain" the same as his father. He represented Charles City in the House of Burges-

ses in 1652 (B. J.) In 1655 a difference between him and Col.
Edward Hill over land was referred to the Council. He was also
ordered to pay 150 lbs. tbco. to Phillip Lewis (Fleet 10. pp. 1-10).
In 1661 Capt. John Woodliffe as Captain-Lieutenant of the County
was to have command of the Charles City regiment. (Fleet II-100).

In 1665, Capt. John Woodliffe and his son, George testified in
Court that Capt. John Woodliffe was aged 51 years, therefore born
in 1614. George was aged 19, born in 1646. (Fleet 13-42, 74).

Col. Robert Wynne, Speaker of the House of Burgesses, 1661-
1674, made his will in 1675, and mentions his daughter "-----
Woodliffe, " and grandson George Woodliffe.

In 1658, Capt. John Woodlief was appointed to arbitrate a difference between Capt. Robert Wynne and Francis Epes and Thomas Epes concerning the estate of John Sloman. Thomas Epes
married a daughter of Anthony Wyatt before 1658 (Fleet).

It is not known when Capt. John Woodliffe died. It is evident
that his wife was a daughter of Col. Robert Wynne. (14 V-175).

Children of . . . . . . (Wynne) and John [4] Woodliffe:

    I. George, born in 1646, according to his deposition,
        was the only grandson mentioned in Col. Robert
        Wynne's will. Probably, not therefore having any
        brothers, he was evidently the father of the following
        Woodliffes.

        The last mention of George Woodliffe in the
        Charles City records was in 1678 when he was granted
        an attachment against the property of Ralph Poole
        (O. B. 1677-79-271). It is probable that he married
        Elizabeth, eldest daughter of James Wallace who was
        a widow in 1701.

        On Oct. 24, 1701, John Butler received a grant of
        land "as marrying Mary Butler one of the daughters
        of Mr. James Wallace, decd. , for and of his said
        wife Mary, who was the youngest daughter of said
        Wallace, and ELIZABETH WOODLIFFE, widow and
        eldest dau. of said WALLACE, a tract of land con-
        taining 950 acres in Charles City County, on second
        swamp of the Blackwater and S. side of said swamp
        . . . " (G. B. 9 p. 388).

        James Wallace's (Wallis') name was used as a
        headright, June 7, 1651, by James Ward who patented
        150 acres on Powell's Creek, S. & W. upon James
        Peebles. . . (C. P. 216). James Wallace married the
        relict of John Bannister, who died in 1653. (Fleet
        II, p. 93.)

        In 1664, James Wallace and Joan, his wife, sell
        to Caesar Walpole parcel of land on Burcher's Creek,

same being a dividend to JOANE WHEELER relict of
THOMAS WHEELER. (Fleet 13, p. 99).

Thomas Wheeler's first grant of land in Charles
City was for 200 acres, Sept. 29, 1637, on a neck of
land..... between two creeks, S. upon land of Mrs.
Perry. (C. P. 74). On Nov. 10, 1638 he obtained
another grant of land at head of Merchant's Hope Creek,
due by assignment from Serjeant Richard Tisdale who
married Mary Baynham, dau. and heir of Ancient
Planter John Baynham, of Surry, (Col. Surry P. (C.
P. 149)). On August 23, 1643 he obtained a grant of
990 acres at head of Powell's Creek, N. upon land at
Merchant's Hope, adj. Cheney Boyce, due by assignment from Richard Milton and Richard Tisdale. (C. P.
145).

It is not known when Elizabeth Woodliffe received
her share of Thomas Wheeler's land. She was holding
844 acres in Prince George in the Quit Rents of 1704.

Children of Elizabeth and George Woodliffe:

1. John, on Dec. 4, 1679, was security for
   Wm. Vaughn as administrator of the estate
   of Samuel Johnson (O. B. 1677-79 p. 271).

   In June 1690 he was issued a certificate for
   600 A. in Charles City. (Do. p. 296). In the
   Prince George Quit Rents of 1704 he was holding 644 acres and John Woodliffe, Jr. was
   holding 750 A. In 1714 Elizabeth Epes sued
   Peter Wynne and John Woodliffe was security
   for the Plaintiff (Epes, B K 63). A John Woodliffe had 212 acres surveyed in 1720, (Survey,
   1710-26.) In 1738 John Woodlief and Thomas
   Harrison qualified as executors of the will of
   John Woodlief, deceased.

2. Edward, m. Sarah....... In June, 1690
   Edward Woodlief and Sarah his wife, Wm. Hay-
   good & Joan his wife, and Ann Osborne state
   that Ferdinando Jarrett, with "Force and Armes"
   did enter into a plantation of theirs on Martin
   Brandon. (D. B. 1677-79, -287). Edward Woodlief made his will in Prince George Sept. 20,
   1718; probated Feb. 1719. His legatees were:
   wife Sarah; sons, Joseph, John, Edward;
   daughter...... Pace and three daughters not
   named.

   (1) Edward Woodlief, Jr., evidently his son,
   patented 204 acres in Prince George in 1720 and

339 acres in 1739. Edward made his will, probated 1759, in Prince George and mentioned a brother "Thomas Woodlief" and his son "Edward", a nephew. He had four sisters one of them being a "Sarah Pace". Edward Woodlief, whose will was probated in 1719, had four daughters and one of them was "a dau. Pace"; but this Edward had no son Thomas mentioned in his will of 1719. Was "Thomas" his eldest son and heir not named in his will, as he would inherit any land not bequeathed?

Edward Jr.'s will, probated 1759, was as follows: to Bro. Thomas Woodlief...... to Joseph Ledbetter and Richard Burge; to nephew Edward Woodliffe, son of Thomas; to sisters, Sarah Pace, Ann Ledbetter, Susanna Woodlief and Mary Louise; to Joseph Ledbetter..... Witnesses: Francis Holden, George Williams, Thomas Whetsone. (IIW (2) -42). It is probable that his four sisters were the "daughter Pace" and the three other unnamed daughters named Edward Woodlief's will in 1719.

Explanation of the Harris Chart

The first person who suggested that Thomas Harris, who came to Virginia on the ship "Prosperous" in May, 1611, and settled in Henrico County, was a son of Sir William Harris of Crixe, Essex, was Dr. Alexander Brown. Dr. Brown stated in his "Genesis of the United States" (Vol. II, p. 913) that "Thomas Harris, Gent., subscribed and paid £ 25 to the Second Virginia Company in January and November 1609. He may have been the son of Sir William Harris. I think he was the person of that name who went to Virginia with Dale in 1611, and was living at the neck of land in Charles City February 1625, aged 38, with his wife Anne, aged 23."

In the will of Sir William Herris, alias Harris of Crixe, dated Dec. 21, 1615, his sons Thomas and John are given £ 1500 the same as the other younger children and no place of residence is shown for any of the children. Same was probated Nov. 20, 1616, by Sir Arthur Herris, his eldest son. (P.C.C. 119 Cope).

Sir Arthur, born 1584, subscribed £ 37, 10 s. to the Third Virginia Co. He died Jan. 9, 1632, leaving children and did not mention any brothers in his will.

William, b. 1585; d. 1622, as William Herris or Harris, matriculated at Pembroke, Cambridge, Easter 1608, aged _____. He made his will March 28, 1622. He mentions his brothers Arthur and John but does not mention his brother Thomas. This will was proved May 11, 1622. (P.C.C. Savile 42) John Harris was residing in Charles City County February 16, 1623, with his wife Dorothy and two infants when the Virginia Census was taken. (Hotten 170). He returned to England soon afterwards, for the Parish Registers of St. Dustan in the East show that on May 1, 1624, "John, son of John Harris of Virginia, gent., and his wife Dorothy, born in the house of Edward Lymbery, of Lyme House, mariner, and the same day baptized." It is very probable that he returned to England to claim his legacy. John Harris does not show in the Census of February 1624-25 taken in Virginia; but was residing in Charles City in 1626 where he had 200 acres patented. He was a Burgess from Shirley Hundred, 1627-30. The records show he had a wife and daughter, both named "Dorothy." (Hotten 268). This John Harris was evidently a member of the Virginia Company, as he was in London June 26, 1624, when he wrote Sir Peter Courteen in Holland, "That the Virginia Company was moved, but Could not prevail" in regard to his request. (Calandar State Papers, Colonial, Vol 1675-76 pp. 64,65.)

Thomas Harris was a member of the House of Burgesses in 1623-24 and he signed his name "Harries" and "Harris", very similar to the spelling of Sir William Harris of Crixe. (B. J.) His date of birth was in the year 1587 as shown by the above census of 1625. This exactly coincides with the date of birth of Thomas the third son of Sir William Harris.

Miss Helen Thacker, record searcher, whose address is 29 Linden Gardens, London W. 2, England, advised that she has searched the records of the P. C. C., London and Essex courts for the will or administration of this particular Thomas Harris and that it can not be found therein.

Under the circumstances, although not directly proven, it appears that Thomas Harris may have been the third son of Sir William Harris. We are concerned only with Thomas Harris as there is no direct proof in Virginia records that Thomas and John of Charles City were brothers.

These notes are taken from a carbon copy of an article on the Harris family which the writer sent to Mr. William Ligon and it appears in full in his book on that family (pp. 837-844) with the exception that Joan "Osborn" was added as a second wife of Thomas Harris, and that Adria Harris was not married in England but was betrothed and married in Virginia. In the Witchcraft trial of Jone Wright, Rebecca Gray said that goodwife Wright did tell her that "Thomas Harris should bury his first wife then betrothed unto him, which came to pass...." (see page 843) (Col. Surry, p. 77.).

Robert Harris was added as a son of Thomas' first wife and there is no authority for naming Thomas' second wife, Joan "Osborne". (At the Ligon reunion in Richmond, Va. in 1937, the writer asked the person who was responsible for this statement first appearing in print where she obtained her information and she said she did not have any; that she had to give a name to Joan so she selected "Osborne" because Thos. Osborne was a neighbor. Once a statement is in print it is difficult to stop it from "just rolling along".)

Authorities for Accompanying Chart.

1. For Percy-Harris connection see chart Brennan's History of the House of Percy, Vo. 1, p. 169.
2. For Drury-Walgrave-Harris see Brydges Collins Peerage, Vo. 4, p. 235-236.
3. For Stapleton-Calthorpe see the Complete Peerage, Vol. 7, p. 34.
4. For Drury-Woodliffe see Burke's Extinct and Dormant Baronetcies (1838), p. 169.
5. For Drury see chart Nichols Bibliotheca Topographica Brittannica, Vo. 5, p. 115.

WOODLIFFE AND HARRIS CHARTS

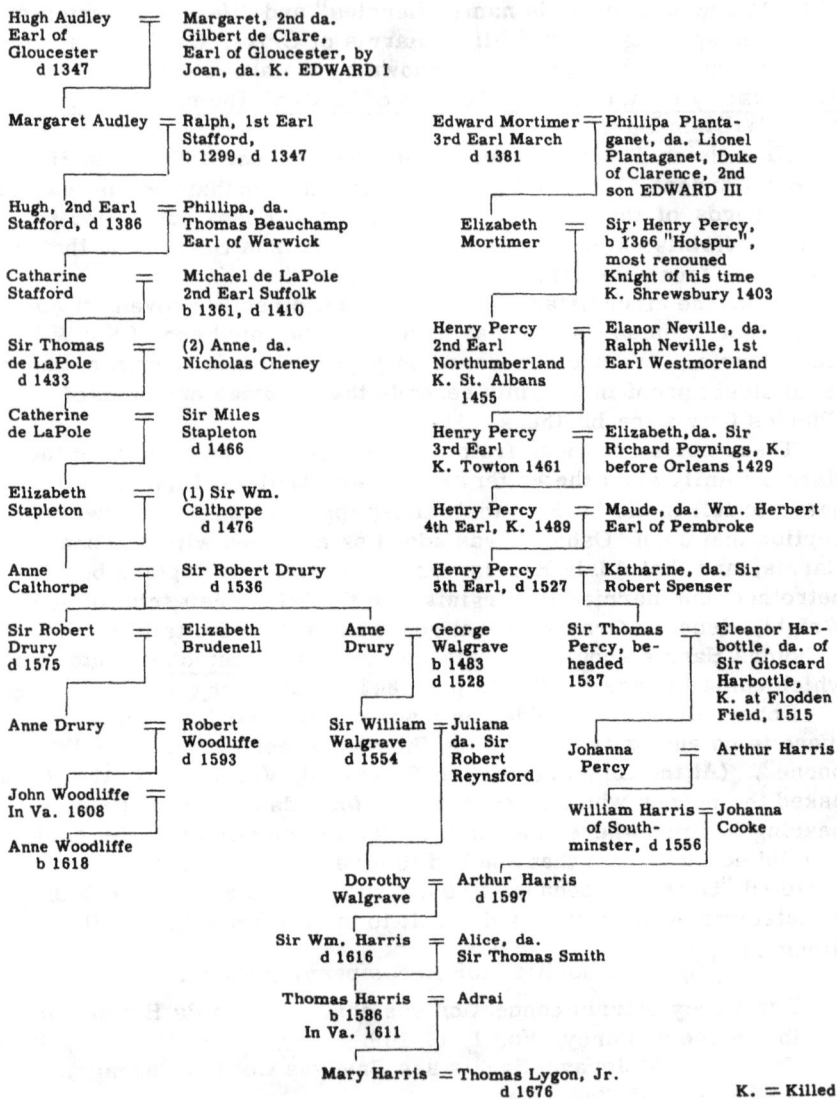

Hugh Audley
Earl of
Gloucester
d 1347
= Margaret, 2nd da.
Gilbert de Clare,
Earl of Gloucester, by
Joan, da. K. EDWARD I

Margaret Audley = Ralph, 1st Earl
Stafford,
b 1299, d 1347

Hugh, 2nd Earl
Stafford, d 1386
= Phillipa, da.
Thomas Beauchamp
Earl of Warwick

Catharine
Stafford
= Michael de LaPole
2nd Earl Suffolk
b 1361, d 1410

Sir Thomas
de LaPole
d 1433
= (2) Anne, da.
Nicholas Cheney

Catherine
de LaPole
= Sir Miles
Stapleton
d 1466

Elizabeth
Stapleton
= (1) Sir Wm.
Calthorpe
d 1476

Anne
Calthorpe
= Sir Robert Drury
d 1536

Sir Robert
Drury
d 1575
= Elizabeth
Brudenell

Anne
Drury
= George
Walgrave
b 1483
d 1528

Anne Drury = Robert
Woodliffe
d 1593

John Woodliffe =
In Va. 1608

Anne Woodliffe
b 1618

Sir William =
Walgrave
d 1554
Juliana
da. Sir
Robert
Reynsford

Edward Mortimer
3rd Earl March
d 1381
= Phillipa Planta-
ganet, da. Lionel
Plantaganet, Duke
of Clarence, 2nd
son EDWARD III

Elizabeth
Mortimer
= Sir Henry Percy,
b 1366 "Hotspur",
most renouned
Knight of his time
K. Shrewsbury 1403

Henry Percy
2nd Earl
Northumberland
K. St. Albans
1455
= Elanor Neville, da.
Ralph Neville, 1st
Earl Westmoreland

Henry Percy
3rd Earl
K. Towton 1461
= Elizabeth, da. Sir
Richard Poynings, K.
before Orleans 1429

Henry Percy
4th Earl, K. 1489
= Maude, da. Wm. Herbert
Earl of Pembroke

Henry Percy
5th Earl, d 1527
= Katharine, da. Sir
Robert Spenser

Sir Thomas
Percy, be-
headed
1537
= Eleanor Har-
bottle, da. of
Sir Gioscard
Harbottle,
K. at Flodden
Field, 1515

Johanna
Percy
= Arthur Harris

William Harris
of South-
minster, d 1556
= Johanna
Cooke

Dorothy
Walgrave
= Arthur Harris
d 1597

Sir Wm. Harris
d 1616
= Alice, da.
Sir Thomas Smith

Thomas Harris
b 1586
In Va. 1611
= Adrai

Mary Harris = Thomas Lygon, Jr.
d 1676

K. = Killed

GODWYN OF WELLS AND WOKEY
Somerset, England, and Nansemond, Virginia

The Godwins and Bennetts settled in Nansemond County, Virginia, 1640-1650. The Bennetts were related to the Bournes of Wells. (See Bourne.) Investigation finds that the Bournes and the Godwins intermarried several times in Wells. It is probable therefore that the Godwins of Nansemond came from that city.

A pedigree of the Godwyn family is shown in the Visitations of Somerset, 1623 (Harl 11, 41.) It is signed by James and Robert Godwyn. They were cousins and from wills subsequently found the pedigree appears substantially correct.

Another pedigree is shown in the Visitations of the same County in 1573 (Weaver, p. 25). This carries the family back four generations previous to that date.

Collinson in his "History and Antiquities of Somerset" (Vol. III, p. 84) carries the pedigree of the family back to the time of Edward II.

He says "The family of Godwyn were long Lords of Bower, and gave it the name of 'Godwyn's Bower.' In the time of Edward II (1307-1327), Hugh Godwyn, Burgess of Bridgewater, possessed lands in Bridgewater, Bower, and Dunwere, and by Margery his wife had John Godwyn who died 20 Edward III (1347) leaving by Joan his wife, daughter of Robert de Bradford (who survived him) John his son and heir.

"John was living 21 Edward III and bore on his shield 'a chevron between three leopards heads.'

"The arms are identical with the arms shown by James and Robert Godwyn in 1623, above. John was succeeded in his estates by William Godwyn his son and heir, and he by another William Godwyn who died 21 Henry VI (1443) seized of the manor of 'Godwyne's-Boure,' and certain lands and tenants in North-Boure, parcel of the same manor, held under Alexander Hody, as of his manor of Otterhampton.'

"William Godwyn, son of the last named William was living I, Edward IV (1461) and had issue William Godwyn, called in his father's life time 'William Godwyn, the Younger.'

"William Godwyn, the younger, was the father of Christopher Godwyn, and the grandfather of Thomas Godwyn, who sold this manor and that of Bagborough, to John Brent, of Cossington, esq., who died seized of same, and the manors of Dunwere, East-Bower, others, 16, Henry VIII (1525) all of which descended to William Brent his son and heir. These manors were afterwards sold by the Brents and dispersed into other families. "

John Brent who died in 1557, buried at Bixley in Kent, married a daughter and heir of Thomas Godwin (Collinson III-436).

William Godwyn of Wells is the first of the family shown in both pedigrees—that of 1573 and 1623. He married a daughter and heir of _____ Swayne and seems to have lived during the time of Richard III and Henry VII (1483-1509). His arms were the same as the family of Godwyn's Bower. John, son of William Godwyn, was living in the time of Henry VIII (1509-1547). He is shown as having two sons by the name of William and one named Richard. Here the recorded wills begin and we are on firmer ground.

Children of John Godwin:

I. William, m. Christian, daughter of _____ Burges or Bruges of Batcombe, Somerset. (See later).

II. William may be the William Godwyn who entered Hart Hall, Oxford in 1571 aged 19. His disposition is unknown.

III. John, Jr., not shown in Pedigree because not in the direct line, may have been a son. A John Godwyn of Wells was the supervisor of the will of William Joyce of St. Cuthbert, Wells in 1532 (Wells wills 1528-36, p. 186).

A John Godwyn, burgess of Wells, made his will July 12, 1551, and as he mentions his brother WILLIAM GODWIN, he may have been the son of William's father, John.

The will of John, the burgess, was proven by his son Michael who probated same May 3, 1582. John desired to be buried in St. Cuthbert near his wife Margaret. He gave to Joane Isacck, daughter of Walter Wall, the best gown late her mother's, rest of his estate to son Michael. John Godwin, the mercer and William Godwin, "my brother to be overseers. (Brown 5-61)

John Godwyn of Wells, the mercer, made his will September 26, 1570, proven November 30, 1581, by his daughter, Christian Deverell alias Godwin, Isabel the relict being dead: (Somerset 46 Darcy). He gave his lands after his death to his heirs male, William Boureman, esq. and Richard Godwin, gent., Overseers, wife Isabel.

Isabel Godwyn, who was deceased prior to the probate of her husband's will (above) made her will October 1578, admn. to John Deverell, Sr., during minority of John Deverell, Jr., June 1579. She gave legacies to her son Adrian Godwin and his son Hugh, to son Nicholas and his children John and Ann; Son-in-law John Deverell and daughter Christian Deverell; daughter-in-law Joan Godwin. Friend Richard Godwin the elder, (See #4) and William Lewis overseers.

John and his wife Isabel were seemingly closely related to the Godwins of this pedigree as they both make Richard Godwin (#4) an overseer of their will.

A John Godwin, Devereaux, or Deverell Godwin, Elizabeth Godwin, Edward Drew and Mary his wife, William Whittington and Mary his wife came to Northampton Co., Va., where Captain William Whittington was granted 800 acres in 1653 for transporting them to Virginia (C. P. 294). "Devereaux" could be taken for "Deverall," or vice versa "ll" for "u."

IV. Richard, the elder, m. Margery, daughter of _____ Broadrib. He is shown as the third son of William in the Visitations and he had sons James and John. This is verified by his will made as of Wells, Som., January 1, 1577, probated by wife Margery February 14, 1583 (28 Butts) (Brown).

Children:

1. James, m. Maud, daughter of Richard Williams of Cleve, Som. He made his will October 19, 1616 as "James, the elder" of Wells, Som, proved December 18, 1616 (120 Cape; Brown 2-28). He desired to be buried "in the north side of the south side of the South Isle in St. Cuthberts Church between the tomb of my brother John Godwyn and the wall in the said ile." He mentions brothers-in-law Richard Cox and George Richards of Bristol. Appoints Edward Wykes, Edmund Bower, etc., overseers. Most of his will is given to a description of the tomb he wishes built over his resting place. (Not a vestige of this tomb remains.)

Children:

(1) Margery, £ 500 to be given her by his brother John Godwyn; (2) Mary 500 marks; (3) Elizabeth £ 20; (4) John; (5) James.

2. John died before 1616.

I. William, shown as the first son of John in the pedigrees, m. Christian Burges of Batcombe, Som. She married secondly _____ Drew. He is shown in the pedigrees as of Wells but on February 25, 1548, he leased the Rectory at Wookey or Wokey, from William Bowerman, the sub-dean, at an annual rent of £ 23 for 80 years and the family held it for 170 years. (Holmes, Hist. of Wookey, p. 150). The date of his death is not known but the Visitation of 1573 shows him with eight children. Besides the three shown below there were Gilbert; William; Agnes m. Anthony Chappell; Margaret and Mary.

Children:

1. Richard, m. Margaret, daughter of Robert May of Charter-house. On August 20, 1581 Richard and Margery his wife of Wells sold to John Maye of Charter House, land and tenements in Wells formerly in possession of Richard Godwyn, the elder of Wells and Christian Drew, mother of Richard Godwyn.

   On October 1, 1582, Richard Godwyn of Wells sold to his brother Anthony of Wookey for £ 300 land in tenure of Margery Godwyn of Wells, widow and Christian Drew, mother of said Richard. His will was dated January 1, 1577 and probated 1583.

2. Isabel m. Nicholas Wykes of Wells, Somerset, Gent. (Tis. 1623 Harl Vol XI p. 120) He made his will Jan. 12, 1611, proved November 20, 1611 by Isabel, widow. He mentions his sons Edward and William; sisters Jone Oliver, widow, and Margery, wife of Thomas Hill, JOHN OLIVER and NICHOLAS HILL, their sons, cousin Thomas Godwin and his sisters Christian Huishe, their sons, and Mrs. Ann Maye, wife of John Maye (Brown (1-8.)

   Children:

   (1) Edward Wykes, m. Jane, daughter of GILBERT BOURNE of Wells. Jane was a first cousin of Mary Bourne who married EDWARD BENNET, the London merchant who established the plantation called "Bennetts Welcome" in Isle of Wight Co. in Virginia in 1622. Edward Bennett's daughter married COL. NICHOLAS HILL of Isle of Wight. JOHN OLIVER was also an early resident of that county.

3. Anthony Godwyn of Wookey, Somerset, second son of William and Christian (Burges) Godwyn was heir to the Rectory in Wookey but seems to have fallen in troublesome times. He left Wookey and died in 1609 in London where he is buried in St. Clement Danes. His will was dated November 20, 1609 and proved March 8, 1609-10 (26 Wingfield; Brown 1-4).

   His first wife was Joan Goad whom he married in 1579. He married, secondly, in 1588 Elizabeth, daughter of Robert Maye of Charterhouse. (See May Chart) The Maye family is shown in the Somerset Visitations of 1573 (p. 49) and the one of 1623 (p. 73).

   He stated in his will "I have had manifold troubles

and suits of law. I am indebted for the payment of same to my brother-in-law, John Maye, Esqr. " He mentions his son Robert who inherited the Rectory lease. He gave "ten pounds out of the Rectory to my son William Godwyn, whom I heartily pray unto God to convert and make an honest man. "

"My daughters Christian Hewes and Alice Parfait 40 s. each for a ring. Residue to wife Elizabeth. Brother-in-law John Maye and Nicholas Wykes overseers. "

Children of first wife Joan Goad, with dates of baptism given by Holmes:

(1) William, b. 1581

(2) Christian b. 1582 m. Edward Hewisch (Huisch) son of John Hewische of Doniford and Grace his wife, dau. of Richard Walrond (for Hewishe, see Som., Arch. Soc. Prec., Vol. 43,(2) p. 11). Edward was a notary of Wells and his will was proven June 14, 1624. He mentions several children and relatives. Among them were his son Anthony and his brother-in-law Robert Godwyn (Brown 1-12). Anthony his son, received his M. A. at Magdalen Hall Oxford, 1616 and succeeded his uncle Thomas Godwyn as head master of Royce School in Abingdon. His wife Christian is buried in the Chancel of Brightwell Church with an inscription as follows:

> Here rests the body of
> Christian, daughter of Anthony
> Godwyn of Wokey, in the County
> of Somerset, Gent., first the wife
> of Edward Hiuish, of Wells, in the
> County of Somerset, Gent.
> Afterwards the wife of Adrian
> Bower, of the same, Gent. She
> died, September, the XV. MDCXXXV

(3) Alice, b. 1584, m. Edward Parfait of Pilton, Som.

(4) Thomas, b. 1587, m. (1) Frances Tesdale, (2) Phillippe BOURNE, daughter of GILBERT BOURNE. He entered Magdalen College, Oxford, May 7, 1602, aged 15. B. A. 24 Jan. 1607, M. A. October 11, 1609; B. D. June 1616. D. D. 18 Nov. 1636. First Fellow of Pembroke College 1624. He was appointed head master of Roysse's School in Abingdon, Berkshire, September 23, 1608; Chaplain to the Bishop of Bath and Wells

1616; Rector of Brightwell Berks on the presentation of the Bishop of Bath and Wells 1626. (Preston's St. Nicholas Abingdon, pp. 333-335) Preston did not know of Thomas' marriage to Phillipe Bourne so he confused the two wives in his history.

Thomas was succeeded as Headmaster by his nephew Anthony Hewishe. Frances, his first wife, was buried in the church yard near the west end of St. Helen's Church, Abingdon, with the following inscription on a gravestone which has since disappeared:

Here lyeth Frances
The wife of Tho. Godwin
Rector of Brightwell
She died Nov. the 11th M D C X...
in the 21st. year of her Age.

Thomas died 20, March 1642/3 and was buried in Brightwell Church, where there is an inscription Latin (nearly illegible) and his arms "Arg. a chevron, ermine, between 3 Leopards' heads, a crecent.

This monument was erected by his wife Phillipe (Bourne) who afterwards married Mr. Bower. Phillipe's first husband was Richard Adams, Canon Residentiary of Wells, who died in 1634. (will, Brown 1-92) Phillipe's will was proven April 9, 1657. She desired "to be buried at Brightwell, Berks, in the Chancel, near my husband, Dr. Godwyn, but if not convenient, then by my former husband Dr. Adams, in St. Andrews Church, Wells."

Thomas Godwyn had two children by his first wife: (1) Anthony, bapt. at St. Nicholas August 16, 1612; (2) Alice, bapt., June 10, 1616. (Reg. St. Nicholas Abd.)

Children of Anthony Godwyn and second wife, Elizabeth Maye
(5) Robert, b. 1589, m. Elizabeth Smythies (See later).
(6) John, b. 1590, d. 1594
(7) Joan b. 1592, d. 1594
(5) Robert Godwyn, b. 1589, d. 1664, m. Elizabeth, dau. of John Smythies of Wrington Som., and his wife Joan, dau. of _____ Dorington of Dorington, Som. John Smythies was buried at Wrington June 26, 1626. Mr. Smithies also, in his will, speaks of his son-in-law Robert Godwin, as "A man not conformable to the laws of the Church of England."

This opinion is confirmed by the fact that in 1641 he paid a tax of £ 2 "as a recusant." (Holmes 150) Joan Smithies in her will dated May 2, 1638, probated July 2, 1639, mentions her daughter Elizabeth Godwyn, and also her daughter's children; Edmond, Elizabeth, Anna, Joane and THOMAS Godwyn. (Smythies family, p. 173, Misc. Gen. and His. Vol. IV, 4th Series).

Robert made his will as of Wookey, Som., gent. October 31, 1661. He stated he was old and infirm. (He was 72) The only child or relative he mentioned was his son Joseph. He mentioned Henry Walrond, George Walrond, Thomas Georges as trustees to pay certain sums to certain person named. (He evidently had made a trust before his death) (80 Bruce; Brown 5-106)

The children shown in the Visitations of 1623 were, Joseph, aged 9, Edward, Mary and Elizabeth. Mr. Holmes in his "History of Wookey" shows Joseph, John and Marie. It is evident that the three last named children in Joan Smithies will were born between 1623 and 1638 (date of her will.)

Children:

(1) Joseph, b. 1615, m. Susan Walrond.
Joseph inherited the Rectory lease at Wookey. From the will of his brother Edwin (Edward of Edmond) he appears to be somewhat overbearing. His will was proven in 1668. Holmes shows only two sons for him (1) Joseph, b. 1649, d. 1725, m. Eleanor Huks and had 12 children--all enumerated by Holmes (p. 150); (2) Henry, b. 1651 (date unknown)

(2) Edwin of Wraxall, Som., gent., made his will January 8, 1660, same proven May 6, 1661, by relict, Elizabeth. (Brown 3-43) He provided that his wife and child Elizabeth should enjoy the tenement lately purchased of his brother, Joseph Godwin, in the March near Highbudge, "if Robert Godwin and Joseph Godwin, his father and brother do not cozen them out of it."
The other children of Robert and Elizabeth Smithies Godwyn were: (3) John, b. 1616, (4) Marie, 1617 (5) Elizabeth (6) Anna,

(7) Joan, (8) THOMAS. (See later)

Thomas Godwin, not mentioned in the Visitation of 1623, was evidently born sometime after that date. He was mentioned in the will of his grandmother, Joan Smithies in 1638 and appears to be just about the age of the Thomas Godwin who came to Nansemond County, Virginia and settled near Philip, Robert and Richard Bennett.

Thomas Godwin of Nansemond County, Virginia settled there about 1650. He patented land in Rappahannock County in that year but sold it in 1656 (C. P. 319) He appears as a Burgess from Nansemond in 1654. His children were; (1) Thomas, m., 1679, Martha Bridger (2) Edward or Edmond, m., Sarah, daughter of Thomas Bembridge; (3) Elizabeth, who married (1) James Webb and had a son, James Webb; then married (2) Joseph Woory, nephew of Sir John Yeamans of Bristol, England. Her third husband was Samuel Bridger.

The date for his birth appears to coincide with that of Thomas, son of Robert and Elizabeth Godwin of Wookey. It is somewhat difficult to point out a particular person across the water and say that he is the person of the same name who appears over here. The names "Thomas, Edmond, Robert, James, Joseph," similar to those of the Godwins of Wells and Wookey are repeated among his children and grandchildren. No will or administration of this particular Thomas of Wookey or Wells is found among the Somerset records.

Captain Thomas Godwin of Nansemond was a Burgess during the Commonwealth period when Richard Bennett, his neighbor, a Puritan, was governor. Robert Godwin, father of the Thomas of Wookey, as stated before, was a non-conformist, probably a Puritan.

Richard Bennett of Nansemond turned Quaker. (17 C. 287) The Godwins frequently attended the Quaker meeting in Chuckatuck. The Southern Historical Association has published the records of the Quaker meetings in Nansemond at Chuckatuck. At the marriage of Thomas Jordan and Elizabeth Burgh, 6th day, 10th month, 1679, some of those present were Edmond Godwin, Thomas Godwin; Joseph Woory, Justice, brother-in-law of Edmond and Thomas Godwin; and Elizabeth Woory, daughter of Captain Thomas Godwin. This was the entire family of the first Thomas Godwin. (Vol. 7, pp. 96, 97, 99)

THOMAS
ISLE OF WIGHT COUNTY
VIRGINIA
and
NASH COUNTY N. C.

The first one of this family in Isle of Wight County was Philip Thomas who came to Virginia before 1635. He and his family consisting of himself, Evan and Sarah Thomas, were brought over by William Hunt wo received a grant of 800 acres at the head of Beverdam Branch, a branch of the Western Branch of the Nansemond, on Dec. 16, 1635, for the transportation of sixteen persons, among whom were the Scott family, who later became Quakers (C. P. 238).

William Boddie, upon coming to Isle of Wight some thirty years later, evidently received a grant of 3350 acres adjacent or near William Hunt's for Boddie's grant was "at the head of the Cypress and Western Branches of the Nazemond beginning at Beaver Dam Branch. (C. P. 475) William Hunt's daughter, Mary, married (1) Robert Edwards, (2) Owen Griffin; (3) William Boddie as his third wife.

Philip Thomas was a creditor of the estate of Nicholas West in 1668. In October 1677, he signed a petition to the King's Commissioners, then in Virginia, praying for the pardon of William West," a rebel taken in arms, whose father had been barbarously murdered by the Indians." (17 C. p. 163). In 1679 he witnessed the will of John Daniel.

Philip Thomas, evidently aged, made his will Nov. 3, 1702, and same was probated Feb. 9, 1702/3. He gave one shilling to his daughter Mary Goodson and the same to his son William. To son John he gave "all that I die seized of that pertains to me and mine." (W. B. 2p. 456). John Thomas, his son, was executor and the witnesses were Margaret and Judy Edwards. They were the step-daughters of William Boddie who had married their mother Mary (Hunt) Edwards.

Children of Philip Thomas.
> I. John, m. Susanne, dau. of John Portis, and relict of John Frizzel. (see later).

II. William, (2) m. Elizabeth Hill, dau. of Sylvestra (Bennet) and Gol. Nicholas Hill. (see later).

III. Mary (2), m. Edward Goodson before 1702 and removed to Bertie county, N. C., later Northampton. In 1737, Edward Goodson, probably a son of the above, married Mary, dau. of Thomas Mandue, of Bertie, formerly of Isle of Wight. (I. W. D. B. 5-152) Also in 1737 George Goodson, probably another son, married Sarah Mandue. A George Goodson was a juror in Bertie in 1740.

I. John Thomas, son of Philip Thomas, married Susanna, dau. of John Portis and relict of John Frizzell. On October 9, 1693, the court ordered "that John Thomas and Susanna his wife, the late wife of John Frizzell, decd., John Portis Jr., Wm. Frizzell and Thomas Sawyer come to the next court for the presentation of the estate of said Frizzell." (O. B. 1693-1695 p. 2).

In 1693 John Portis, Sr., made a deed of gift to his daughter Susanna Thomas of land next to Thomas Moore and Thomas Tooke. (D. B. 1-65) On Nov. 22, 1704, Debora Portis, widow of John Portis, Jr., deeded a certain tract of land given by John Portis, Sr., to Susanna wife of John Thomas on April 4 1693, which was afterwards assigned to John Portis Jr. by John Thomas and his wife, (D. B. 2-238). On Sept. 2, 1697, John Thomas of L. P. made a deed of gift of 100 acres, lying between Col. Smith and Thomas Parnell, to Henry and Mary Martin his wife. (D. B. 1-228)

About twenty years previously, William Boddie made a deed of gift of cattle to Thomas Dixon, Henry Dixon and Henry Martin, the children of Henry and Mary Martin, and her former husband, Thomas Dixon. (D. B. 2-205). There appears to be a relationship between these families.

In 1699, Henry and Mary Martin deeded three hundred acres, to Robert Brock, part of a patent of 2100 acres to Edmund Palmer, 700 of which had been granted to his father Henry Martin next to John Thomas 100 A., to line of Hugh Brassy and William Boddie.

In 1697 and 1698 John Thomas deeded land "lying next to Mr. William Boddie" (D. B. 1-232, 281) On June 9, 1705, John Thomas witnessed a deed from William Boddie to James Mercer-for 4000 lbs. tbco. paid by James for purchase of a plantation which James Mercer bought of William Boddie, June 2, 1704-now assigned by Mercer to Lowry (D. B. 2, 1704-1715, -2) John Thomas bought 580 acres from Joseph Parnell, part of a patent of 2800 acres to Edmund Palmer, Feb. 8, 1672, and deeded by said Palmer to Thomas Parnell father of Joseph in 1679. Deed was dated Oct. 7, 1707. On August 8, 1710, John Thomas appointed John Giles to represent him in a law suit. Witness- William Thomas. (D. B. 2-7, 13) On Feb. 9, 1711, Thomas Pitt sold Matthew Lowry 100 acres, part of a patent granted William Boddie July 12, 1665, for 3350 acres, witnessed by Arthur Smith and John Thomas. (Do. 14).

John Portis Sr., father of Susanna Thomas, together with Henry West, patented 900 acres of land, next to John Sherrer, Sept. 25, 1673. (17c.-690.) John Portis' will was probated in Isle of Wight in 1707, and John Jr's in 1704.

John Thomas made his will Dec. 12, 1725. His wife named in will appears to be "Hannah" instead of "Susanna" so he may have been married the second time. He gave wife Hannah 100 acres "I now live on son Richard 100 acres between West, Portis, John Clarke and John Sherrer; son Samuel 'I have already given him land '; to be taken care of by Joseph Weston, Joseph Weston to be executor". (G.B.-196)

Children:

I. Richard, m. Elinor Sherrer (Sherrod or Sherwood). He bought 250 acres on the Western Branch from John Boddie, Jan. 21, 1737. (D.B. 5-223) In 1738 he returned the inventory of Elizabeth Sherwood; also in 1738 he and his wife Elinor deeded land bought from John Boddie to Richard Hurst of Gloucester. In 1743 Robert Sherrod deeded him land. In 1745 he bought land of Giles Kelly.

Richard Thomas made a deed of gift to his son John in 1757. He mentions Mary Gale, Sarah Haywood and Moses Exum in his will but the relationship is not shown. Children: (1) John m. Mary dau. of Philip Moody; (2) William; (3) dau. m. Moses Exum; (4) Tabitha m. William Gale; (5) Richard, who as son of Richard Thomas, made a deed of gift in 1756 to "William Haywood and Sarah his wife, my niece". He may have been dead in 1761 as he is not mentioned in his father's will. (6) Mary, m. Whitney Gale. She is mentioned as "my niece" in deed of Samuel Thomas of N.C. in 1764.

II. SAMUEL, m. Elizabeth Sherrer and removed to Northampton County, N.C. In 1754 he sold 100 acres to Whitney Gale which had been given him by his father John Thomas. He is said to have had a daughter Alice, who married a Bryan.

III. JACOB, m. Mary Norsworthy. In 1767 Tristram Norsworthy was guardian of his orphan children. Anne and Tabitha Thomas were called "Granddaughters" in the will of Elizabeth Harrison in 1773. His orphans were: John, Anne, Haywood, Tabitha and Polly Thomas.

An important Norsworthy deed was found in Norfolk county, inasmuch as the records of Nansemond County are destroyed. John Norsworthy, gent., of Nansemond Co., on Nov. 6, 1717, as "eldest son of Col. George Norsworthy, of the same county, who was eldest son of Major George Norsworthy, who was eldest son of Tristram Norsworthy" deeded to George Newton for 44 shillings 73 1/2 acres, part of land patented by "my great Grandfather, Tristram Norsworthy, 19 August, 1650 in Lower Norfolk. " (D. B. 9-633).

II. William Thomas, son of Philip Thomas lived in the Lawne's Creek district or Upper Parish of Isle of Wight. He married before 1692, Elizabeth Hill, daughter of Col. Nicholas Hill, Burgess for Isle of Wight 1659-1666. This marriage is shown in the will of John Jennings, Jr., son of the old Clerk of Isle of Wight, who was ordered to be banished by Berkeley for taking part in Bacon's Rebellion. Jennings Sr. died before his transportation could be effected.

Elizabeth Hill's mother was Sylvestra Bennett, daughter of Edward Bennett, the wealthy London merchant, who established the first permanent plantation in 1622. (see 17c.) Edward represented his plantation, "Bennett's Welcome", in the House of Burgesses in 1628.

The plantation of Edward Bennett was divided between his two daughters and co-heirs, Sylvestra Bennett and Mary Bland. Mary had been married previously to James Day. This division is shown in a grant to Major Nicholas Hill and Sylvestra, his wife, for 750 acres in the Upper Parish of Isle of Wight "being a moiety of 1500 acres appertaining unto Silvestra and her sister Mary Bland, who were daughters and co-heirs to Mr. Edward Bennett, decd., beginning upon the top of a bank of James River and running to a place called 'The Rocks. '" (C. P. 144)

Nicholas Hill patented 100 acres in Elizabeth City county, Nov. 26, 1637. (C. P. -77), and sold same to Williams ap. Thomas who repatented same June 2, 1648 (C. P. 175). Nicholas was Burgess for Isle of Wight 1659-60, 1663-1666. (17c-102, 703). In 1666 Peter Green of Surrey sold him 70 acres in Surry, part of a patent of 160 acres granted Greene Feb. 21, 1663. In 1667 he was a Justice of the County Court, Adjutant and Major of Militia. (do. -704) In 1670 he patented 670 acres at Blackwater near Parson's bridge on the Beaver Dam Branch. (do. -6910)

Col. Hill's will was dated April 19, 1675, probated Oct. 20, 167£

He desired to be buried as near his deceased wife and children as may be; to wife Silvestra for life my plantation in Isle of Wight being bounded between the cart path that goes from the well of Mr. George Hardy towards the church and swamp commonly called the Meadows with liberty to use the timber on land bought of Col. Wm. Bernard, decd. after her death to my son RICHARD HILL and his heirs, together with the woodland on West of said swamp by Mr. Richard Briggs' and Edward Beckeno's land; to son RALPH HILL land bounded by cart path that goes from the mill towards the church at the head of Lawn's Creek, with all woodland of 70 acres

bought of Mr. Peter Green decd. on north side of said creek in
Surry County; to son RALPH Hill the codd of land at Blackwater between Branch and William Miles, from John Parson's bridge to
Left. George Branch; to son GEORGE HILL all my woodland between the land Col. Bacon bought of Thomas Harris and my land;
to son GEORGE HILL "after my wife's decease, or sooner, if
she please, " that plantation of 750 acres granted to me and my
loving wife in Upper Parish of Isle of Wight commonly called "The
Rocks" and running for breadth down towards Pagan Creek; two
negroes to wife Silvestra for life then to son GEORGE; negro to son
Ralph; 8000 lbs. Tbco. to dau. AGNES HILL, to dau. MARTHA one
scarlet mantle; to wife Silvestra my silver tankard with what money
and rings she is possessed of; to wife one third of personalty, residue
to my children GEORGE, MARTHA, MARY, ANNA, RICHARD
and ELIZABETH HILL; to son NICHOLAS 10,000 lbs. tbco;
to son Ralph 5,000 lbs. of tbco. ; to my wife and her six children
all my lands monies etc. not mentioned in this will belonging to
me either in England or Virginia; my three children by a former
wife having an equal proportion of what may fall to me in the Bay;
wife extrx. for that part of the estate belonging to her and her six
children; friends Mr. THOMAS TABERER, Major JAMES POW-
ELL, Mr. WM. BRISSEY and JOHN JENNINGS to be overseers.
(7W-238).

John Jennings, Jr. who married Mary, daughter of Silvestra
and Col. Hill, made his will Dec. 31, 1692, same probated in
1695. (Bk. 1688-1704, 261.) He gave to sister Sarah Luck "a
gold ring"; (She married, first John Luck, who died in 1711.
She then married Philip Weadon) (G. B.-646); to "son GEORGE
JENNINGS all land at Warrisqueak Bay at Lawne's Creek, to
mother SILVESTRA HILL, 40 shillings". He made her executrix
and "BROTHER WILLIAM THOMAS" executor. The witnesses
were FRANCIS MANGUM, MARTHA THROPP and WILLIAM
THOMAS.

William Thomas' marriage to Elizabeth Hill is shown in Mrs.
Chapman's "Marriages of Isle of Wight" (p. 50). The authorities
given for same are "D. B. 1, p. 201, and W. D. Bk. 2. p. 408 ."

William Thomas' wife was named "Elizabeth" as shown by the
following transaction. On Jan. 2, 1696, William Prosser of Surry deeded to William Thomas "the tract of land I now live on" containing 50 acres (Surry D. B. 1694-1709-252). On Nov. 27, 1702
"William Thomas and his wife Elizabeth" sold Joseph Thropp of
Surry the above mentioned 50 acres. (do. 252).

Mrs. Silvestra Hill, on June 9, 1701, made a deed of gift to
William Thomas as follows "Articles of agreement between Mrs.
Silvestra Hill, Upper Parish of Isle of Wight, and William Thom-
as, same Parish. Mrs. Hill lets to William Thomas land on the
James River adjoining Mr. Day's land running south along river

side to Thomas Elmes, and from the river southerly by the plantation which William Thomas formerly lived upon, at his death to return to Mrs. Hill, the said William Thomas paying one ear of corn every New Years day". Wits. Charles Edwards, Martha Thropp. (Bk. 1, 1688-1704, p. # 355.)

Thomas Elmes, who will be mentioned in a later deed, bought land adjacent to Richard Bennett, esq. (17c-277). This was next to the patent for 750 acres Mrs. Hill had received in 1664 from her father Edward Bennett. (17c.-277.)

Col. Nicholas Hill in his will in 1675 gave the plantation he lived upon to his wife Silvestra for her life, and after her death to his son George. On Sept. 12, 1695, Silvestra deeded her life interest to Lewis Burwell as follows: "Silvestra Hill widow, relict of Lt. Col. Nicholas Hill, for £ 20- paid by Lewis Burwell, sells a little above Lawne's Creek, the plantation where Col. Hill formerly lived and by his will gave to Silvestra for life." (17c-623) Mrs. Hill in her will dated Oct. 17, 1706, (will indistinct) probated Jan. 9, 1707, gave to her Goddaughter, Mary Baker, land she lives upon, known as The Rocks, and all the rest of that neck of land, that is to say the plantation of William Thomas and others. She also gave 300 acres to the poor of Isle of Wight. This land was sold by the Trustee of the Charity, the Reverend Alexander Forbes, Oct. 26, 1714 to Thomas Hill who owned land adjacent to same and who may have been a grandson of Col. Hill by his first wife. (D. B. 2, 1704-15).

The above mentioned "Plantation of William Thomas" does not appear to be the one Mrs. Hill deeded to William Thomas for his life, as he outlived her. It seems to be the plantation he "Formerly lived upon" which was adjoining the one she gave him. The one given to William Thomas seems to be the one deeded later by his son John in 1719.

The 300 acres bought by Thomas Hill is mentioned in his will, dated May 23, 1719, as follows: "I give and bequeath the plantation I now live on, together with all my land bought from Mr. ALEXANDER FORBES containing by estimation 300 acres formerly belonging to Mrs. SILVESTRA HILL, I give the whole tract to my son THOMAS HILL and for want of heirs to my son JOSEPH HILL, then to daus. ANN and MARY; to son THOMAS pistole, belt, trumpet and colors and silver headed cane, except things given by my mother unto my children, son THOMAS to come of age or marry."

That Col. Hill had other children living at the time Silvestra died is shown in a deed made in 1710 by Ralph Hill of Prince George and Nicholas Hill of Norfolk, son and heir of Ralph. They sold the 70 acres in Surry that Col. Hill had bought from Peter Greene in 1666. (7 W (1) -262.) Thomas Hill could have been a second son of Ralph and therefore not an heir under the law of primogeniture.

Previous to this, in 1686, Ralph Hill and Hanna his wife sold to Nicholas Wilson a parcel of land at the head of Lawne's Creek (17c. -585). Also in 1688 Ralph sold to Henry Baker a parcel of land at George Hardy's mill. (do. -597). Richard Hill, son of Col. Nicholas, died before 1680. (do. -585.).

A further connection between the Hill and Thomas families is shown in the will of Humphrey Marshall made on Dec. 18, 1711. He gave three silver spoons to John Thomas, son of Elizabeth Thomas; and £ 20 to his mother Elizabeth Thomas. (G. B. 2-533) Mary Hill, wife of Thomas Hill of the above will, was a daughter of Humphrey Marshall.

In 1719, John Thomas of the Upper Parish of Isle of Wight, gent., had a lawsuit with Philip Wheadon and Sarah his wife concerning the boundries of their property. The suit was decided by an Isle of Wight jury. Sarah Wheadon was formerly Sarah Luck, the sister of John Jennings, Jr. Jennings' wife was Mary Hill, daughter of Silvestra and Col. Nicholas Hill, and heretofore stated. John Jennings, Jr. had bequeathed his wife's inherited property to his only son George who later died intestate. George's heir would be his only sister, Sarah (Luck) Wheadon.

On Nov. 7, 1719, "John Thomas of the Upper Parish of Isle of Wight, gent., deeded to Thomas Day" a plantation lying and being in the U. P. of Isle of Wight bounded as follows: Beginning at ye head line of the land whereon Thomas Day now liveth (Which land was purchased by him of William DeLoach and Elinor his wife, and Francis Lee) running south along a line of marked trees which parts this land from the land of James Burwell to a red oak on John Harrison's line and along the said line to a corner tree of John Murrey's and Philip Wheadon's in Bayly's Swamp and from thence to ye dividing line the jury made between the land of John Thomas and Philip Wheadon and his wife Sarah, and along the line to the head line of Thomas Day's to the planation whereon John Hobbs now liveth, now is in possession of said John Thomas. Nov. 7, 1719. Wits: Samuel Davis, Wm. Drew, John Chapman. (G. B. -321-22).

William Thomas held 250 acres in Isle of Wight in the Quit Rents of 1704. He was the only person named "Thomas" holding land in Isle of Wight or Surry. His last appearence in the records seems to be as a witness to a deed of John Thomas his brother, in 1710. (ante). He was evidently deceased by 1711, when his wife Elizabeth was mentioned in Humphrey Marshall's will. There is no record of the administration of his estate. Most of the order books of Isle of Wight are missing. The known children of William and Elizabeth Thomas were: (I) John, who is mentioned as a son of Elizabeth Thomas in Humphrey Marshall's will which is also proven by John Thomas' subsequent deed of 1719 to the Hill-Bennett lands; (II) Elizabeth, who married (1) John Boddie, (2) Col.

John Dawson.

(III) Barnaby Thomas, who in his will, 1735, calls Col. John Dawson his "brother in law", also mentions his "brother Philip Thomas. " The witnesses to his will were: William Thomas, John Dawson, and Jacob Thomas.

(IV) Phillip, who was mentioned as a "brother" in the will of Barnaby Thomas.

(V) William, who was closely associated with the other four children in North Carolina.

(See below #I to V consecutively.)

Children of Elizabeth (Hill) and William Thomas.

I. John. After the sale of the Bennett-Hill lands in 1719, heretofore mentioned, John Thomas moved with his three brothers and his sister, Elizabeth-Boddie-Dawson to the fertile river valleys of North Carolina and settled in what was Bertie county, now Northampton. He married Anne Cotton, Daughter of John and Martha (Godwin) Cotton. John Cotton made his will in Bertie in 1728 and mentioned his son in law "Captain John Thomas". John Cotton's children named in the will were, John, William, Thomas, Samuel, James, Arthur, Joseph, Alexander, Priscilla, Susanna, and Ann who married Captain John Thomas.

James Cotton, son of John and Martha Cotton, made his will in Bertie County Jan. 14, 1758, same was probated April 1758. He gave "plantation where I now live" to son James, and legacies to other sons, Henry, Solomon, Theophilus, and daughter Christian Cotton. Wife and executrix, Sarah, with brothers Arthur and John Cotton, executors. Wits.: Samuel Cotton, Thomas Roche, Mary Roche. (Grimes 78.)

Samuel Cotton, the above witness and also brother of James, made his will in Northampton, Jan. 16, 1774 probated May 18, 1774. He gave son Samuel his manor plantation, and legacies to son John Cotton and Thomas Thomas. Executrix was wife Lidia together with Robert Hilliard, executor. Wife's children: Elizabeth Cotton Ewell, Sally Cotton Ewell, Roderick Cotton Ewell, were mentioned. (Grimes 83). Samuel, Jr., had a son named Micajah Thomas Cotton.

Solomon Cotton and Samuel Cotten were mentioned in the will of Micajah Thomas, Jr. in 1788. (see later).

Martha Cotton, wife of John, Sr., by Nov. 10, 1731 had married Wm. Green. They prayed for a division of John Cotton's estate according to his will. Capt.

Thomas Bryant and William Bennett were executors. (O. B.)

The three brothers, John, Philip, and William Thomas, had the following acreage in the Quit Rents in Bertie in 1729-32, John 200, Philip, 337, William, 170. (N. C. Col. Rec. 22, p. 243.)

On May 1, 1736, William Evans sold John Thomas 350 acres east of Mill Creek swamp in Bertie for £ 35 (D. B. "D"-270.) On Dec. 8, 1736, for £ 80, John Thomas sold the 200 acres he held in 1732 to Isacc Sanders. Wit., Philip Thomas.

John Thomas made his will in Northampton March 18, 1745, pro. May 1746. He gave his plantation to his son Joseph and made his wife Ann his executrix. Witnesses were India Edwards, John Goodson, Matthew Lowry. Names are similar to those of his relatives and neighbors in Virginia. (Grimes -374)

On July 3, 1759, Joseph Thomas, gent., of St. George Parish, Northampton, and Anne his wife, sold to Wm. Fleming for £ 200, 350 acres which had been granted to Wm. Pope Apl. 1, 1723, who deeded same to William Evans and said Evans deeded to John Thomas, father of Joseph Thomas, and John Thomas in his last will left to his son Joseph. (D. B. 3 -25) On May 21, 1759, Joseph sold 100 acres to Thomas Godby. Wits. Barnaby Thomas.

The known children of John Thomas were (I) Joseph Thomas who moved to Johnston county, N. C. (2) Micajah Thomas of Edgecombe and Nash, probably eldest son and heir at law, was a wealthy man. His son, Micajah, Jr., willed property to his Cotton relatives.

A Joseph Thomas made his will in Edgecombe Oct. 15, 1757, pro. June court 1758. He names daughters, Mary, Priscilla, Charity, and Mourning. His wife Mourning and brother John Thomas were executrix and executor. Witnesses were Micajah Thomas and Mourning Thomas.

The Mourning Thomas who witnessed the will was not the testators wife as has been stated. She was the wife of Micajah Thomas. Also it will be noted that Joseph Thomas, son of John Thomas of Northampton, made a deed the year after this Joseph was deceased. He was probably a relative of Micajah's.

George Crudup, son of Mourning Crudup - Thomas by her first husband John Crudup, married Priscilla Thomas daughter of the above Joseph Thomas, May 3, 1761, in Edgecombe county. (Bible record) George Crudup made his will Mar. 21, 1764, and mentioned his wife,

Priscilla, brother Josiah, and daughter Mary Crudup.

Micajah Thomas' Bible is now in the possession of
Mrs. Jenkins Cooper of Nashville, N. C. and some of
the entries have been previously quoted. (Boddie Family p. 91). A few are mentioned below as follows:
"Micajah Thomas was born the 13th day of February
1725. He married Elizabeth Veale 11th day of April
1751 which Elizabeth Thomas died on the 7th day of
July 1752.

"Micajah Thomas was married to Mrs. Mourning
Crudup, October 9, 1753. Mourning Thomas was born
November 10th, 1722. "

Mourning Crudup was Mourning Dixon of Isle of Wight,
daughter of Penelope and Thomas Dixon. Thomas Dixon
made his will in Isle of Wight in 1747. (W. B. 5 -141)
This Thomas Dixon was the son of Thomas Dixon who
died in Isle of Wight in 1670 leaving wife Marie and sons
Thomas and Henry. An appraisal of this estate was
sworn to Oct. 25, 1670, by Henry Martin who had married the relict. (17c -220)

Mourning Dixon's first husband was John Crudup who
died in 1752. She presented the inventory of his estate
Aug. 1753. Mourning Crudup then married Captain Micajah Thomas who died in 1769. She then married James
Smith. By her first husband, John, Crudup, she had
George, Josiah and Chloe Crudup. By her second she
had Bathesheba and Micajah Thomas, Jr.

Chloe Crudup was reared by her mother and step-
father, Micajah Thomas, Sr. Micajah's step-daughter,
Chloe Crudup, in 1760 married Nathaniel Boddie.

The deaths of Mourning Smith and her daughter Chloe
Boddie are recorded in the Thomas Bible.

"Mourning Smith, mother of Micajah Thomas, 2nd,
deceased on Friday on the 29th of June, A. D. 1781,
about six o'clock in the afternoon. She died of a flux -
sick thirteen days. "

Chloe Boddie did not long survive her mother. "Chloe
Boddie died of the Hysterical fever enjoined with a -
fever on Wednesday the 12th of September, 1781, about
eight o'clock at night. She lingered near seven months. "

The births and deaths of the children of Mourning and
Micajah Thomas are recorded in the Bible as follows:
"Bathesheba Thomas, born November 3rd, 1754, died
April 12, 1770. Micajah Thomas, Jr., born January
3, 1757. Captain Micajah Thomas deceased November
14, 1769. "

Micajah Thomas, Jr., married Ann Hawkins sister of U. S. Senator Benjamin Hawkins. Their marriage and children are shown as follows:

"Micajah Thomas married Anne Hawkins 7th day of June, 1778. She was born the 5th of June, 1754.

"Basheba Thomas, daughter of Micajah Thomas and Ann his wife was born 19th of September, 1778, and died 23 November, 1778, about one o'clock.

"Philemon Hawkins Thomas, son of Micajah Thomas and Ann his wife was born 19th day of February, 1780, and died the 10th of June, 1780, about midnight, of convulsions.

"Anne Thomas deceased on Monday the 12th day of March about twelve o'clock in the forenoon in 1781. She dyed of the most violent consumption which had been seized upon her for the space of two years but blessed with her senses until the last moment. Parson Crupples preached the funeral service over her on Wednesday the 2nd of May. He took for his text out of the fourth chapter of First Thessalonians and 18th verse, 'wherefore comfort one another' ".

Captain Micajah Thomas, Sr., represented Edgecombe in the Provincial Congress. He made his will Dec. 4, 1769, pro. Feb., 1770, as follows: "wife Mourning, negroes and use of plantation where I now live and one other plantation on Tar River bought from Thomas Kearney, also use of the other plantation bought of Thomas Pollard. To dau. Bathesheba negroes and the tract bought of Thomas Henderson and two bought of William Harris lying on Peach Tree creek in Edgecombe containing 1340 acres, also one other tract bought of Willoughby Tucker, 200 A. on Back swamp, 100 A. bought from Peter Hedgepath on Pig Basket, 700 bought from Joshua Wombell, 540 from Thomas Richardson.

To son Micajah all the land not given away and remaining negroes. Elisha Battle and Nathan Boddie, exrs. Wits: Duncan Lamon, Nathan Boddie, William Boddie. "

Micajah Thomas, Jr., married, first, Elizabeth Crafford of Surry county, Va., June 5, 1776. (Col. Surry - 220). His second wife was Ann Hawkins whom he married Jan. 7, 1778. She was a sister of Col. Benjamin Hawkins, the first United States Senator from North Carolina. Micajah Thomas, Jr., represented Nash county in the General Assembly from 1784 to 1787.

Wheeler, in his "History of North Carolina" (p. 430), has the following to say about Micajah Thomas, "As an additional evidence of Col. Benjamin's disinterestedness, Micajah Thomas, Jr., who had married his sister Ann and received by her a handsome patrimony, and who (Ann) had died long before leaving no child, and was a man of very large fortune sent especially for Col. Hawkins, when upon his death bed, to visit him. He told him upon his arrival that he had sent for him to write his will and give him a large portion of his estate. Mr. Thomas was surrounded by many respectable friends at that time. Col. Hawkins told him he would write no such will; that he valued his friendly feelings thus expressed, but that he was sufficiently provided for, and as Mr. Thomas had blood relations he advised him to give his estate to them. When Mr. Thomas found he could not get him to accept of the offered legacy he entreated him to accept of five hundred guineas, which he also positively refused, and he wrote his will <u>giving his property to his relatives.</u> "

Mr. Thomas' will was a very long one. Among his relatives he remembered George Boddie with 5000 acres and gave 1000 acres and two years schooling to Solomon Cotton, his first cousin.

His will was dated and probated in 1788 (pp. 32-35). He bequeathed to, "my half brother Josiah Crudup one sorrel horse raised on my plantation near Capt. Samuel Bryants, and wearing apparel; to my niece Mourning Arrington two negroes, to my niece Rhoda Ricks small negro girl and bay mare; to my nieces Temperance and Mary Perry a suit of mourning; to my father-in-law Philemon Hawkins, negroes; to my daughter Mary Crawford, child of the late Elizabeth Crawford (Crafford) in Surry County, Virginia, all my slaves on the north side of the Roanoke River in Northampton county and land which I purchased of Samuel Cotton and estate of Frederick Ruffin containing 1500 acres; if she dies before marriage then to Margaret Thomas Jackson, if she dies to her sisters Mourning Thomas and Temperance Thomas Jackson. XXX. To - King 200 acres; to Solomon Cotton 1000 acres and two years schooling; to nephew George Boddie 5000 acres in Tennessee; to nephew Bennett Boddie a gray mare and my favorite gray horse. "XXX.

II. Elizabeth, daughter of William and Elizabeth (Hill) Thomas, m. (1) John Boddie of Isle of Wight who died 1720, (2) Col. John Dawson. Her children by her first husband were John and William Boddie who came to North Carolina with their mother and step-father Colonel John Dawson.

William Boddie married Mary Bennett, daughter of Captain William Bennett of Northampton heretofore mentioned as an executor of John Cotton's estate.

William and Mary Boddie were the parents of Nathaniel Boddie who married Chloe Crudup, step-daughter of Micajah Thomas, Sr.

Explanation of some relationships shown in
the will of Micajah Thomas, Jr.

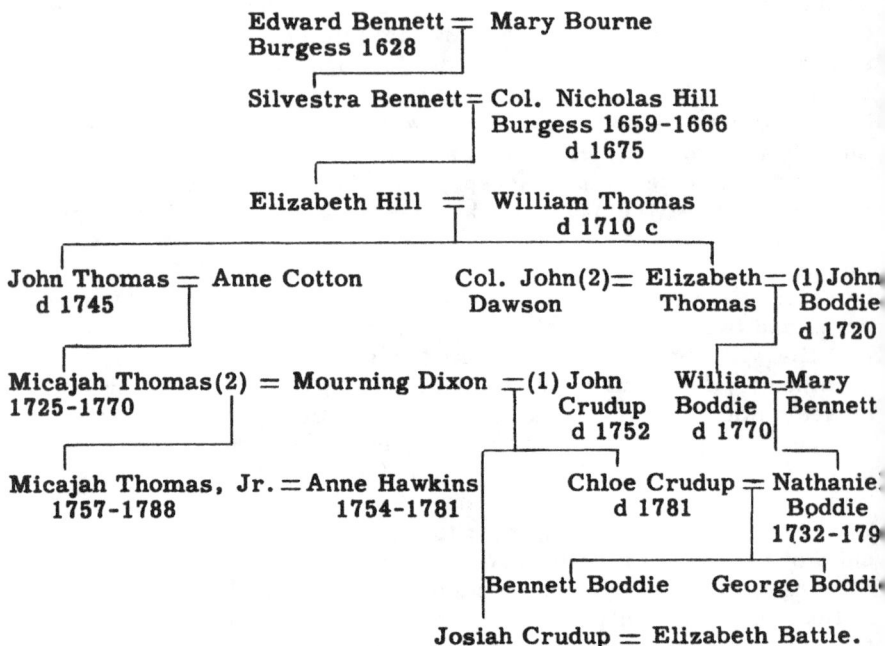

```
        Edward Bennett ═ Mary Bourne
        Burgess 1628
        ┌─────────────┘
      Silvestra Bennett ═ Col. Nicholas Hill
                          Burgess 1659-1666
                             d 1675
        ┌───────────────────┘
      Elizabeth Hill  ═  William Thomas
                            d 1710 c
  ┌─────────────────────────┴─────────────────────────────┐
John Thomas ═ Anne Cotton          Col. John(2)═ Elizabeth ═(1)John
   d 1745                             Dawson       Thomas  │ Boddie
                                                           │ d 1720
  ┌──────────┘                             ┌───────────────┘
Micajah Thomas(2) ═ Mourning Dixon ═(1)John   William═Mary
1725-1770                            Crudup   Boddie │ Bennett
                                     d 1752   d 1770 │
  ┌───────────────┘                                  │
Micajah Thomas, Jr. ═ Anne Hawkins   Chloe Crudup ═ Nathaniel
   1757-1788          1754-1781         d 1781       Boddie
                                                   1732-179

                     Bennett Boddie    George Boddie

           Josiah Crudup ═ Elizabeth Battle.
```

III. Barnaby Thomas, m. Sarah_____. On March 16,
     1723, he paid £ 15 to Lazarus Whitehead for 250
     acres in Bertie Precinct (D.B. "A" 83). In 1726 he
     bought land from Col. John Dawson, his brother in
     law. (D.B. "B" - 95). On Aug. 2, 1729, he patented
     170 acres in Bertie in the woods north of Morratock.
     (G.B. 3 - 211).

         Barnaby made his will in Bertie Oct. 5, 1735,
     same probated Dec. 11, 1735, as follows: "as to
     all my barren cattle my will is that my brother Philip
     sell same for ready money or a slave. I give my ne-
     groes to be equally divided between my son Elisha
     Thomas my planation whereon I now live. As for my
     plantation where Mary and Josuah Lamb now dwelleth
     if they fail to make payment according to reasonable
     time after notice to be given them by my brother in
     law John Dawson then I give plantation to my child
     unborn. I give use of my plantation to my wife Sarah
     for twenty years. my children to have schooling to
     be paid out of my estate. my loving brother Philip
     Thomas to be sole executor. Teste. William Thomas,
     John Dawson, Jacob Carr.

Children:

1. Elisha of Northampton on May 12, 1760, for £ 70 sold to Britton Dawson of Southampton Co., Va., 170 acres granted to Barnaby Thomas Aug. 1, 1729, adjoining John Bridgers. (D.B. 3-72). Elisha moved to Johnston County, N.C. in 1761.

2. Barnaby was the unborn child mentioned in Barnaby Thomas' will, 1735. On Sept. 7, 1762, Barnaby Thomas deeded 200 acres to Solomon Pace in Northampton, "part of a tract said Thomas' father bought of John Dawson." (Do., 206.)

IV. Philip was executor of his brother Barnaby's will in 1735. On Sept. 8, 1722, Philip patented 337 acres in Yamahaw Woods, beginning at a white oak on Henry Sims' corner. (G.B. 3-). This tract was sold later by his son, Mathew Thomas. In 1739 Philip was overseer of the road from Bridger's Creek to Wheeler's Mill. On May 1, 1736, he witnessed a deed from William Evans to John Thomas for 350 acres east of Mill Creek Swamp in Bertie. (D.B. "B." -270.)

On July 22, 1739, Philip Thomas, "living in Bertie," for £ 40 bought 180 acres from William Thomas (See William Thomas), being half of the tract granted Henry Sims by patent March 1, 1719, lying in Wamahaw Woods north side of Moratuck Woods. Wits. John Dawson, John Boddie. (Bk. E-474.) This tract of 360 acres had been sold by Henry Sims to William Thomas Aug. 20, 1722, and evidently joined upon the land of his brother Philip. (Bk. A-2.)

Philip was deceased before February 16, 1749.

Children:

1. Mathew evidently was the oldest son of Philip, for on Feb. 27, 1749, he sold to Philip Winbourne for £ 50 337 acres which belonged to his father, Philip Thomas, decd. (D.B. I, 259.) On Oct. 4, 1756, he also sold to Philip Winbourne the 180 acres deeded Philip Thomas by William Thomas (Do.-372.) Also, on February 26, 1749, he paid William and Ann Hall a certain sum for the right of dower in the land of Philip Thomas, decd., father of the said Mathew in Northampton County. (Do-411) His mother had evidently married William Hall.

2. Philip was evidently another son, for on March 16, 1744/45 he patented land in Northampton county "beginning at a corner white oak in his FATHER PHILIP THOMAS' line and Richard Pace's to an oak tree on William Thomas' line, along line to said father's corner in William Thomas' line, then along father's line to beginning." (G.B. 5-149.)

V. William Thomas, m. Christian ----. On April 9, 1706, Thomas Joyner sold him 200 acres on Seacock Swamp in Isle of Wight County. (DB 2, 1704-16, p. 10.) This land was adjacent to the grant of 3350 acres to William Boddie in 1665 whose patent ran to the corner of Thomas Joyner. (17 c-682.)

William Thomas on Sept. 5, 1723, patented 290 acres on the east side of Seacock Swamp adjacent to "William Thomas' old lines and Thomas Williams and James Barnes." (G. B. XI. -257.) On the same day he also patented 130 acres on east side of Sea- cock Swamp to corner tree of Randell Revels. (Do. -259.)

William Thomas soon afterwards moved to North Carolina, for on the "2nd day of the 9th month, 1725," as "William Thomas of N. C.", he deeded Thomas Summerall 490 acres in Isle of Wight, 200 acres bought of Thomas Joyner in 1706 and 290 acres granted by patent Sept. 5, 1723. (Great Bk. - 724.) On Nov. 23, 1725, Christian Thomas, his wife, relinquished her dower rights (Do. -725). On August 20, 1722, Henry Sims of Chowan County, N. C., sold 360 acres in Bertie to "William Thomas of Isle of Wight." (A-2.) From September 29 to March , 1732, William Thomas was in arrears in Quit Rents for 337 acres in Bertie. (N. C. Col. Rec. 22, -243.)

In 1735 William Thomas witnessed Barnaby Thomas' will. On July 22, 1739, William Thomas sold to Philip Thomas "living in Bertie," for £ 40, 180 acres "being half of the tract granted Henry Sims by patent March 1, 1719, lying in Yamamaw Woods north side of Moratuck Woods. Wits. John Dawson, John Boddie". (E. -474.)

This deed was evidently made to his brother Philip and not to his son Philip as has been stated, for there was a consideration involved.

On October 4, 1745, he sold for £ 44 another 180 acres to Matthew Thomas (ante) "being the plantation I lately lived on." This was evidently the other half of the tract mentioned in the above deed. Matthew was a son of Philip.

William Thomas patented 200 acres in Bertie March 1, 1742/ 43. (G. B. 5 - 114.) He left a will which has been lost.

Children:
1. John. On February 29, 1756, John Thomas sold to Bartholomew Figures 100 acres, part of a patent granted Henry Charles, 1714, and devised to him by his father, WILLIAM THOMAS, in his last will and testament, situated on S. side of Meherrin River and north side of land granted Henry Charles. (B. 2, 1741-51, 259.)
2. Philip evidently moved out of the county, for on Jan. 4, 1762, as "Philip Thomas of Granville County, N. C.",

he sold to William Winbourne for £25,200 acres in Northampton County, "running to a white oak on his FATHER WILLIAM THOMAS' line", and Richard Paces, being a patent of March 1, 1742/43 and an estate of inheritance. (D.B. 3-174.)

NOTE:

Mr. Solomon Buxton Williams furnished the Bible records of the Bennett family shown in the "Bennetts" on Pages 85 and 86 of "Boddie and Allied families." Also the data in the footnote on page 305 of "17th Century Isle of Wight", and in the text of page 332 of the same book. His information seems to have been very correct.

He also at that time stated that the mother of William Boddie, (1710-1772) who married Mary, daughter of William Bennett, was also a "Bennett." He said that William Bennett's three daughters were "double Bennetts" and were called "the three Graces." (The youngest daughter was named "Grace".) The two Bennett families, according to his narrative, came from London, and were kin.

It now seems this information was incorrect only in the respect that William Boddie's grandmother was a "Bennett", and not his mother.

He said this information came from his own mother. At the time his long ago notes were read it was considered best not to leave anything to tradition. (See last phrase of preface to "Boddie and Allied Families.": "...nothing is left to tradition.")

A book called "The Lost Tribes of Carolina" has much erroneous information on the Thomas and Hawkins families. The descendents of the Thomas families of Isle of Wight, Nansemond, and Surry are mixed together. No authorities are shown or citations given. They are so involved there is no object in mentioning them.

However, the ancestry of the Hawkins family of Granville appears incorrect. (p. 287.) Philemon Hawkins probably came from Spottsylvania County, Virginia, for on November 16, 1742, Joseph Hawkins, son and heir of John Hawkins, late of Spotts., made a deed to his brother PHILEMON HAWKINS of said county. Joseph stated that the last will of John Hawkins was recorded in King William. He mentions his mother, Mary Hawkins, George Smith and Elizabeth, his wife, and Phebe Hawkins.

This family probably connects with Hawkins of Spotts. and Orange. (I T 255.) Capt. Thos. Hawkins (d. 1677) was Burgess from Warwick, and John Hawkins (d. 1726) Burgess from Essex.

Edward Jones' will was proved in Warren Co., N.C. in April, 1750. He names wife Abigail and children: Sugar, James, Edward, Daniel, Sarah Obedience, Kabon and Priscilla Mason. ("Lost Tribes," p. 216.) Sugar Jones' will was probated in Granville July 15, 1761.)

In "Lost Tribes" it is stated that "The name of Edward Jones' wife was Abigail Sugre, a member of a Huguenot family at Manikintown," and that Edward Jones came from Richmond County, Va.

Now on page 32 of Blanch Adams-Chapman's abstracts of "Isle of Wight Wills" is the will of Jonn Sugars (sometimes spelled "Sheugar"), recorded September 25, 1727. His legacies were: daughter, Elizabeth Bynum, daughter ABIGAIL JONES' land upon which EDWARD JONES lives; dau. Priscilla; grandson SUGAR JONES, wife Elizabeth.

The above John Sugars is probably the John Sugar or Shugar who married about 1680 (1) Elizabeth, relict of Thomas Clay in Surry. (W. B. 2, p. 40.) His second wife was also named "Elizabeth." She was the widow of John Drew. (B. K. -1711, p. 48.)

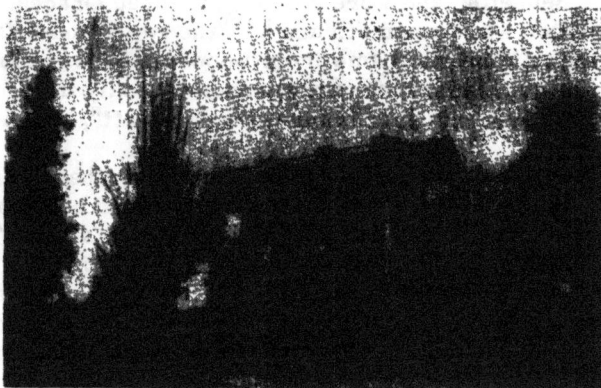

Rose Hill

BENNETT - BODDIE CHART

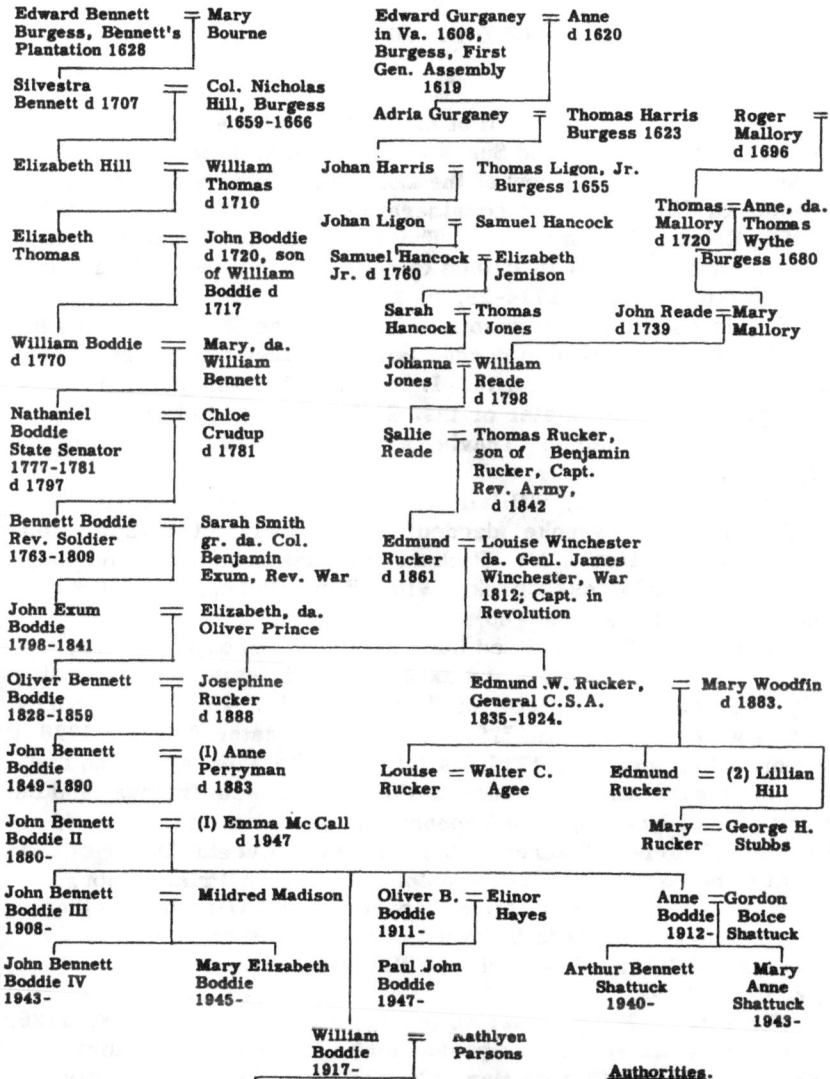

Edward Bennett = Mary Bourne
Burgess, Bennett's
Plantation 1628

Edward Gurganey = Anne d 1620
in Va. 1608,
Burgess, First
Gen. Assembly
1619

Silvestra Bennett d 1707 = Col. Nicholas Hill, Burgess 1659-1666

Adria Gurganey = Thomas Harris, Burgess 1623   Roger Mallory d 1696

Elizabeth Hill = William Thomas d 1710

Johan Harris = Thomas Ligon, Jr. Burgess 1655

Thomas Mallory d 1720 = Anne, da. Thomas Wythe Burgess 1680

Elizabeth Thomas = John Boddie d 1720, son of William Boddie d 1717

Johan Ligon = Samuel Hancock

Samuel Hancock Jr. d 1760 = Elizabeth Jemison

William Boddie d 1770 = Mary, da. William Bennett

Sarah Hancock = Thomas Jones

John Reade d 1739 = Mary Mallory

Johanna Jones = William Reade d 1798

Nathaniel Boddie State Senator 1777-1781 d 1797 = Chloe Crudup d 1781

Sallie Reade = Thomas Rucker, son of Benjamin Rucker, Capt. Rev. Army, d 1842

Bennett Boddie Rev. Soldier 1763-1809 = Sarah Smith gr. da. Col. Benjamin Exum, Rev. War

Edmund Rucker d 1861 = Louise Winchester da. Genl. James Winchester, War 1812; Capt. in Revolution

John Exum Boddie 1798-1841 = Elizabeth, da. Oliver Prince

Oliver Bennett Boddie 1828-1859 = Josephine Rucker d 1888

Edmund .W. Rucker, General C.S.A. 1835-1924. = Mary Woodfin d 1883.

John Bennett Boddie 1849-1890 = (I) Anne Perryman d 1883

Louise Rucker = Walter C. Agee

Edmund Rucker = (2) Lillian Hill

John Bennett Boddie II 1880- = (I) Emma McCall d 1947

Mary Rucker = George H. Stubbs

John Bennett Boddie III 1908- = Mildred Madison

Oliver B. Boddie 1911- = Elinor Hayes

Anne Boddie 1912- = Gordon Boice Shattuck

John Bennett Boddie IV 1943-   Mary Elizabeth Boddie 1945-

Paul John Boddie 1947-

Arthur Bennett Shattuck 1940-   Mary Anne Shattuck 1943-

William Boddie 1917- = Kathlyen Parsons

Jill Kathryn Boddie b. Jan. 5, 1954

Authorities.
1. 17th Century I. of W., pp. 319-374.
2. Ligon Family, pp. 326-328; 553-560.
3. Thomas Family, herein.

GRIFFIS OF SUSSEX

Thomas Griffis, the first of his family in Sussex, was deeded land in Prince George and Surry (later Sussex) as follows: "John Nickeels, late of Va., now of the London merchants, deeds to Thomas Griffis of Va., in consideration of £ 100, sterling, paid by Mr. Robert Hodson for Mr. Thomas Griffis, 450 acres, lying part in Surry and part in Prince George, north side of main Blackwater Swamp. (P. G. 1714-28, p. 206).

Travis Morris, later mentioned in Thomas Griffis' will as his "brother in law" was also deeded land in Prince George about the same time as Thomas Griffis. It is difficult to tell whether Morris married Griffis' sister or that Griffis married his sister. Griffis had a son named "Travis" and Morris had a son named "Griffis".

On Dec. 12, 1715, William Short and Elizabeth, his wife, of P. G. Parish of Wyanoke, deeded Travis Morris of the same 100 acres along the line of Mr. Richard Pidgeon and Thomas Adams, then to mouth of Cross Creek. Wits. Wm. Bishop, Robert Short, Thomas Harrison. (do. -86)

Thomas Griffis appointed his wife and his brother-in-law, Travis Morris, executrix and executor of his estate, so he probably married, Mary, sister of Travis Morris. He moved to Surry County where he died in 1726. His will was dated April 8, 1726, and probated Sept. 21, 1726, as follows: "to wife Mary land and plantation extending to Frenchman's Branch; son Thomas land on other side of Branch, also Troopers arms and saddle; sons Edward and Travis 100 acres of land on Three Creeks in Isle of Wight to be equally divided; son John all land in Prince George; daus. Jane, Mary and Elizabeth, personalty. Wife and brother-in-law Travis Morris to be executors. Wife to have care of children until 21. Wits: Edward Holloway, Thos. Eldridge." (Bk. 7, p. 649).

His widow, Mary, married Gilbert Hay, for on Oct. 19, 1726, inventory of his estate was presented by Mary Hay, executrix. (Bk. 7, p. 650). Gilbert Hay, who had no children, evidently raised his young step-children and survived his wife. His will was probated in Surry April 18, 1758. (Wills 1754-58, part 1, p. 138). He seems to have given his step-children property inherited from their mother and then remembered his own relatives.

He gave to his "son-in-law" (step-son) John Griffis 2 negroes;
"to Thomas Griffis, son of Edward Griffis, my plantation in Sussex
whereon Edward Griffis now lives with 125 acres of land. *** To
Betty Prince, wife of Nicholas Prince, the labor of 3 negroes
during her life, also feather bed, rug, a mare and filly and a chest.
To my cousin (nephew) Gilbert Hay, son of Charles Hay, 125
acres in Sussex joining the land I first gave Thomas Griffis, it
being the lower end of my land. *** To Nathan Prince one negro girl
after his mother's decease. *** To Nicholas Prince one negro boy,
after his mothers decease; To Jane Jarrett, wife of Nicholas Jarrett my negro boy Robin. To my sister Ruth Slowman, wife of
William Slowman, a negro boy. To Stephen Johnson one feather
bed, etc. To James Holloway, son of John Holloway, my best
horse. To Mary Weaver, wife of Edward Weaver, a negro girl.
To Edith Griffis, dau. of Thomas Griffis, feather bed, etc. To
brother Richard Hay my still. To Betty Tatum, one negro boy.
Rest of estate not devised to be sold and proceeds equally divided
among my godchildren, Gilbert Hay, Lucy Cotton, Richard Cor-
lisby, Jane Jarrett, Stephen Johnson, James Holloway, Lucy Griffis
and Betty Prince. Exrs., Edward Weaver, James Holloway. Wits.
Wm. Cooke, James Cooke, John Johnson.

Children of Thomas and Mary Griffis:
    I. Thomas, made his will in Sussex in 1764.
   II. Edward, m. Catherine_____. Gilbert Hay gave his son
       Thomas a plantation. Edward Griffis' will was probated
       1763, on Jan. 4th. He mentions his wife, Catharine, and
       son, Thomas Griffis. Wit. Henry Ivey, Richard Hay,
       Frances Hay.

Children from Register:
     1. Thomas, b. Sept. 5, 1749.
     2. Edward, b. Dec. 26, 1753.
     3. John, b. Feb. 2, 1755.
     4. William, b. Mar. 8, 1758.
     5. Ede, b. Mar. 26, 1761.

   III. John, lived in Prince George.

   IV. Travis, m. Ann, dau. of John SLEDGE. He patented
       146 acres in Sussex in 1756.

Children from Register:
     1. Rebecca, b. April 29, 1751.
     2. Allen, b. Nov. 16, 1758.
     3. Joshua, b. Mar. 9, 1762.

V. Jane, m. Nicholas Jarrett.

Children from Register:
1. Mary, b. Dec. 18, 1750.
2. Lucy, b. June 6, 1753.
3. Henry, b. Sept. 12, 1755.
4. Nancy, b. Oct. 16, 1762.

VI. Mary, m. Edward Weaver, son of John Weaver and
_____COOK. Edward Weaver's will was probated in
1772.

Children from Register:
1. Edward, b. Feb. 7, 1738, will pro. 1777.
2. Susanna, b. June 6, 1741.
3. Travis, b. Mar. 18, 1743.
4. Amy, b. Sept. 17, 1746.
5. Lucy, b. Sept. 29, 1749.
6. William, b. Nov. 16, 1752.
7. Winney, b. Oct. 12, 1755.
8. John, b. Feb. 26, 1760.

VII. Elizabeth, m. Nicholas PRINCE. Two children, Nathan
and Nicholas Prince are mentioned in Gilbert Hay's will.

EXPLANATION
of the
PECHE-CORNISH-EVERARD-MILDMAY CHART

The Peche family became Barons by writ in the time of Edward I, and therefore are shown in the Peerage of England. Also, they were Knights in the days of Edward I and appear in the "Knights of King Edward", published by the Harleian Society.

Hamon Peche, who died about 1185, married Alice, daughter of Robert Peverell. She was the second of four sisters who became co-heirs of their brother, William Peverell. (The Complete Peerage by G. E. Cokayne, vol. X, p. 333) (Knts. King Ed. I, Harl Soc. Vol. 83, p. 23).

Gilbert Peche, his eldest son, who died in 1212, married Alice, daughter of Walter Fitz Robert and sister of Robert Fitzwalter, the famous Magna Carta Baron.

Hamon, son of Gilbert, died in 1241. He married "Eve, a foreigner". (G. E. C.)

Gilbert Peche, their son, married first, Maude de Hastings, secondly Joan, daughter of Simon de Creye and widow of Richard de Dover. (do). Maude de Hastings was the elder daughter of

Henry de Hastings who married Ada, daughter of David, Earl of Huntington, son of David I, King of Scotland, 1124-1153. (do).

Gilbert Peche, eldest son of Gilbert by his first wife, Maude, was summoned to Parliament as Lord Peche, 1299. He married Isolde, and died in 1322. His eldest son, Gilbert, 2nd. Lord Peche died leaving a son, Roger, 3rd. Lord, who died in 1360 without heirs. The Barony fell in abeyance between the heirs of his sister Katherine. (do)

Sir Simon Peche, second son of Gilbert, 1st. Lord Peche, was given the manor of Great Thrillowe in Suffolk and 1/2 of a Knights fee in Polingsworth by his father. (Harl. 83, p. 24) He was living about 1350, and married Agnes, daughter of Sir Simon Holme. Margaret, their daughter and sole heir married John Hunt. (Harl. 13, p. 8) Morant, the Essex historian, says John Hunt held 1/2 of a knights fee in Springfield, 1358-1370 (Vol. 1, pg. 173). Iodena Hunt, his daughter, married Thomas Cornish. (Harl. 13, pg. 8) Morant says that a John Cornish held a moiety of the Manor of Langleys in 1398. He also says that on Jan. 7, 1515, another John Cornish, son and heir of John Cornish, son and heir of Thomas Cornish and Iodena his wife conveyed their part of the manor to Thomas Everard who had married his daughter and sole heir. (Morant, 2, p. 87)

In 1450 a pardon was issued to Thomas Cornish and John Cornish of Great Waltham, Essex; also to Thomas Bedell and William Everard for their engagement and conflict in the late rebellion against the King. (P.R. 1450, p. 370.) This may have been Jack Cade's rebellion, or the opening of the War of the Roses.

The above William Everard married Isabel Bedell. He was the grandfather of Thomas Everard who married Joan, granddaughter of Thomas Cornish. (Visitation of Essex, Harl. 13, p. 8) The Visitations, however, show only one "John Cornish" in the pedigree, leaving out one other intervening John Cornish mentioned by Morant in his deed of Jan. 7, 1515, which makes Joan the great granddaughter. (See Chart.)

The last John Cornish, the one who made the deed of 1515, was evidently the John Cornish who received a grant for life of the office of the Keeper of the Park of Hatfield Bradock, Essex, "sometime of Humfrey, late Duke of Buckingham." (P.R. 1484 p. 378).

On May 16, 1482, Thomas Everard sold a part of the Manor of Langleys (Merant 2, p. 86.) This may have been the moiety held by John Cornish in 1398.

Thomas Everard's daughter, Mary, married Walter Mildmay of Writtle, in Essex. (Harl. 13, p. 193) This agrees with the pedigree of Mildmay, which shows that Walter Mildmay of Writtle, living in 1483, married a daughter of Thomas Everard of

Much Waltham. (Har. 13, p. 250) and also Visitation, 1634 (Burke's Peerage, 1938, p. 1737). The pedigree also shows that his father Thomas Mildmay, living in 1465, married Margery, daughter of John Cornish of Much Waltham. Evidently, Walter Mildmay married his first or second cousin.

An effort to verify the Mildmay ancestry shown in the Mildmay pedigree previous to Thomas Mildmay, was without success. Not a one could be found mentioned in the Calendar of State Papers. It was seemingly artificially constructed.

Sir Thomas Mildmay, of Chelmsford, in Essex, son of Walter and Mary (Everard) Mildmay, was Auditor of the Court of Augementations at the time Henry VIII confiscated the Monasteries. He augmented his fortune extensively by acquiring such property, which also founded the fortunes of many other noble families in England. He married Anne Reade, and died in 1566. She died in 1557.

John Mildmay, third son of Sir Thomas, is said to have married Joan, daughter of Sir Giles Allington. (Vis. 1612, Harl. 13, p. 250) However, on acquiring a copy of the will of Sir Giles Allington, (P. C. C. Windsow 49) it was found that his daughter married Henry Mildmay and not John. Henry was John's brother. John married, instead, Frances, daughter of Rainbow of Ipswich. (Vis. Essex 1634). Thomasine Mildmay, their daughter, married John Boddie, "sea captain of Queen Elizabeth". He died in 1591 and his son married his first cousin, Mary Mildmay. (See 17th. Cent. Isle of Wight for descendants).

Explanation of Harcourt-Crispe Chart.

The Harcourt generations down to and including Sir John Harcourt, d. 1330, are verified in The Peerage by G. E. Cokayne. The generations beginning with Henry Crispe of Stanlake who married Matilda, da. of Sir John Harcourt, down to Margaret Crispe who married John Crayford of Mongeham, are according to the pedigree of "Crispe" in Harleian, vol. 42, p. 73, and Berry's Kent. The pedigree in Berry's Kent is correct, according to a certified copy of the original (in Latin) made 1619 by John Philipot, Rouge Dragon. (College of Arms MS. C-16, p. 166).

The Crispe lineage may have been made by Philipot from documents then in possession of the family. The marriage between Matilda Harcourt and Henry Crispe is not verified by the Peerage, but very often daughters were not mentioned in the early pedigrees. The Crispe family lived in the County of Oxford near the Harcourts and the names in the Crispe pedigree are not fictious for reference to the Calendar of State Papers of England finds that the persons named therein were living at the times stated. A search for additional evidence is being made by interested persons.

PECHE-CORNISH-EVERARD-MILDMAY-HARCOURT-CRISPE CHART

```
DAVID I, King  =         Walter Bigod   = Ida
SCOTLAND,                Earl of Norfolk,
1124-1153               M.C.B. d 1221.

David, Earl of  = Maude, da.    Margaret = William    Sair de     = Margaret, da.
Huntington        Hugh, Earl    Bigod      de         Quincy        Robert, de
d 1219            of Chester               Hastings.  1st Earl      Beaumont,
(See Aston Chart)                                     Winchester,   3rd Earl
                                                      M.C.B.        Leicester
Ada, de        = Sir Henry Hastings                   d 1219.       d 1196
Huntington       d 1250                                             (See Mallory
                               Arabella  = Sir Richard Harcourt      Chart)
                               de Quincy   d 1228.

Maude de  = Gilbert       Hillary de  = Sir William Harcourt,
Hastings    Peche         Hastings      Stanton-Harcourt, Oxford.
            d 1291                      d 1258.

Gilbert, 1st Lord = Isolde    Richard de Harcourt  = Margaret, da.
Peche. d 1322.                d 1293.                Sir John Beke.

Sir Simon Peche  = Agnes, da. & heir   Sir John de  = Margaret, da. Eudo La
of Suffolk,        Sir Simon Holme     Harcourt       Zouche. (See Mallory
2nd son.                               d 1330.        Chart)

Margaret Peche  = John Hunt     Matilda de  = Henry Crispe, the elder,
da. & Heiress     d 1370.       Harcourt      of Stanlake, Oxford.
                                              (living in 1400, P.R.)

Iodena Hunt  = Thomas Cornish   John Crispe  = Anna, da. Wm. Phillips
               (living 1440-1450)  of Cobcotr

John Cornish =                  Henry Crispe  = Joan, da. Nicholas Dyer.
eldest son.

Margaret  = Thomas    John  = Agnes, da.   John Crispe  = Agnes, da. & sole
Cornish     Mildmay   Cornish  & sole heir  of Quekes in   heir of John
            (living 1465)       of Humfrey   Thanet, Kent.  Quekes of Quekes.
                                Walden.

    Mary  = Thomas Everard                John Crispe  = Avica, da. & heir
    Cornish  of Much Walton.              son & heir     Thomas Denne of
                                                         Kingstone.
Walter Mildmay  = Mary Everard
of Writtle, Essex                     Margaret Crispe  = (I) John Crayford
(living 1483)                                              of Mongeham
                                                          (See Crayford of Eng., Key Chart)
Sir Thomas Mildmay, of  = Anne Reade.
Chelmsford, Essex,        d 1557
    d 1566.

John Mildmay      = Frances, da.
3rd Son of          Rainbow
Critingham,         of Ipswich
d 1580

Thomasine  = John Boddie      Thomas  = Olive, da.
Mildmay      Sea Captain       Mildmay   Robert Nuttal
             d 1591

             Thomas Boddie  = Mary
             BricknacrePriory  Mildmay
             Essex, d 1627      d 1634

John Boddie  = Mary      Robert        Anne  = Richard
Ingatestone    b 1608    Boddie        Boddie  Heaward
d 1640                   b 1616                of Virginia
                         of Virginia
William Boddie
of Virginia
```

CRAYFFORD - CRAFFORD
of
GREAT MONGEHAM, KENT

The Crayfford family was long seated at Great Mongeham in
Kent. Hasted, in his History of Kent (Vol. IV, p. 137), says,
"The Crayford House, alias Stonehall, was a mansion, situated
a small distance westward of the church (of Great Mongeham).
For many descents (it) was the property and residence of the
family of Crayford, whose estates in this neighborhood were
very considerable. They were written in very ancient deeds, de
Mongeham Magna, and in more modern ones, of Great Mongeham.
In an old roll which gives an account of those Kentish gentlemen,
who were with Richard Nevill, Earl of Warwick, in the year 1460,
at the Battle of Northampton, fighting on behalf of the then vic-
torious House of York, mention is made of William Crayford,
esq.; who was then made knight banneret by K. Edward IV, for
his eminent service performed there, and at different times before; and bore for his arms: 'or, on a chevron sable, 3 eagle's
heads erased argent.' From this Sir William Crayford, knight-
banneret, the seat and estate descended down to William Crayford
of Great Mongeham, esq., who died possessed of it in K. Charles II's reign, and seems to have been the last of his family who
resided here."

The visitations of Bedford and Kent give the following line of
descent from the above Sir William Crayfford. (Harl 19, p. 167.)

1. Sir William Crayford, made a knight-banneret at the
   Battle of Northampton 1460, lived during the time of
   King Edward IV. His son was

2. Guy Crafford of Great Mongeham, who had

3. John Crafford of G. M. in Kent married a daughter of
   Monyngs and had

4. John Crafford of G. M. in Kent m. a daughter and heir
   of Edward Wood of London and had

5. John Crafford of G. M., Usher to the Privy Chamber
   of King Henry VIII, m. Margaret, dau. of John Crispe
   of Thanet, Kent, and had

6. Edward Crafford of G. M. m. Mary, dau. and heir of
   Henry Atsea of Herne, Kent, and had

7. Sir William Crafford of G. M., died 15 August 1623
   aged 68. He married Anne, daughter of John Norton

of London and Suffolk who died May 26, 1624. The arms of Norton were "azure, a manch? ermine." Hasted says, "In the 7th year of K. Edward VI, Sir William Craford of Mongeham, kt., son and heir of Edward Craford, by Mary, one of the sisters and co-heirs of Henry Atsea above mentioned was found to hold by inquisition the third part of all the lands and tenements that were Anthony Atsea's."

The children of Sir William and Anne, taken from parish register of Great Mongeham were as follows:

- I. Edward, bapt. June 24, 1577. (See later.)
- II. Thomas, bapt. Aug. 21, 1578, dsp.
- III. Sir William, bapt. August 20, 1579, of Ampthill in Bedford, Kt.; m. Margaret, dau. of Abraham Campion of London.
- IV. Anne, bapt. May 21, 1581; m. Aug. 2, 1591, John WARREN, gent., of Ripple Court. (See Warren.·)
- V. Margaret, bapt. Sept. 30, 1582.
- VI. Elizabeth, bapt. Dec. 1, 1683; m. Oct. 9, 1604, William Boetler or Butler of Higham Abbey near Rochester, Kent.
- VII. Alice, bapt. May 16, 1585; m. Jan. 13, 1613/14 John MERIWETHER of Sheperdswell, Kent.
- VIII. Aphera, bapt. June 22, 1587; m. Capt. Thomas Mansell of Vandy in Bucks.
- IX. John, bapt. Feb. 9, 1588/9, dsp.
- X. Sir Robert, bapt. Mar. 3, 1589/90, of London, m. Anne, dau. of Robert Russell of Grinsted in Norfolk.
- XI. Richard, bur. Jan. 22, 1608/9.

ABSTRACT of WILL of WILLIAM CRAYFORD

Con. 46 p. 66   Proved 22 August 1623

WILLIAM CRAYFORD of Great Mongeham, Knight.

Dame ANNE his wife to whom he wills all those Lands, Tenements, etc. which he had in Sholden by lease or by any other means, Conveyances from the Archbp. of Canterbury and all his interest and term of years in the same, to hold during her natural life towards the payment of his debts; and for the like purpose he gave and devised to her the rents and issues of all his Lands and Tenements etc. whatsoever as far as he could by Law devise to hold during her life - Mr. Robert Blechenden his uncle - his cosen George

Blechenden - his Grandchild Elwyn Mansell. And he wills that
after the decease of his wife, his son Robert should have all the
Messuages, Lands, Tenements, Leases, and terms of years heretofore bequeathed to his wife for her life as above, to hold to him
and his heirs for ever - to hold in Tail general remainder to his
cosen JOHN CRAYFORD and his assigns for evermore - his daughter Aphra wife of Thomas Mansell Esq. - His Grandchild Anne
Boteller.

In Definitive Sentence, pronounced 13 Dec. 1623, mention is made
of Sir William Crayford, Knight, junior; Robert Crayford of
Great Mongeham, Esq.; Anne Crayford als. Boys, wife of Edward
Boys, Gent., of Goodnestone; Alice Crayford als. Merriweather,
wife of John Merriweather of Shepherdswell, gent.; and also Affra
Crayford, als. Mansell wife of Thomas Mansell, gent.; the children of the said Sir William Crayford, Knight, senior, the Testator; and also William, George and Richard Crayford of the Parish
of Smeeth gents., John Crayford of Sutton by Dover, and Anne
Crayford of Ulcombe, the children of Edward Crayford, Esq., deceased, the son of the said Testator; as also Henry, Anne and Elizabeth Boteler the children of Elizabeth Boteler als. Crafford, deceased, the daughter of the said Testator.

Lady Anne Crayford's will was proven June 11, 1624 as follows:
(abstract) "DAME ANNE CRAYFORD, widow, late wife & sole ex-
ecutrix of the will of SIR WILLIAM CRAYFORD of Great Mongeham,
Knight, wills to be buried near to her said husband - ANNE WARREN
her grandchild - ANNE BOTELER her grandchild - her daughter
MANSELL - her grandchild EDWYN MANSELL - her son ROBERT
CRAYFORD her sole executor. Her grandchild, ELIZABETH,
wife of ABRAHAM HEGESON - Edmund Randolph a witness - signed
with her mark.
"A definitive sentence on the above will mentions SIR ROBERT
CRAYFORD, Knight, her son; SIR WILLIAM CRAYFORD, Knight;
ANNE CRAYFORD alias BOYS; ALICIAN CRAYFORD alias MER-
RIWEATHER; AFRA CRAYFORD alias MANSELL; children of the
said testatrix - GEORGE, RICHARD, JOHN, WILLIAM, and ANNE
CRAYFORD, children of EDWARD CRAYFORD, Esq., deceased,
son of the said testatrix - HENRY, ANNE, and ELIZABETH BOT-
ELER, children of ELIZABETH BOTELER alias CRAYFORD, de-
ceased, daughter of the said testatrix."

8. Edward Crafford, eldest son and heir of Sir William,
died before his father and was buried at Great Mongeham
Sept. 29, 1615. He married Anne, dau. of Sir Rowland
Hayward, thrice Lord Mayor of London. There is a
memorial to him in the church at Great Mongeham. It

depicts in Alabaster a man in armor and his wife kneeling at a faldstool, with five sons and one daughter below.

Children:

I. William, b. 1609; m. 1635 (1) Cordelia, dau. of Sir Roger Nevison, who died in 1673 by whom he left no surviving issue. He married (2) Ursula, dau. of William Horsemanden. His children by his first wife were Maria and Robert. He was the last of his line that resided at Great Mongeham. He was buried there July 19, 1676.

II. George, b. 1611, d. 1661; m. 1641, Margaret, dau. of Edward Boys of Betshanger.

Children:

1. Edward of Canterbury, m. Susan Peters, dau. of Dr. Peters of Canterbury, and died in 1713.
2. Margaret, m. John Bayley.
3. Robert of Canterbury, dsp. ?
4. George of Canterbury, m. Margaret_____.
5. Vincent, gent., m. Mary Howe April 10, 1676 at G. M. Cordelia, their daughter, was bapt. at G. M. Mar. 30, 1677 and bur. April 3, 1677.

III. Richard. Edward, son to Richard, was bapt. at G. M. Jan. 6, 1637/8.

IV. John, bur. Aug. 8, 1672.

V. Anne.

The spelling of this family in the Bedford Visitations is clearly shown as "Crayfford" and "Crafford" with the double "ff's". The latter spelling, the more modern version, "Crafford", is exactly the way the name was spelled in the Surry, Virginia records. Scribes, clerks, writers, and historians have persistently spelled the name with one "f", or changed the name altogether to "Crawford".

WARREN of KENT, ENGLAND
and
SURRY, VIRGINIA

The pedigree of the Warrens of county Kent, England, is well authenticated from the latter half of the fifteenth century. Their coat of arms - Azure, a cross, in each of the dexter chief and sinister base points a martlet, in each of the sinister chief and dexter base points a chaplet, all gold - appears in the catalogues of British arms for no other family than the Warrens of Dover and Ripple. There are reasons to believe that they were of foreign derivation and that these Warrens were descended from the Varennes (Guarennes) of Picardy, in France, who bore the similar, but simpler coat of - Gules, a cross gold (Dictionaire de la Noblesse ... France, tome 19). No evidence has been discovered connecting the family with the ancient Earls of Warren and Surrey, but it is quite possible that they were a cadet branch of the same Norman stock.

1. William[1] Warren was 'Chief Customer of Sandwich, Dover, and the Members thereof,' that is, principal customs officer of the Cinque Ports; and he is recorded in the municipal records as mayor of Dover in 1493. He died in 1506 and was buried in the church of St. Peter, Dover, 'within the Chapel of our Ladie ... before her image there.' After bequests toward the reparation of the parish church, and for a yearly obit to be said for him by the master and brethren of the Maison Dieu, William Warren left all of his 'houses and lands as well within the Towne, Port, & Libertie of Dover as within the Shyre of Kent, and alsoe ... lying in the Lordship of Marke & within the Marches of Calaye, to his wife, Joane, for life; with reversion to his son, John, in tail general. The visitation pedigrees confirm that the only surviving son of William Warren was:

    2. i. John

2. John[2] (William[1]) Warren married Jane, daughter of John Moninges of Waldershare, Kent, Esquire, by his wife, Battel Anstey. John Warren was three times mayor of Dover during the period 1525-1540 and sat for that town in three Parliaments between 1529 and 1541. He acquired lands called Greuawaye and Palmers in the parish of Ripple, Kent, in 1538; but he seems to have continued a resident of Dover, where he died in 1546, being interred with his father in the church of St. Peter. His

238

wife survived him for many years and by her will, proved in 1572, she provided for her burial in the Lady Chapel of St. Peter's, as near as might be to her husband, John Warren. Mrs. Jane Moninges Warren's principal beneficiaries were her son, Thomas Warren; James Brooker and Thomas Finneas, sons of her daughter, Elizabeth; and Mary, daughter of her deceased son, John Warren. Issue of John and Jane Moninges Warren.

- I. John; died before 1536 as evidenced by a reference in that year to the lands of his heirs, that is, his son, Edward, who died without issue, and his daughter, Mary, living in 1572:
- II. Elizabeth; married 1) Henry Brooker of Canterbury, Gentleman; 2) William Finneas of Huffam, Gentleman:
3. III. Thomas.

3. Thomas[3] (John[2], William[1]) Warren married Maria Christian, a daughter of the family of Close of Calais. He was born about 1510 and lived in Dover during most of his life; apparently he was that Thomas Warren who was 'Clerk of the Call' while Sandgate Castle was building in 1539-40. Thomas Warren was mayor of Dover for five terms and represented that town in five Parliaments during the period 1549 to 1575. He complained in his will that his wages for attending Parliament had not been paid and that he had to bear his own expenses at the coronation of Queen Elizabeth. Thomas Warren seems to have spent his latter years at Ripple, about five miles from Dover, and he was buried in the church of Ste. Mary the Virgin, Ripple, where a brass plate to his memory is inscribed:- 'Here lieth Buried the body of Thomas Warren/ Sonne of John Warren Esquier/ Who was sonne of William Warren Esqr/ sometymes chief Customer of Sandwich/ Dover & the Members thereof/ Which said Thomas died the XXIIII daye of Aprill/ Ao Dni 1591/ Being of thage of LXXX years.' On the brass appears the Warren arms quartering an unidentified coat consisting of a single six-pointed star. Other records evidence that the shield should be red and the star silver.

After the death of Thomas Warren it appears that his widow, Christian, did not wish to accept the legacy given her by Thomas, and threaten to sue her son John for a greater portion of his father's estate. This is related in a deposition made by Sir William Craford July 14, 1619, as follows:

Extract from
CATHEDRAL LIBRARY DEPOSITIONS Ref. X 11, 13, 197b.

Sir William Craford of Great Mongeham, born there, aged 64.

This deponent hath seen the last will and testament of THOMAS WARREN made by the testator 28 years ago or thereabouts immediately or not long before his death. The testator appointed his son JOHN WARREN to be his only executor.....

Legacies given to ANN MITCHELL als HOLMES....

When CHRISTIAN WARREN his widow came to know and understand that the said testator had given only £ 30 per annum for life she utterly refused to content herself with said gift and would not by any means stand unto her husband's will, but would sue her son JOHN WARREN and recover from him a far greater widow-right or dowry ....

"JOHN WARREN, greatly to content his said mother, and partly to avoid the danger of recoverye of her whole dowry, was compelled to fall to a composition and agreed to pay her £ 40 a year for life out of the testators lands during his life and after his death by ANNE WARREN executrix of said JOHN WARREN'S will. "

The only surviving issue of Thomas and Maria Christian Close Warren was:

4. I. John.

4. John[4] (Thomas[3], John[2], William[1]) Warren was born, probably at Dover, about 1561. There are references to him as a resident and parisioner of Ripple in 1595 and 1606.

John Warren is the only son of Thomas shown in the visitations. He predeceased his mother who mentioned only her "daughter in law, Anne, " his wife, in her will. John Warren married at Great Mongeham, Aug. 2, 1591, Anne, daughter of Sir William Crafford. She was baptized at Great Mongeham May 21, 1581.

An unusual circumstance that will be noted here is the age of Anne at her marriage. Twelve years was the legal age of marrige for girls in 17th century Virginia and probably in England. Anne may have been born a long time before her baptisim, maybe a year or more. She had a sister, Elizabeth, baptized Dec. 1, 1583 who married William Butler Oct. 9, 1604. (Great Mongeham registers). (See Crafford family).

It may be that these baptisms occurred a long time after birth, for if the family were Puritans the baptism of their children would probably be delayed until admonished by the parish priest. However, Anne Crafford married in 1591, ten years after her baptism, did not have a child until 1597, when she would have been sixteen.

Anne had twelve children by John Warren and had been a widow about seven years when she married her second husband

Edward Boys in 1621. At that time her age was stated in the marriage license to be "about 38", when in reality she was over 40.

John Warren was buried at Ripple, Jan. 24, 1612/13. On May 17, 1621, his widow married Edward Boys. The marriage license record is as follows: "Edward Boys the elder of Goodnestone, widower, about 40, and Anne Warren of Dover, widow, about 38; relict of John Warren deceased about 7 years since." (Cant. Marriages p. 123).

His monumental inscription there sets forth both his ancestry and the names of his children:- 'Here Lyeth Buried the body of /John Warren Esqr sonne of Thomas Warren Esqr/ Who was sonne to John Warren Esqr/ Who was sonne to William Warren Esqr/ Sometymes Chief Customer of Sandwich/ Dover & the Member thereof/ Which sayd John Warren dyed/ The 21 day of January 1612/ Being of the Age of 50 yeares and had Issue/ Willm.. Tho . John . Edward . and/ Elizabeth . Alice . Affrie/ Dead before him/ Jane . Mary . Battell . ' The quartered arms of Warren as above described are engraved upon the monument, impaling (Gold) on a chevron (vert) three hawk's heads erased (silver), for Crayford.

Children from Ripple Register:
I. William, bapt. Mar. 7, 1596/7, m. Katharine Gookin.
II. Anne, bapt. June 17, 1598.
III. Elizabeth, bapt. Oct. 7, 1599, m. July 24, 1626, John Hugeson of Dover.
IV. Mary, bapt. July 12, 1601, bur. July 23, 1601.
V. Battel, bapt. and buried 1602.
VI. Thomas, bapt. Feb. 13, 1603/4.
VII. John, bapt. 1605, bur. May 23, 1605.
VIII. Jane, bapt. 1606, bur. Dec. 4, 1606.
IX. Alice, bapt. 1608.
X. John, bapt. Jan. 28, 1609/10, living 1634/35.
XI. Affra, bapt._____ 1610/11, m. Jan. 13, 1628, William Inger, goldsmith of London, age 27.
XII. Edward, bapt. Sept. 3, 1612.

5. William[5] (John[4], Thomas[3], John[2], William[1]) Warren was baptized at Ripple on 7 March 1596/7; he married in 1619, Catherine, daughter of Thomas Gookin of Ripple Court, Kent, Esquire, by his wife, Jane, daughter of Richard Thurston of Challoke, Kent, Esquire. Catherine Gookin Warren was a niece of Daniel Gookin (1582-1633), Esquire, who was the founder of Newport News, Virginia, in 1621; and whose son, Major General Daniel Gookin (1612-1687), succeeded him there but later removed to Massachusetts. William Warren is recorded as a

parishioner of Ripple in 1621, and as a liberal benefactor of the
local church. He died intestate in 1631, administration of his
estate being granted that year to his widow, Catherine Warren
of the parish of Ripple. As 'Katherine Warren of Ripple, Widow,
32,' she married secondly, in 1632, John Sewall of Halstead,
Essex, Gentleman. According to the parish registers, the surviving children of William and Catherine Gookin Warren were:

     I.   Albert; baptized 1622; a resident of Halstead, Essex,
         as late as 1663:

6.   II. Thomas; baptized 30 January 1624, emigrated to Vir-
         Virginia with his cousin, Daniel Gookins II, on his re-
         turn voyage.

    III. Mary; baptized 1627; beneficiary in 1640 under the will
         of her step-father, John Sewall; as 'my well beloved
         friend Mistress Mary Warren, daughter of William
         Warren, late of the parish of Ripple in the county of
         Kent, Gentleman, deceased,' she was named sole heir
         and executrix in the will, 1651, of John Dering of
         Charing, Kent, Gentleman.

    The following article is by Mr. Lundie W. Barlow: "The er-
roneous ancestry long attributed to Thomas Warren was corrected,
and some account was given of the origin and descent of Smith's
Fort Plantation and the brick manor house there, in the first
volume of this series. (Colonial Surry) The engaging story of
this oldest dwelling house in Virginia to which a definite date can
be assigned, and of its restoration and maintenance as an historical shrine by the Association for the Preservation of Virginia
Antiquities, has been charmingly told by Mrs. Anne Page Johns
in an APVA pamphlet reprinted from volume 43 of The Virginia
Magazine of History and Biography; some further details regarding
Thomas Warren and his immediate family were recorded by Dr.
B. C. Holtzclaw in volume 47 of the same magazine. The account herein is based principally upon the pedigrees taken at the
heraldic visitations of Kent, parish register entries, family wills,
publications of the Kent Archaeological Society, gleanings from
local histories, landgrant and legislative records of colonial
Virginia, and the manuscript record books preserved at Surry
Courthouse. While no document can be cited in which it is
specifically stated that Thomas Warren of Kent, England, was
identical with Thomas Warren of Surry, Virginia, the attendant
circumstances, and the reasonable deductions from them, are
sufficiently convincing:

    1) Between 1625 and 1640 there is no entry of the death of
        Thomas Warren in the parish registers of Ripple, Kent,
        or of Halstead, Essex;

    2) Although there are several records of the continuing
        residence in England of Albert and Mary, only brother

and sister of Thomas Warren, no reference whatever can be found there to him after 1640;

3) Thomas Warren was listed with the other members of Daniel Gookin's family incident to their coming to Virginia in 1640; and no evidence appears of anyone of that name, other than the Thomas Warren born at Ripple in 1624-5, who was living in 1640 and could have been a relative of Daniel Gookin;

4) In the will of John Sewall, 1640, a step-father of Thomas Warren, the clause relative to the estates of his wife's Warren children is so phrased as to indicate that a settlement had just previously been made with Thomas; and therein probably is the explanation as to how a sixteen year old orphan lad would be possessed of the rather substantial means necessary to purchase headrights and acquire land immediately after his arrival in Virginia;

5) A careful checking of the colonial records has disclosed no Thomas Warren in Virginia, other than the later resident of Surry, who could have been identical with the young boy brought over by Daniel Gookin;

6) In 1661 it was estimated by the Clerk of the Surry Courts that Thomas Warren was then 'aged 40 or thereabouts,' which reasonably accords with his actual age of 37 years at that time;

7) Thomas Warren of Surry was of the same social class as the Warrens of Kent, being always referred to in the records as 'Mister' or 'Gentleman'; many of his fellow settlers in Surry were from Kent, including the Barhams, Crayfords, and Meriweathers, all of whom were neighbors and family connections in England of the Kentish Warrens.

WARREN
of
WARREN HOUSE and BACON'S CASTLE

Thomas Warren who built the famous brick house in Surry, now called the "Warren House", owned and operated under the auspices of the Association for the Preservation of Virginia Antiquities, evidently came to Surry before February 3, 1640, for that is the date of a grant to him for 450 acres on the eastern branch of Smiths Fort Creek in Surry.

It appears that he was the Thomas Warren who was brought to Virginia by his kinsman Daniel Gookin and that Thomas was the son of William of Ripple Court in Kent and his wife Catherine Gookin.

Daniel Gookin of Nansemond received a patent for 1400 acres of land November 4, 1642, on the north side of the Rappahanock River for the transportation of 28 persons among whom were, "Himself, Daniel Gookin twice, Mrs. Mary Gookin, Samuel Gookin, Thomas Warren, " etc. (See chapter entitled the Warren House) Patents at that time were customarily granted several years after the arrival of the grantors. (See 17th Cent. p. ____).

In fact Thomas Warren had seven years in which to pay for his land and the patent issued July 3, 1648, was for only 290 acres. (See Warren House in "Colonial Surry")

William Warren of Ripple Court who married Catherine, daughter of Thomas Gookin of Ripple in Kent, had a son Thomas, baptized at Ripple January 30, 1624/25. Christenings then as now were often several weeks after births and he may have been born in 1623.

Now Thomas Warren of Surry received no grant for his own transportation which tends to show he was transported by some - one else. Mrs. Nugent's records (C. P. Index) show that three Thomas Warrens were brought to Virginia and the one brought by Daniel Gookin is the only one whose time would approximate that of the coming over of Thomas Warren of Surry. Also Thomas Warren of Surry stated that he was "aged 40 or there-abouts" in a deposition made in the County Court May 3, 1661.

(See Warren House for discussion of question of the variation of ages in depositions)

The Variations allowed by the word "thereabouts" might well place him as the Thomas Warren of Ripple Court. This connection is further substantiated by the intermarriages shown between the Warrens, Crayfords, Meriwethers and other Kent families who afterwards migrated to Surry.

A coincidence of family names is also shown. Thomas Warren of Ripple was the son of William Warren and Thomas Warren of Surry named his oldest son "William". His second son was named "Thomas". The name, "Thomas", may have been derived from grandfather Thomas Gookin.

Besides the grant mentioned above Thomas Warren of Surry received a grant of "200 acres on the Blackwater Swamp adjoining a branch which divides this land from that of Martin Sheppard", September 20, 1667; and another one of 450 acres November 1, 1669, adjacent to his own land, (Pat. Bk. 6, p. 263). He was a member of the House of Burgesses in the sessions of March 1, 1658-59; December 1662 to September 10, 1663, and October 23, 1666.

THOMAS WARNE was Burgess for James City in 1644-45, and not THOMAS WARREN. THOMAS WARNE and others patented 1550 acres on the Chickahomy River, in James City in 1638 for the transportation of 31 persons, among whom was THOMAS WARNE. (C. P. 99-100)

Thomas Warren was married three times. The name of his first wife and the date of her death is unknown. His second wife was Mrs. Elizabeth Shepard, widow of Major Robert Shepard and daughter of William Spencer, Member of the House of Burgesses, 1624.

A marriage contract between "Mr. Thomas Warren of Smith's Fort, Surry, Gent. and Mrs. Elizabeth Shepard, widow, of Lower Chippoakes", was made September 23, 1654. This document states that Thomas Warren is to have and enjoy all the estate of Major Robert Shepard, deceased, now in possession of the said Elizabeth his relict, except the land and the following articles which Mrs. Elizabeth shall dispose of at her own pleasure, viz. one gold seal ring marked D. S., one pair of silver tongs marked R. S., one silver ink horn marked I. S., and she may appoint feofees in trust to oversee her children's estate and it is agreed that on September 29, 1656, Mr. Thomas Warren shall give to Anne, John, Robert and William Shepard certain horses and sums; and to Priscilla and Susanna Shepard their full share of their father's estate, besides give each a cow and calf, etc. This contract was recorded November 9, 1654, after the marriage. The witnesses were Edward Ffoliott and William Cockerham. The feofees appointed for the children were Mr. John Cocker,

Mr. William Cockerham, Mr. Ffoliott and Mr. Caufield.

Thomas Warren's second wife, Elizabeth (Spencer) Shepard died before 1659 as Thomas Warren, Jr., eldest son of third wife, was born in that year. His third wife was Jane, widow of John King, who married thirdly, Samuel Plaw.

Thomas Warren made his will March 16, 1669 and same was probated April 21, 1670, by his son William. If the will was recorded in Surry the recording has been lost.

Children by First Wife.

I. William, granted probate of his father's will April 21, 1670, was dead before 24 September, 1670, dsp.

II. Alice, aged 32, in 1677 (Deposition) married Matthias MARRIOTT. This is proven by the following agreement dated September 24, 1670. (Bk. 1, p. 377)

"An agreement between Jane Warren, relict of Mr. Thomas Warren, deceased, late of Surry County, of the one part, and Matthias Marriott who hath married Alice Warren, the only sister by the whole blood of William Warren, deceased, son of the aforesaid Mr. Thomas Warren, of the other part, witnesseth: That said Jane Warren and Matthias Marriott are and have been at controversy and variance about the division of the aforesaid Thomas and William Warren, their estates: Now to the end that perpetual partitition shall be had and made between said parties of and in the aforesaid Thomas and William, their estates, both personal and real, it is covenanted, concluded and agreed between the said parties to those presents in manner and form following: first that Mrs. Jane Warren shall have her thirds out of the whole estate of the above said Mr. Thomas Warren, his estate, and if Thomas Warren, son of the above said Mr. Thomas Warrin, and Jane, his wife, should happen to die before he comes to the age of 21 years, that the land which was given to him by his father's will is then to fall to William Warren, the youngest son of said Thomas Warren and Jane, his wife, during his natural life, and when he dies said land is to fall to Matthias Marriott and his heirs forever. It is also agreed that Thomas, a negro man, is and shall remain Matthias Marriott's and his heirs forever, said Matthias Marriott paying unto the above said Jane Warren the sum of 1667 lbs. of legal tobacco and casks out of his share of the estate and likewise it is further agreed between said parties that said Matthias Marriott shall have a white mare and her foal, one feather bed and furniture, one gold ring and one caster hat, all of which were the estate of William Warren, and that the above said Matthias Marriott shall have a full share of with the children out of the abovesaid Thomas Warren, deceased, his estate, and that the manour house wherein said Thomas Warren did live and the whole devident of land whereon it is situated with all houses, orchards and other appurtenances thereunto belonging is and shall remain in fee simple unto Matthias Marriott and his heirs forever; it is further agreed betwixt said parties that said Jane Warren shall peacably and quietly use, occupy and enjoy the one-third of the aforesaid manour house and of all other houses, orchards and the devident of land thereunto belonging with free egress and regress in and upon said land during her life, said Marriott to have him his share of the crop 2 bushels of wheat and 2 bushels of oats. In witness whereof the parties above specified have hereunto set heir hands and seals the day and year above written."

Jane Warren   The seal,
red wax

Mathias Marriott

In 1672 Mr. Marriot was fined for contempt of the county court as shown by the following order:

"Atte a courte houlden at Southwarke for the county of Surry the 4th day of September 1672... Mathias Marriott haveinge in Contempt of an order of this Courte, grounded upon an Act of Assembly for the restraint of of servaunts walking abrode on Sundayes or other dayes, gave his Negroe a note to goe abrode & having noe business; and alsoe renderinge scurrilous language to the Court both yesterday & todaye; the said Marriott is ordered to pay unto the sherifs for use of the county, Two Hundred Poundes of Tabacco & Caske with Costs..." -(V.7 -314).

On July 23, 1673, Mathias and Alice Marriot sold a tract of land "on which they now live" to JOHN SALWAY, "...same formerly in possession of Mr. THOMAS WARREN commonly called 'Smith's Fort' being 400 acres on Gray's Creek, adjacent WILLIAM MARRIOTT'S land lying on south side of James River". (R. B. 1671-84. p. 30.)

This was a deed to the present "Warren House" which became Mathias' under the above prenuptial agreement. It came to Alice upon the death of her brother William Warren in 1670.

In consideration for the above property, John Salway

and his wife Elizabeth deeded to Mathias Marriot a tract of land lying at the head of Grey's Creek "nigh unto the church". (Do. -31)

Alice Marriot made a deposition Sept. 15, 1677, in which she stated she was aged "32 or thereabouts".

Mathias Marriott's will was dated June 12, 1707 and probated Sept. 2, 1707. He gave his wife, ALICE, the manor plantation for her life, at her death to go to son WILLIAM. He mentions daughters MARGARET FLAKE, ELIZABETH HILL, MARION CHIPS, grandson THOMAS FLAKE, son of ROBERT FLAKE. (R. B. 1694-1708, p. 374).

WILLIAM MARRIOT was an only son and as he was named executor, he was therefore probably a minor when his father's will was written in 1707 but he proved a document under oath in 1710 and must have been of legal age at that time. It would appear that he was born about 1688.

William Marriot was married before November 16, 1725, as he was joined by his wife SARAH COLLIER in making a deed of that date. Their marriage and her identity are further evidenced by the will of her father THOMAS COLLIER, dated February 15, 1728 ".... my Daughter SARAH MARRIOTT, wife of WILLIAM MARRIOTT .. my Grandaughter MARY MARRIOTT..... my Grandsons WILLIAM and THOMAS MARRIOT..... their father..... my son-in-law WILLIAM MARRIOTT. "

"Major William Marriot", who obviously was a kinsman and at various times was a member of the Surry Court, High Sheriff of the County, and Vestryman of Southwarke Parish had an only surviving child, Mary, married to Mr. Samuel Thompson who, in his will written in 1720, bequeathed to WILLIAM, son of MATHIAS MARRIOTT, " my seal ring that was my wife's father's ring. "

In his will, dated September 20, 1765, and proved January 20, 1767, WILLIAM MARRIOTT did not mention his wife, who must have died before the will was written. The major part of his propert, including land in Brunswick County Virginia, was left to his sons THOMAS and MATHIAS, and to JOHN and WILLIAM, sons of his deceased son BENJAMIN MARRIOTT. A bequest of land in Brunswick was made to WILLIAM MARRIOTT'S grandson, WILLIAM DAVIS, his son-in-law HENRY DAVIS was given negroes and other personal property; and there was provision for "the maintanance and education of my daughter MARY DAVIS' five Smallest Children". (1754-1768,

p. 436.) He also provided that STEPHENSON BUXTON and his wife ELIZABETH enjoy the dwelling "where they now live" until his grandson WILLIAM MARRIOTT was 18.

It is possible that Elizabeth Buxton was William Marriott's sister. Mary Marriot, only daughter of William' Marriott, married Henry Davis. (See later.)

Children of Thomas Warren by Second Wife, Mrs. Elizabeth (Spencer) Shepard.

III. Elizabeth, m. John Hunnicutt. The marriage contract between the two was dated Feb. 26, 1670/71. (D & W 1644-71. p. 38). John Hunnicutt also receipted Mathias Marriott for the estate of his wife, Elizabeth, daughter of Thomas Warren, decd. (do 389). John Hunnycutt died intestate in 1699. His inventory, signed by Elizabeth Hunnycutt, his wife, was dated April 17, 1699. The tithables for 1702 show the names of WILLIAM, JOHN, and THOMAS HUNNICUT as tithables in her household and over 16, thus indicating them as sons. (For Hunnicutt see W   )

Children by Third Wife, Jane

2.   IV.   Thomas, b. January 9, 1659, d. 1721. (See later)

3.   V.   Allen, b. 1663, d. 1738. (See later)

4.   VI.   Robert, b. 1667, d. 1721. On September 29, 1688, he made a deed to John Watkins of "100 acres of land, part of 450 acres granted my father, Mr. Thomas Warren, November 1, 1669, who did by his last will and testament give and bequeath same to me". (Bk. 4, p. 89.) He also on January 5, 1690, deeded Luke Meizele 350 acres - wife Anne relinquished dower. Administration of his estate was granted to Robert Warren, probably a son, May 15, 1728. (Bk. 7, p. 810.)

5.   VIII.   William, b. 1669/70, d. 1702. He receipted his brother Thomas for his share of father's estate, 15214 lbs. of tobacco, April 25, 1691.

Administration on his estate was granted to James Warren, probably his son, June 2, 1702. (Descendants untraced.)

2.   Thomas Warren, Jr., was born January 9, 1659, which is proven by the following order dated June 4, 1680: "Thomas Warren, son of Thomas Warren, will be of age on the 9th day of this instant. Samuel Plaw is to deliver him his part of his father's estate on the 15th of this month". (O. B. 1671-90, p. 329.)

The Court also ordered Samuel Plaw to give him the shares of the three other orphans of Mr. Thomas Warren.

On April 20, 1684, Francis Lord Howard, Governor, granted Thomas Warren "280 acres of land situated about a mile and half above Ware Neck Mill in the Upper Parish of Surry County, 190

acres thereof being part of a patent of 290 acres granted his
father Mr. Thomas Warren, died July 3, 1648, the remaining 90
acres being waste land." (Pat Bk. 7, p. 367.)

Thomas Warren's will was probated August 16, 1721. (Bk. 5,
p. 362.) His wife was Elizabeth, who made her will in 1724;
same probated 1730. She names the four sons named in her husband's will, and in addition - grandson Thomas Warren, granddaughter Mary Warren, grandson James Davis. (Bk. 8, p. 80.)
Children, with land bequeathed by father:

I. William, "land where I live and between the two swamps
and 80 acres after death of my wife." He and wife to be
executor and executrix.

II. John, "land called 'Rich Neck' where he now lives".

III. Joseph, "land lying upon Peterfells and Buck Point,
between Hog Pen Swamp and Wild Swamp, 90 acres."

IV. Robert, "land between Hull Cabins and Shee Cabins, 40
acres."

15. V. Elizabeth, m. Thomas Davis who died 1720. (See later.)

3. Allen Warren, born 1663, died 1738, receipted to his
brother Thomas, May 31, 1684, for 5214 lbs. of tobacco "left
me by my father". (Bk. 4, p. 212). On October 19, 1714, he
deeds "Allen Warren, the younger" for 40 shillings, 130 acres
of land on the Blackwater being part of a patent dated September
20, 1667." (Bk. 1209-15 p. 216.)

Allen Warren lived to about 81 years of age as proven by following documents. Deed dated and recorded April 19, 1738 from
Allen Warren of Southwark Parish, Surry County, "for the natural
love and affection I have and bear to my grandson, Allen Warren,
I give him 70 acres of land in Lawnes Creek Parish being part of
a patent granted my father Thomas Warren for 200 acres, dated
September 1667, adjacent to 130 acres which I sold my son Allen
out of same patent." (C. B. 1730-38, p. 867.)

He made his will March 15, 1737/38; same not probated until
January 16, 1744. He mentions his wife, but does not name her
and names his son, Benjamin, executor. (Will & Deed Bk. 1738-
54, p. 488.)
Known Children:

4. I. Allen II (See later.)

II. Benjamin

4. Allen Warren II predeceased his father. He made his will
"as of Lawnes Creek Parish", December 16, 1732. Same probated August 13, 1733. He gave his son Allen "all land I hold
in this county and my trooper's arms." His wife, Anne, married
John Little, who joined her in administrating upon his estate in
1738. (Bk. 9, p. 47.)
His children were: Allen III, (see later #5); Robert, not 18;

Sarah; Elizabeth; Lucy; Mary.

5. Allen Warren III grew to old age in Surry. His will was dated February 9, 1780 and was probated March 28, 1780, as follows:

"Sick and weak but in perfect sense and memory xxx to son William Warren 120 acres where he now lives, also negroes; to son Arthur Warren 145 acres wherein he now lives; to son John Warren 80 acres, adjacent to Stephen Bells, William Edwards, and the land given to sons William and Arthur, etc., to son Jesse Warren land and plantation where I now live (after wife's decease) containing 180 acres, other three sons are to have liberty to cut cypress timber out of the swamp on said place, xxx , negroes to daughters, Martha White and Mary Murfee; a trunk to granddau. Rebecca White. Executors: sons, William and Jesse. Teste: Wm. Hart, Eldred Edwards, Stephen Bell, Jr." (W. B. 1778-83, p. 123). Testators also gave by name a large number of slaves to his wife and each of his children.

His children were: William d. 1804 (see later #6); Arthur; John; Jesse, (see later #7); Martha, m. Mr. White; Mary, m. Mr. Murphee.

6. William Warren made his will May 3, 1804, and same was probated September 25, 1804, as follows: "In low state of health, to dau. Sally Bell £20; to dau. Polly Bell £20; to son James H. Warren plantations of 120 acres where he now lives; to son Samuel Warren 120 acres adjoining James H. Warren; to dau. Selah Judkins, negroes, to son Allen Warren tract of land of 140 acres called 'Caesars' joining Jesse Browne and Richard Carter; to son William Warren £200; to son Jesse Warren £200, to son John Phillips Warren, plantation where I now live. Wife, son James H. Warren and John H. Bell, executors. Teste: Drewery P. Warren, Micajah Bell, John Lane." (W. B. 1804-15, p. w.)

His children were: 1. Sally, m. John H. Bell; 2. Polly, m. James Bell; 3. James, m. Becky Lane; 4. Samuel; 5. Selah, m. Joseph Judkins; 6. Allen; 7. William Wilson; 8. Jesse, m. Martha P. Thompson (see later #8); 9. John Phillips.

8. Jesse Warren, born in Surry County, 1791, died in 1832; married December 12, 1812, Martha Phillips Thompson, born 1788, died December 19, 1863. Martha was the daughter of Sally (Hunnicut) and Joel Thompson (Will 1799). Children:

    I. John, b. 1814, m. Julia Anne Mathew.

9. II. William Allen, b. April 15, 1820, m. Sarah E. Dashield.

   III. James Samuel, b. 1822, m. Lucy Caroline Clarke.

   IV. Jesse Albert, b. April 5, 1829, m. Betty Bell.

9. William Allen Warren, born April 25, 1820, in Surry, died in Richmond, Virginia, July 2, 1914. He married Febru-2, 1854, Sarah Elizabeth Dashield born September 16, 1833, died at Bacon's Castle January 1901. Sarah Dashield was the daughter of Sarah Hunnicut (Davis) and James Dashield.

Mr. Warren lived to be 94 years of age. During his long and useful life he acquired "Bacon's Castle" which the family still own. Mr. Warren gave this venerable mansion to his son, Charles W. Warren, who married Carrie A. Pegram, daughter of Major Blair Pegram. It is now owned by their son, Walker Pegram Warren of Smithfield, Virginia. Thus the Warrens, having built the Warren House, the oldest mansion in Surry, in the course of three centuries have moved only a few miles away to Bacon's Castle. the next oldest mansion.

Children:
  I. William Wallace, b. November 8, 1854, dsp.
  II. James Albert, b. August 4, 1856, dsp.
  III. Charles Walker, b. November 7, 1859, m. Carrie A. Pegram.
  IV. Virginia Davis, b. January 4, 1861, m. William Pegram Wilson.
10. V. Martha Jessie, b. March 30, 1864, m. Robert Lee Powers

10. Martha Jessie Warren, born March 30, 1864, at Wall's Bridge, married November 25, 1890, at Bacon's Castle, Robert Lee Powers, born January 2, 1865, at Richmond, Virginia, died January 11, 1944.

Children:
  I. Sarah Virginia Powers, born December 23, 1900, lives in Richmond.

7. Jesse Warren, son of Allen Warren III, was commissioned a Lieutenant in Captain Wilson's Company of Surry County Militia, August 26, 1777. (O. B. 1775-85.)

He married Martha _____ and died in 1794. On January 27, 1795, his wife, Martha, was appointed administratrix of his estate. (O. B. 1795-1800, pp. 1, 95.) On September, 1795, she was appointed guardian of the following children: 1. Edwin; 2. Patsy (Martha); 3. Jesse Phillips (see later No. 11); 4. Elizabeth (Warren) Gwaltney; 5. Avarilla.

11. Jesse Phillips Warren, married January 25, 1814, Sally C. Bell, daughter of Benjamin Bell, Ensign in the Navy in War of 1812. Mr. Bell died in 1821.

Mr. Warren's will was dated August 28, 1829, and recorded in Surry County. (W. B. 1827-30, p. 506.) His wife's will is recorded in Will Book 1834-40, page 525.

Children:
- I. Joseph B.
- II. Rebecca Anne
- III. Elizabeth
- 12. IV. Lucy Caroline, m. William Major West. (See later)
- V. Sally Angeline Phillips

12. Lucy Caroline Warren, married September 26, 1836, as his second wife, William Major West, born 1806, died January 22, 1866.

Children:
- I. Sara West, m. 1. Scott, 2. Freer.
- II. Washington Josephus West, m. Miss Newcomb.
- III. Othello Jesse West, m. Virginia (Jannie) Newcomb.
- IV. Alice West, m. Joseph Ramey.
- V. Coltha West, m. Emmett William Maynard.
- VI. Martha Louella (Pinkie) West, m. Samuel Tinsley.
- 13. VII. Samuel Edwin West, m. Oceana Winifred Gwaltney.
- VIII. Lucy Major (Kate) West, m. John Hunnicutt.

13. Samuel Edwin West, born 1838, married Oceana Winifred Gwaltney of Isle of Wight County, daughter of Sara (Holland) and William Gray GWALTNEY. Mr. West was a soldier in the Confederate Army.

Children:
- I. Elliott Edwin West, m. Mary Hunnicutt
- II. Sarah Caroline West, m. 1. Edwin Warren, 2. George W. Brown.
- III. Mollie West, m. Nathaniel Barryman.
- IV. James Thomas West, m. Elizabeth Jones.
- V. Eugene Gordon West, m. Oneta Hardin.
- 14. VI. Grace West, m. James Robbins McClamroch.

14. Grace West, born September 7, 1874, in Surry County, married February 27, 1901, James Robbins MacClamroch, son of Sarah Ellen (Foster) and Julius Lawrence MacClamroch, born November 16, 1870 at Mocksville, Davie County, N. C., died December 16, 1935, at Greensboro, N. C. (For an account of his life, see Vol. V, p. 593, of Dr. Archibald Henderson's History of North Carolina, "The Old North State and the New".)

Children:
- I. James G. W. MacClamroch, born December 1, 1901, is an attorney at Greensboro, N. C., and is a graduate of the University of North Carolina (A. B.) and of Yale (LLB); member of the American Bar Association, Sigma Chi Fraternity at North Carolina, Phi Delta Phi at Yale; Sons of American Revolution and of Confederate Veterans; Societies of the War of 1812, of Colonial Wars; Society

of Genealogists of London, Eng., and of the Harleian
Society of England. To Mr. MacClamroch is due credit
for furnishing material on the Warren Family, particularly that concerning the building of the "Warren House"
mentioned in "Colonial Surry", and also for obtaining of
valuable information about the Warrens from Kent County,
England.

II. Julian Westwarren MacClamroch, born February 10, 190-
III. Virginia Gwaltney MacClamroch, born November 9, 1907
married James F. Hoge and lives in New York City. Mrs
Hoge is a graduate of Hollins College (B. A.), President of
Dramatics Club and of Delta Delta Delta Sorority in senio:
year; member of Junior League of New York City; of the
National Society of Colonial Dames; D. A. R. and United
Daughters of the Confederacy, all of New York State.
(See New York Social Register).

Their children are:

I. James Fulton Hoge, Jr., graduate of Buckley School,
N. Y., student at Phillips Academy, Exeter.
II. Warren MacClamroch Hoge, student at Buckley School.
III. Barbara Hume Hoge, Senior at Chapin School, N. Y.
IV. Virginia Howe Hoge, student at Chapin.

DAVIS
of
Surry, Georgia and Alabama

Thomas Davis was in the Surry County Militia in 1687 and appears as a tithable in 1688. In 1694 he had James Robinson in his household. In 1702 he had four tithables: himself and Mingo, Jack and Peg, negroes. (Col. Surry.) On Mar. 3, 1689/90 he bought fifty acres from Adam Heath and his wife Sarah, which land Heath had purchased from Samuel Thompson. (DB4- p. 159.) On Mar. 11, 1703/4 he made a deed of gift to a negro boy named Will to his grandson Mathew Ellis, son of Elizabeth (Davis) Ellis and Mathew Ellis. This was witnessed by Allen Warren and Thomas Warren (II). (DB, 1694-1709, Part 2 -296.) He bought 150 acres in Surry from William Rhodes and Susanna, his wife, on May 17, 1706, for 5000 lbs. of tbco. (Do.-349.) He made his will on Sept. 28, 1716, probated Dec. 21, 1720. He gave son JAMES DAVIS all land and houses he possessed, wife to have use of same for life; and legacies to grandson MATTHEW ELLIS and THOMAS ELLIS; grandaughters ELIZABETH and ISABEL ELLIS; grandchildren: THOMAS DAVIS, negro boy Roger; JANE DAVIS, negro girl Betty; JAMES DAVIS, negro boy Mingo; HENRY DAVIS, negro girl Peg; ELIZABETH ELLIS, a good Bible; son JAMES DAVIS, negro woman Sarah. Wits.: Samuel Thompson, Thomas King, Zachariah Madderra. (W&D. 1715-30-287.)

James Davis, son of Thomas and Elizabeth Davis, on Feb. 16, 1722, received a grant of 330 acres in Surry next to Capt. Henry Harrison. 100 acres were for importing his father and mother many years before, and the balance for 25 shillings. (P. B. II-1719-24, p. 193.) Inasmuch as his father had been living in Surry for nearly 40 years, this grant must have been for a return trip from England.

James Davis married Elizabeth Warren, daughter of Elizabeth and Thomas Warren II. His son James was mentioned as a "grandson" in the will of Mrs. Elizabeth Warren, dated 1724, recorded in 1730. (ante) Some authorities claim it was he and not his son who was the "James Davis" mentioned in the will of Mrs. Warren; that "James" was the only son the above Thomas had, whereas this James, the son of the subject of this sketch, had several brothers and sisters. Others claim that Thomas Warren II, who was born Jan. 9, 1659/60 (47V329), was of the same generation as Thomas Davis, who first appeared as a tithable in 1674 at the age of 16, showing that he was born in 1658. (Col. Surry, p. 185.) Thomas Davis had two sets of grandchildren when he made his will in 1716. It does seem somewhat improbable that his wife could have been a daughter of Thomas Warren II, inasmuch as he, Thomas Davis, was aged enough to mention several grandchildren in his will. (There were several distinct families of Davis in Surry and Isle of Wight in the 18th. century.)

James Davis, Sr. made his will Sept. 4, 1746, witnessed by Thomas Warren, John Warren and John Slate, recorded Jan. 21, 1746/47. (W B 3-546)

Children of James Davis (d. 1746) were;

1. Thomas Davis (d. 1748) of Isle of Wight Co., Va.
2. Jane Davis, who married a Warren.
3. John Davis (of Brunswick Co., Va. ?)
4. James Davis (d. 1783) of Surry County, Va.; m. Elizabeth Baldwin, dau. of William Baldwin. (see later.)
5. Henry Davis (d. 1767), of Surry Co., Va.; m. Mary Marriott, dau. of Wm. Marriott and Sarah (Collier) Marriott.
6. Robert Davis (d. 1749) of Pasquotank Co., N. C.; m. Sarah Chapman?
7. Nathaniel Davis (d. 17-) of Hyde Co., N. C. (?)
8. Anne Davis, m. ca 1740 (?), James Nicholson (d. 1793) and had James Nicholson, who m. Elizabeth Woodruff.

Henry Davis married Mary Marriott, dau. of William Marriott who was the son of Mathias Marriott and his wife Alice, dau. of Thomas Warren. (see ante)

Henry Davis made his will Feb. 18, 1767; same was probated Mar. 17, 1767. In it he referred "all that is due me from the estate of William Marriott". He gave legacies to his children: William, Ann, Hannah, Benjamin, Isham, Randolph, Elizabeth, Henry, Kezia, Marriott, Silvia, and James Davis, who were listed in that order. His brother James and his son Benjamin were executors. (B. K. 1754-68, p. 448.)

5. Benjamin Davis of Brunswick County, Virginia, Planter, son of Henry and Mary Marriott Davis, married Tabitha, daughter of John Rose of Brunswick County, Planter. The second of their seven sons was also named Benjamin. Tabitha Rose Davis died before 1810 and her husband in April of 1817.

He seems to have removed permanently to Brunswick County after his father's death in 1767, having purchased a small plantation there in 1770 and being executor of the will of his brother, William Davis of Brunswick, two years later. In 1775 he and his brother, Randolph, were witnesses to the marriage bond of Elizabeth Davis, their sister, and John Rose, junior, brother of Tabitha, wife of Benjamin Davis. By a deed dated 20 May 1777, Benjamin Davis sold the above mentioned land and was joined in its execution by his wife, Tabitha, evidencing that they were married before that date. In 1792 he was executor of the will of John Rose, junior.

By his will dated August 7, 1780, John Rose, senior, of the County of Brunswick and Parish of Saint Andrew, Planter, named his son, John Rose, junior, as residuary legatee and executor and bequeathed "unto my daughter Tabitha Davis ... the Plantation on which she and her husband now lives ..." Apparently, Tabitha Rose Davis died prior to 1810 as she was not included as a member of Benjamin Davis' household in the United States census returns of that year. Benjamin Davis acquired a substantial holding of land and slaves during his residence in Brunswick, and he died there between April 8, the date of his will, and April 28, 1817, the date of its probate. His surviving children, as named in his will and in several subsequent powers of attorney and land deeds incident to the settlement of his estate, were William, Elizabeth (wife of John Brown), John, Martha, (wife of Littleberry Baugh), Benjamin, Henry, Thomas and Merritt Davis. (6T 110)

As set forth in the minutes of a Brunswick County Court held on April 23, 1782, Benjamin Davis gave aid to the American Revolution by furnishing supplies and thereby affords eligibility for membership in the National Society of the Daughters of the American Revolution. In an account of the Davis family, he is referred to as "Major Benjamin Davis ... who lived in Brunswick County, Virginia, and was an Officer in the Revolution". His name is also included in a list of Revolutionary War officers published in Volume six of the Alabama Historical Quarterly. No confirmation of this service has been found in the Virginia records but the family tradition is strong and it is probable that Benjamin Davis was an officer of the Georgia Militia during the early years of the war. It must certainly be more than mere coincidence that after selling the only land he is known to have owned in 1777, he is not mentioned again in the Brunswick records until 1780; that he had a brother, Randolph, and that men named Benjamin and Randolph Davis appear in the Georgia Certified List of Revolutionary Soldiers; that a Benjamin Davis applied for by proxy and was granted land in Georgia in 1784 as a refugee soldier entitled to a bounty; and that in 1809 Benjamin Davis, junior, son of Benjamin Davis of Brunswick, sold a portion of what seems to have been the same land.

6. Benjamin Davis of Autauga County, Alabama, Planter and

Merchant, son of Benjamin and Tabitha Rose Davis, was born on April 25, 1784. He was married in 1816 to Martha, daughter of Benjamin Taylor of Oglethorpe County, Georgia, Planter. Their fourth child and second daughter was Louisiana Caroline Davis. Benjamin Davis died in Autauga County of June 29, 1863 and his wife died there in September of 1873.

Benjamin Davis removed as a young man to Oglethorpe County, Georgia, and served as First Lieutenant in the Georgia Militia during the War of 1812. He was usually referred to as "Major" but it is unknown whether this was a courtesy title or arose from subsequent military service.

"State of Alabama)   The 24th of August, Anno Domini, one thou-
  Autauga County)   sand eight hundred and fifty five: Person-
ally appeared before me, Thomas C. Monroe, Justice of the Peace within and for the County and State aforesaid, Benjamin Davis, aged seventy years, a resident of Autauga County in the State of Alabama, who, being duly sworn according to Law, de- clares that he is the identical Benjamin Davis who was a First Lieutenant in the Company commanded by Captain Burwell Pope, in the Regiment of Militia commanded by Colonel Jett Thomas, in the War with Great Britain declared by the United States on the 18th day of June 1812 ...

"He makes this Declaration for the purpose of obtaining ... bounty and to which he may be entitled under the Act approved the 3rd day of March, 1855 ... (s) Benjamin Davis."

In 1818, Major Davis and his wife, Martha Taylor Davis, moved from Georgia to Alabama, settling first in Shelby and a few years later in Autauga County. He was appointed Justice of the Peace (member of the County Court) on November 20, 1818 and he and his father-in-law, Mr. Benjamin Taylor, are shown by the census records as residents of Shelby in 1820 and of Aut- auga in 1830 and subsequent years. The following is quoted from the account of the Davis family in volume three of Dr. Thomas McAdory Owen's Dictionary of Alabama Biography: "DAVIS, BENJAMIN, planter and merchant, was born April 25, 1780, in Brunswick County, Virginia, and died June 29, 1863, in Autauga County; son of Major Benjamin and Tabitha Davis who lived in Brunswick County, Virginia. Mr. Davis served in the war of 1812 and came to Alabama ... was elected to the State Legislature from Autauga County about 1828, when the capitol was at Tusca- loosa, and served two terms. At one time he was tax collector of Autauga County. He was a Democrat and a Methodist ... married May 28, 1816, Martha, daughter of Benjamin Taylor, who came to Alabama from Georgia and settled in Autauga County. She died in 1873 at the age of seventy-seven years. Children: 1. Mary Elizabeth, m. Cary L. Newman; 2. Merritt Warren, killed at nine years by a falling tree; 3. Benjamin F., M.D., m. Eliza-

beth Frith; 4. Louisiana Caroline, m. John H(arvin) Barlow;
5. Thomas Asbury, physician, served in the C.S. Army as Captain of Co. G, Sixth Alabama Infantry, then as Surgeon of the
Regiment, later as Brigade Surgeon under General Gordon, m.
Dora Motley; 6. Robert Henry, died when twenty-one years
old; 7. Laura Taylor m. William Caver; 8. Martha Aurelia,
m. George W. Zeigler; 9. John William, physician, ... m.
Astoria ... Shackleford ...

7. Louisiana Caroline Davis, daughter of Benjamin and
Martha Taylor Davis, was born in 1824 and was married on December 22, 1841, to John Harvin Barlow of Lowndes County, Alabama, Planter. Their youngest child was John Davis Barlow.
Louisiana Caroline Davis Barlow predeceased her husband and
he died on October 9, 1871. (note g) He was born February 9,
1816, in Laurens County, Georgia, but became a resident of
Autauga after his marriage, removing thence about 1860 to the
adjoining county of Lowndes where his home plantation was called
Pleasant Hill. The children of John Harvin and Louisiana Caroline Davis Barlow were Martha Annie, Thomas Wade, William
Franklin, Robert Merritt, Mary Emma (wife of Jesse Deane
Boring), James Judson, Ella Amelia (wife of William Buchanan),
and John Davis Barlow.
    John Harvin married secondly, in 1864, Louisiana, daughter
of James Deats and widow of William Archer Butler. By her he
had three children, Janie Lanier (wife of B. C. Morrison), Laura
Harvin (wife of W. J. Suggs), and Joseph Foster Barlow. After
the death of their father, these children removed to Texas with
their mother and several of their half brothers and sisters.
    Being too old for active duty during the War between the
States, John Harvin Barlow served with the Lowndes County
Home Guards. His eldest son, Thomas Wade Barlow, enlisted
when only sixteen years of age in the Alabama Battery of the Jeff
Davis Artillery; was captured at Spotsylvania Court House on May
1, 1864; and died in an army hospital the following year. John
Harvin Barlow was a Mason; a Deacon of the Baptist Church; and
a Justice of the Peace of Lowndes County. He died in Americus,
Georgia, on October 9, 1871. The following notice of his death
appeared in The Weekly Sumter Republican, the Americus news-
paper of that time: "Mr. John Barlow, an esteemed citizen of
Alabama, died in this place on Monday night last. He had been
on a visit to his brothers, Doctors W. W. and W. J. Barlow,
and contracted the disease from which he died. He leaves a wife
and nine children. His remains were escorted to Oak Grove
Cemetery by the members of the Masonic Fraternity and a large
number of mourning friends in vehicles. The solemn Masonic
rites were held over the remains".

8. John Davis Barlow of Anniston, Alabama, Merchant, son of John Harvin and Louisiana Caroline Davis Barlow, was born in Autauga County on November 20, 1859. He was married on September 7, 1883, to Josephine Erwin, daughter of Allen Weathers, Alabama, Planter and Manufacturer. Their eldest son is Lundie Weathers Barlow. Josephine Erwin Weathers Barlow died on March 17, 1932 and her husband on March 17, 1942. In 1881, John Davis Barlow went to Texas and resides with his sister, Mary Emma Barlow Boring. He returned to Alabama about 1890 and located at Anniston where he became a wholesale produce merchant and operator of iron ore mines. John Davis Barlow was Lieutenant of the Anniston Rifles, Alabama National Guard, at the time of the Spanish-American War, but was not called to active service. He was a Mason, a Steward of the Methodist Church, and a leading citizen of Anniston for many years.

Josephine Erwin Weathers was born in Weathers, Clay County, Alabama, on May 22, 1868. After the death of her parents she lived in Anniston with her brother, Mr. Lundie M. Weathers, and she and John Davis Barlow were married there in 1893. They had three children, Lundie Weathers; John Davis, junior, born 1897, died 1899; and Robert Allen Barlow, born 1900.

During their latter years, John Davis and Josephine Erwin Weathers Barlow lived in Florida. She died in Pompano and he in Jacksonville, but they are buried in Miami.

9. Lundie Weathers Barlow of Boston, Massachusetts, Banker, son of John Davis and Josephine Erwin Weathers Barlow, was born on January 27, 1896, in Anniston, Alabama. On August 9, 1920, he was married to Emmelina Jernigan, daughter of Matthew Howell Moore of White Plains, Georgia, Educator. They are the parents of Joanne Moss Barlow.

Lundie Weathers Barlow was educated in the private and public schools of Anniston, Alabama, and Lakeland, Florida, and at the University of Florida. During World War I, he served as Second Lieutenant of Field Artillery, United States Army. Thereafter, he was engaged for a short ime in building construction and in the Atlanta architectural offices of his uncle, Mr. Lundie M. Weathers. In 1921 he was employed by the Federal Reserve Bank of Atlanta, going from there in 1923 to Florida where he held official positions with two Miami banks during the ensuing six years. After four years as Vice President of Page Trust Company of North Carolina, Lundie Weathers Barlow became a member of the original staff of the Federal Deposit Insurance Corporation. He has subsequently held assignments with it as Bank Examiner in North Carolina and Virginia; Assistant to the Chief, Division of Examination, in Washington; and District Supervising Examiner in Richmond and Boston.

Emmaline Jernigan Moore was born in White Plains, Georgia,

on February 8, 1901, and was educated in the primary schools there and in Greensboro, and at the Georgia State College for Women, Milledgeville. She and Lundie Weathers Barlow were married in Athens and their children are Joanne Moss Barlow Williams and Lundie Weathers Barlow, junior, M. D., who was born in Miami, Florida, on October 4, 1923.

10. Joanne Moss Barlow, daughter of Lundie Weathers and Emmaline Jernigan Moore Barlow, was born in Atlanta, Georgia, on May 24, 1921. She was married on November 4, 1942, to Francis Deane Williams, junior, of Richmond, Virginia, Manufacturer.

Joanne Moss Barlow recieved her education in Carthage, North Carolina, and Washington, D. C., and at Westhampton College, Richmond, where she was graduated, B. S., in 1942.

Francis Deane Williams, junior, was born and reared in Richmond and is a graduate of Episcopal High School, Alexandria, and of the University of Virginia where he attained membership in Phi Beta Kappa. He served during World War II as a Naval Lieutenant, principally in the South Pacific. He is a Director and Vice President of The Tredegar Iron Works which was established and has been operated by his family for four generations.

Joanne Moss Barlow and Francis Dean Williams, junior, were married in Richmond, where they now live, and are the parents of Cary Leigh Williams, born July 9, 1946. and Sallie Archer Anderson Williams, born June 20, 1947.

RUFFIN
of
SURRY

William[1] Ruffin, who at the age of 18, embarked for Virginia at Gravesend, England, July 24, 1635, on the ship "Assurance"; Master, Issac Bromwell, (Hotten p. 113) and died in Isle of Wight County, Virginia, in 1674, was the progenitor of the Ruffins of Virginia and North Carolina. He left no will, but his death in 1674 is indicated by the fact that on January 9, 1674/5, administration on his estate was requested by Robert Ruffin as son and heir, with Capt. William Oldis and Mr. William Boddie as surities. (Isle of Wight Will & Deed Book 2, page 34, reverse.) The earliest record of him in this country appears to be his signature as a witness to the will of Edward Chetwyne in Isle of Wight County Sept. 7, 1649. This first signature was "Gulielm. Ruffin". According to family tradition, his name was originally William Ruthvin. Apparently he had Latinized it, in accordance with the fad in those days, especially among the University graduates; some weight is given to this surmise from the fact that the name "Ruffin" has not been found abroad. "Gulielmus" soon reverted to "William" but the "Ruffin" stuck. In 1666, William Ruffin patented 750 acres of land in Isle of Wight County, at ye Cypress Swamp, adjoining Ambrose Bennett. In 1668, William Ruffin sold to Thomas Pope 450 acres out of 900 acres patented by him and Robert Coleman. In 1670, William Ruffin assigned 200 acres to Mrs. Katherine Thornton (b. 1634), with reversion to her two children, Arthur Whitehead and Rebecca Thornton.

William[1] Ruffin married _____ before 1651, probably about 1645, and had one son -

Robert[2] Ruffin (ca. 1646-1693) who died in Surry County, Virginia. He was born in Isle of Wight County before January 1, 1651, when "Robert Ruffin the son of William Ruffine" was a legatee in the will of William Jewry which was witnessed by his father William Ruffin. The fact that his father gave him a power of attorney on February 8, 1667/8, indicates that he was then of age and therefore was born in 1646 or before. (Isle of Wight Book 1, p. 107.) On June 7, 1669, William Oldis and Robert Ruffin patented 2050 acres of land between the branches of the

Blackwater adjoining the land of Col. Pitt". On January 21, 1675/6, Robert Ruffin "of the County of Surry" deeded to Thomas Giles of Nansemond County "my plantation on which my decd. father William Ruffin of Isle of Wight lived, except 200 acres which my decd. father made over to Katherine Thornton". This deed was witnessed by William Oldis and Edmond Prime, and consented to by Mrs. Elizabeth Ruffin. (Surry County Book 2, p. 99). In 1677, Robert Ruffin confirmed this sale as "sole heir and administrator of William Ruffin". (Isle of Wight Book 1, p. 355). In May, 1678, the Court appointed Mr. Robert Ruffin and Capt. Robert Spencer to serve as Sheriffs until the pleasure of the Governor be known. In May, 1684, Mr. Robert Ruffin by order of the Governor was sworn in as Sheriff of Surry County. He was a Justice of the Peace from 1680 on. In 1687 the Surry County Justices of the Peace were Mr. Robert Ruffin, Major Samuel Swann, Mr. Francis Mason, and Mr. Robert Randall.

Robert [2] Ruffin married, 1675, the widow of Capt. George Watkins, nee Elizabeth Prime, daughter of Edmond Prime and his wife (name unknown but probably a Ridley). They had five children, apparently in the following order:

1. Olive [3] Ruffin (ca. 1676-1722), m. ca. 1693, William Chambers (d. 1718) ... 6 (?) children.
2. Elizabeth [3] Ruffin.
3. Robert [3] Ruffin (1681-1720), m. 170, Elizabeth _____ . . . 7 children.
4. William [3] Ruffin (ca. 1683-1739). (See below)
5. Jane [3] Ruffin.

"William Ridley (d. 1671), Mrs. Charles Barham, Mrs. Edmond Prime, and possibly Nathaniel Ridley (d. 1719), may have been children of Peter Ridley of James City County who was granted land in Martins Hundred in 1639 and served as Burgess from James City County 1644-48.

Edmond Pryme, aged 16, embarked July 4, 1635, at Gravesend, England, on the ship "Transport" of London, master, Edward Walker. (Hotten p. 103)

Robert [2] Ruffin in his will dated May 8, 1693 and proved July 4, 1693, (witnessed by Wm. Chambers, Wm. Newsum, and Roger Rawlins) left legacies to his wife Elizabeth, to his sons Robert and William, and to "my daughter Elizabeth's first borne childe". That he had more than one daughter is shown by instructions to his wife to bestow portions on his daughters as they come to age or are married. Mrs. Elizabeth Ruffin in her will dated July 29, 1711, and proved August 18, 1714, (witnessed by William Gray, Jr. and Olive Chambers) left legacies to her unmarried daughter Jane Ruffin (named as executrix) and to her sons William and Robert Ruffin. The omission of specific mention of Jane in her father's will was probably due to her being very young at the time,

and the omission of Elizabeth from her mother's will was probably
due to her having either married or died. The omission of Olive
from both wills was probably due to her having received her share
of the estate when she married. That she was a daughter is proved
by the wording of a deed recorded in Surry County Book 1694-1709,
page 408, as follows: "Indenture between Robert and William Ruffin of Surry to Will Edwards, March 1, 1708- for divers good
causes and considerations and 61s. by sd. Edwards to William
Chambers we release all our claim or right to our sister Olive
Chambers to a tract on the mill dam for 6 acres to build a mill".
This deed was witnessed by William Drew and Thomas Harris.

Olive [3] Ruffin married William Chambers probably before
May 8, 1693, when he was a witness to her father's will. She was
a second wife, the first having been Rosamund Beighton. In his
1718 will, William Chambers mentions, without stating by which
wife, six children: 1. John Chambers (d. 1727), 2. William Chambers, 3. Elizabeth Chambers, 4. Mary Chambers (m. Richard
Hardy who died 1756 in Isle of Wight County leaving two children:
Richard Hardy who married Marcella Davis, and Sarah Hardy),
5. Olive Chambers, and 6. Martha Chambers. This will was
proved by William Edwards (age 39) and Robert Ruffin (age 37).

Robert [3] Ruffin (1681-1720), of Surry County, Virginia, married 170_, Elizabeth_____ and had seven children: John[4],
Joseph[4], Benjamin[4], Edmond[4], Mary[4], Martha[4], and Elizabeth[4]
Ruffin. John Ruffin (170 -1775), of Surry and Mecklenburg
Counties, Virginia, married Patty Hamlin; a son was Robert Ruf-
fin who married Mrs. Mary (Clack) Lightfoot; a son was Sterling
Ruffin who married Alice Roane; and their son was Thomas Ruf-
fin (1787-1870), born in King & Queen County, Va., who moved
across the border in 1807, married Anne Kirkland, and was Chief
Justice of the Supreme Court of North Carolina from 1833 to 1852.

William [3] Ruffin (ca. 1683-1739) was born in Surry County, Virginia, but settled in Bertie County, N. C. (then known as Bertie
Precinct of Albemarle County) in the section which in 1741 (after
his death) became Northampton County. In Bertie County Deed
Book E, p. 329, there is recorded a deed from William Ruffin
and Sarah his wife to Robert Ruffin; this is dated Nov. 14, 1738.
In the N. C. Historical Commission at Raleigh, N. C., there is
filed the inventory of the estate of "William Ruffin, late of Bertie
County decd. Feb. 10, 1738/9" (showing 11 negroes, 78 head of
cattle, 61 head of hogs, 11 sheep, etc.). The executors were
his sons William and Robert Ruffin.

William [3] Ruffin married 1st, ca. 1707, Faith Gray (ca. 1688-
ca. 1720), daughter of William Gray and his wife Elizabeth_____.
They had at least four children, apparently in the following order:

     1. William Ruffin (ca. 1708-1781), of Northampton Co, N.C.
        m. _____.....4 children.

2. Ethelred Ruffin (ca. 1710-1777), of Northampton Co.,
   N. C. m. Martha_____ .....4 children.
3. Robert Ruffin (ca. 1712-1767). (See below).
4. Samuel Ruffin (1716-ca. 1779), of Edgecombe Co., N.C.,
   m. _____Lamon. (See later).

William 3 Ruffin married 2nd, 1725, Mrs. John Newsum (nee
Sarah Crafford).....No children.

Will of William Gray, of Surry County, Va., dated June 3,
1719, proved Nov. 18, 1719:
Sons: William Gray, Gilbert Gray.
Daughters: Mary Gray, Priscilla Gray, Faith Ruffin.
Grandchildren: Wm. Andrews, Elizabeth Edwards, Willm.
           Ruffin, and William, Robert, Joseph, and
           Thomas Gray.
Executor: Gilbert Gray.   Witnesses: Nichl. Maget, Robt.
           Judkins, Saml. Maget.

Capt. William[3]Gray (1661-1719) was the son of Capt. Francis[2]
Gray (d. 1679; wife Mary), who was the son of Thomas[1]Gray (1593-
1658), emigrant to Virginia in 1608, and his wife Annis (i. e.
Agnes).

In the "North Carolina Colonial Records" we find in Vol. 22,
p. 243, that William Ruffin, Junr. (note the "junior") paid quit
rents in Bertie County, N. C. in 1735 (which rents were in arrears
for 1729-1732); in Vol. 4, p. 521-2 that William, Robert, and
Samuel Ruffin were jurymen, in the list for Bertie and Edgecombe
counties, in February, 1740; that Robert Ruffin had land grants in
1741, 1742, and 1743, and that Samuel Ruffin had land grants in
1743 and 1745; that William Ruffin was a witness in Northampton
County in 1763; that Samuel Ruffin was a Member from Edgecombe
County in the General Assembly in 1762, also sheriff and justice
of the peace for Edgecombe County; that Ethelred Ruffin was a
justice of the peace and contested an election in 1776; etc. In
"Grimes' Abstracts of N. C. Wills, 1690-1760" we find: (a) Robert Ruffin a witness to the will of James Moore of Bertie Precinct
in 1735 (executor was John Dawson; a witness was John Brown);
(b) Ethelred Ruffin and Robert Ruffin were executors of the will
of John Hart of Bertie Precinct dated 1741, proved 1746 (John
Lamon and Howell Browne were witnesses); (c) Samuel Ruffin was
an executor (with Col. John Dawson and others) of the will of Joseph Howell of Edgecombe County dated 1749, proved 1750.

Robert [4] Ruffin (ca. 1712 (?)-1767) lived in Northampton County,
N. C. His will, dated March 28, 1767, proved at August Court
1767, was witnessed by Henry Dawson, Mary Cotten, and John
Hull. He married, 1733, Anne Bennett, daughter of Capt. William
Bennett and his wife Grace_____ . (See 17c.)

Children:
1. Faith Ruffin (1733-1733)
2. William Ruffin (1735-1781) (See below.)
3. Anne Ruffin (1737-1801), m. 1753, Arthur Smith (d. 1789) of Halifax Co., N. C. ... 11 children.
4. Olivia Ruffin (1739-1803), m. 1760, William Barrow (d. 1787) of Edgecombe Co., N. C. ... 8 children.

William 5 Ruffin (1735-1781), of Bertie County, N. C., married, 1762, Sarah ("Sallie") Hill, (1743-ca. 1813), daughter of Capt. Richard Hill, of Sussex County, Va., and his wife Margery Gilliam (daughter of William Gilliam and his wife Susanna Green). Children:
1. Robert Ruffin (1763-1786) ... d. s. p.
2. Thomas Ruffin (ca. 1764-17) ... died young.
3. Sallie Ruffin (ca. 1766-17), m. 17 , William Rhodes, ... 2 daughters.
4. Hannah Ruffin (1768-1848) married 1st. 1786, Marmaduke Norfleet (1766-1818) q. v., married, 2nd., 1820, James Gee (d. 1834) ... No children.
5. Rebecca Ruffin (ca. 1770-17) ... died young.

Mrs. Sarah (Hill) Ruffin married 2nd., 17--, Capt. James Smith (d. 1811) of Halifax County, N. C., but had no children by him.

That this first born was named "Faith" after her grandmother has been inferred from the mother's mourning ring that has been handed down in the family (and is now, 1945, in the possession of W. A. Graham Clark) inscribed "F. R. ob 9 Decm. 1733 AE 14 days". (See first line above.)

Samuel Ruffin, (1716-1779), son of Elizabeth Grey and William Ruffin of Surry County, Va., had land grants in what is now Edgecomb Co., in N. C. in 1743-45. He represented Edgecomb in the General Assembly of 1762 and later was also sheriff and Justice of the Peace. He died in 1779, and he and his wife, said to have been a Miss Lamon, had children, 1. Lamon; 2. Ethelred, b. 1744. (There may have been others.)

Ethelred Ruffin, son of the above Samuel Ruffin, married MARY, daughter of Col William Haywood, and his wife, Charity Hare. Col. Haywood was Colonel of the Edgecombe Militia in the Revolution and a member of the Halifax Convention which declared for Independence April 4, 1776. (Wheeler) The children of Ethelred and Mary Ruffin were (1) Henry John Grey, b. May 9, 1782 (see later); (2) Wm. Haywood, (3) Samuel; (4) Sarah, m. Henry Haywood; (5) Charity Ann, married first ----Ward; second, --- Henderson; (6) Margaret Elizabeth; (7) James, m. Miss Staunton and had Wiley, who died unmarried.

Col. Henry John Grey Ruffin, b. May 9, 1782, at Louisburg,

N. C., died March 8, 1854; m. Mary Tartt, b. April 29, 1791, died March 10, 1879. Col. Ruffin was a member of the House of Representatives in 1812 and was also State Senator in 1828, He served as an officer in the Militia in 1812. Henry John Grey and Mary (Tartt) Ruffin had children (not given in order of birth): (1) Pinnah, m. Dr. John K. Ruffin; (2) Lamon, Confederate States Army, died in service; (3) Ethelred, born 1832, Confederate States Army, d. in service; married 1853 Elizabeth Lee Kennedy, and had Mary Lee, married to John Exum Woodward and had Mary Lee Woodward, who married Cushing B. Hassel of Wilson, N. C.; (4) Sally Blount; (5) Patrick Henry; (6) Lafayette; (7) Dr. George W., Confederate States Army, died in service; (8) Thomas, b. Sept. 9, 1820; member of Congress 1853-55, and of the Provisional Congress of the Confederate States; entered the C.S.A. and when colonel of the First N.C. Cavalry was mortally wounded near Bristow Station, Oct. 15, 1863; (9) Mary Haywood, m. Samuel G. Williams; (10) Samuel, m. Ann, daughter of U. S. Senator William H. Haywood; (11) William Haywood, b. Feb. 22, 1817, m. Agnes K. Chadwick (see later).

Dr. William Haywood Ruffin, II, born at Louisburg, Feb. 22, 1817, d. April 25, 1879, m. Agnes Chadwick. Dr. Ruffin graduated in medicine at the University of Pennsylvania, rode twice to California on horseback during the gold rush period, bought a plantation in Alabama and served in the C.S.A. as a Brigade Surgeon.

His children were: (1) William Haywood III, b. July 19, 1864, (see later); (2) Samuel, m. Blanch Foster; (3) Chadwick, unmarried; (4) Mary T. m. Mark Stamps; (5) James; (6) Thomas; (7) Sarah Drum.

William Haywood Ruffin III was born in Sheffield, Ala., July 19, 1864, and died at Louisburg, N. C. March 12, 1926. He married at Louisburg, June 28, 1893, Sally Johnson White, b. at Louisburg Oct. 13, 1866, died there Dec. 17, 1922. She was the daughter of Thomas White and his wife Mary Louisa Shaw.

Mr. Ruffin was educated at Louisburg Academy. He practiced law in the city and became President of the First National Bank of Louisburg.

His children were: (1) Thomas White, b. 1896; m. Leona Lamberton; (2) Wm. Haywood IV, b. Feb. 8, 1899, (see later); (3) Henry John Grey, b. May 2, 1904, d. May 18, 1926.

William Haywood Ruffin IV was born at Louisburg, N. C., Feb. 8, 1899. He married Oct. 20, 1929, at Salisbury, Rowan Co., N. C., Josephine Craige Kluttz, born Oct. 14, 1908, at El Paso, Texas, daughter of Wm. Clarence Kluttz and his wife Josephine Branch Craige.

Mr. Ruffin is President and Treasurer of the Erwin Cotton

Mills Co., of Durham, N. C., and also a Director of the Durham Bank & Trust Co. He was educated at the University of North Carolina and served as an officer in World War I.

Children:

1. William Haywood V, b. May 10, 1932;
2. Josephine Branch Craige, b. July 30, 1934;
3. Burton Craige, b. Nov. 5, 1939.

5. Edmund Ruffin, son of Elizabeth and Robert Ruffin, was born in 1713 in Surry and died in 1790 in Prince George County. He married Mrs. Anne Edmunds, widow of Thomas EDMUNDS and daughter of John Simmons, Burgess for Isle of Wight 1736-49. She died in Sussex in 1749.

Children from Albermarle Register:

    I. Mary, b. Dec. 24, 1739.
    II. James, b. July 23, 1741.
    III. Eliz. b. Sept. 22, 1742.
6. IV. Edmund, b. Jan. 2, 1744.

6. Edmund Ruffin of Prince George County, married (1) Jane Skipwith, daughter of Sir William Skipwith, born 1707, died 1764, 6th Bart.; married (2) 1733, Elizabeth Smith, dau. of John Smith, Sheriff of Middlesex Co., Va. Mr. Ruffin was a member of the House of Delegates 1777-1787; member of Constitutional Conventions 1788, County Lieut. 1789; Sheriff 1797.

Children:

7. I. George Ruffin, m. (1) Jane Lucas, (2) Rebecca Cocke. (See later).

7. George Ruffin of Evergreen, Prince George Co., Va., born Jan. 29, 1765, died May 12, 1810, married (1) Jane Lucas of Surry, (2) Rebecca Cocke, daughter of Col. John COCKE of Surry. Mr. Ruffin was a planter in Prince George and a member of the House of Delegates, 1803-1806.

Children:

8. I. Edmund, m. Susan H. Travis. (See later.)
    II. Elizabeth, was the first wife of Lieut. Henry Harrison Cocke, U. S. N.

8. Edmund Ruffin was born January 5, 1794, died June 15, 1865. In 1813 he married Susan H. Travis of Williamsburg. He served as a private in camp at Norfolk during the War of 1812.

He was a noted agriculturist. It was at the Coggin's Point farm which the recent death of his father had brought him "that he began the agricultural experiments which were to bring him fame and restore his section to prosperity." (D. A. B.)

He was one of the founders of the Prince George Society of Agriculturists and became famous for his writings and publications on agricultural subjects. In 1841 he was appointed to the first Virginia State Board of Agriculture. In 1842 he became agricultural surveyor of South Carolina and in the atmosphere of that belligerent state he became an early advocate of Secession.

In 1843 Mr. Ruffin moved to a new estate, "Marlbourne", in Hanover County. He was always interested in politics and served three years in the Virginia Senate (1823-26). He originated the League of United Southerners, secured and presented one of John Brown's pikes to the governor of each of the Southern States and volunteered to serve with the Palemetto Guard of Charleston. On account of his services to the cause of Secession he was selected to fire the first shot from Morris Island against Fort Sumter. He also served with this company at the first Battle of Bull Run. (D. A. B.)

Children:

9.   I.   Edmund, b. 1816, m. (1) Mary Cooke Smith, (2) Jane M. Ruffin.
      II.   George Champion, died young.
      III. Agnes, m. Dr. Thomas S. Beckwith.
      IV.   Jane, died young.
      V.   Julian Calx, m. Charlotte Meade.
      VI.   Rebecca, m. John T. Bland.
      VII. Elizabeth, m. William Sayre, of Kentucky.
      VIII. Mildred C., m. B. B. Sayre, brother of Wm.
      IX.   Jane, am. John J. Dupuy.
      X.   Ella
12.   XI.   Charles Lorraine, b. Sept. 10, 1832; m. Henrietta Alice Harrison (see later).

9.   Edmund Ruffin, born 1816, died August 19, 1876, at "Marlbourne", Hanover County; married (1) Mary Cooke Smith, daughter of Anne (Dabney) and Thomas Gregory Smith; (2) Jane Ruffin, dau. of Judge Thomas Ruffin of N. C.

Mr. Ruffin was a Captain C. S. A. He wrote the editor of The Richmond Daily Dispatch: "Sir: Please have me put down as a subscriber to the iron-clad gunboat scheme, for the protection of the James River. I will give $1, 000 if the whole matter is put into the hands and under the control of the Confederate government, and the scheme be prosecuted without unnecessary delay. Very respectfully, etc., E. Ruffin, Jr. April 4, 1862."

Children: (first wife):

      I.   Virginia, b. October 8, 1837, died 1844.
      II.   Edmund Quintus, b. March 25, 1839, d. 1853.
      III. Anne, b. January 1, 1841, d. July 25, 1853.
      IV.   Thomas Smith, b. 1843, d. 1873, m. Alice Lorraine.

He was a member of his father's cavalry company,
enlisting at 18.

V. George Champion, b. March 3, 1845, d. 1913; m.
Alice Cooke.

VI. Susan, b. June 30, 1846, d. 1931; m. (1) William Will-
cox, (2) E. C. Harrison.

VII. Mary Smith, b. 1848, d. 1942; m. Rev. E. V. Jones.

10. VIII. John Augustine, b. Feb. 25, 1853; m. Jane Cary Harrison.

10. John Augustine Ruffin was born February 25, 1853, at
"Beachwood", Prince George County, and died November 3,
1926, at "Evelynton", Charles City County. He was married
May 22, 1888, at Westover, to Jane Cary Harrison, born June
20, 1855, at "Riverside", Charles City County, died April 18,
1909, at Evelynton. Mr. Ruffin was a planter and resided at
"Evelynton", which was named for Evelyn Byrd of "Westover".

Children:

11. I. Susan, b. May 5, 1889, m. Lyon G. Tyler.

II. Carolina Kirkland, b. May 7, 1891, m. R. B. Saunders.

III. Mary Harrison, b. Aug. 13, 1893, m. A. G. Copeland.

IV. John Augustine, b. August 17, 1895, m. Mary B. Saunders.

11. Susan Ruffin, born May 5, 1889, at "Evelynton", mar-
ried September 12, 1923, at Westover Church, Dr. Lyon Gardiner
Tyler, born August, 1853, at "Sherwood Forest", Charles City
County, died February 12, 1935, at "Lions Den", Charles City
County.

Dr. Tyler was a son of Julia (Gardiner) and John Tyler,
tenth President of the United States. He was A. B. University
of Virginia, 1874; A. M. 1875; member Virginia House of
Delegates 1887; President of the College of William and Mary,
1888-1919; made president-emeritus, 1919.

Dr. Tyler was also noted for his authorship of historical
writings dealing principally with Virginia; was editor and proprietor of the William and Mary Quarterly, founded 1902, and of
Tyler's Quarterly, founded 1919; also wrote "Letters and Times
of the Tyler's", and "The Cradle of the Republic". Virginia is
indebted to Dr. Tyler for the preservation of its early history
more than to any other man.

Children of Susan (Ruffin) and Dr. Lyon Gardiner Tyler:

I. Lyon Gardiner, b. January 3, 1925, entered Naval
Reserve at age of 17, commissioned Ensign, Sept. 14,
1944; served in World War II.

II. Harrison Ruffin, b. November 9, 1928.

III. Henry, b. January 18, 1930, d. January 26, 1930.

12. Charles Lorraine Ruffin, born Sept. 10, 1832, died January 9, 1870, at "Rose Cottage", Prince George, married April 28, 1864, Henrietta Alice Harrison, born June 29, 1843, died Sept. 14, 1925, at Richmond, Va., daughter of Mary (Boisseau) and Alexander Harrison.

Mr. Ruffin received a degree of C. E. at the V. M. I. and was in General Beauregard's command at Bull Run.

Children:

    I. Charles Lorraine II, b. May 21, 1866 (see later).
    II. Mary, b. 1868.

Charles Lorraine Ruffin II, born May 21, 1866, in Prince George, married April 24, 1895, at Baltimore, Maryland, Mary Levering, born Jan. 23, 1875, dau. of Nellie (Denmead) and Robert Levering of Baltimore. Mr. Ruffin was educated at the V. M. I. and is president of the Sand and Gravel Co., of Richmond, Va. He resides at 6314 Chopt Road.

Children:

    I. Mary Denmead, b. Aug. 8, 1896.
    II. Henrietta Harrison, b. Feb. 2, 1899, m. Dr. W. R. Comthwarte.
    III. Charles Lorraine, b. Feb. 20, 1901, m. Elizabeth Thornton.
    IV. Ella Levering, b. Feb. 6, 1902, m. Dec. 30, 1933, David Adam Wallace, son of Sophie Willis (Adam) and David Duncan Wallace, born Dec. 31, 1901, killed in action March 10, 1943, leaving one son, David Duncan Wallace, b. March 8, 1936.

ASTON
of
Tixall, Staffordshire, and Charles City, Va.

It seems somewhat far fetched to carefully trace the English pedigree of a family that became extinct in the male line in Virginia in the second generation. However, many descendants through female lines survive. This family is traced back to Charlemagne, in the chart heretofore shown, mainly to show how easily families can be traced back to royalty. Nearly every American family that goes back to the visitation pedigrees of England more than likely has a pedigree leading back to royalty. Royal pedigrees are the oldest in Europe and all royal lines lead back to Charlemagne. The one herein shown does not descend through the royal family of England.

The family of Aston owned the Manor of Heywood in Staffordshire, England. The records of this family extend back to the time of Henry II and are fairly numerous during the time of Richard I and King John. The line begins with Ralph de Aston, who lived in the time of Henry III. (For more about this family see the the William Salt Society Annals of Staffordshire, Vol. III, p. 133, also Vol. VI, part 1, p. 209).

SIR JOHN[9]ASTON of Heywood and Tixall in Stafford, ninth in line from Ralph de Aston, was the eldest son an heir of John Aston and his wife Elizabeth Delves.

He was a member of Parliament for Staffordshire 1495-96-97-1504-10-15-23. He was also Sheriff of Stafford in 1500-01, 1508-09; 1513-14; and of Warwick and Leicester 1510-11.

He was made a Knight of the Bath at the marriage of Prince Arthur, eldest son of Henry V, in 1501.

He was in the Staffordshire Contingent in France and accompanied Henry VII in his expedition into Brittany. He was present at the seiges of Terrouenne and Tournay. For his bravery at the Battle of Spurs he was made a knight banneret by the King on the field of battle.

Before he departed overseas he made his will dated April 24, 1513, beginning as follows: "intending to depart over see with our most dreadde soverayne in his royall armee". This will was proven April 25, 1523 (P.C.C. 6 Bodfille).

Sir John Aston died March 28 in the 14th year of reign of Henry VII (1523) seized of lands and tenements in Wollaster and Orne which he held of the King as of his manor of Church Eyton by his fealty only of the value of 100 S., the said manor of Church Eyton having come into the King's hands by the forfeiture of Edward, late Duke of Buckingham, attained for high treason.

He married Joan, daughter of Sir William Littleton, son of the famous Chief Justice Thomas Littleton (See Littleton Viscount Cobham, Burke's Peerage 1929), from whom Joan inherited Tixall; and from her mother Helen and coheir of Robert Welsh, Esq. and his wife Margery, daughter and coheiress of Sir Richard Byron, she inherited Wanlip in Leicester.

Children:

    I. SIR EDWARD
    II. WILLIAM, mentioned in his father's will to have Mill-wich for life.
    III. ISABEL, left £ 200.
    IV. ELIZABETH, left £ 200.

SIR EDWARD [10] ASTON of Tixall was son and heir of Sir John Aston and his wife Joan Littleton. He was born in 1494 and died in 1568.

He married, first, Mary, daughter of Sir Henry Vernon. She died without issue, and he married secondly, Jane, daughter of Sir Thomas Bowles. He was a member of Parliament for Stafford in 1523-36-39 and 40. He was Justice of Peace from 1526 to 1565, and was Sheriff of Stafford in the years 1528-9, 1534-5, 1540-01, and 1556-7. He was knighted at Calais in 1532 (Shaw) and built the mansion at Tixall in 1555.

Children:

    I. MARIA, married Simon Harcourt of Stourton.
    II. KATHERINE, married William Gresley of Colton.
    III. ANNA
    IV. FRANCES, married Robert Needham.
    V. SIR WALTER ASTON, married Elizabeth Levison and was grandfather of Walter Aston, created Lord Aston of Forfar in Scotland.
    VI. LEONARD, married Elizabeth Barton, widow of Thomas Creswell.

LEONARD[11] ASTON, according to the Visitations of Staffordshire for 1583, was born in Tixall and was the second son of Sir Edward Aston of Tixall and his wife Jane Bowles. The Visitations of London for 1534 are in error in showing him as the son of Sir Walter Aston, as the records plainly show that he was his brother.

The Feet of Fines for Stafford (Vol. XI, p. 285) show that there was a fine levied in 1542 concerning land in Milwich in which it was stated that the land was to go to William Aston for life, and then to Leonard Aston, son of Edward, for life. This William Aston was the second son of Sir John Aston (d. 1523) and Edward Aston was the elder son who inherited Tixall. Leonard is here clearly shown to be the son of Edward Aston, which verified the Visitation of Stafford for 1583 and contradicts that of London 1634.

Leonard Aston married Elizabeth Barton, relict of Thomas Creswell, by whom she had two daughters. (Chancery Proceedings 1560-70, Salt Vol. IX, N. S. p. 168.)

There were several fines levied by Leonard Aston and his wife, Elizabeth, concerning land in Longdon about the end of Queen Elizabeth's reign.

WALTER [12] ASTON, son of Leonard Aston and his wife Elizabeth Barton, lived at Longdon. He married Joyce, daughter of Nason of Rougham in Warwickshire.

He dealt rather extensively in land in Longdon, as he and his wife Joyce made many fines concerning land in Longdon. In 9 James I (1612) Walter Aston, gentleman, and Joyce, his wife, sold 54 acres of land to Edward Hill. Shortly after that Walter Aston, Knight, sold land to Walter Aston, gentleman, and Joyce, his wife, 434 acres in Longdon. (Salt Vol. III, N. S. p. 41.)

In 12 James I, Walter Aston and Joyce, his wife, of Longdon, sold land to John King in Longdon. (Salt Vol. IV, N. S. p. 73.)

WALTER [13] ASTON was the son of Walter Aston, gent., and his wife, Joyce Nason, of Longdon in Staffordshire. (Vis. London 1634.) He is shown in the Visitation of London 1634 as being "now in the West Indies". (W&MQ 4, p. 144.) Virginia, in those days, was frequently referred to as the "West Indies". From an inscription on his tomb at Westover, he was born in 1607, and died April 6, 1656. The first record we find of Walter Aston is from the land grant records, where it is shown that he pattented 590 acres of land, as follows:

"Sir John Harvey to WALTER ASTON, 590 acres, July 26, 1638, page 578. Gent. Charles City Co. between Sherly Hundred and land of Nathaniel Causey. Due for personal adv. of himself, wife Warbowe, and ten other persons." (C. P. 93.)

He further patented in 1646, 1040 acres, 200 of which acres he had formerly bought from John Causey Feb. 7, 1634. This John Causey was probably the son of Nathaniel Causey, who had patented this land in 1620. Nathaniel Causey was an old soldier who came in the first supply in 1608.

Walter Aston's first wife was named "Warbowe" and she, as shown by the above patents, came over with him. He married, secondly, Hannah Jordan, (Major's, p. 27) who after his death married Col. Edward Hill.

Walter Aston represented Sherley Hundred Island in 1629-30 in the House of Burgesses. He represented Sherley Hundred, Mr. Farrars and Chaplains in February 1631-32; Charles City County in 1642-43. He was a Justice and also was Lieutenant-Colonel of the Charles City County Militia. Captain Thomas Pawlett, in his will dated January 12, 1643-44, a brother of the Marquis of Winchester, mentions Thomas Aston, his godson, and his loving friend "Mr. Walter Aston. " (W&M 4, p. 152).

He was buried at Westover which afterwards passed into the hands of the Byrd family, and his tomb with the following inscription is still intact at Westover (W&M 4, p. 144):

Here Lyeth interred the body of Leftenant
Colonell Walter Aston who died the 6th
April 1656. He was aged
49 years and
lived in this country 28 years
Also here lyeth the Body of Walter Aston
the son of Leftenant Collonel Walter Aston
who departed this life ye 29th of Ianuari 1666
aged 27 years and 7 months.

Children:

    I. SUSSANAH, was a relict in 1655 of Lieut. Col. Edward Major. In her will in Nansemond in 1662 she names her nephews John Cox (Cocke) and Thomas Binns and niece Susan Binns and her son-in-law (step-son) Wm. Major. (Majors, p. 25).

    II. WALTER, b. 1639 of "Causeys Care" was unmarried. He made his will December 21, 1666, probated February 4, 1666/67, (Byrds Book of Title Deeds.) He gave to Hannah Hill, his mother, that parcel of land called the "Level"; to godson John Cocke, the son of Richard Cocke, decd., 4,000 pds. tbco. to be paid in 1668, to godson Edward Cocke, son of the aforesaid Cocke, 6,000 pds. tbco. to be paid in 1669. To sisters Mary Cocke and Elizabeth Binns 20 shillings apiece for a ring.

    III. MARY, m. Lt.-Col. Richard Cocke.

    IV. ELIZABETH, m. Thomas Binns, and had son, Thomas and daughter Susan Binns; (see Binns) mentioned in will of Sussanah Major.

    V. THOMAS, probably d.s.p.; mentioned in will of Captain Thomas Paulett, 1643.

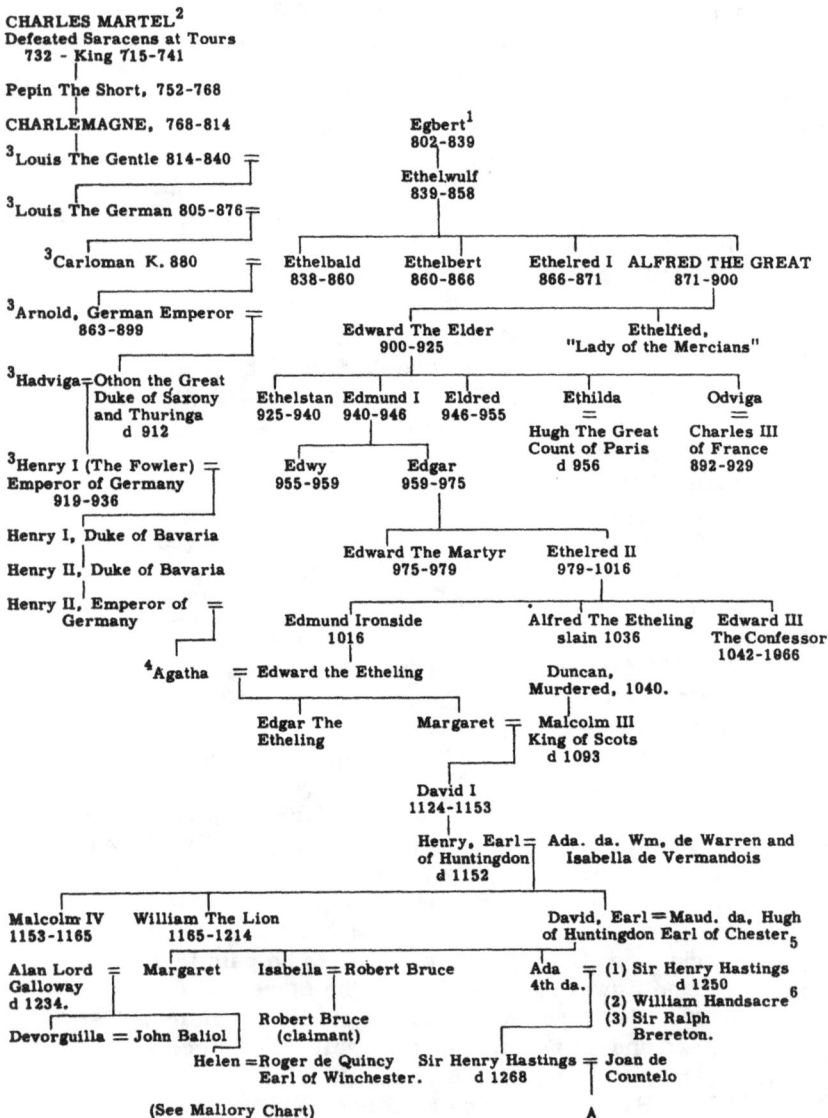

ASTON

CHARLES MARTEL[2]
Defeated Saracens at Tours
732 - King 715-741

Pepin The Short, 752-768

CHARLEMAGNE, 768-814

[3]Louis The Gentle 814-840 =

[3]Louis The German 805-876 =

[3]Carloman K. 880 =

[3]Arnold, German Emperor =
863-899

[3]Hadviga=Othon the Great
Duke of Saxony
and Thuringa
d 912

[3]Henry I (The Fowler) =
Emperor of Germany
919-936

Henry I, Duke of Bavaria

Henry II, Duke of Bavaria

Henry II, Emperor of =
Germany

[4]Agatha = Edward the Etheling

Egbert[1]
802-839

Ethelwulf
839-858

Ethelbald   Ethelbert   Ethelred I   ALFRED THE GREAT
838-860   860-866   866-871   871-900

Edward The Elder   Ethelfied,
900-925   "Lady of the Mercians"

Ethelstan   Edmund I   Eldred   Ethilda   Odviga
925-940   940-946   946-955   =   =
                                     Hugh The Great   Charles III
                                     Count of Paris   of France
Edwy   Edgar   d 956   892-929
955-959   959-975

Edward The Martyr   Ethelred II
975-979   979-1016

Edmund Ironside   Alfred The Etheling   Edward III
1016   slain 1036   The Confessor
                                                1042-1966
                         Duncan,
                     Murdered, 1040.

Edgar The   Margaret =   Malcolm III
Etheling   King of Scots
                                   d 1093

David I
1124-1153

Henry, Earl = Ada. da. Wm. de Warren and
of Huntingdon   Isabella de Vermandois
d 1152

Malcolm IV   William The Lion   David, Earl = Maud. da, Hugh
1153-1165   1165-1214   of Huntingdon Earl of Chester[5]

Alan Lord = Margaret   Isabella = Robert Bruce   Ada   = (1) Sir Henry Hastings
Galloway   4th da.   d 1250
d 1234.   (2) William Handsacre[6]
                         Robert Bruce   (3) Sir Ralph
Devorguilla = John Baliol   (claimant)   Brereton.

Helen =Roger de Quincy   Sir Henry Hastings = Joan de
      Earl of Winchester.   d 1268   Countelo

(See Mallory Chart)   A

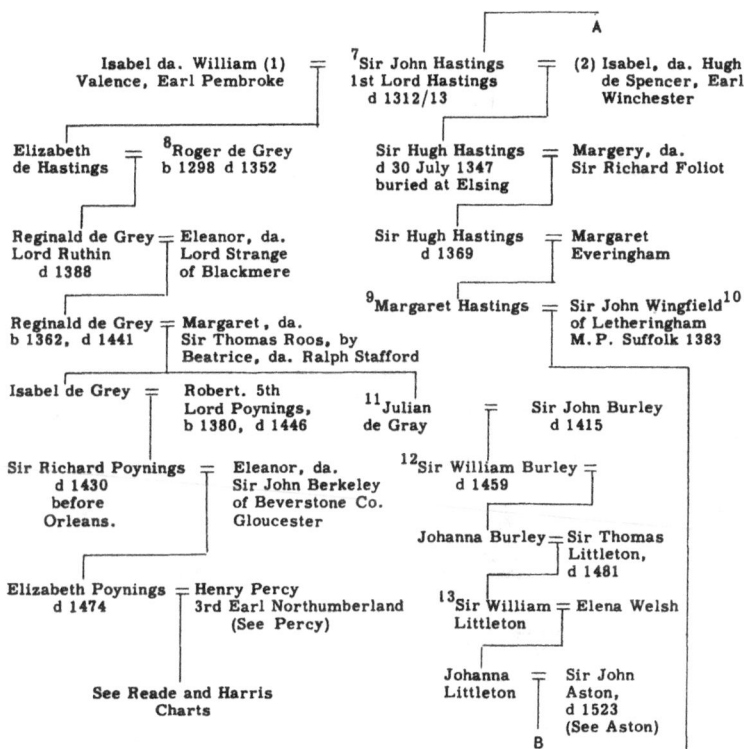

A

Isabel da. William (1) = [7]Sir John Hastings = (2) Isabel, da. Hugh
Valence, Earl Pembroke   1st Lord Hastings   de Spencer, Earl
  d 1312/13   Winchester

Elizabeth = [8]Roger de Grey   Sir Hugh Hastings = Margery, da.
de Hastings   b 1298 d 1352   d 30 July 1347   Sir Richard Foliot
  buried at Elsing

Reginald de Grey = Eleanor, da.   Sir Hugh Hastings = Margaret
Lord Ruthin   Lord Strange   d 1369   Everingham
d 1388   of Blackmere

Reginald de Grey = Margaret, da.   [9]Margaret Hastings = Sir John Wingfield[10]
b 1362, d 1441   Sir Thomas Roos, by   of Letheringham
  Beatrice, da. Ralph Stafford   M. P. Suffolk 1383

Isabel de Grey = Robert. 5th   [11]Julian = Sir John Burley
  Lord Poynings,   de Gray   d 1415
  b 1380, d 1446

Sir Richard Poynings = Eleanor, da.   [12]Sir William Burley =
d 1430   Sir John Berkeley   d 1459
before   of Beverstone Co.
Orleans.   Gloucester

   Johanna Burley = Sir Thomas
  Littleton,
  d 1481

Elizabeth Poynings = Henry Percy   [13]Sir William = Elena Welsh
d 1474   3rd Earl Northumberland   Littleton
  (See Percy)

   Johanna = Sir John
  Littleton   Aston,
  d 1523
See Reade and Harris   (See Aston)
Charts

B

Katherine = Michael de la Pole
Wingfield   1st Earl of Suffolk
  1330-1389.

Michael de la Pole = Catherine
2nd Earl of   Stafford
Suffolk

See Woodlief Chart

Authorities

1. History of England, Larson, p. 57 and 176.
2. Leading Facts French History, Montgomery, p. 300.
3. Allstrom's Dictionary, Royal Lineage, p. 326-419-328-575.
4. Hume History of England, Vol. I, p. 136.
5. Complete Peerage by C.E.C., Vol. 6, p. 345.
6. Banks Baronage in Fee. Vol. 1, p. 211.
   Omerods Cheshire, Vol. III. p. 88.
7. Complete Peerage, G.E.C.
8. Complete Peerage, G.E.C.
9. Coppingers Manors in Suffolk, Vol. 3, p. 77.
10. Visitation of Norfolk, Vol. I. p. 79.
11. Owens & Blakenaye Shrewsbury, Vol. II. p. 139
12. Shropshire Archaeology, Vol. 44, p. 15.
    (Sir Wm. Burley was Speaker, House of Commons.
    1433 and 1444)
13. Visitation Staffordshire, 1583.

278

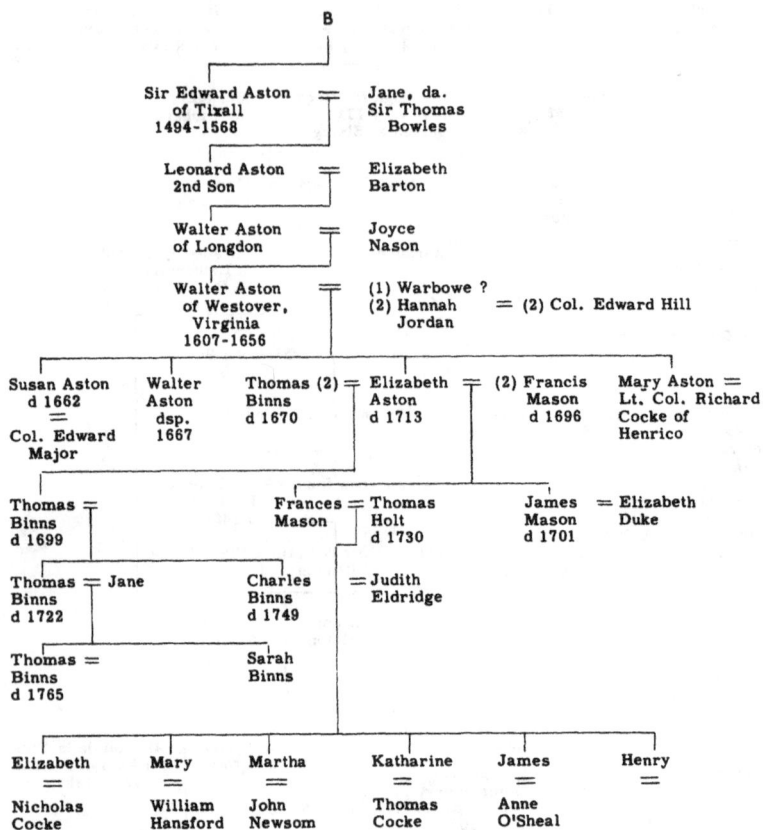

ELDRIDGE
of Surry

The first one of the Eldridge family from whom descent can be traced was Thomas Eldridge of Henrico, a lawyer, who was deputy clerk of that county in 1716 and clerk of the House of Burgesses from April 23 to April 28, 1718. (V. M. 32, p. 136.)

He married Judith, daughter of Richard Kennon of "Conjures Neck", Henrico, and his wife, Elizabeth, daughter of William Worsham. Richard Kennon was a Justice in Henrico, 1678, and was Burgess for that county in 1685. He died in 1696 and gave his daughter Judith and her husband Thomas Eldridge 657 acres at Rochdale, now in Chesterfield County. (V. M. 32, p. 390.)

Thomas Eldridge patented 830 acres in Brunswick in 1727. (B 13, p. 182.) He was probably then residing in Surry County, where he died November 4, 1740. His will was dated August 17, 1739 and proven May 20, 1741. He gave his wife, Judith, all land in Brunswick - at her death to go to sons William and Richard. Land at Hunting Quarter in Surry was to be divided between his daughters. His son Richard was to have Rochdale in Henrico and land purchased of James Dickins; William, not 21, was to have the home place. He also gave grandson, Thomas Eldridge and granddaughter Judith Eldridge £15 each. Son Thomas was to have land in Prince George on Warwick Branch. Judith (Kennon) Eldridge died October 14, 1759. Her death was certified by her son, William Eldridge.

Children:

2. I. Thomas, m. (1) Martha, daughter of Mary (Kennon) and John Bolling, (2) Elizabeth Jones.
3. II. William, m. Ann Jones. She afterwards married John Cargill III.
    III. Richard
    IV. Judith, m. Charles BINNS.
    V. Elizabeth died September 15, 1745, certified by Thomas Eldridge.
    VI. Mary
    VII. Anne, m. Sterling Clack of Brunswick. He was born in Gloucester but removed to Brunswick, where he became

Deputy Clerk September 17, 1734. He succeeded Drury Stith, the first Clerk of Brunswick, on June 5, 1742. On November 10, 1740, he purchased from Robert Mumford 1000 acres of land. (B 2, p. 238.) In 1746 he gave the land where the Court House was built. He was a Church Warden of St. Andrews in 1749; made his will January 9, 1750, same probated March 26, 1751, and provided that the 1000 acre plantation was to go to his son, Eldridge Clack. Ann, his wife, died in Sussex January, 1754.

According to the will of Mrs. Judith Eldridge of Sussex, 1760, Ann was her daughter, and Mrs. Eldridge mentioned Mary, Elizabeth, Judith and Ann Sterling Clack as her grandchildren.

Eldridge Clack, married in Sussex, November 3, 1769, Betty, daughter of John Hunt, decd.

VIII. Martha, m. August, 1748, John Harris of Surry, whose will was dated December 26, 1770, was probated Surry, March 19, 1771. Legatees: daughter, Pamela McRae, two negroes; sons, Richard Kennon and Eldridge Harris; daughters, Mary Harris and Ann Kennon Harris. Directs lands at Ware Neck be sold and proceeds divided among his three sons. Appoints his particular friends, Rev. Christopher McRae, rector of Southwark Parish, Michael Nicholson and William Eldridge of Surry, Executors.

Children:
1. Pamela Harris, b. June 11, 1749, m. March 29, 1768, Rev. Christopher McRae.
2. Ann Kennon Harris, b. April 6, 1758.
3. Eldridge Harris, b. May 19, 1764.
4. Richard Kennon Harris.
5. Kennon Harris.
6. Mary Harris.

2. Thomas Eldridge, II, married (1) Martha, born 1713, died October 23, 1749, daughter of Mary (Kennon) and John Bolling, married (2), Elizabeth Jones. His first wife was a descendant of John Rolfe and Pocahontas.

Thomas Eldridge died in Sussex December 4, 1754. Inventory of his estate was filed in Sussex 1755.

Children of first wife (V. M. 46, p. 275):
I. Thomas III, m. Winifred Jones of Goochland.
II. Jane, d. s. p.
III. John, b. April 22, 1741.
IV. Judith, (twin) b. March 11, 1743, m. James Ferguson, who made his will in Amelia 1769.

   V. Mary, (twin) b. March 11, 1743, m. Thomas Branch.

  VI. Rolfe, b. December 29, 1744, m. November 26, 1773 (Brunswick Bonds), Sarah Everard Walker. He was Clerk of Buckingham from 1770 until his death in 1806.

Children of second wife:

 VII. Sarah, b. 1754, d. 1836, m. November 25, 1771 (Brunswick Bonds) Colonel Thomas EDMUNDS of Brunswick (1748-1825).

3. Captain William Eldridge married Ann Jones, sister of Robert JONES. She married secondly, Swptember 15, 1774, John Cargill III. Captain Eldridge died April 2, 1772, and his will, dated January 24, 1772, was probated in Sussex May 21, 1772. He made his wife and his brother-in-law, Robert Jones, executrix and executor. (W. B. "B", p. 350.) Her will, as Anne Jones Cargill, was dated October 27, 1780, and probated September 15, 1784. (W. B. "C", p. 393.)

Eldridge children:

4.   I. Elizabeth, m. July 24, 1779, with the consent of her mother, Ann Cargill, John Massenburg. (See later.)

     II. Mary, III. Ann, IV. Robert, V. Thomas, m. April 21, 1769, Elizabeth Pennington, a widow.

4. Elizabeth Eldridge married John Massenburg, July 24, 1779. He served in the Revolutionary War for three years as a seaman on the ship "Henry" in the Virginia Navy. (Brumbaugh, pp. 16 & 69).

He was a Justice of the County Court, 1798-1801. Their children were: John; William E.; Richard K.; Thomas (1798-1845) m. Tabitha Hamlin Powell (see later #5); Benjamin H.; Barbara m. John Parham; Eliza E.; and Robert.

5. Thomas Massenburg, born March 1798, died February 9, 1845; married February 21, 1825, Tabitha Hamlin Powell, born October 5, 1803, daughter of Martha and William Hewitt Powell of Greensville County. He was a planter and Justice of the Sussex County Court in 1837.

Children:

     I. Martha Jane Massenburg, b. November 19, 1825, m. Richmond F. Dillard.

    II. Elizabeth Eldridge Massenburg, b. February 9, 1827, m. Col. James S. Gilliam.

  III. Thomas Hamblin Massenburg, b. Aug. 9, 1829, d. s. p.

  IV. John William Massenburg, b. June 7, 1831, d. s. p.

    V. Charles McKie Massenburg, b. Mar. 10, 1833, d. s. p.

6. VI. Agnes Cocke Massenburg, b. April 3, 1836, m. William A. Trotter. (see later.)

  VII. Virginia Kennon Massenburg, b. Jan. 3, 1838.

 VIII. Lucy Robertson Massenburg, b. Nov. 28, 1839.

  IX. Richard K. Massenburg.

6.   Agnes Cocke Massenburg, born April 13, 1836, at Coman's
Wells, Sussex, died June 1916, in Greensville County, married
Feburary 23, 1858, William Augustus Trotter, born May 16,
1832, in Brunswick, died May 21, 1912, in Greensville.   Mr.
Trotter was educated at Randolph Macon College.   He was a plan-
ter and served in the Confederate Army, 1861-65.
Children:
   I.   McKie Massenburg Trotter, m. Virginia Purdy.
   II.   Isham Edward Trotter, m. Irma Cousins.
   III.   Thomas Trotter, m. Bessie Kirkland.
   IV.   Agnes Trotter, m. Robert A. Raney.
   V.   Martha Dillard Trotter, b. February 12, 1867, m.
         James Woods.
7.   VI.   William Augustus Trotter, Jr., b. August 22, 1868, m.
         Betty M. Raney (see later).
   VII.   John Herbert Trotter, b. March 17, 1870, m. Hattie
         McWhorter.
   VIII.   Bagley Meredith Trotter, b. February 25, 1877, m.
         Mary Jackson.
   7.   William Augustus Trotter, Jr., born August 22, 1868,
died October 5, 1940, at Lawrenceville. Virginia; married
November 1893, Betty Mallory Raney, born March 13, 1871,
at Smoky Ordinary, Brunswick County, daughter of Betty (Mal-
lory) and Dr. George Monroe Raney.   Mr. Trotter was a banker
and resided at Lawrenceville.
Children:
   I.   George Monroe Trotter, b. September 21, 1894, m.
         Esther Solomon.
   II.   William Augustus Trotter, III, b. August 8, 1896, m.
         Frances Seay.
8.   III.   Louise Trotter, b. August 22, 1900, m. Sterling Wooten,
         (see later).
   IV.   Virginia Elizabeth Trotter, b. May 25, 1902, m. John
         A. Brosnaham.
   V.   Isham Edward, b. Oct. 24, 1904, m. Louise Harper.
   VI.   Agnes Baugh, b. March 10, 1907, m. Andrew F. Sams,
         Jr.
   VII.   Carleton Heath, b. August 19, 1908, m. Ruby Wilson.
   VIII.   Leigh Raney, b. November 17, 1910, m. Louise Jones.
   8.   Louise Trotter, born August 22, 1900, at Smoky Ordinary,
Virginia, married June 24, 1933, at Lawrenceville, Sterling
Dillon Wooten, born March 20, 1901, at Kinston, Lanoir County,
N. C., son of Lillian (Dillon) and Arthur Speight Wooten.   They
reside in Goldsboro, N. C., at 811 E. Beech Street.
Children:
   I.   Louise Trotter Wooten, b. March 9, 1935.
   II.   Sterling Dillon Wooten, Jr., b. April 6, 1939.

BINNS
of Surry

Thomas Binns was the first of this family in Surry. On February 25, 1653, he patented 343 acres of land "on S. side of James River from Mr. Bishop's corner tree to the head of Reedy swamp and south to Mr. Edward's land for the transportation of seven persons." (C. P. 231). He married Martha (name unknown) before 1665 - her date of death is unknown.

His second wife was Elizabeth Aston, daughter of Lt. Col. Walter ASTON. He was a Justice in 1668 and in that year had ten tithables in the tax list - the largest number in Surry. On May 4, 1669, "Mr. Thomas Binns was sick with distemper, is unable in to appear in court in case against William Marriott and Col. Jordan's business against himself." (B. 1, p. 336) Thomas Binns evidently did not recover, as his wife was appointed administratrix of his estate in 1670. This date is known from a law suit brought against her in the General Court in that year.

It was on March 25, 1655, that William Brereton and Temperance, his wife, sold to Thomas Binns and John Bishop "Grindalls Old Forte or Middle Plantation ground" in Surry. (B. 1, p. 72) Previously, Montjoy Evelin, gent., had patented part of this land in 1651; "150 acres of which had been granted to Edward Grendon December 5, 1620, and 300 granted to Mr. George Sandys in 1624, purchased of Thomas Grendon by Captain George Evelin August 3, 1649, who gave same by deed to his son the said Mountjoy April 28, 1650". (C. P. 401.) It seems that these two titles conflicted. The General Court order of 1670 was that "The difference between Major William Andrews, guardian of George Evelyn, orphan of Mountjoy Evelyn, plaintiff, and Mrs. Elizabeth Binns, admnx. of Thomas Binns, decd., about Grindall's Hill is dismissed. The said Mrs. Binns to remain in possession neither of the orphans being of age". (W. M. 20, p. 190.)

By 1673 Mrs. Elizabeth (Aston) Binns had married Colonel Francis MASON, who died in 1696. In 1701, Mrs. Mason divided 777 acres, patented by her in 1679, among her grandchildren, Frances Holt, Francis Mason, and Charles Binns. She died in 1713. (See Mason).

In the "Reliques of the Rives", p. 496, it is stated that Thomas Binns II was a son of Thomas Binns I and his first wife, Martha,

instead of his second wife, Elizabeth Aston. This is an error, for
Susannah (Aston) Major, aunt of Thomas Binns and relict of Col.
Edward Major, mentions her nephew and niece, Thomas and Susan
Binns, in her will in 1662. (See Aston). Other evidence in the
records of the Binns, Mason and Holt families bear this out.
Children of second wife:

     I. Susannah, mentioned in will of her Aunt, Susannah Major,
        1658.

2.   II. Thomas Binns

     III. Mary Binns, m. JOHN HOLT.

    2.   Thomas Binns was the son of Elizabeth (Aston) and Thomas
Binns. On July 1, 1679, he acknowledges receipt from Mr. Francis
Mason of 85,850 lbs. of tobacco, being his part of his father Binns
estate (B 2, p. 229). This would place his date of birth in 1658.
Thomas Binns died in 1699, for on July 4, 1699, James Mason,
his half brother, was appointed executor of his estate. James
Mason, in a deed in 1701, calls him "his brother" (W. M. 20,
p. 190). In 1704, Captain Thomas Holt held 950 acres in the Surry
Quit Rents for Thomas Binns orphans.
Children:

3.   I. Thomas Binns (See later)

4.   II. Charles Binns (see later)

    3.   Thomas Binns married Jane, last name unknown. He made
his will October 18, 1722, same probated November 20, 1723. He
gave his plantation to his wife for life and after her death to son
Thomas, for want of heirs to daughter, Sarah Binns - and for want
of heirs to his brother Charles Binns; wife and brother executors.
(W. B. 7, p. 484)
Children:

     I. Sarah; II. Thomas, m.   . He was mentioned in the
will of his Uncle Charles Binns in 1749. He made his will in 1765
in Sussex.

    4.   Charles Binns married Judith, daughter of Judith (Kennon)
and Thomas Eldridge I. John Holt, who made his will in 1723, provided that his "brother" Charles Binns shall assist his executor.
Charles was a Justice in Surry in 1732 and High Sheriff of Surry
in 1747.

    Charles Binns made his will Oct. 16, 1749, and same was pro-
bated March 20, 1749/50. He gave son Charles Binns two small
tracts of land, one bought from Thomas Moreland and the other
from Joseph Delks, also £100 current money when 21 and £15 per
annum for his schooling during his minority. To dau. Elizabeth
Binns £100; to daus. Martha and Lucy £100. If child in esse is
a female she was to have £100, if a male he was to have land at

the fork of the Nottoway and Blackwater in Nansemond.   "To nephew Thomas Binns, my woolen clothes; to Sally Binns one gold ring; to Sarah Shands 50 sh.   To Jean Gwaltney, who was brought up by me 50 sh. in goods.   To John Champion 15 sh. in Books of Divinity.   Nephew Thomas Binns to be guardian of son Charles, if he die loving brother Thomas Eldridge to be guardian. " Children are under 18 years of age and wife to be executrix.   Teste: John Newsum, John Harris, Joseph Newsum. (B 9, p. 626)

It has been said that "Brother Thomas Eldridge" was Thomas Eldridge III. A glance at the Eldridge family herein will show that he was Thomas Eldridge II. Judith, wife of Charles Binns, was a daughter of the first Thomas Eldridge and not of the second one who married Martha, daughter of John Bolling, a Pocahontas descendant.

Judith, widow of Charles Binns, married secondly Dr. John Hay of Sussex which is proven by a mortgage made between Thomas Eldridge of Prince George and Dr. John Hay and Judith his wife, executrix of the will of Charles Binns, decd. (O. B. 1752-54, p. 61.)

Dr. John Hay died April 27, 1760, and Judith Hay died Aug. 1, 1762. One child, Margaret Hay, is shown in the Albermarle Register as bapt. on Nov. 5, 1751. She married in 1775, Peter Cole HARRISON.

Children of Judith and Charles Binns:
I. Charles, untraced.
II. Elizabeth, m. July 22, 1758, Col. John Jones, Burgess from Brunswick 1773; member Va. Convention 1778; president of Va. Senate.

Children (maybe others)
1. Betsy Jones, m. Mr. Wilkins.
2. Charles Jones
3. Nancy Jones, m. John Claiborne
4. Capt. John Jones, Jr. m. Lucy Binns CARGILL.
5. Binns Jones, m. 1781, Elizabeth CARGILL. He was a 2nd Lieut. 15th Va., Nov. 25, 1776; Regimental Qm. May 6, 1778; regiment designated 11th Va., Sept. 14, 1778. Was in Service 1780. His will was dated Feb. 8, 1791, probated May 23, 1791. (W. B. 5, p. 425.) He appointed his wife, his father, and two brothers, Charles and John Jones, executrix and extrs. His Revolutionary bounty land was divided among his heirs in 1834. (See Burgess, p. 518).
Children:
(1) John Cargill Jones had children, Virginia, m. M. M. Fletcher; Binns; Sarah Eliz.
(2) Sally Jones, m. John Massenburg. Their children

were Cargill and Eliz. C. Massenburg.
(3) Richard Jones, dsp.
(4) Elizabeth Cargill Jones, m. Drewery Burge and
had one child, Sarah Ann, m. Mr. Cox.
III. Lucy, m. John CARGILL III.
6. IV. Martha, m. in 1773, Timonthy Rives. (See later.)
V. Margaret, m. Mr. Steverson.
6. Martha Binns, born 1748, died December 30, 1778, married February 8, 1773, Timothy Rives of Sussex. He married secondly February 4, 1780, Rebecca Mason; no children by second wife. He died in Sussex Dec. 1803.

Children:
I. Charles Binns Rives, b. Feb. 14, 1774, m. Mrs.
Nancy (Colyer) Goodwin and had Robert Binns Rives
and Nathaniel Eldridge Rives.
II. Archibald, bapt. June 9, 1775.
III. Anthony Rives, b. November 22, 1776, d. 1834, m.
Mary Browne Green. He is an ancestor of Mr. J.
Rives Child who wrote that excellent book on the Rives
family, entitled "Reliques of the Ryves."

MASON
of Surry

Captain James Mason was the first of this family in Surry. He is said to have been a son of Lieutenant Francis Mason of Lower Norfolk County, but this is unproven. He is probably the James Mason who was brought to Surry before November 10, 1638, for on that date Thomas Crouch patented 150 acres on Tappahannock Creek for the transportation of three persons among whom was a James Mason (C. P. 98). It will be noted that Captain James Mason patented land later in that same vicinity.

On July 8, 1648, he patented 250 acres at the head of Grey's Creek adjacent Thomas Grey. On February 27, 1653, he and John Bishop patented 50 acres on the S. E. side of Tappahannock Creek for the transportation of Mary Wade. It seems from an abstract of the patent in Cavaliers and Pioneers that she later became Mary Mason (C. P. 281). In 1657 this land was re-granted to William Edwards and the land was then said to be located on Crouche's Creek. (C. P. 353).

James Mason was a Burgess for Surry in 1654. He died about 1670, leaving a son Francis, born about 1647. It seems that Capt. Mason had a second wife, Elizabeth, for in 1655, Thomas Binns filed a complaint against Mrs. Elizabeth Mason, wife of Mr. James Mason, in defense of his (Binns') wife, Martha. (Bk. 1, p. 70.) (Col. Surry.)

2. Colonel Francis Mason, aged 21 years, made a deposition about a horse in 1668. He testified that the horse in question was his father, James Mason's, horse. This suit was about two horses. Mr. Arthur Allen and James Mason had gone to Jamestown - each one bought a horse. One horse died on the way back and each one claimed that the dead horse was on the other fellow.

On September 26, 1678, Francis Mason patented 300 acres near the head of Crouch's Creek. He married about 1673, Mrs. Elizabeth Binns, widow of Thomas Binns and daughter of Lt. Colonel Walter ASTON. He was a Justice of the County Court and a Major and later Colonel of the county militia. In 1692 he represented Surry in the House of Burgesses and died in 1696. In 1701, his widow, Elizabeth, divided 777 acres located in Lawne's Creek Parish next to George Blow's, patented by her in

1669, between her grandchildren, Frances Holt, Francis Mason and Charles Binns.

When she died in 1713 she did not mention any grandchildren in her will other than her seven Holt grandchildren. That may have been because her Mason and Binns grandchildren had received their share in the above division of land. Charles Binns, shown above, was alive at time of the making of her will and was not mentioned. (See Binns)

Colonel Francis Mason in his will dated October 4, 1696, probated March 2, 1696-97, gave to his son James one-half of 300 acres of land formerly belonging to John Bishop; to daughter Frances, wife of Thomas Holt, property in Hog Island; "...to wife all the land where I live for life, then to son James Mason; wife Elizabeth executor. "

Children:
3.   I.   James, m. Elizabeth Duke.
        II.   Frances, m. Thomas Holt of Surry.
    3.   James Mason, son of Elizabeth (Aston) Binns-Mason, died young. He made his will June 9, 1696, probated July 18, 1701, (B. 6, p. 73) mentions his sister "Holt" and his "niece", Mary, daughter of Captain Thomas Holt, his "brother" (half brother) Thomas Binns, deceased, and gave balance of his property to his son Francis and child in esse. His son Francis seemingly died in infancy; possibly he had other children. James inherited 150 acres on Tappahanna or Crouche's Creek from his father in 1696 and his son Francis was given one-third of 777 acres in 1701, as heretofore related. This property should be traced.

James' wife was Elizabeth Duke, daughter of Henry Duke and his wife, Lydia, daughter of Charles HANSFORD (pg. 25, Duke-Symes History). After James' death, she and her second husband, Elthelred TAYLOR, presented an inventory of his estate. On May 4, 1705, Taylor filed a supplemental inventory.

In 1701 Thomas Holt and Frances, his wife, "Administrators of Thomas Binns, deceased", gave a receipt for her legacy to Ethelred Taylor and Elizabeth, his wife, "administrators of James Mason, decd. " With his death it appears that this Mason family became extinct.

CLARK

Colin Clark (March 18, 1750 - Feb. 18, 1808) was born and and raised, and died, a Scot. He sailed from Limekilns, Fifeshire, Scotland, on August 18, 1770, and going by way of Barbados arrived late in the same year at Plymouth, North Carolina. Here he began trading up and down the coast, starting with one vessel, the "Martin", of which he was captain. Later he bought other vessels and living ashore, first at Plymouth in Tyrrell County and then at nearby Windsor in Bertie County, became a commission merchant, sending his ships to Norfolk, New York, and the West Indies loaded with tobacco and other local produce and bringing back manufactures and other merchandise needed in the colony.

He married, at "Rosefield" (the Gray home) near Windsor, on October 18, 1771, Janet McKenzie (Nov. 22, 1750-Nov. 25?, 1778), daughter of Rev. John McKenzie and his wife Janet Gray (daughter of John Gray and his wife Anne Bryan). They had four sons:

2.   I. David Clark (1772-1829). (See below).
     II. Kenneth Clark (1775-1815). Never married. Enlisted as a Lieutenant in the War of 1812. While stationed near Norfolk, Virginia, during an epidemic of yellow fever he spent his fortune buying medicines and medical care for the poor soldiers of his command, and in tending them he was himself stricken and died.
     III. John McKenzie Clark (1776-1803). Never married. Was a student at the University of North Carolina. Died at Buckfield (the Bryan home) in Bertie County, N. C.
     IV. William McKenzie Clark (1778-1836). Graduated, 1801, at the University of North Carolina. Lived in Martin and Bertie Counties, N. C. He married, 1813, Martha Boddie Williams (1796-1843), daughter of Gen. William Williams and his wife Elizabeth Williams (daughter of Capt. Solomon Williams and his wife Temperance Boddie). They had 11 children.

Colin Clark was an energetic young Scot and he was rapidly amassing a fortune when the Revolutionary War broke out. His wife's people (the McKenzies, Grays, Bryans, Hunters, etc.) born and raised in America, actively espoused the colonial cause. Colin Clark, however, had taken the oath of allegiance to the

British Crown then required before one could leave the old country, and besides he could not join in an uprising against his own people in a colony in which he had lived for but a short while. He tried to continue his export-import trade without taking sides but finding this impossible he gave up the business he had worked so hard to establish and left in the Spring of 1778. Before leaving he made what provision he could for the family he had to leave behind him, and he later made various attempts to send money and supplies for their support; some of this got through but most of it was taken en route. His fourth son was born, after his departure, on Nov. 15, 1778, and his wife died shortly thereafter and was buried at "Rosefield". Of Colin Clark's life abroad we have little information but he appears to have been ill for a long time. Eventually he married again but the name of this wife is not known to us. He is reported to have been drowned in 1808 in Liverpool harbor by the capsizing of a row boat when he was taking ship to return to see his children in America.

The ancestry of Colin Clark has not been established but he was probably a son of David Clark who was listed in Scotch records as "shipmaster at Limekilns".

In a letter written in 1791 by Colin Clark to his brother-in-law William McKenzie he sent his regards to "my cousin Thomas Clark, merchant at Buckfield near Windsor". This Thomas Clark may have been a son of the Thomas Clark who married Amelia Gray (1739-1814), a sister of Mrs. Janet (Gray) McKenzie. This would make Thomas Clark, Sr. of Bertie County, N. C., a brother of David Clark of Scotland, and would confirm the family tradition that Colin Clark and his wife Janet McKenzie were cousins.

2. David Clark (Oct. 25, 1772-Sept. 23, 1829) was born at Plymouth, N. C. After his mother's death in 1778 he and his three brothers were taken by their childless uncle and aunt, Capt. William and Margaret (Cathcart) McKenzie, and raised on their "Skewarky" estate where is now Williamston, N. C. In token of gratitude David Clark requested that the name "McKenzie" be always kept up by his descendants; so far this has been done. When he reached manhood David Clark went to Plymouth and as his father did before him he became a commission merchant and had boats which took local produce as far north as New York and as far south as the West Indies and brought back other goods. He was very successful in this and after his marriage when he moved to Halifax County he continued to export and import his own ships (as did his son after him) although his main interests became those of a planter. His wife had inherited land on the Roanoke River and David Clark added to this by extensive purchases until he had one of the largest plantations in the State, and 376 slaves to work it. He built a home, "Albin", at Scotland Neck in Halifax County. Here

he died and was interred under a marble mausoleum, as was his wife and their sons Colin and William, in the family burying ground on the estate.

David Clark married, at Scotland Neck, N. C., on September 2, 1806, Louisa Norfleet (Feb. 28, 1789-Jan. 4, 1828), daughter of Marmaduke Norfleet and his wife Hannah Ruffin (daughter of William Ruffin and his wife Sarah Hill). They had 11 children.

   I. Colin McKenzie Clark (1808-1868), m. 1830, Eliza L. Bond (1811-1870) ...... No children.
   II. William Ruffin Clark (1809-1861), m. 1837, Martha Godwin (1815-1897) .... No children.
   III. Kenneth Norfleet Clark (1811-1811)
   IV. Janet Rebecca Louisa Clark (1812-1842), m. 1831, Dr. Alexander Hall (1806-1851) ... 2 sons.
   V. Frances Helen Clark (1814-1866), m. 1833, Andrew Barrett White (1807-1861) ... 2 daughters.
   VI. Sarah Laura Hill Clark (1816-1861), m. 1836, Henry Francis Bond (1814-1881) ... 8 children.
   VII. David Clark (1818-1819)
3. VIII. David Clark II (1820-1882). (See below).
   IX. Ann Olivia Clark (1822-1877), m. 1845, John Davis Hawkins (1821-1902) ... 4 sons.
   X. Mary Alethea Clark (1825-1850), m. 1844, Dr. William James Hawkins (1819-1894) ... 2 sons.
   XI. Lucy Norfleet Clark (1827-1867), m. 1855, Dr. William James Hawkins (1819-1894) ... 2 daughters.

3. Gen. David Clark (Feb. 11, 1820 - Oct. 4, 1882) was born at "Albin" near Scotland Neck, N. C. He was a planter, owning thousands of acres on the Roanoke River and many slaves. He built a winter home, "Ventosa", on the Roanoke River, and a summer home, "Airlie", on higher ground in the northwest section of Halifax County south of Littleton. At the outbreak of the Civil War he was made Colonel of the 17th Regiment, and then promoted to Brigadier-General and put in charge of the militia of Halifax, Warren, Northampton, and Edgecombe Counties, and saw active service within the State, time and again foiling raiding parties of the enemy from Plymouth and the Albemarle country, and participating in the battle of New Bern. He died at "Airlie" and was buried, with his wife, in the Thorne-Clark Burying Ground at Bethel Hill near there.

Gen. David Clark married, at "Prospect Hill" (the Thorne home) on October 1, 1845, Anna Maria Thorne (March 3, 1824-March 7, 1899) daughter of William Williams Thorne and his wife Temperance Williams Davis (daughter of Archibald Davis and his wife Elizabeth Hilliard). They had 13 children:

4.   I.   Walter Clark (1846-1924). (See below).
       II.   David Clark (1848-1862).
      III. Samuel Thorne Clark (1850-1854).
      IV. Louisa Mabbette Clark (1851-1904), m. 1880, Frank
            Ballard (1849-1932) ... 1 son.
       V.   Anna Leila Clark (1852-1924), m. 1890, Rev. Joseph
            David Arnold (18--, 1920) ... No children
      VI. Edward Thorne Clark (1855-1932), m. 1st. 1880, Mar-
            garet Lillington (1855-1924) ... 3 children. m. 2nd.
            1926, Elise Bradley ... No children.
     VII. Alice Eudora Clark (1857-1933), m. 1885, Joseph Wright
            Nicholson (1854-1915) ... 1 son (d. inf.)
    VIII. Henry Norfleet Clark (1859-19). Never married.
      IX. Martha Thorne Clark (1860-1937), m. 1882, Robert
            Boyd Patterson (1855-1890) ... 1 son.
       X.   Lucy Norfleet Clark (1862-1936) ... Never married.
      XI. Sallie Hill Clark (1864-1936). m. 1914, Maj. W. A.
            Graham (1839-1923) ... No children.
     XII. David Clark II (1866-1866)
    XIII. Mary White Clark (1868-1879).

    4. Chief-Justice Walter Clark (Aug. 19, 1846- May 19, 1924)
was born at "Prospect Hill" (the Thorne home) in Halifax County
not far from Littleton, N. C. At the outbreak of the Civil War
when he was 14 he became a drillmaster with rank of Second
Lieutenant in the 22nd N. C. Regiment, and the next year was
promoted to Adjutant and First Lieutenant in the 35th N. C.
Regiment. He participated in the first Maryland campaign, the
capture of Harper's Ferry, and the battles of Second Manassas,
Sharpsburg, Fredericksburg, etc. His brigade being ordered
back to North Carolina in 1863 he resigned from the Army, entered the Senior Class at the University of North Carolina and
graduated with the first honor in June 1864. He immediately
rejoined the Army and was elected Lieutenant-Colonel, of the
70th N. C. Regiment, at the age of 17, being the youngest officer of that rank in either army. Participated in the battles of
Fort Branch, Bentonville, etc. After the war he lived in Halifax
County, practicing law and managing his plantation, until November 1873 when he moved to Raleigh. In 1881 he made an extensive tour of Europe, and in later years a special study of Mexico.
Elevated to the Bench in 1885 he was a Superior Court Judge,
1885-1889; an Associate Justice of the Supreme Court, 1889-
1902; and Chief Justice of the Supreme Court, 1903-1924, a record length of service. He was author of an "Annotated Code of
Civil Procedure" which passed through three editions; annotated
reprints of 164 volumes of N. C. Supreme Court Reports; com-
piled and edited 16 volumes of "North Carolina State Records"

and 5 volumes of "Histories of North Carolina Regiments, 1861-1865"; translated, from the original French, Constant's "Memoirs of Napoleon" in 3 volumes; and was author of numerous addresses and magazine articles. He was an indefatigable student and writer and a profound thinker; very progressive in his ideas he initiated many reforms. He died in Raleigh, N. C., and is buried there, with his wife, in Oakwood Cemetery.

He married, at Hillsboro, N. C., on January 28, 1874, Susan Washington Graham (March 9, 1851-Dec. 10, 1909), daughter of Gov. William Alexander Graham and his wife Susannah Sarah Washington (daughter of John Washington and his wife Elizabeth Heritage Cobb). They had 8 children:

    I. Susan Washington Clark (b. 1875), m. 1908, Joseph Ernest Erwin. (Morganton, N. C.). 4 children.

    II. Capt. David Clark (b. 1877), m. 1916, Aileen Butt, (Charlotte, N.C.) No children.

5. III. W. A. Graham Clark (b. 1879). (See below).

    IV. Anna Thorne Clark (1883-1884).

    V. Capt. Walter Clark (1885-1933), m. 1918, Mary Johnston (Charlotte, N. C.) 3 daughters.

    VI. John Washington Clark (b. 1887), m. 1919, Nannie Elizabeth Wright (Greensboro, N. C.) 5 children.

    VII. Thorne Clark (b. 1889), m. 1913, Mabel Gossett (Lincolnton, N. C.) 4 children.

    VIII. Eugenia Graham Clark (b. 1892), m. 1922, Rev. John Allan MacLean (Richmond, Va.) 1 son (d. inf.)

5. W. A. Graham Clark, of Washington, D. C., was born Aug. 14, 1879, at Raleigh, N. C. Graduated at North Carolina A. & M. College and at Cornell University. Engaged in cotton manufacturing until 1906 when he was sent abroad by the Government to study foreign markets for American textile manufactures, and the manufacturing methods of competitors. He visited and reported on the textile industry, trade, and tariffs of 37 countries, including all of those in the Western Hemisphere, and circled the globe twice, once by way of India and once by way of Siberia. From 1917 to date (1945) he has been Chief of the Textile Division of the U. S. Tariff Commission, directing the work of a staff of textile experts. He has written extensively along textile lines.

He married, at Raleigh, N. C., December 6, 1911, Pearl Chadwick Heck (Jan. 28, 1889 - June 30, 1939) daughter of Col. Jonathan McGee Heck and his wife Mattie Anna Callendine (daughter of Martin Beaver Callendine and his wife Anna Chadwick). They had two children:

    I. Margaret Heck Clark (b. July 9, 1915), m. May 3, 1940,

Guy Edwin Crampton, Jr. They have one son, Guy Clark Crampton (b. March 25, 1944).

6. II. Graham Montrose Clark (b. 1922). (See below).

6. <u>Graham Montrose Clark</u> was born March 12, 1922, at Washington, D. C. Graduated June 9, 1943, at U. S. Naval Academy. He married, at Washington, D. C., on June 10, 1943, Jane Arleigh Blue (b. Dec. 28, 1922), daughter of Col. Franz S. Blue and his wife Myrtle Arleigh Holmes. As Ensign and then Lieutenant (j. g.) on a destroyer in the Pacific he has seen active service from Kwajalein to Leyte and Iwo Jima, and beyond.

CRAFFORD
of Surry

Some families find it difficult to preserve the identity and the true spelling of their names, for genealogists or record searchers, looking over old records two or three centuries later, conclude that they really did not know how to spell their own names properly, and so they change the spelling. In this way it is probable that the ancient family of Crayford (Craford-Crafford) in Kent becomes the noble family of the Earls of Crawford of Scotland. (Burgess, Vol. 2, p. 465.)

The Craford family of Surry, without the "y" and more often shown as "Crafford" with two "ff's", is nevertheless nearly always changed to "Crawford" by writers.

1. Robert Crafford, b. 1660, ("Craford" in Quit Rents 1704) came to Surry before March 6, 1682/3, as the records show that on March 6, 1682/3, his wife, Elizabeth, was the daughter and heiress of George Carter, deceased. (O.B. 1671-90, p. 401.) On November 1, 1684, Robert Crafford and Elizabeth, his wife, deed land in Surry which was originally granted to William Carter, her grandfather, May 21, 1638.

It may be that David Crafford of New Kent was his father. David had a daughter, Elizabeth, who married Nicholas MERI-WETHER. The Crafford and Meriwether families also inter-married in Kent. There was also another family of Craffords in Virginia, for on March 8, 1652, George Smith patented 200 acres of land on south side of York River for bringing over himself, Phillip, John and Elizabeth Crafford. (C.P. 271)

William Carter, grandfather of Elizabeth Carter, the wife of Robert Crafford, appeared before the Council and General Court on March 1, 1622/3, and several times thereafter. On May 20, 1636, he patented 700 acres in James City (see later Surry), 50 acres being due for personal adventure of his first wife, Avis Turtley; 50 for his second wife, Anne Mathis; and 50 for his third wife, Alice Croxon. This and later patents totaled 1000 acres.

In a deposition made in Surry, May 2, 1654, he stated he was 54 years of age and his wife, Alice Croxon, was then aged 55. He was dead before October 18; 1655, for on that date his widow, Alice Carter, made an agreement with Edward Pettaway who had married the relict of William Carter, Jr. "son-in-law to me Alice Carter", that he was to enjoy the use of 500 acres of land bequeathed to William Carter, Jr. only during the life time of his wife, Elizabeth.

295

Mrs. Alice Carter, married (2) Captain Giles Parke, Justice of Surry and (3) Edward Warren.

George Carter, son of William, Sr., born about 1638, died about 1665. His widow, Mary, married (2) William Hare, who on June 26, 1665, gave bond for the estate of Elizabeth Carter, orphan. (See article by Dr. B. C. Holtzclaw, pp. 74-75, V. M. 48.)

Robert Crafford held the 1000 acres of Carter lands in 1704, and his son, Carter, held 100 acres (Quit Rents). It is probable that Elizabeth Carter, his wife, was deceased by January 25, 1708/09, when Carter Crafford, her eldest son, and Sarah, his wife, deeded some of these lands. (D. & W. 1693-1709, p. 400.)

Robert Crafford had remarried by September 8, 1712, when "Robert Crafford, Miller, of Surry," and Margaret, his wife, deeded land in Isle of Wight.

Robert Crafford made his will in Surry October 26, 1714, same probated January 19, 1714/15 (D. & W. 1709-14, p. 220.) His wife, Margaret, was probably the widow Davis at the time of her marriage to Robert, as Robert mentions his son-in-law (stepson) Davis, in his will, also Peter Davis, in his will made in Bertie, N. C. (1723) mentions his "cousins", Arthur and Henry Crafford, who were Robert's sons by his second wife.

Margaret Crafford, the second wife, was married to Ellis Braddy of Isle of Wight before 1719, for she and Ellis, November 17, 1719, deeded land given her by Robert Crafford in his will. Margaret Braddy made her will in Southampton in 1750 and mentions her son Henry Crafford and daughters.

Children of Elizabeth (Carter), first wife:

2.   I. Carter, b. 1682, d. 1744, m. Sarah Swann.
- II. Elizabeth, b. 1685, m. Thomas NEWSOM.
- III. Sarah, m. John NEWSOM.
- IV. Robert, will probated 1735, gives his "cousin" (nephew) Carter Crafford, Jr. 200 acres; mentions "cousin" Mary, brother Carter's daughter. He desires "a sermon to be preached at my funeral and to be buried by my father and mother."
- V. William; VI. Jane; VII Agnes; VIII Mary; IX Hester.

Children of second wife, Margaret:
- X. Henry; XI Arthur; XII Martha, m. Philip.

2. Carter Crafford married Sarah, daughter of Matthew Swan. (D & W 1693-1709, p. 401). He first appears a tithable in 1699 at the age of 16. He made his will August 5, 1743; same probated February 15, 17.43/4. (B. 9, p. 458). He gave his son John "the plantation where I now dwell on Sunken Marsh at John Ruffin's line, to son, Carter, the land where John lately lived adjacent

to where Catharine Peacock lived, now in possession of John
Drew", wife and sons extrs.
　　Children:
　　　I. John
3.　　II. Carter, m. Elizabeth Kearney
　　　III. Faith, m. Hart
　　　IV. Constance.

　　3.　Carter Crafford married Elizabeth Kearney, daughter of
Elizabeth (Godwin) and Captain Barnaby Kearney of Nansemond
County. Captain Kearney, who died about 1737, was in Nanse-
mond in 1684. (See 17th Cent., p. 471.)
　　Elizabeth Kearney was born June 17, 1724. Carter Crafford
made his will in Surry 1782.

　　Children:
　　　I. Elizabeth, m. Pettway.
　　　II. Martha, m. Joseph Arrington
　　　III. Captain Henry Crafford, dsp., in Surry 1825.
4.　IV. Leah, b. 24 August 1743, m. Major Isaac Hilliard.

　　4.　Leah Crafford, born August 24, 1743, died October 1825,
married Major Isaac Hilliard, born July 28, 1739, died June 25,
1790. He was a captain in the Nash county militia and fought at
the Battle of Guilford Court House. (N. C. Army Accts., Vol. X,
p. 1, folio 3). His plantation was located 11 miles west of Rocky
Mount, where he moved shortly before the Revolution and called
the place "Woodlawn".
　　Children:
　　　I. Isaac Hilliard, m. Mary Murfee
　　　II. James Hilliard, b. 30 October 1768, m. Mourning Bod-
　　　　die, b. 26 February 1778, d. 25 February, 1847, daugh-
　　　　ter of Nathan Boddie of "Rosehill" in Nash County. (See
　　　　later #9).
5.　III. John Hilliard, b. 1785, d. 1841, m. Elizabeth Tunstall.
　　　IV. Betty Hilliard, m. Archibald Davis.
　　　V. Martha Hilliard (1788-1847), m. (1) James Branch (2)
　　　　1810, Nathaniel Macon Hunt (1782-1866).
　　　VI. Robert Carter Hilliard, m. Amarilla Hunt.
　　　VII. William Hilliard, Henry, Nancy and Polly Hilliard, all
　　　　dsp.

　　5.　John Hilliard (Black Jack) born 1785, died 1841, married
Elizabeth Tunstall, born 1789, died November 1830, daughter of
Ann Eliza and Edmund Vickery Tunstall.
　　Mr. Hilliard was a planter and resided in Nash county where
his will was probated in 1841.

Children:

6. I. Robert Carter Hilliard, b. December 1808, m. Mary
Harrison Walker.

6. Dr. Robert Carter Hilliard, born December 31, 1808, at
Hilliardston, Nash County, died September 10, 1867, at New
Iberia, Louisiana, married December 20, 1837, Mary Rebecca
Harrison Walker, born December 2, 1819, died September 3,
1897, daughter of Dr. Mumford Walker and his wife Lucy
CARGILL Jones.

Dr. Hilliard was a physician and at one time a member of
the North Carolina Legislature before moving to Louisiana.

Children:

I. John Tunstall, b. 1841, killed at Shiloh.
7. II. Robert Lucy, b. June 22, 1843, m. Chas. McVea,
1866. (See later)
III. Susan Douglas, b. January 18, 1856, dsp.
IV. Edmund Thastrell, b. September 29, 1849, m. Ina
Graham.
V. Robert Barker, b. 1847, dsp.
VI. Baby, d. 1845, dsp.
VII. Audubon, b. July 8, 1854, m. Ida Campbell 1877.
VIII. Henry Peebles, b. February 8, 1859, m. (1) Estelle
Bremand November 10, 1886, (2) Elizabeth Bissell,
January 17, 1911.
IX. May, b. February 25, 1864, m. Chas. W. Frader
1883.

7. Robert Lucy Hilliard, born June 22, 1843, in Brunswick
County, Virginia, died August 13, 1875, at San Antonio, Texas.
She married December 4, 1866, at New Iberia, Louisiana, Charles McVea, born March 1832 at Bayon Sara, West Feliciana Parish, Louisiana; died October 4, 1886, at Baton Rouge.

Judge McVea was educated at Centenary College and studied
law in New Orleans. He was first a Judge of the District Court,
and then was elected to the Circuit Court where he served 16
years.

Children:

I. Robert Hilliard McVea, b. December 4, 1867, dsp.
II. Charles McVea, b. Feb. 1869, m. Pearl Lobdell.
III. William Walker McVea, b. Mar. 3, 1871, m. Sadie Link.
IV. Mary Virginia McVea, b. January 26, 1873, m. E.
Dunbar Newell.

8. Mary Virginia McVea, born January 26, 1873, at Clinton,
East Feliciana Parish, Louisiana, married February 2, 1898,
at Baton Rouge, Dr. Edward Dunbar Newell, born February 2,

1873, at Newellton, Louisiana.

Dr. Newell is a graduate of the Louisiana State University and of Tulane. He served in World War I as a Lieutenant Colonel, Medical Corps. He is a surgeon and member of the American Medical Association; resides at 703 Battery Place, Chattanooga, Tennessee.

Children:

I. Marjorie Newell, b. January 6, 1900, m. May 8, 1924, R. Houston Jewell. Children: 1. Robert Houston Jewell, Jr., b. February, 1925; 2. Ed. Dunbar Jewell, b. May 1927; 3. William Henry Jewell, b. May 1930.

II. Bert McVea Newell, b. October 5, 1901, m. June 1, 1922, Dr. Earl R. Campbell. Children: 1. Mary Virginia Campbell, b. July, 1923; 2. Earl R. Campbell, Jr., b. February 1929.

III. Catharine Wade Newell, b. October 7, 1903, m. October 16, 1923, Edward W. Oehmig. Children: 1. Francis West Oehmig, b. January 1925; 2. Catharine Newell Oehmig, b. May 1926; 3. Elizabeth Dunbar Oehmig, b. October 1927; 4. Edward West Oehmig, b. May 1930; 5. Dunbar Newell Oehmig b. July 1931.

9. James Hilliard, son of Leah (Crafford) and Isaac Hilliard, was born at "Woodlawn", Nash County, N. C., Oct. 30, 1768, and died at "Hilliardston" July 6, 1832. On Sept. 25, 1798, he married Mourning Boddie, daughter of Nathaniel Boddie of "Rose Hill, Nash County". She was born Feb. 26, 1778, and died Feb. 25, 1847.

In the Nash County census of 1790, James Hilliard appeared as the head of his late father's family with eighty-four slaves, the largest number in the Nash County. He attended a northern college and upon his return he ran the Hilliardston Academy employing northern teachers. He was an early advocate of public school teaching in N. C.

Children:

I. Isaac Hilliard, b. Feb. 25, 1801, m. Lucy Emily Hilliard, dau. of Elizabeth (Tunstall) and John Hilliard.

10. II. James Crafford Hilliard, b. Nov. 5, 1806, m. (1) Mary Ann Ruffin. (see later).

III. Elizabeth Jane Hilliard, b. Feb. 1, 1809, m. Jonas Johnston Carr.

IV. Elijah Boddie Hilliard, b. 1815, m. Rebecca Brown Powell.

V. Mary Temperance Hilliard, b. Nov. 16, 1816, m. John Buxton Williams.

VI. Leah Hilliard, b. May 2, 1819, m. Dr. Algernon S. Perry.

10.   James Crafford Hilliard, born at "Hilliardston", Nov. 5, 1806; died at "Woodlawn", Nash County, April 13, 1860; married Feb. 10, 1813, died Dec. 11, 1843, daughter of Mary Ann (Johnston) and Samuel Ruffin of Edgecombe County. Mary Ann Johnston was a daughter of Colonel Jonas Johnston who was killed at the Battle of Stono Creek in the Revolution.

Mr. Hilliard was educated at the University of Virginia and operated a large plantation in Nash County. He married secondly Martha Ann Pitts of Halifax County. All their children died unmarried.

Children of first wife:

I.   Mourning Boddie Hilliard, b. Dec. 21, 1835, m. James M. Vaughan.

II.   Elizabeth Maud Hilliard, b. May 18, 1838, m. William Pegram.

11. III.   Samuel Ruffin Hilliard, b. Nov. 10, 1840, m. Sallie Jones. (see later)

IV.   Jonas Johnston Hilliard, b. Nov. 14, 1842, d. June 6, 1862.

11.   Samuel Ruffin Hilliard, born Nov. 10, 1840, at "Woodlawn",. died Oct. 2, 1922, at Rocky Mount, N. C., married Jan. 17, 1894, Sarah (Sallie) Elizabeth Jones, born Nov. 28, 1866, at the "Old Roger's Place", Wake County, died Dec. 9, 1926, at Rocky Mount, daughter of Sarah (Rogers) and Alexander Clay Jones.

Mr. Hilliard attended Horner Military Academy, and Union College, now Duke University. At the outbreak of the Civil War he left college and enlisted as a private in Company K, 15th N. C. Regiment. He was wounded at the battle of Malvern Hills and was later made Captain and Quartermaster of the 2nd N. C. State Guard. After the war he returned to Woodlawn and operated his plantation.

Children:

I.   Isaac Marvin Hilliard, b. Oct. 10, 1894.

II.   James Byron Hilliard, b. Jan. 15, 1897, was educated at the Rocky Mount High School and N. C. State College. In World War I, he was a corporal in the 113th Field Artillery, 30th Division and served in the defense of the Toul Sector, Aug. 27th to Sept. 11, 1918; was at Battle of St. Michiel, Sept. 12-14, 1918, in the Woevre offensive Nov. 8-11, 1918. Mr. Hilliard is now a Tobacconist with the G. R. Garrett Co., at Rocky Mount, N. C.

III.   Mary Ruffin Hilliard, b. April 3, 1899.

IV.   Elizabeth Rogers Hilliard, b. Oct. 1, 1900.

V.   Samuel Jones Hilliard, b. Sept. 18, 1902.

VI.   Foy Lynn Hilliard, b. April 18, 1907.

FLOOD

Col. John[1]Flood (ca. 1595-1658), of James City and Surry Counties, Virginia, arrived in 1610. In the "Muster Rolls, of Settlers in Virginia, 1624/5" is: The MUSTER of John Fludd: John Fludd arrived in the 'Swan' 1610, Margaret his wife in the 'Supply' 1620, Frances Finch her daughter in the 'Supply' 1620, William Fludd his son aged 3 weeks." John Flood was living in Charles City in 1616 and at "Jordan's Journey" in 1625; in 1638 he patented land and settled in James City County just across the river from Jamestown in the section which in 1652 became Surry County.

The above mentioned patent, dated May 12, 1638, was issued to "John Fludd, Gent." and was for 2100 acres "E. upon land of Capt. Henry Browne, N. upon the maine river, S. into the maine woods & W. upon Benjamine Harrisons marked trees being upon the W. side of Sunken Marsh Cr.", for transportation of 42 persons. On June 7, 1650 "Capt. John Flood, Gent." surrendered this patent and was given another of 1100 acres "on S. side the side the river, bounded S. E. S. upon land of Capt. Henry Browne, N. W. by N. upon land of Mr. Charles Foord and Richard Baven." Among his headrights were listed: John Flood, an Ancient Planter, Margt. his wife, Frances Finch her daughter, John Flood, Junr., Eliza.Browne, John Lawrence, John Wright, Wm. Wood, and others. ("Cavaliers and Pioneers", pages 86 and 194).

On Jan. 12, 1643/4, John Fludd witnessed the will of Capt. Thomas Pawlett (owner of Westover) who left one silver spoon and one sow shote apiece to his god-children Wm. Harris, John Woodson, Tho. Aston, Thomas Fludd, Henry Richley, John Bishop, Tho Woodward, Tho. Boyse, Tho. Poythers, and William Bayle. ("Title of Westover", by Dr. Lyon G. Tyler, in William & Mary College Quarterly, Vol. 4, p. 151).

The Grand Assembly held at James City October 5, 1646, enacted- "That upon any occasion of message to the Gov'r. or trade, the said Necotowance and his people the Indians doe repair to fforte Henery alias Appmattucke fforte, or to the house of Capt. John ffloud, and to no other place or places of the south side of the river, att which places the aforesayd badges of striped stuffe are to be and remaine." *** "Be it also inacted that Capt. John ffloud be interpreter for the collony, and that for his service therein and transporting such Indians as shall be employed from time to tyme to the Gov'r. in message or otherwise, he is to

be allowed from the publique the salary of four thousand pounds
of tob'o. yeerly."

The Grand Assembly held at James City July 5, 1653, or-
dered- "And the commissioners of York are required that such
persons as are seated upon the land of Pamunkey or Chickahominy
Indians be removed according to a late act of Assembly made to
that purpose, and Coll. John Fludd to go to Tottopottomoy to
examine the proceedings of busines and to deliver it upon his
oath."

John Flood was only a boy when he came to Virginia but he
was active and energetic and rose to high honors. He was Burgess for Flowerdieu Hundred in 1630, for Westover, Flowerdewe
Hundred, and Weyanoake in February 1632, and for Westover and
Flowerdue Hundred in September 1632; he was one of the Burgesses for James City County in 1643, 1645, and 1652. He was
Captain in 1643 (and probably earlier), Lieutenant-Colonel in
1652, and Colonel in 1653. At his death in 1658 he was Chairman
of the Surry County Commission which held Court and administered the affairs of the county; the other commissioners at that
time were Lt. Col. Thomas Swann, Capt. George Jordan, Capt.
Benjamin Sidway, Mr. George Stephens, Mr. Thomas Warren,
and Mr. James Mason. He was also Speaker of the House of
Burgesses in 1652. (5 V. 185)

Col. John Flood died in Surry County in 1658 not long before
the marriage of his daughter Mary to John Washington. He was
living in June 1658 when he sold to Anthony Holburt a red cow
formerly belonging to Eliz. Lother; this sale was witnessed by
Thomas Flood. He was dead, apparently, before Nov. 14, 1658,
when Thomas Flood deeded to William Jennings "the tract and
houseing, whereon he now lives, which he formerly held by lease
from my father Col. John Flood, adjoining John King and sd.
Jennings." (Both deeds are recorded on page 131 of "Surry County Records, 1645-1672"). The Grand Assembly held at James
City March 7, 1658/9 passed the following resolution: "WHERE-
AS, Coll. John fflood hath long and faithfully served this country
in the office of an interpreter and being now deceased, It is en-
acted, That Thomas fflood, son to the said Coll. John fflood,
being recommended to the Assembly for his ability in the Indian
tongue, shall be received in the place of his father and have the
same salary." (Hening, Vol. 1, p. 521). The will of Col. John
Flood has not been found but extracts therefrom are quoted in
various recorded deeds. In 1670 Lt. Col. George Jordan confirmed a land sale as the surviving trustee or overseer of the
last will and testament of Col. John Flood decd.

Col. John[1]Flood married, 1st. ca. 1624, Mrs. William
Finch (nee Margaret_____) and had at least four children:

I. William Flood (1625-   )

II. John Flood (ca. 1727(?)-ca. 1672), m.____and had three children: (1) John Flood (d. 1678), m. 1678, Mary Creede; (2) Jane Flood, m. 1667, Thomas Lane (d. 1710); and (3) Elizabeth Flood who m. 1st. Thomas King (d. 1679) and m. 2nd. 1680, Nicholas Smith (d. (1719).

III. Capt. Thomas Flood (ca. 1629(?)-ca. 1677), m.____ and had at least one child: Capt. Thomas Flood (ca. 1651(?)-1718), m. ca. 1672, Ann Rose (d. 1728). (See later.)

IV. Mary Flood (ca. 1635(?)-ca. 1678), who married four times. (See below.)

Col. John[1]Flood married, 2nd. ca. 1645(?), Fortune Jordan (ca. 1623(?)-1669) and had at least two children:

V. Jane Flood (ca. 1646-1669), m. 1665, John Cary (1645-1701) and had two children: (1) Thomas Cary (1667-1716), m. Esther Hudson, and (2) Mary Cary (1669-1732) who married 1st.____Young and m. 2nd. Nathaniel Harrison (1677-1727).

VI. Walter Flood (1656-1722), m. ca. 1677, Anne Browne (ca. 1661-1723). (See below.)

(Mrs. Fortune Flood m. 2nd. ca. 1660, James Mills but had no children by him).

Mary Flood (ca. 1635(?)- ca. 1678) was the daughter of Col. John[1]Flood by his first wife, Margaret _____, widow of William Finch. The first record of her, as shown in "Early Virginia Immigrants", by G. C. Greer, reads- "Mary Flood, 1650, by Capt. John Flood, Gent., and John Flood, an Ancient Planter, James City County." This seems to indicate that Mary Flood, who had been to school or on a visit to England, had her return passage paid by her eldest brother and her father. Mary Flood married four times; as stated by Dr. Tyler- "She must have been a very attractive woman".

Mary Flood married:

1st. ca. 1655, Richard Blunt (1616-1656) of Surry County, Va., and had one son; Thomas Blunt (1656-1709).

2nd. 1657, Charles Ford (d. 1657) but had no child by him.

3rd. 1658, John Washington (1623-ca. 1660) and had one son: Richard Washington (1659-1724).

4th. 1661, Henry Briggs (1635-1686) and had at least five children: Henry Briggs (1662-1739), Charles Briggs (1664-1730), Marie Briggs, Samuel Briggs (ca. 1673-1737), and George Briggs (1676-1699).

When Richard Blunt died in 1656 his estate was claimed by the administrators of Thomas Jauncey decd., to repay loans made

by Jauncey for financing the plantation which he and Richard
Blunt owned jointly. The widow, Mary (Flood) Blunt and her infant son would have been left penniless but for the fact that Capt.
George Jordan, attorney for the Jauncey interests, decided "out
of charity for her maintenance" to permit her to retain not only
what belonged to her self (including wearing clothes and linen) but
also a main servant, two cows, two heifers, poultry and turkeys,
corn, etc., and part of the tobacco from the crop next ensuing.
Capt. George Jordan was a brother of her stepmother Mrs. Fortune (Jordan) Flood, and apparently to avoid suspicion that his
decision in her behalf was unduly influenced by the relationship
he called in four arbitrators, Tho. Swann, Wm. Butler, Ben.
Sidway, and Wm. Edwards, and they confirmed his allotment
to the widow. (Surry County Records, 1645-1672, p. 91).

In 1657 Mrs. Mary (Flood) Blunt married Charles Ford, a
neighbor whose land adjoined that of her father. On April 9,
1657, he made a report, as county coroner, with respect to a
man found dead; among his panel on this case was John Flood
(junior?), Arthur Jordan, Thomas Gray, etc. On July 7,
1657 "John Maire, servant unto Mr. Charles fforde" testified
in Court. Mr. Charles Ford died, apparently in the latter part
of 1657, without issue. This is the last reference to him alive.

In 1658 Mrs. Mary Ford, widow, married John Washington.
The marriage contract, dated Nov. 15, 1658, provided that
John Washington deliver unto Robert Stanton,-clarke (i. e. min-
ister), feoffe, a filly for the sole use and behoof of Thomas
Blunt, son of said Mary, when he should attain to ten years of age.
Witnesses were Benjamin Sidway, John Allen, Edmund Shipham,
Thomas Flood, and John Flood. Col. John Flood had recently
died but this marriage contract with his daughter Mary was witnessed by her brothers Thomas and John Flood. Of the other
witnesses it may be noted that Capt. Benjamin Sidway was a
member of the Surry County Commission of which Col. John
Flood had been chairman. He had married Mary, widow of Benjamin Harrison (the first of the name), and in 1662 Capt. Thomas
Flood was guardian to her son Benjamin Harrison. John Allen
was a member of the Allen family, neighbors and close friends
of the Floods. With respect to Edmund Shipham no information
appears available. John Washington apparently died without leaving a will. He was living April 6, 1659, when he and Benjamin
Sidway were witnessés together on a deed, and "Mr. Jno. Wash-
ingtons house" is mentioned in the records of July 6, 1659. Date
of death is uncertain but it was probably in the latter part of 1659.

(John Washington, the second son of Sir John Washington, of
Thrapston, England, was living in England in 1673. He was there-
fore not the above John Washington. See Washington Family-
Burke's Landed Gentry, 1939, p. 2960.)

Mrs. John Washington (nee Mary Flood) appears to have married Henry Briggs in 1661 for their son Henry Briggs, Jr., was born in 1662.

In 1662 George Jordan and Mary Briggs witnessed James Mills' bond to Mr. Robert Spencer. (Surry County Records, 1645-1672, p. 211). In 1664 Nathaniel Knight, Mary Briggs, and Jane Flood witnessed bond of James Mills relinquishing all right in the personal property of his wife Fortune or in the land and house formerly belonging to Col. John Flood; at the same time Fortune Mills and George Jordan relinquished any claim to the personal property of James Mills. (Ibid, p. 249).

Thomas Blunt and Richard Washington were named by Henry Briggs as tithables in the Surry County list of June 1678. (Surry County Book 2, p. 188).

On March 1, 1677/8 Thomas Blunt deeded to Thomas Drew, son of Richard Drew, land which had belonged to his father Richard Blunt and had been held indirectly by one Richard Harris until the November last past when the said Thomas Blunt being come to full age was on application to the Court put in possession of his lawful inheritance. This deed was witnessed by George Jordan and Arthur Allen. Thomas Blunt's mother, Mary, and her then husband Henry Briggs, relinquished all right and claim they had in the property. (Surry County Records, 1671-1684, p. 167). This is the last time that Mary (nee Mary Flood) appears in the records. She died before 1681, probably in 1678.

Henry Briggs married, second, Mrs. Margery Gilliam (widow of John Gilliam) before July 5, 1681, as on that date he and his wife Margery deeded 150 acres of land to Thomas Blunt, Planter. This was recorded Nov. 1, 1681. (Surry County Book 2, p. 296). Henry Briggs in his will dated Sept. 26, 1681, recorded July 6, 1686, mentioned his "son-in-law" (i. e. stepson) Thomas Blunt.

Walter[2] Flood (1656-1722), of Surry County, Virginia, was the son of Col. John Flood by his second wife, Fortune Jordan. The first mention of him in the records appears to be in 1666, in a deed reading as follows:

"Whereas Coll John fflood decd did by his last will & testamt leave orders that the dwelling house, orchard & land thereunto belonging should be sold pvided that two good breeding mares were paid & delivered unto his sonn Walter fflood at the age of sixteene years, & tenn thousand weight of good tobb: & caske at the age of 21, Now know all men by these psents that wee Fortune Mills the relict of the sd. Coll:fflood as alsoe Capt Thomas fflood & Lt Coll George Jordan with whose advice the sd house land & orchard is to be sold, Have accordingly sold & sell over unto John Cary whoe marryed Jane the daughter of Coll John fflood aforesd the sd dwelling house orchard & land thereunto belong. ****** April 19, 1666. " Fortune Mills, Geo. Jordan, Tho. fflood. (Surry County Records, 1645-1672, p. 350.)

On Dec. 27, 1669, John Cary patented 230 acres in Surry County adjoining said Cary, Capt. Thomas Flood, and Arthur Jordan, and being part of a grant to Col. John Flood, decd., and conveyed to said Cary by the relict of said Col. John Flood. (Virginia Land Office, Book 6, p. 269). In early 1670 John Cary, leaving Surry County for England, took with him, to school there, his young brother-in-law Walter Flood, of whom he was guardian. For the latter's estate in his possession he gave bond to Lt. Col. George Jordan and Capt. Thomas Flood. On Jan. 15, 1677/8 Walter Flood recorded in Surry County a discharge to John Cary for his estate; this was witnessed by George Jordan and Christopher Foster. Walter Flood was a legatee in the 1678 will of his uncle Lt. Col. George Jordan (who left most of his property to his 7 nephews and 1 niece then living). The will of Walter Flood, dated Oct. 14, 1722, proved Nov. 21, 1722, named Nathaniel Harrison and William Browne as executors and was witnessed by Nicholas Maget, Richard Price, R. Smith Woobank, and Nathaniel Edwards.

Walter² Flood married, ca. 1677, Anne Brown (ca. 1661-1723), daughter of Col. William Browne, of "Four Mile Tree", and his wife Anne Browne.

 Children:
  I. Fortune Flood (ca. 1678-1753), m. ca. 1695, Capt. Hinshaw Gilliam (ca. 1663-1734) q.v.
  II. John Flood (ca. 1682-1711), m. 170-, Mary Blunt, (dau. of Thomas Blunt). 1 daughter.
  III. Walter Flood (ca. 1684-1720), m. ca. 1705, Sarah Simmons. 3 children.
  IV. Mary Flood (ca. 1689-1733) d.s.p.
  V. Ann Flood (ca. 1693-174-), m. 1st. ca. 1724, William Cocke (d. 1732). 2 daughters. m. 2nd. ca. 1734, Thomas Hamlin (d. 1750). 2 children.

Descendants of Capt. Thomas Flood, son of Col. John.

Captain Thomas Flood was apparently dead by June 1670, as the tithables of that year show his widow, Mrs. Faith Flood, without him (Book 1, p. 121). She was dead by Mar. 5, 1671/2, when John Emerson appears as executor of her will (Order Bk. 1, p. 1). John Emerson gave an account of the estate of Capt. Thomas Flood and Faith his relict Mar. 5, 1677/8 (Book 2, p. 167). Capt. Flood was still living on April 19, 1670, when it is stated that he was ill and made a deed to Nathaniel Knight (Book 2, p. 272). Thomas and Faith Flood apparently had only one son, Thomas Flood, who was still mentioned as "orphant of Capt. Thomas Flood, decd." on Sept. 4, 1677 (O.B. 1, p. 156).

Thomas Flood, Jr., witnessed the will of Francis Hogwood Jan. 3, 1676/7 (Book 2, p. 121), but it is probable that he was not of full age till John Emerson handed in the account of the estate of his father and mother early in 1677/8. This would put his birth date as about 1656, the same age as his uncle Walter.

Thomas Flood, Jr., apparently married Ann, daughter of William and Anne Rose of Surry Co. William Rose was born 1616-17, as he gave his age as 38 on Mar. 27, 1654/5 (Book 1, p. 41). William Rose and Anne his wife made a deed of gift in 1666 to their children Jane, William, Anne, and Mary Rose (id. p. 272-2). In addition to the above children, there was a son Richard Rose, as the following records show. Richard Rose married Elizabeth SOWERBY, daughter of Francis and Katherine Sowerby (see Sowerby family). Jane Rose married Richard Avery, whose will, dated Sept. 12, 1685, and probated in Surry Co. Jan. 5, 1685/6, mentions his sons, George, William, Thomas and John, his wife Jane, and his brothers, William Rose and Thomas Flood. The son George Avery died in Surry in 1692, his will, dated May 22, 1692, and probated July 5, 1692, mentioning his uncles Thomas Flood and Richard Rose, and his brothers Thomas and John Avery (Book 3, p. 269). In 1688 the records show that Jane, widow of Richard Avery, had married Edward Bookey and that William Rose was guardian of John Avery (W. & D. 1687-94, p. 61). Jane Rose Avery Bookey had died by 1692, and Edward Bookey was married to Fortune, daughter of Samuel Maget, whose will dated May 5, 1692, and probated Jan. 3, 1692/3, mentions his two children, Nicholas and Fortune wife of Edward Bookey (id.; p. 302). William Rose, Jr., m. Lucy, sister of Wm. Corker and widow of Thomas Jordan.

Thomas and Anne (Rose) Flood apparently had only one son, Harry Flood and two daughters, Faith and Jane Flood. On Feb. 20, 1733, John Nicholson and Elizabeth, his wife, daughter of Jean Watkins, who was daughter of Thomas Flood, decd., and Thomas Ricks, eldest son of Faith Ricks, another daughter of Thomas Flood, deeded land (D. & W. 1730-38, p. 360). . It is uncertain which of the sons of John and Elizabeth (Spencer) Watkins of Surry married Jane Flood. Faith Flood married Richard Ricks (Reekes), whose will, dated Jan. 10, 1708, and probated in Surry July 5, 1709, mentions his son, Thomas Reekes, daughters, Elizabeth and Jane, and wife Faith.

Faith (Flood) Ricks married (2) William Phillips of Surry Co., whose will, dated Dec. 5, 1734, and probated Jan. 15, 1734/5, mentions his daughters Mary, Sarah and Faith, and son John. The will to Thomas Reeks, dated Feb. 15, 1744, and probated in Surry Feb. 20, 1744/5, mentions his sisters Elizabeth Collier, Mary Dawson, Sarah Howser and Faith Dudley;

William Collier, son of his sister Elizabeth; and brother John Phillips. William Phillips, second husband of Faith Flood, was probably the son of William Phillips who married Mary, daughter of Matthew Swan of Surry Co., and died in 1721 in Surry, his will, dated Feb. 14, 1720/21, and probated April 19, 1721, mentioning his sons John, William, Swan and Matthew, and his daughters Anne, Mary and Elizabeth, and his wife Mary.

Anne (Rose) Flood, widow of Captain Thomas Flood, Jr., died in 1728. Her will was dated Nov. 25, 1728, proved March 19, 1728/29. Daughter Faith Phillips; grandaughter Elizabeth Collier; grandaughter Elizabeth Watkins, "a gift made me by Mrs. Potter"; grandaughter Jean Ricks; grandson Thomas Reeks; granddaughter Mary Phillips. Executors, my daughter Elizabeth Collier and her husband, Thomas Collier. Witnesses: John Cargill, Benjamin Chapman Donaldson, Richard Rose. (Surry Book 1715-30, p. 915).

Harry Flood (who may have been a son of Capt. Thomas Flood, Jr.,) married Mrs. Joanna (Joyce) Nicholson, widow of Robert Nicholson, III, (d. 1719). He was married twice and had a daughter by his first wife who married Robert Nicholson, son of his second wife. Harry Flood made his will Dec. 18, 1739, proved Oct. 15, 1740, as follows: ... to daughter Ann Flood in England, if living; daughter Elizabeth Nicholson and her six children; Henry, Robert, Mary, George, James and Anne Nicholson. Executor: Son-in-law Robert Nicholson, under direction of Col. Allen. Witnesses Thomas Hamlin, L. Delong Elizabeth Rookings. (Surry Book 1738-54, p. 228)

His wife Johanna (Joyce) Flood made her will Oct. 21, 1720, same probated May 18, 1743, as follows: I give to John Nicholson the Great Bible that was his father's which is properly mine; son Robert Nicholson; daughters Joice and Anne Nicholson, under age (in 1720), daughter Elizabeth. Capt. Henry Harrison to have daughters Joice and Elizabeth and their estate until they are of age; Capt. Thos. Cocke, son of Mr. Walter Cocke to have Anne until she is of age; Capt. Thos Cocke to be Executor. Witnesses: Nicholas Cocke, Mary Dawson, Mary Allstin. (Surry Book 1738-54, p. 433).

GRAY

Thomas[1] Gray (1593-1658), of James City and Surry Counties, Virginia, arrived as a boy of 15 in 1608. He survived the "year of starving", the Indian massacres of 1622 and 1642, and all the other trials and tribulations of the earliest English settlers of what is now the United States. His first marriage was apparently in Virginia in 1618. In the "Musters of the Inhabitants in Virginia 1624/5" (Hotten, p. 228) there were listed: "Thomas Graye, Margrett his wife, Jone their daughter aged 6 yeres, William their sonn aged 3 yeres".

In 1635 Thomas Gray patented 550 acres in James City County "On S. side of the maine river over against James Citty, adj. on the E. to the plantation now in his possession & to land of Capt. Perry, running along by Rolfes Cr. & S. into the woods upon the Cross Cr., 100 acres due as an Ancient Planter at or before the time of Sir Thomas Dale, 50 acres for the personal adventure of Anis Gray his first wife, 50 acres for the personal adventure of Rebecca Gray his now wife, and 350 acres for trans. of his two sons, Wm. Gray & Tho. Gray, and 5 servants: Jon. Bishopp, Robt. Browne, Robt. Welshe, Luke Misle, Jon. Banckes". (Virginia Land Office Book 1, p. 283.) This patent is identical with one issued - apparently a reissue - May 26, 1638, except that, as shown in "Cavaliers and Pioneers", p. 105, the name of his first wife was stated as "Avis"; this was probably not an actual change but a slight difference in the appearance of the written word. Others have interpreted the word as "Annis".
In 1639 Thomas Gray patented 400 acres in James City County, upon the head of Gray's Creek, for the transportation of 8 persons: Richard Deane, Francis Fiveash, Allen Sadome, William Short, John Hancoke, and 3 negroes. In 1642 Thomas Gray patented 100 acres in James City County on the east side of Gray's Creek, adjoining his own land, for the transportation of two persons: George Graves and William Browne. On March 14, 1652, Thomas Gray patented 800 acres in Surry County, on south side of James River at the head of Smiths Fort Creek, adj. land of John Kemp; 400 acres thereof were granted sd. Gray July 30, 1639, and 400 acres were purchased by sd. Gray of Samuel Abbott. (Land Office Book 3, p. 158). On March 7, 1653, Thomas

Gray, Senr., aged 60 years or thereabouts, deposed that Daniel
Hutton (In the Valentine Papers, p. 556, this name is printed as
"Daniel Shelton") in the time of his sickness not long before his
departure did bequeath his whole estate to Rebecka his wife verbally. (Surry County Deed Book 1, p. 41).

Thomas [1] Gray married twice. The name of his second wife
was Rebecca. The name of his first wife, who was probably the
mother of his five children, was listed in the "Muster" of 1624/5
as "Margaret" but his may have been an error on the part of the
recorder as in land patents by her husband her name appears to
have been "Avis" or "Anis" or possibly "Annis".

Thomas Gray had five children, in the following order:

I. Jane Gray (1619-16), m. John Hux (1613-16).
II. William Gray (1622-1714), m. ca. 164 , Mary ____.
    4 children.
III. Thomas Gray (ca. 1625-1676) d. s. p.
IV. John Gray (ca. 1627-1683) m. Mary____. 1 daughter.
V. Francis Gray (ca. 1630-1679). (See later.)

William [2] Gray (1622-1714) lived in Surry County, Va. In
1677 William Gray and John Gray, planters of Surry County,
being joint heirs of Thomas Gray, sold Col. Thomas Swann
100 acres lying between Col Swann's and the mouth of a creek
formerly called Smiths Fort Creek but now called Gray's Creek.
Witnesses: Thos. Busby, Robt. Penny. (Surry County Deed
Book 12, p. 145). In 1860 William Gray patented 680 acres
in Surry County adjoining Mr. Richard Briggs, Mr. William
Edwards, and Mr. Robert Ruffin, being part of 800 acres granted
in 1668 to William Harris of Surry County and by him sold in 1679
to the said William Gray. (Virginia Land Office Book 7, p. 27).
In 1679 William Gray sold to Robert Kae of Isle of Wight County
and Nicholas Wilson of Surry County a 99-year lease, of a water
mill, made to sd. Gray by Robert Parke and Mary his wife.
(Surry County Deed Book 12, p. 252). In 1688 William Gray sold
to Mr. Chas White 136 acres which had been patented in 1654 by
Eliza Hutton and which had descended to the sd. William Gray as
next cousin and heir. (D. B. 3, p. 3). In 1689 William Gray
sold to Robt. Caufield 680 acres, of which 490 acres had been
purchased of Wm. Harris, son of Thomas Harris, decd, and
the remainder patented by the sd. William Gray in 1680. Witnesses: Arthur Allen, Wm. Smith. (D. B. 3, p.). William
Gray in his will dated February 8, 1710, recorded October 20,
1714, gave a cow to Henry Clark and a cow to Chas. Judkins,
and left the remainder of his estate to be equally divided between
his wife and his son Thomas Gray. Witnesses were Wm. Foster and David Andrews. (D. B. 5 p. 212).

William Gray married, 164 , Mary_____and had four

children: (1) Lydia Gray. She was probably the Lydia who
m. 1st. Samuel Judkins (d. 1672), and m. 2nd. Capt. Thomas
Pitman. (2) Gilbert Gray (ca. 164 -ca. 1710) d. s. p. (3)
John Gray (ca. 1650-1708) d. s. p. He left legacies to "my sister Lidia, my brothers Thomas and Gilbert, and my father".
His father William Gray was executor. (4) Thomas Gray (ca.
1652-ca. 1717), married _____ and left one son, Thomas Gray,
who was an orphan in 1717 and chose William Foster as a guardian.

Thomas[2] Gray (ca. 1625-1676), of Surry County, Va., apparently never married. In his will dated April 16, 1676, and
proved May 2, 1676, he gave to his brother Francis Gray 3
draughts of hogs, to the wife of Francis Gray his linen cloths,
to his brothers John and William Gray his plantation with all
the land belonging therewith, and to his three brothers, Francis,
John, and William Gray the remainder of his estate to be equally divided. Witnesses were Nathl. Knight and Jno. Ironmonger.
On May 2, 1676, his will was proved by Mr. Nathl. Knight and
John Jennings, and Francis Gray qualified as administrator, with
Thos. Sorsby and George Foster as his securities.

John[2] Gray (ca. 1627-1683) lived in Surry County, Va. On
Nov. 2, 1675, John Gray, Senr., was ordered to pay to Wm.
Tooke 500 lbs. tobacco according to will of Ridley, decd. 1671,
for the services of John Gray, Jr., one year more. (Surry
County Order Book 1671-90, p. 104). On Nov. 4, 1678, John
Gray confessed judgment to Mr. Robert Ruffin for 400 lbs. of
tobacco. (O. B. 1671-90, p. 241). John Gray in his will dated
May 16, 1683, proved July 3, 1683, gave one-third of his
estate to his wife, and the remainder (except for his housing
and land) to his daughter with reversion, should she die before
coming of age or marrying, to the children of his brother Wil-
liam Gray. His housing and land he gave to his "cousin" John
Gray, son of William Gray. He gave a cow to his "cousin"
William Gray, son of Francis Gray. He made his wife executrix,
and desired his brother William Gray and his "cousin" William
Gray to see that his will was performed. Witnesses were John
Foster and Thomas Bage. (D. B. 12, p. 330). On July 3, 1683,
Mary Gray was granted probate on the will of John Gray decd.
John Moreing, Mr. Geo. Foster, and Mr. Thos. Crews were
appointed appraisers of the estate. (O. B. 1671-90, p. 408).
The widow, Mrs. Mary Gray, married 2nd. 1683, Robert Nichol-
son.

Capt. Francis[2] Gray (ca. 1630 (?)-1679), of Surry County,
Virginia, was the youngest son of the immigrant Thomas Gray
(1593-1658). On Nov. 3, 1658, Francis Gray for a consideration
assigned his right in certain land patents to his brother, Thomas
Gray. Witnesses were Jno. Gittings and Sam. Swaine. (Surry

County Deed Book, 1, p. 175). In 1662 William Browne, William
Simmons, Nathl. Knight, Henry Francis, Francis Gray, etc.
on a special jury panel. (D. B. 1, p. 185). In 1662 Francis
Gray bought a heifer of Henry Briggs. (.D. B. 1, p. 210). On
Jan. 26, 1662/3, Francis Gray deeded to John Tatum 100 acres
in Surry County of Chippoakes Creek adj. sd. Tatum's land
lately purchased of John Rawlings. Witnesses: Elias Osborne,
Selby Sparrow. (D. B. 1, p. 213). On Sept. 4, 1666, Francis
Gray acknowledged his deed to his brother Thomas Gray of the
plantation on which Mr. Hely lived and which his said brother
Thomas Gray had since let to Mr. Dickerson. (D. B. 1, p. 275).
In 1668 Thomas Gray and Francis Gray in the list of tithables
taken by Mr. George Jordan. In 1673 Francis Gray confessed
judgement to Harry Francis for 400 lbs. tobacco & caske with
costs. (O. B. 1671-90, p. 22). In 1674 Francis Gray, defendant, vs. Col. Thomas Swann; judgment for plaintiff 2769 lbs.
tobacco. (O. B. 1671-90, p. 72). In 1675 Francis Gray and
Mary Gray sold to Thomas Crews a parcel of land in Surry
County bounded by lands of Thomas Gray, George Foster, and
Col. Thomas Swann, near the mouth of Gray's Creek. Witnesses: Wm. Thompson, Fra. Sumner. (O. B. 1671-90, p. 69).
On May 2, 1676, Francis Gray qualified as administrator of
the estate of his brother Thomas Gray decd., with Thos. Sorsby
and George Foster as his securities. (O. B. 1671-90, p. 126).
In 1677 Francis Gray in the list of tithables of Surry County.
Capt. Francis Gray apparently made no will. He died in 1679
and his widow, Mary Gray, qualified as administratrix; she
gave bond for 40, 000 lbs. of legal tobacco, with Roger Potter and
George Foster as her securities. Witnesses: Thos. Jordan, Wm.
Edwards. Recorded June 25, 1679. (D. B. 1, p. 1).

Capt. Francis Fray married, 165 , Mary_____and had one
son, Capt. William Gray who died in 1719, and three daughters.
The latter have not been positively identified but they appear on
the basis of available data to be those shown in the following list.

    Children:
    I.   Margaret Gray, m. William Harris (d. 1720), m. 2nd.
         Thomas Taylor.
    II. Mary Gray, m. Edward Moreland (d. 1723)
    III. Elizabeth Gray, m. James Nicholson (d. 1723)
    IV. Capt. William Gray (1661-1719). (See below.)
    (Mrs. Mary Gray m. 2nd. 1679, Owen Myrick).
    Capt. Willam[3] Gray (1661-1719), of Surry County, Virginia,
was the only son of Capt. Francis Gray who died in 1679. He was
sheriff in 1700, a Justice of the Peace in 1710, and a member of
the House of Burgesses in 1710, 1712, 1713, 1714, and 1715. He
was a member of the Court in 1716. (O. B. 1713- 1718, p. 93).

In 1685 William Gray, planter, of Southwark Parish, Surry County, sold Samuel Plaw 400 acres, recently purchased of Sion Hill, adj. Holly Bush Swamp near Mr. Warren's line. Witnesses: Robt. Ruffin, Wm. Newsum. Mrs. Elizabeth Gray gave Robert Ruffin power of attorney to relinquish her dower rights and this was proved by William Williams. (Surry County Deed Book 2, p. 39). On Nov. 7, 1690, Willam Gray, aged 28 years or thereabouts, testified as to the processioning of the lines between the lands of Capt. Robert Randall now in the possession of Thomas Swann and the lands of Thomas Crews. (D. B. 3, p. 184). In the Virginia Quit Rent Rolls for Surry County in 1704, Capt. William Gray was listed with 1750 acres and William Gray, Junr. with 1050 acres. In 1710 Capt. William Gray sold to William Browne 4 acres in Surry County at Horse Bridge on the head of Grays Creek, 3 acres thereof being on the south side and the remainder granted to the sd. Wm. Gray by the Court of Surry County for the purpose of building a water mill. (D. B. 5, p. 14). Capt. William Gray, in his will dated June 3, 1719, proved Nov. 18, 1719, left legacies to his son William and to the latter's four sons (William, Robert, Joseph and Thomas Gray); to his son Gilbert Gray, then unmarried; to his daughters Mary Gray, Priscilla Gray, and Faith Ruffin; and to his grandchildren Wm. Andrews, Elizabeth Edwards, Wm. Gray, and Willm. Ruffin. His son Gilbert Gray was appointed executor. This will was witnessed by Nichl. Maget, Robt. Judkins, and Saml. Maget.

Capt. William ^{3} Gray married, ca. 1682, Elizabeth_____ and had at least seven children. Order of birth not recorded but apparently about as indicated below.

Children:
I. Willam Gray (1682-1736), m. 1702, Mrs. Mary (Crawford) Seward (d. 1756). 7 children. (see later).
II. Elizabeth (?) Gray (ca. 1684(?)-17), m. William Andrews. 2 (?) sons.
III. Lucy(?) Gray (ca. 1686 (?)-17), m. John (?) Edwards.
IV. Faith Gray (ca. 1688(?) - ca. 1720), m. ca. 1707, William Ruffin (ca. 1683-1739) q. v.
V. Mary Gray (ca. 1690(?)-17)
VI. Priscilla Gray (ca. 1692(?)-17), m. Capt. Thomas Hill (1686-1737).
VII. Gilbert Gray (ca. 1696(?)-1764), m. ca. 1720(?), Margaret_____(d. 1767). 7 children. (See later.)

William Gray (1682-1736) married 1702, Mrs. Mary (Crafford) Seward, daughter of Robert Crafford and widow of John Seward. On March 31, 1701/2, Mary Gray was executrix of the estate of John Seward. Her account was audited by Robert Crafford and Robert Jarrett. William Gray was Sheriff of Surry in 1718. His securities were William Browne and William Edwards. He was also Burgess from Surry 1723-1726.

He made his will March 10, 1731, same probated June 16, 1736. His will is that of a wealthy man as he bequeaths large tracts of land and many negroes. He gave sons, William, Robert, Joseph, Thomas, "land and plantations where they now live". Also to Robert he gave "land left me by my father called Babb's land and land purchased by me of my brother Gilbert." To Joseph he gave land "purchased of Charles Jones and wife." To son Edmund "land purchased of Robert Scott lying in Isle of Wight County."

Mrs. Mary Gray's will, dated 1756, showed daughter Lucy, wife of Howell Briggs; granddaughter Eliza Rose; sons, William, Edmund, James, Robert, Joseph and Thomas Gray; also son, William Seward. Witnesses, Gray Briggs, Susannah Gray, and William Thorp.

Children:
  I. William, Jr. (1703-1744) (see later).
  II. Robert, (1705-1777). Sheriff of Surry 1740, married Miss Claiborne, moved to Edgecombe County, N. C.
  III. Joseph, (1707-1771), m. Sarah, dau. Col. John Simmons (see later).
  IV. Thomas
  V. Edmund, under 21 in 1731, given land in Isle of Wight.
  VI. James, (1715-1788), under 21 in 1731. m. Sarah____, children: Josiah, m. Betsy West; James; Sarah, m. Richard Powell Davis; Ann; Elizabeth; Susannah, Nathaniel.
  VII. Lucy, (1711-   ), m. Howell Briggs.

William Gray, (1703-1744), son of William Gray (1682-1736), was known at first as William Gray, Jr. On January 16, 1734, Thomas Foster of Surry and John Clements of Isle of Wight, deeded him 175 acres in Surry whereon Thomas Foster now lives being the head of a branch and adjoining Ogburn, Allen Warren, William Marriott and Mary Boston. (D. B. 1730-38, p. 515).

He married Elizabeth, daughter of Captain William Browne (1671-1746), widow of William Chamberlayne of New Kent and removed to that county where he was a Justice in 1742. On December 9, 1740, as "William Gray of New Kent" he deeded John Harris of Surry the 175 acres above mentioned, "being the land that John Clements, deceased, gave to Thomas Foster by will dated May 12, 1704, and purchased by the said William Gray of the said Thomas Foster and John Clements the younger. Teste, J. Gray, Gilbert Gray, Robert Gray. (D. B. 3, p. 273) (see Clement's family).

In 1739, William Gray patented 5000 acres in Goochland where some of the name still resides. December 4, 1744, he again deeded land in Surry "left him" by the will of William Gray, dec. by will dated March 10, 1731. His children were: Ethelred who married a daughter of Captain William Drew; Lucy mentioned in will of Captain William Browne.

4. Gilbert Gray, son of William Gray, Sr., (1661-1719), lived in Surry County where he made his will Alril 8, 1758, probated December 10, 1764, (WB 9). Same is as follows: "To son, Joseph Gray 550 acres given testator by the will of said testator's father, exclusive of that known as Babbs, containing 360 acres, also gives said Joseph Gray a tract purchased by said testator of the Vestry of the Parish of Southwark, adjoining said 550 acres. Daughter, Eliza Marriott, wife of Mathias Marriott, 3 negroes. Daughter Sarah Gray, 3 negroes, one bed and furniture. Daughter Mary Gray, 3 negroes, one bed and furniture. Daughter Lucy Gray, 3 negroes, one bed and furniture. Son John Gray, son James Gray 4 negroes, one bed and furniture and the tract of land known as Babbs given the testator by the will of said testator's father. Wife, Margaret, the remainder of his estate during her natural life or widowhood. Executrix, testator's wife; Executor, testator's son Joseph Gray. Witnesses: Robert Gray, Hartwell Cocke, George Dawson."

Children:
I. Joseph, m.
II. John, m. Mary.
III. Eliza, m. Mathias Marriott (17-1774).
IV. Sarah, m. Thomas WASHINGTON, Jr.
V. Mary, m. Christopher (?) Clinch.
VI. Lucy, dsp. 1773, left legacies to brother John Gray and James Gray, the latter under age.
VII. James.

Joseph Gray, (1707-1771), m. 1st December 14, 1729, Sarah Simmons, daughter of Colonel John SIMMONS. The name of his second wife whom he married in 1748 is unknown. Colonel Gray was Burgess from Isle of Wight 1736-1749. His land fell in Southampton County where he was one of the first Justices of the County Court, 1749; Sheriff 1751, Burgess 1755 to 1769. His will was dated August 30, 1769 and proved June 13, 1771.

Children of 1st wife. (V. M. 30, p. 64).
I. William (1732-1750) dsp.
II. Mary, (1734-   ), m. (1st.) Littleton Tazewell, m. (2nd.) Rev. William Fanning.
III. Elizabeth, (1736-1761).

IV. Anne, (1738-   )
V. Sarah, (1739-   ), m. Major James Wall.
VI. John, (1741-1760).
VII. Edwin, (1743-1790) (see later).
VIII. Peter, (1745-1761)
IX. James, (1747-1807).

Children of 2nd. wife:
X. Joseph, (1749-1754).
XI. Lucy, (1751-   ), m. 1769, Col. John Flood Edmunds, of Brunswick Co., Va.
XII. Jane, (1753-1754).

Colonel Edwin Gray married Julia, daughter of Thomas Godwin of Nansemond. He was a member of the House of Burgesses 1769-1774, of the Virginia Conventions of 1774, 1775, and 1776; and of the House of Delegates and State Senate. He made his will September 23, 1788 and same probated June 1790.

Children:
I. Joseph, will proven in Southampton, 1820. Children: Sons, James and Joseph; Daughters, Sally and Nancy Gray.
II. Edwin, m. (1) Julia Gray (2) Mrs. Gray nee Lewis. He was Member of Congress from Southampton, 1799-1813.
III. Thomas, m. Mrs. Brewer nee Cocke. His will was dated September 6, 1831, and proven in Southampton September 9, 1831. Children: Catherine, m. Richardson; Edwin, m. (2) Charlotte Langston; Joseph, m. Evelyn Davis; Anne; Robert, m. Mary Nicholson; Thomas Ruffin, m. Mary Gray.
IV. Mary, m. September 1788, Daniel Simmons.
V. Henry Mills, m. Martha Hynes, made will 1814.

JONES

The coat-of-arms of this family, as given by Robert Jones, Attorney-general of North Carolina, who was a descendant, was: Ermine three Lions (Wm. and Mary Quarterly, 1st Series, 19, p. 291). These are the arms of the Jones family of Kent and London. The first positively known ancestor of the family was James Jones of Charles City and Prince George Cos., who was born about 1640-42 and died at an advanced age in Prince George Co. in 1719. James Jones was first granted land in Charles City Co. March 1, 1663 (Nugent, p. 504), his land being very close to that of Rev. Richard Jones, who may have been his father. However, it seems slightly more probable that both these men were sons of David Jones, b. 1594, d. in Charles City Co. between 1665 and 1673, who was settled in Virginia as early as 1624 (cf. Hotten, p. 214; Nugent, pp 25, 167, 535; Order Book 1655-65, pp. 104, 343, 529; Order Book 1672/4, p. 524). The above references show that David Jones had a son John, who died in 1657 and left a son John; and two daughters Mary and Ann; but since his land was in the Parish of Weyanoke, close to that of James Jones and Rev. Richard Jones, it is not improbable that they were, also, his sons. The names David and Richard were both perpetuated in the family of James Jones.

James Jones is mentioned in the will of Christopher Lewis, dated Sept. 1, 1673, and probated Oct. 20, 1673, in Surry Co., who left a legacy to Mary Jones, daughter of James Jones, and appointed Mr. Jones his executor (Surry D. & W. 1672-84, p. 35). As executor, he deeded away the land that had belonged to Mr. Lewis July 7, 1696 (D. & W. 1693-1709, p. 99). The above may indicate a relationship to Mr. Lewis, perhaps through James Jones' first wife, whose name is otherwise unknown. The wife, Sarah Jones, referred to in his will, was probably his second wife and not the mother of his children. James Jones was again granted land in Charles City Co., in Weyanoke Parish in 1683 and 1684, and he had a grant in Surry Co. in 1702 (Grants Bks., 7, p. 329, p. 488; 9, p. 497). The will of James Jones, dated April 6, 1719, and probated in Prince George Co. May 12, 1719, leaves his property to "my loving wife and my wife's two sons"; daughter Mary Darden and her

son Charles Williams; daughters Elizabeth, Hannah, and Rebecca;
granddaughter Elizabeth Glover; grandson Thomas Chappell;
granddaughter Jane Cooke, daughter of John Cooke; and son
James. (Prince George D. & W., 1713-28, p. 350). A letter
from Sarah Jones April 20, 1719, states that she is satisfied
with the provisions made for her in the will (id., p. 311).
James Jones hand only the one son, James. Of his four daughters the following is known.

I. Mary Jones was born prior to 1673, as she is mentioned in the will of Christopher Lewis in that year.
   She married (1) John Williams, and had three sons,
   James, Charles and John Williams. These three men,
   stated to be sons of John Williams, deceased, were
   granted land in Bristol Parish, Prince George Co.,
   April 25, 1702 (Grant Bk. 9, p. 451). John Williams,
   the son, died Jan. 16, 1725 (Bristol Psh. Reg.). The
   mother, Mary (Jones) Williams married (2) Richard
   Darden (Prince George D. & W. 1713-28, p. 864).
   The son Charles Williams, mentioned in the will of
   James Jones, was also left land by his uncle-in-law,
   Thomas Chappell, in Surry Co., which he and his
   wife Anne deeded away Feb. 12, 1721 (D & W. 1715-30,
   p. 416). The children of Charles and Ann Williams,
   as shown by the Bristol Parish Register, were:
   1. Charles, b. May 26, 1722.
   2. Sarah, b. Sept. 20, 1725
   3. Lucy, b. May 6, 1727
   4. John, b. Mar. 17, 1729
   5. Mary, b. Aug. 5, 1731
   6. John, b. May 14, 1734.
II. Elizabeth Jones m. (1) Thomas CHAPPELL (d. 1702/3),
    by whom she had four sons, Robert, Thomas, James
    (b. 1694), and Samuel Chappell (b. 1696)(see Chappell
    Family). She married (2) in 1704, Thomas Taylor, by
    whom she had four children, John Taylor, Thomas
    Taylor, Elizabeth, m. John Chambliss, and Katherine
    m. Edward Holloway, Jr. (cf. Prince George D. & W.
    1713-28, p. 861; pp. 1108, 1109; Surry D. & W. 1730-
    38, p. 628).
III. Hannah Jones, mentioned in James Jones' will merely
     as "my daughter Hannah", may have been the wife of
     John Cooke and the mother of Jane Cooke, the grand-
     daughter mentioned also in the will. John Cooke died
     in Surry Co. in 1715, his inventory handed in by William
     Cooke, being dated Jan. 18, 1715. (Surry D. & W. 1709-
     15, p. 255).

IV. Rebecca Jones married William Cooke. Thomas Chappell deeded to William Cooke, Jr., June 19, 1722, 100 acres of land in Surry Co. left to Chappell by the will of James Jones (D. & W. 1715-30, p. 402). On Sept. 20, 1727, William Cook and Rebecca, his wife, deeded to William Briggs for their sons James and Reuben Cook the land left Rebecca by her father James Jones, deceased (id. p. 753-4). William Cook's will, dated May 1, 1740, and probated Nov. 19, 1740, in Surry Co., mentions sons William, Reuben and James; daughters Elizabeth wife of Thomas Tomlinson, Rebecca wife of James Andrews, Sarah wife of Henry Mitchell, Mary wife of William BRIGGS, Susannah, wife of Miell Hill, Hannah wife of William Gary, and Amy wife of John Maclin. Of the sons, William Cook, Jr., m. Elizabeth _____, and lived in Albemarle Parish, three of his children's births being recorded in the Parish Register, namely, Thomas, b. Dec. 4, 1741; Sarah, b. Oct. 6, 1744; and Henry b. Feb. 26, 1750. William Cook's will, dated Nov. 8, 1764, and probated in Sussex Co. Dec. 20, 1764, mentions his daughters Hannah Goodwyn and Elizabeth Irby, sons William, James and Thomas Cook, daughter Sarah Cook, sons Foster and Henry Cook, and wife Elizabeth (Sussex W. B. "B", p. 17).

There was another William Cook with wife, Naomi, the births of whose children are recorded in the Albemarle Parish Register as follows: Mercurius, b. April 12, 1742; Lazarus, b. April 30, 1744; Samuel, b. April 30, 1744; Ephraim, b. July 30, 1751. He may have been a son of John Cooke. Reuben Cooke, son of William and Rebecca (Jones) Cook, m. Anne_____, and died in Sussex Co. in 1764. His will, dated June 23, 1764, and probated Aug. 19, 1764, mentions his wife Anne, daughter Mary Briggs, son Richard Cook, daughters Sarah and Elizabeth Cook, son Henry, and daughter Amy. The Albemarle Parish Register shows the following children of Reuben and Anne Cook: Joseph (?), b. Nov. 21, 1741; Richard, b. Aug. 1, 1744; Sarah, b. June 24, 1746; Elizabeth, b. June 11, 1748, Henry, b. Aug. 22, 1750. Another Reuben Cook, possibly a son of the above who predeceased his father, died in Sussex Co. in 1760, his will, which was probated Dec. 19, 1760, mentioning his wife, Mary, children William, John and Sarah, and brother John Reeks. The children were born as follows: William b. Dec. 3, 1755; John, b. Jan. 12, 1758; Sarah, b. 1760, christened April 6, 1760.

James Jones II, son of James Jones, married Rebecca ____,

and died in Prince George Co. in 1725. On Feb. 2, 1720, he
deeded to James Jones, Jr. and Robert Jones part of the land
patented in Surry Co. by his brother-in-law Thomas Chappell
Oct. 10, 1701, and conveyed by Chappell to Jones, June 3, 1702,
(D. & W. 1715-30, p. 295). His will, dated Feb. 20, 1724, and
probated in Prince George Co. July 13, 1725, mentions his sons
James and Robert, daughters Elizabeth Glover and Rebecca, sons
David, John, and Richard, wife Rebecca, "mother-in-law Sarah
Jones" (also called "my mother Jones"); wife Rebecca and son
Richard, executors (D. & W. 1713-28, p. 832). The following
is known of James Jones' sons:

I. James Jones married Sarah, daughter of Howell Edmunds,
and lived in Surry Co. He. d. Aug. 22, 1742, and his
wife Sarah Mar. 11, 1750/51, both deaths being reported
by their son James Jones (Alb. Psh. Reg.). James
Jones' will, dated Aug. 22, 1742, and probated in Surry
Co. Feb. 16, 1742/3, mentions sons James, Howell,
John and Thomas, daughter Elizabeth, wife Sarah,
unborn child, and his brother Robert Jones and cousin
Robert Jones. The "unborn child" of the will was Edmunds Jones, b. Dec. 13, 1742 (Alb. Psh. Reg.).

II. Robert Jones, b. 1694, member of the House of Burgesses for Surry, 1752-1755; married Elizabeth____,
died Feb. 14, 1775, in his 81st year (alb. Psh. Reg.).
Robert Jones' will, dated Nov. 25, 1774, and probated
in Sussex Co., April 20, 1775, mentions his daughter
Elizabeth Gray, son David and the latter's son David,
son John, son Jesse's children, sons Peter and Nathaniel, son Richard's daughter Mary, daughter Rebecca
Hancock and her daughter Elizabeth Green Hancock.
The births of two of the children of Robert and Elizabeth Jones are recorded in the Albemarle Parish Register, namely, Abraham, b. Sept. 3, 1739, and Rebecca, b. April 17, 1743. Robert Jones' eldest son
was Robert Jones, Jr., Attorney-General of North
Carolina (see later).

III. David Jones m. Susannah _____, and they had the
following children recorded in the Albemarle Parish
Register:
1. James Boisseau, b. May 23, 1731. (7 children in
register.)
2. Rebecca, b. Feb. 4, 1732/3.
3. David, b. Nov. 6, 1734, m. Sarah____. (See below.)
4. John, b. Dec. 10, 1736.
5. Harris (?) b. Jan. 24, 1739/40.
6. Susannah, b. Jan. 13, 1740/1.
7. Sarah, b. Aug. 8, 1743.

8. Elizabeth, b. May 18, 1745.
9. Mary, b. Feb. 4, 1747/8.
10. Robert, b. Nov. 17, 1752.
The children of David Jones, Jr. and wife Sarah are given as follows:
1. David, b. Sept. 27, 1752.
2. Rebecca, b. Aug. 9, 1754.
3. Abram, b. June 1, 1756.
4. Holmes, b. June 15, 1758.
5. Robert, b. Nov. 1, 1760.
6. Littlebury, b. May 15, 1765.
7. Charlotte, b. Sept. 11, 1767.
This David Jones, Jr. may have been the son of Robert Jones, Sr., however, rather than David, Sr.

IV. John Jones was apparently identical with a John Jones who died in Surry Co. in 1743 and left no male heirs. His will, dated March 9, 1742/3 and probated in Surry Co. Aug. 17, 1743, mentions his daughters Mary, Betty and Rebecca Jones, his wife Sarah, and her father William Batte, and make his brother Richard Jones and Holmes Boyseau executors.

V. Richard Jones was apparently identical with a Richard Jones who is recorded in the Albemarle Parish Register as dying Feb. 18, 1774, in his 72nd year. Ann, his wife, died Feb. 21, 1774, in her 66th year, and the statement is made that they had been wedded about 50 years. A Richard Jones, Jr., who died in Sussex Co., in 1772, may have been a son of this couple. His will, dated Dec. 28, 1771, and probated Jan. 16, 1772, mentions his wife Sarah, sons Howell, Richard and Samuel, daughters Ann and Martha Myrick Jones, and brother Robert Jones.

Children from register:
1. Howell, b. July 25, 1760;
2. Anne, b. Mar. 16, 1762;
3. Richard, b. Feb. 17, 1765;
4. Martha Myrick, b. 1768;
5. Samuel, b. Mar. 18, 1771.

Robert Jones, Jr. (1718-1766), son of Robert Jones, Sr. (1694-1775) of Sussex County, married Sarah, daughter of Robert Cobbs and his wife, Elizabeth Allen of York County, Va. (V. M. 3, p. 196). He lived in Sussex until shortly after 1750 as the births of four of his children are shown in the Albermarle Parish Register . He removed to Northampton Co., N. C. and became Attorney General of North Carolina. The

Albermarle Parish Register records his death as follows:
"Robert Jones, son of Robert Jones of this Parish and Attorney
General of North Carolina in his 49th year, Oct. 2, 1766."

He married secondly, Mary, daughter of Colonel William
Eaton, who mentions his daughter "Mary, wife of Robert Jones"
in his will, probated in 1759. (Grimes, p.. 108). Mary Eaton's
mother was Mary, daughter of Captain William Browne and his
wife, Mary, daughter of Francis Clements.

His will was probated Nov. 1776, as follows: "To wife,
Mary, plantation for life and to son Willie Jones, after decease
of wife. To my two sons, Allen and Willie, land in Halifax
County; daughter, Martha, wife of Thomas Gilchrist, slaves;
friend Joseph John Alston, personalty. The amount of sales
of my land in Rowan, Orange and Granville counties to Wm.
Wynne of Virginia." Codicil of September 20, 1766, names
daughter Elizabeth. (Bk. A, part 1, pg. 90).

Children:
I. Allen, b. Dec. 24, 1739. (see later).
II. Willie, b. May 25, 1741. (see later).
III. Martha, b. Aug. 22, 1743, m. Judge Thomas Gilchrist.
Their daughter, Grizelda, m. Oct. 15, 1789, Col. Wil-
liam Polk, b. July 9, 1758, d. Jan. 14, 1834. William
Polk, while a student at Queens College, Charlotte, was
appointed a second lieut. of S. C. Troops and was woun-
ded at the battle of Reedy River. He was appointed Ma-
jor of 9th Regt., N. C. Line, Nov. 27, 1776, and joined
Washington in New Jersey where he fought in the battles
of Brandywine and Germantown and wintered at Valley
Forge. Transferred to 3rd. Regt., N. C. Line as
Colonel commanding he fought in the South at Eutaw
Springs and in other battles. (D. A. B.)
His first wife died in 1799 and he married secondly,
Sarah, dau. of Philemon Hawkins, Jr. He had two
children by his first wife, one of whom was Dr. William
Julius Polk, who married his cousin, Mary Rebecca
Long, granddaughter of Allen Jones.
IV. Carlotta (Charlotte), b. Sept. 7, 1746.
V. Robert, b. 1749-50, christened Feb. 2, 1749-50.

Daughter of 2nd. wife, Mary Eaton:
VI. Elizabeth, b. 1766, m. Gov. Benjamin Williams (1754-
1814) eleventh and fourteenth governor of N. C. (1799-
1802 and 1807-08). Gov. William succeeded his brother-
in-law, William R. Davie, as governor. He was 1st
Lieut. 2nd N. C. Sept. 1st, 1775; Capt. 19 July, 1776;
served until 1780 and was made Colonel of State Militia;

fought at Battle of Guilford C. H. Mar. 15, 1781. (Heitman). He was a member of Congress, 1793-95, before being elected governor. He died in Moore County, N. C. (D. A. B.)

Allen Jones, b. Dec. 24, 1739; d. Nov. 14, 1807; son of Robert Jones, Jr., Attorney General of N. C., married (1) Jan. 21, 1762, Mary Haynes, married (2) Sept. 3, 1768, Rebecca Edwards, dau. of Col. Nathaniel EDWARDS of Brunswick Co., Va., m. (3) Mary, by whom he had no children. He was a member of the House of Commons, 1773-75, from Northampton. In 1771, he aided Gov. Tryon in suppressing the Regulators.

His services in the Revolution were numerous. He was on Committee of Safety for Halifax District 1775, and represented Northampton in the Provincial Congresses 1774-76. He was appointed Brigadier General of Militia 1776. From 1777 to 1779 he was in the State Senate and was speaker in 1778-1779; was a member of the Continental Congress 1779-1780. In 1783, 1784 and 1787 he was a member of the State Senate. He was an advocate of the ratification of the Federal Constitution and, unlike his brother, Willie, who was Anti-Federalist, was defeated for the conventions of 1788 and 1789. In 1790 he was the owner of 177 slaves, the fourth largest holding in the state (D. A. B.) His widow married William Wright of Southampton County, Va.

His will dated July 4, 1807, was probated Jan. 15, 1808, as follows (abstract):

"To wife Mary, for the support of herself and gr. daus, Rebecca Jones Long and Mary Rebecca Allen Long - - -. Wife and grandchildren to remain during that time (until debts are paid) at Mount Gallant and to be supported as usual, and to have the same servants carriages and horses. After debts are paid land called Mount Gallant and other tracts (named) to wife, and at her death to gr. dau. Mary Rebecca Allen Long. If the latter dies without issue, the land to gr. sons Allen Jones Green and Allen Jones Davie.

" gr. son Hyder Allen Davie
" " " Wm. Richardson Davie
gr. daus. Mary, Sarah, and Rebecca Davie
gr. sons, John Sitgreaves
gr. daus, Amarilla and Emily Sitgreaves
dau- Martha Cobb Hall, land now in possession of Dr. Hall
**
Wife Mary, friend Lunsford Long, guardians to the estate

devised to gr. daus. Rebecca Long Jones and Mary Rebecca
Long, and it is my wish that they remain with my dear wife
who has been a tender parent to them.

Friends Lunsford Long and Doctor Thomas Hall, Exrs,
and they to receive 100 lbs. Va. money for their trouble.

Having divided my estate with all the justice in my power,
I once more recommend my slaves to the care and protection of my Children. "

Children of 1st. wife:
I. Robin, dsp.
II. Martha Cobb, m. 1788 (1) James Green and had one
son, Allen Jones Green; (2) Judge John Sitgreaves.
He was a Lieut. in N. C. Militia 1776, died Mar. 4,
1802. (Heitman).
III. Sarah, m. 1782. Gov. William Richardson Davie, b.
June 20, 1756; d. Nov. 29, 1820. He was born at Egre-
mont, Cumberland, Eng., and was brought by his father,
Archibald Davie, to the Waxhaw settlement in S. C. in
1763. He served under his father-in-law to be, Gen.
Allen Jones in 1777-78 and received successive commissions as lieut., Capt., and Major. He joined Pul-
aski's Legion and was severly wounded at the Battle of
Stono, June 20, 1779. On Jan. 16, 1781, he was appointed Commissary-General to General Greene and
kept his army supplied on its march to Guilford C. H.
After his marriage he served in the Legislature
from 1786 to 1798. In 1798 he was elected Governor
of N. C. and served one term. In 1799 he was appointed by President Adams Peace Commissioner to
France. He had six children (all named in will of Allen
Jones) and died at his plantation "Tivoli" in Lancaster
County, S. C. 1820. (D. A. B.)

Children of Allen Jones by second wife:
IV. Rebecca Edwards, b. 1770, m. Lunsford Long, Commissary-General of N. C. in the Rev., member of
Provincial Congress and State Senate.
Children:
1. Rebecca Edwards Long, m. Col. Cadwallader Jones.
2. Mary Rebecca Allen Long, m. her cousin, Dr. William J. Polk.

Willie Jones b. May 25, 1741, d. June 18, 1801; named for
the Rev. William Willie, beloved Rector of Albermarle Parish;

son of Robert Jones, Jr., Atty. General of N. C., married June 27, 1776, Mary Montfort, dau. of _____ Montfort. He and his brother, Allen, were sent to England to be educated and spent some years at Eton.

Upon his return from England he lived at his home place "The Grove" in the town of Halifax. In 1774 he was elected to the first Provincial Congress and served in five succeeding congresses. He was a member of the House of Commons 1777-1780; senator 1782-84-88. In 1780 he was elected to the Continental Congress. In 1788 he was a member of the Constitutional Convention and was the leader of the movement against ratification having behind him a majority one hundred members. He was elected to the next convention which ratified the constitution but would not attend.

Children:

I. Sarah, m. Gov. Hutchins Gordon Burton (1774-1836), son of John and Mary (Gordon) Burton. He was a student at the Univ. of N. C. 1795-98, and graduated in law. He was elected to the House of Commons in 1809; served as Attorney General of N. C. 1810-16; 1819 to 1824 was a representative in Congress. In 1824 he was elected governor by the General Assembly and was twice re-elected serving until Dec. 1827.

II. Martha, m. Jan. 6, 1809, John Wayles EPPES. (1772-1823). M. C. and U. S. Senator from Virginia. He resigned from the Senate, Dec. 7, 1819, on account of ill health, and died Sept. 20, 1823, at "Eppington" in Chesterfield County. His first wife was Mary, daughter of President Thomas Jefferson, by whom he had one son, Francis Wayles Eppes.

Children of Martha Jones:

1. Mary Eppes, m. Phillip Bolling.
2. Sarah Eppes, m. Edmond W. Hubard of Buckingham, N. C.
3. Dr. Willie Jones Eppes of "Milbrink" Buckingham.
4. John Eppes, dsp.

III. Annie Maria, m. Joseph B. Littlejohn.
IV. Willie, dsp.
V. Robert, dsp.

THE HAYNES FAMILY

The two Haynes brothers, Anthony who married Jane Eaton, and Andrew who married Annie Eaton, daughters of Col. William Eaton, were sons of Thomas Haynes, Jr., Sheriff of Warwick 1716, who died in London in 1742.

The first one of this family in Virginia was Anthony Haynes who patented land in New Kent in 1658. (C. P. 368-369).

His son was Thomas Haynes who married the widow of Robert Clark before November 12, 1666 in York County (B, 3, p. 94) (County Court Note Book, June 1929, p. 18) (See also W. M. 24, p. 43).

Thomas Haynes was the father of Thomas Haynes, Jr., Sheriff of Warwick, whose will, dated September 1742, was probated in London, September 27, 1746. (Tyler 1, p. 68).

Children from will:
I. Anthony, m. Jane Eaton. His wife married secondly, Colonel Nathaniel Edwards of Brunswick. (See Edwards).
II. Thomas, was on Warwick Committee of Safety, 1774. (W. &M. 5, p. 250)
III. Virginia
IV. Richard
V. Andrew, m. Annie Eaton. He is mentioned as deceased in Colonel William Eaton's will 1759, and is said to have died in 1753. (Wm. IV, p. 182).
VI. Elizabeth, m. Edward Cary. (Wm. IV, pp. 47, 182)
VII. Martha
VIII. Mary
IX. Herbert, died 1757 in London (Will PCC). He mentions father Thomas Haynes deceased. (V. M. 15, p. 427.)

The Eaton family originated in York County. John Eaton, father of Col. William Eaton, moved from York to Prince George County. The Colonel's grandfather was John Eaton whose will was probated in York, Dec. 17, 1717. His legatees were sons: John; Samuel, to whom he gave land in Prince George; and William; daughters: Elizabeth, Sarah Woodland (?); and Mary Lepesis, (?) (York Records).

Samuel, the brother of John Eaton of Prince George, on Aug. 19, 1719, as of Yorkhampton Parish, York County, deeded 250 acres in Prince George to John Green "being remaining part of the patent to John Eaton, father of said Samuel Eaton, dated Dec., 1714, of 420 acres, devised to Samuel Eaton in his father's will recorded Dec. 17, 1717. (P.G. Deeds, part II, p. 341.) Samuel Eaton, in his will probated 1719, mentions his brother John.

John Eaton, father of Col. William Eaton, was a Burgess from Prince George 1736-39 and died in 1739. (B. J.) He married Rebecca, daughter of Catherine (Allen) and Benjamin Cocke, of "Bacon's Castle", Surry. Colonel William Eaton lived first in Prince George, but moved to Greenville, County, N. C. In 1742 as "William Eaton of North Carolina," he conveyed to An-

thony Haynes of Prince George, (on record in Amelia which was
formed from Prince George in 1732) 204 acres patented by him
in 1732. Anthony Haynes was his son-in-law. This land probably afterwards fell in Dinwiddie, for on Oct. 14, 1752, William
Walker surveyed lands on both sides of the Nottoway in that
county, "lying next to Anthony Haynes." (Dinwiddie Plot Book
1752-1865).

Colonel Eaton was Colonel of the Greenville County Militia,
and served many years in the Provincial Congress. His will
was dated Feb. 19, 1759, probated Mar. 20, 1759, of St. John's
Parish in County of Greenville, to sons: WILLIAM lands in
Dinwiddie and Brunswick Counties in Va. (Except lands received
of William Scroggins); THOMAS; CHARLES RUST EATON; daus:
JANE, wife of COL. NATHANIEL EDWARDS, whose former husband had been ANTHONY HAYNES, decd., by whom she had children; ANNE HAYNES relict of ANDREW HAYNES, decd., MARY,
wife of ROBERT JONES; SARAH, wife of CHARLES JOHNSON;
ELIZABETH wife of DANIEL WELDON; MARTHA; grandson
EATON HAYNES. Wife and extrx, MARY. (Grimes 108).

The children of the two brothers, Anthony and Andrew Haynes,
who married Eaton sister, have not been definitely ascertained
as the brothers seemingly died intestate.

Anthony Haynes, probably a son of Anthony who married
Jane Eaton, died in Columbia County, Georgia, 1795. He bought
200 acres, April 2, 1785, in Richmond (later Columbia)
from William Sims who patented it Dec. 6, 1774 on Uchee Creek
"Where said Anthony now lives". (D.A.R. Hist. Colln. of Ga.
p. 294). On May 9, 1794, he gave a power of attorney to William
Sims to secure balance due him from Eaton Haynes of Northampton, N. C., executor of his brother, Herbert Haynes, and from
Andrew Haynes, admn., of his sister, Jean Wood. Anthony's
will was dated June 15, 1795, and probated June 20, 1795. He
gave 20 shillings each to his brothers and one sister, naming
them as follows: HERBERT HAYNES, JANE WOOD, EATON
HAYNES, ANDREW HAYNES. He gave negroes to THOMAS
HAYNES of Columbia County, without naming him as "brother",
and appointed him executor. (W.B. 1790-1804)

Thomas Haynes, the above mentioned executor, may have
been a brother although not named one. He married Frances,
daughter of William Stith in Brunswick County, Va., April 22,
1782, and died in Columbia County, Ga., 1823. His known
children were: (1) Thomas, Jr., m. Cathrine Marie Davis;
(2) Cathrine m. John Bonner; (3) Mary, m. Dennis Laurence
Ryan; (4) Elizabeth, m. Patrick Laurence Robinson. (D.A.R.
records.)

Andrew Haynes, brother of the first Anthony, as stated before, married Annie, dau. of Col. William Eaton. Andrew

died before 1759, the date of Col. Eaton's will, evidently intestate.

His children, from wills and deeds were as follows, although
he may have had more children than are shown below:

I. Thomas, of Halifax, married Cathrine Allen Bradby,
in Surry, Sept. 24, 1776. (Colonial Surry, p. 219.)
It may have been his nephew, Thomas, who married
Cathrine Allen Bradby. She apparently predeceased
him, and they had no children, for he did not mention
a wife or child in his will dated Halifax, May 2, 1796,
and probated the same month. His legatees were:
nephew, CHRISTOPHER, son of WILLIAM HAYNES; to
nephews JOHN and THOMAS, sons of JOHN GORDON,
600 acres of land on Cumberland River in Davidson
County, Tenn; to nephew JAMES son of JOHN GORDON,
one horse and saddle; nephews THOMAS and EATON
HAYNES, sons of CHRISTOPHER HAYNES; sister
MARY HAYNES; nephew CHRISTOPHER HAYNES executor (Bk. 3, p. 267).

II. Mary (?), b. Dec. 11, 1751, m. (1) W. R. DAVIE,
(2) John Daves. (See later.)

III. Anna, b. Jan. 26, 1755, m. John Gordon. (See later).

IV. Mary, m. Allen Jones, (see ante).

V. William, m. ____, had a son Christopher, who m.
Lucy, daughter of Ambrose Pitman, so named in Am-
brose Pitman's will probated in Halifax, Feb. 1787.
(Bk. 3-122) Christopher was a sergeant in Dawson's
Company, 7th. Regt. N. C. Troops, discharged in 1777.
(Rev. Records, Vol. 16, p. 1082). He made his will
in Halifax, Mar. 24, 1787, probated Feb. 1788, lega-
tees, wife LUCY; daus. LUCY NOBLIN and MARY BAR-
ROW; executors, wife, WILLIAM NOBLIN, and ROBERT
BARROW. (Bk 3-127).

VI. Christopher, had two sons, Thomas and Eaton Haynes,
legatees in his brother Thomas' will. A Thomas Haynes
was a soldier in Capt. Thomas Sitgreave's company of
state militia at Newberry, N. S. in 1771. (N. C. Col.
Rec. 22, p. 422). His wife may have been named
"Mary" for William Jarvis, in his will probated Feb.
1785, in Halifax, gave a legacy to "Eaton Haynes, son
of Mary Haynes".... (Bk. 3)

Richard Frear in his will probated in Halifax, Nov. 1774,
mentions his daughter MARGARET HAYNES, and his executors
were: Allen Jones and Eaton Haynes. The name of Margaret's
husband does not appear, unless it was Eaton Haynes, probably
of Northampton, for on August 30, 1799, Richard Frear, his

son, and Eaton Haynes of Northampton deeded land. Eaton was
County Court Clerk of Northampton. (Bk. 1793-1802, p. 366).

Mary Haynes, born Dec. 11, 1751, died April 11, 1822; dau.
of Annie (Eaton) and Andrew Haynes; married (1) W. R. Davie;
married (2) April 2, 1782, John Daves, born 1748 in Mecklenburg Co., Va., died Oct. 12, 1804, in New Bern, N. C.

Mr. Daves was captain of the 3rd Regiment, N. C. Continental Line during the Revolution and was an original member of the
North Carolina Society of the Cincinnati.

    Children:
- I. Sally Eaton Daves, b. April 17, 1783, m. Morgan Jones.
- II. Ann Rebecca, b. Nov. 14, 1785, m. Josiah Collins.
- III. John Pugh, b. July 23, 1789, m. Elizabeth Batchelor Graham. (see later).
- IV. Thomas Haynes, b. Sept. 24, 1791, m. Harriet Hatch.

John Pugh Daves, born July 23, 1789, died Mar. 26, 1838,
at New Bern, N. C., married Elizabeth Batchelor Graham,
born Aug. 3, 1804, died May 9, 1885, at New Bern.

    Children:
- I. Jane Graham Daves, b. Oct. 8, 1830, m. John Hughes.
- II. John Daves, b. Dec. 24, 1831.
- III. Edward Graham, b. Mar. 31, 1833, m. Mary Grace Foster.
- IV. Mary McKinley, b. Jan. 2, 1835, m. John Willis Ellis. (See later.)
- V. Graham, b. July 16, 1836, m. Alice London DeRossett.
- VI. Ann Rebecca Collins, b. Mar. 5, 1838, m. Christopher W. McLean.

Mary McKinley Daves, b. Jan. 2, 1835, died Jan. 23, 1916,
at Pensacola, Fla., married Aug. 11, 1856, John Willis Ellis,
born Nov. 30, 1820, in Rowan County, died July 7, 1861, while
Governor of North Carolina.

Governor Ellis attended the University of N. C. 1837-41, read
law under the noted Richmond Pearson and was admitted to the bar
in 1842; represented Rowan County in the House of Commons,
1844-48; Judge of the Superior Court 1848-58; Governor of N. C.
1858-60; re-elected on Secession Ticket and died six weeks after
North Carolina seceded from the Union.

    Children:
- I. Mary Daves Ellis, b. June 8, 1859, m. William Hyer Knowles. (See later.)
- II. Jane Graham Ellis, b. Oct. 9, 1860, m. William Trent Rossell.

Mary Daves Ellis, daughter of Governor Ellis, born June 8, 1859, at Raleigh, N. C., died April 27, 1927, in New York City; married Nov. 25, 1885, at New Bern, N. C. William Hyer Knowles, born Dec. 27, 1857, at Pensacola, Fla., died April 24, 1939.

Children:
I. John Ellis, b. Oct. 31, 1886, m. Marion Brattle Burbank.
II. Graham Daves, b. Feb. 18, 1886, d. May 20, 1889.
III. Josephine, b. Sept. 15, 1889, m. Joseph Lionel Seligman (see later).
IV. Jeanie Graham, b. July 1, 1894, m. Julian Augustus Fay.
V. Peter, b. June 10, 1899, m. (1) Mary Emily Bailey, (2) Isabel Brantley.
VI. William Hyer, Jr., b. Dec. 14, 1906, m. Frances Sharp.

Josephine Knowles, born Sept. 15, 1889, at Pensacola, Fla; married June 29, 1911, at North Hatley, Quebec, Canada, Joseph Lionel Seligman, born April 18, 1887, in New York City, died April 7, 1944, at Pensacola, Fla., son of Guta (Loeb) and Isaac Newton Seligman. Mrs. Seligman resides at Harborview, Pensacola, Fla.

Children:
I. Joseph Lionel Seligman, Jr., b. November 26, 1913, m. June 13, 1942, Peggy Van Horne. They have one son, Thomas Knowles Seligman, b. Jan. 1, 1944.
II. Muriel Guta, b. May 24, 1918, died Feb. 27, 1920.

Ann Haynes, daughter of Ann (Eaton) and Andrew Haynes, born January 26, 1755, in Halifax County, N. C., died Feb. 25, 1815, married John Gordon of Halifax, born Feb. 12, 1745, died February 27, 1815.

Children:
I. Nancy Gordon, b. May 28, 1774, m. John Harrison. (See later.)
II. John, b. August 29, 1775.
III. Polly, b. June 30, 1777.
IV. James, b. July 2, 1779.
V. Betsy, b. August 12, 1781.
VI. Lucy, b. July 13, 1783.
VII. Thomas, b. February 24, 1786.
VIII. William, b. September 30, 1788.
IX. Joseph, b. Mar. 25, 1791, m. (1) Eliza Rousaville, (2) Matilda Henderson.

X. Elizabeth, b. Oct. 3, 1793, m. Roland Allen.
XI. George Haynes, b. Mar. 27, 1796, m. Martha Boyd, sister of Alfred Boyd.
XII. Sallie.

Nancy Gordon, daughter of Ann (Haynes) and John Gordon, was born May 28, 1774, and married John Harrison July 26, 1792. He died March 10, 1815.

Children:
I. Benjamin Harrison, b. June 30, 1793, m. Martha Wingfield.
II. John Harrison, b. Apr. 23, 1799.
III. Nancy Harrison, b. Aug. 16, 1795.
IV. Abner Harrison
V. Philadelphia Harrison, m. T. Jameson
VI. Mary Harrison, m. _____ Barnes.
VII. Ann Harrison
VIII. Lucy Amis Harrison, b. Dec. 12, 1806, m. Alfred Boyd (see later).

Lucy Amis Harrison, born December 12, 1806, died March 14, 1847, married October 19, 1824, Alfred Boyd, born in Trigg County, Ky., Oct. 9, 1802, died at Mayfield, Ky. 1874. Mr. Boyd served in the Mexican War and was a member of the Kentucky Legislature.

Children:
I. John Harrison Boyd, b. Sept. 28, 1825, m. Sarah Cook.
II. George Boyd, b. Sept. 24, 1827.
III. Abram Boyd, b. Jan. 26, 1830, m. Bettie Jones (see later).
IV. Agnes Boyd, b. July 2, 1832, m. Jas. T. Grimes.
V. Adelaide Linn Boyd, b. Jan. 18, 1834, m. Thomas Allen.
VI. Martha Gordon Boyd, m. Jay C. Small.

Abram Boyd, born January 26, 1830, at Cadiz, Ky., died March 10, 1900, at Beulah, Ark., married March 8, 1870, at Memphis, Tenn., Bettie Jones, born April 3, 1850, at Paducah, Ky., died July 3, 1938, at Los Angeles, Calif., daughter of Maria Leonard (Halsted) and Henry L. Jones. Mr. Jones was a farmer and an attorney at law.

Children:
I. Alfred Boyd, b. Jan. 7, 1872, m. Alice Dimmick (see later).

   II. Fannie Boyd, b. Mar. 12, 1874, m. Wm. F. Wright.
  III. Rose Boyd, b. Jan. 8, 1876.
  IV. Ernest Boyd, b. Nov. 18, 1877, m. Cora Gibson.
   V. Abe Boyd, b. Oct. 19, 1883, m. Hilda Naslund
  VI. Amie Halstead Boyd, b. Feb. 12, 1888, m. George
      Souther.
 VII. Harry Leonard Boyd, b. Jan. 3, 1894, m. Mae Thomson.

Alfred Boyd, born Jan. 7, 1872, at Evansville, Ind., married
Aug. 31, 1910, Alice Dimmick, born Dec. 26, 1879, at Cincin-
nati, Ohio, daughter of Sarah Louise (Morris) and Benjamin
Franklin Dimmick.

    Mr. Boyd is a civil engineer and a professor of civil engin-
eering. He retired in 1944 as professor of civil engineering at
the University of North Dakota where he had taught for twenty
four years. He now resides in Middlebrook, Mo.

    Children:
    I. Alice Louise Boyd, b. June 4, 1911.
   II. Alfred Gordon Boyd, b. Nov. 8, 1914, m. Etheldreda
       McArthur.

NORWOOD

William Norwood of Surry Co., was a member of the Norwood family of Leckhampton, Gloucestershire, England (cf. Wm. and Mary Quarterly, 2nd Series, 16, p. 289 ff). His English ancestry is given in full in the above article in the William and Mary Quarterly, in the 1623 Heralds Visitations of Gloucestershire, and in C. W. Throckmorton's "History of the Throckmorton Family". William Norwood was a cousin of Col. Henry Norwood, Treasurer of Virginia, and of Capt. Charles Norwood, Clerk of the the Virginia House of Burgesses in the 17th Century. Through his grandmother, Elizabeth Ligon, he was descended in two lines from Edward I, King of England, and through his great-grandmother, Katherine Throckmorton, he was descended from John of Gaunt, Duke of Lancaster, son of Edward III and Philippa of Hainault. Only the paternal line will be given her.

John Northwood of Leckhampton in Gloucestershire married Eleanor, daughter and co-heir of John Gifford of Leckhampton. Their son, Roger Northwood, married Alice, daughter of Sir. John Butler, Kt., of Badminton, Co. Gloucester. Their son was Ralph Norwood of Leckhampton, who married the daughter of a knight of Shrewsbury, and had three sons, John, Henry and Nicholas Norwood. Henry Norwood, son of Ralph, of Leckhampton, married Katherine Throckmorton, daughter of Sir Robert Throckmorton. (See chart.) She married (1) John Williams, by whom she had issue: Robert, Ludovic, William, Richard, Lucy, Eleanor, and Anne Williams. Henry and Katherine (Throckmorton) Norwood had six children, William, Robert, Edward, Henry, Jane and Margaret Norwood. William Norwood of Leckhampton, son of Henry and Katherine (Throckmorton) Norwood, died Sept. 23, 1623; he married Oct. 18, 1569, Elizabeth Lygon, daughter of William Lygon of Madresfield. They had issue: (1) Richard Norwood; (2) William Norwood, d. s. p.; (3) Henry Norwood, father of Capt. Charles Norwood and Col. Henry Norwood, prominent in early Virginia history; (4) Ralph Norwood, soldier in the Low Countries; (5) Thomas Norwood; (6) Maurice Norwood, d. s. p.; (7) Eleanor Norwood m. George Blount of Sellington, Worcestershire; (8) Elizabeth Norwood m. Richard Moore. Richard Norwood, son of William and Elizabeth (Lygon) Norwood,

was born about 1575 and died after 1623; he married Elizabeth,
daughter of Nicholas Stuard, LL. D. , and had the following children: (1) Augustine Norwood; (2) Francis Norwood, whose sons,
Capt. William Norwood and Francis Norwood, were mentioned
in the will of Col. Henry Norwood in 1689; (3) John Norwood;
(4) William Norwood, who emigrated to Surry Co. , Va. ; (5)
Richard Norwood; (6) Edward Norwood; (7) Thomas Norwood,
(8) Eleanor Norwood; (9) Dorothy Norwood. (See Key Chart.)

William Norwood, son of Richard and Elizabeth (Stuard) Norwood, was born in England prior to 1623, as he appears in the
Heralds Visitations of that year. He was exempted from taxes
July 4, 1682, in Surry Co. , Va. (Order Bk. No. 1, p. 378),
showing that he was at least 60 years of age at the time. His
first appearance in the Virginia Records in Oct. 6, 1649, when
Thomas Gyor deeded him land in Isle of Wight Co. , Va. (Isle
of Wight D. & W. No. 1, 1662-1715, p. 396). He was involved
in a lawsuit with Carberry Kegan of Isle of Wight in 1653 and
1654, which is mentioned several times in the Virginia records;
but finally sold the land in dispute to Mr. Kegan Dec. 9, 1656.
On Jan. 23, 1653/54 William Norwood was deeded land in Surry
Co. by John Blackborne (Book 1, p. 66) and he continued to live
in Surry the rest of his life. His wife was named Lydia, but
there is uncertainty about her maiden name. She may have been
connected with the family of Col. George Jordan, as the latter's
nephew, George Jordan, on Mar. 7, 1703, made deeds of gift of
land to William Norwood "my loving friend" (this land being later
inherited by William Norwood's son Richard), and to George Norwood, son of William (cf. D. & W. 1693-1709, pp. 299, 709).
The will of William Norwood, dated Jan. 6, 1702/3 and probated
in Surry Co. March 7, 1703, leaves his property to his sons Edward, George and Richard Norwood; to his daughters Sarah Norwood, Elizabeth Branch, Lydia Sowerby, and Mary Norwood;
to his granddaughter Elizabeth Branch; and to his wife Lydia.
Sarah and Mary Norwood, unmarried at the time of their father's
death, were married respectively to Richard Lewis and William
Glover prior to May 6, 1707, when the two couples sued George
and Lydia Norwood, executors of William Norwood, for their
shares of their father's property. Issue of William and Lydia
Norwood:

    I. Edward Norwood, b. 1662-3 (first appears as a tithable
        1679), m. prior to July 6, 1680, Naomi, daughter of
        Richard Smith of Charles City Co. (Surry Order Bk. 1
        pp. 306, 312), and moved to Chowan Co. , N. C. prior
        to Jan. 11, 1685, when the birth of Jane, daughter of
        Edward and Naomi Norwood, is recorded in the Parish
        Register (Hathaway, III, p. 215). Edward Norwood left
        male heirs, from whom the Norwood family of Perry,

Ga., is descended. General Courtney Hodges, U.S.A., is descended from this family, his mother having been Katherine Norwood.

II. Elizabeth Norwood, m._____Branch prior to 1703, and had a daughter Elizabeth Branch mentioned in William Norwood's will.

III. Lydia Norwood m. John SOWERBY of Surry Co., son of Francis and Katherine Sowerby (see Sowerby Family).

IV. William Norwood, Jr., b. 1672/3 (tithable first 1689), apparently predeceased his father.

V. George Norwood, b. 1676/7 (tithable first 1693), married and moved to Northampton Co., N.C., where he died in 1749. His will, dated April 21, 1749, and probated Aug. 1749 (Grimes "Abstracts", p. 271), mentions his sons Samuel and William; grandsons George and Nathaniel, sons of Nathaniel Norwood; grandson John, son of William Norwood; granddaughters Elizabeth, Mary and Sarah, daughters of Nathaniel Norwood; and makes his sons William, Nathaniel and Samuel his executors.

VI. Richard Norwood, b. 1679-80 in Surry Co. (tithable first 1696), m. Elizabeth_____; received a deed of gift of 80 acres in Surry Co. March 7, 1703, from George Jordan (Order Bk. 2, pp. 249 and 346), which he deeded away in 1729 (D. & W. 1715-30, p. 974); moved to Isle of Wight Co., Va., where he died in 1731 and his wife in 1733. Richard Norwood's inventory was recorded Oct. 25, 1731, in Isle of Wight Co. (W.B. 3, p. 285). The inventory of his wife Elizabeth Norwood was recorded Aug. 7, 1733 (id., p. 386). The will of their son, William Norwood, dated Feb. 8, 1735, and probated in Isle of Wight Co. April 26, 1736, leaves all his land to William Harrison, son of Henry Harrison, and to John Clark, son of Thomas Clark; mentions his sisters Rebecca, Elizabeth Vaughan, Mary and Hannah; and appoints his brothers Henry Harrison and Thomas Clark executors. An account of Richard Norwood's estate, signed by William Norwood, dated Feb. 10, 1734/5 and recorded Mar. 24, 1734/5, mentions payments to Col. Harry Harrison, Mrs. Mary Harrison, Mr. George Norwood and Mr. William Norwood (Wills and Accts., 1733-45, pp. 48-9). The inventory of William Norwood, deceased, was dated June 2, 1736 and signed by Thomas Clark and Henry Harrison, executors (id., p. 120). On the following page (121) there is an account of Elizabeth Norwood's estate which mentions "her dower in my father's estate"; is signed by "Thomas Clark, Executor of

William Norwood, who was Administrator of Elizabeth Norwood"; and recorded June 29, 1736. The inventory of James Norwood, deceased, was recorded in Isle of Wight Co, Oct. 25, 1736 (id., p. 145). From the above records, it appears that Richard and Elizabeth had the following children.

1. William Norwood, d. s. p. 1736.
2. Mary Norwood m. Henry Harrison.
3. Sarah Norwood m. Thomas CLARK, fourth. We know from Thomas Clark's will that her name was Sarah.
4. Elizabeth Norwood m. _____ Vaughan.
5. Rebecca Norwood.
6. Hannah Norwood.
7. James Norwood (probably) d. s. p. 1736.
8. George Norwood (possibly)

VII. Sarah Norwood m. Richard Lewis 1703-1707.
VIII. Mary Norwood m. William Glover 1703-1707.

SOWERBY - SORSBY
of
Surry

Sowerby is a manor in the Hundred of Amournderness in Lancaster, England. The Sowerbys were holding part of this manor 1284 but seem to have been later dispossessed by the Butlers. (Vic. Hist. Lanc. Vol. 7, p. 68). The arms of the Sowerbys were "Barry of six, sa, and gu on a chevron between 3 lions rampant, as, or" (Burke). There was once a family of Sowerbys long seated at Dalston Hall in Cumberland.

Francis Sowerby was one of three brothers who were resident in Surry Co. during the middle 17th century. The eldest of the three was James Sowerby, who first appears in the Surry records Sept. 5, 1652 (Book 1, p. 16). He was born in 1611 (Book 2, p. 127) and died in 1678 or 1679, leaving a wife Ann and daughter Margaret (Book 2, pp. 263, 15, in back of book). The other two brothers were much younger than James. Of these, Thomas Sowerby was born 1632-1634 (Book 1, p. 105, Book 2, p. 154, Book 4, p. 18). His will, dated Dec. 6, 1694, and probated Sept. 10, 1695, leaves his property to his wife Ann and to "Thomas Shrowbery my brother's son" (W. & D. 1693-1709, p. 85). His widow Ann married (2) by Jan. 7, 1695/6 James JORDAN (id., p. 110), and her will dated Sept. 22, 1697, and probated Nov. 2, 1697, leaves most of her property to "my husband Thomas Shorsby's Brother's children" (id. p. 146).

1. Francis Sowerby was probably the youngest of the three
brothers and the only one who left male heirs. He first appears
in the records Dec. 28, 1659 (Book 1, p. 145), and died in 1678
or 1679. His will, dated Nov. 8, 1678, and probated Mar. 4,
1678/9, mentions his wife Katherine, son Francis, "all my sons",
daughters Sarah and Elizabeth, brothers Thomas and James
Sowerby, and daughter Jane Rix (Book 2, p. 197). The widow,
Katherine Sowerby, was married (2) by May 6, 1679, on which
date her second husband, John Vinson, made deeds of gift to
her children, Sarah, Francis, John, Thomas, Elizabeth and
William Sowerby (id., p. 205). John Vinson's will, dated Oct.
20, 1698, and probated July 4, 1699, leaves all his property to
his wife Katherine (D. & W. 1693-1709, p. 171). Katherine
Sowerby Vinson died in Surry in 1705, her will being dated Mar.
26, 1704/5 and probated Nov. 6, 1705 (id., p. 339). It makes
bequests to Thomas Rose son of Richard Rose, to her daughter
Elizabeth Rose, her granddaughter Ann Rose, to Thomas Sower-
by, to her godson Charles Reeks, to Elizabeth Jarrard and
Elias Osborne, and the remainder of her estate to her sons
Francis and John Sowerby. Issue of Francis and Katherine
Sowerby:
   I. Jane Sowerby m._____Ricks, prior to 1678, and had
      a son Charles Ricks mentioned in his grandmother's will.
  II. Sarah Sowerby, apparently died young.
 III. Francis Sowerby m. (1) Sarah_____(cf. D. & W.
      1693-1709, p. 98), and m. (2) Mary JORDAN, daughter
      of Thomas Jordan and his wife Jane Brown, daughter
      of Capt. William Brown. Francis Sowerby died in
      1717, his will mentioning sons Francis and William.
      (His second wife married John Tyus.)
3. IV. John Sowerby (see later).
   V. Thomas Sowerby m. Sarah____(id., p. 334).
  VI. Elizabeth Sowerby m. Richard Rose, and had children
      Thomas and Ann Rose, mentioned in their grandmother's
      will.
 VII. William Sowerby, apparently d. young.

3. John Sowerby, son of Francis and Katherine, was probably
born about 1670. He is shown as an independent tithable in 1693,
and married, probably about 1690-95, Lydia NORWOOD, daughter of William and Lydia Norwood of Surry Co. (See Norwood
Family). His will, dated Jan. 2, 1726, and probated in Surry
July 19, 1727, mentions his wife Lydia, sons Benjamin (see
later), and Henry, daughters Sarah Owen, Jane Deberry, Elizabeth and Mary, and granddaughter Ann Sowerby. Of these children, Henry Sowerby married Sarah------ and moved to Northampton Co., N. C. , where his will, dated June 22, 1747, and

probated August, 1747, mentions his sons John and Henry, wife
Sarah, and apparently other children, and makes Capt. John Deberry (who was his brother-in-law) and Arthur Sherrard trustees. Henry Sowerby's son John made his will in Northampton
Co., N. C. Dec. 22, 1778, and it was probated July, 1778. It
mentions his son Henry, wife Mary, and his daughters, all under
age.

Jane Sowerby, daughter of John and Lydia (Norwood) Sowerby,
married Capt. John Deberry, son of Peter Deberry of Surry and
Isle of Wight Cos. and his first wife, Mary Brantley. Peter Deberry first appears in the Surry records March 6, 1664/5 (Book
1, p. 251). He was in the militia of Surry in 1687 (Wm. and Mary
Quarterly, 1st Series, XI, 83). He married (1) Mary, daughter
of Edward Brantley of Isle of Wight Co. Edward Brantley's will,
dated March 30, 1688, and probated Jan. 9, 1688/9, in Isle of
Wight, mentions his son Edward and the latter's son, James; son
Philip and the latter's son, Edward; son John and the latter's son
John; and daughter Mary, whom he appoints executrix (Chapman,
Wills, I, p. 43). Peter Deberry married (2) Elizabeth_____,
and died in Isle of Wight Co. in 1713. His will, dated Dec. 30,
1712, and probated in Isle of Wight March 28, 1712/13, mentions
his daughter Priscilla, wife of Zacharias Madera, daughter Sarah,
wife of John Warren, son John, wife Elizabeth and brother John
Brantley (Chapman I, p. 76). John Deberry, only son of Peter
and Mary Brantley Deberry, on May 4 and 5, 1716, deeded away
the land in Isle of Wight Co., inherited from his mother Mary
Brantley and his grandfather Edward Brantley (Great Bk. 4, p.
74; D. B. 9, p. 270). He married Jane Sowerby some time prior
to the date of her father's will in 1726/7. On April 20, 1745, he
was granted 200 acres of land in Northampton Co., N. C., and
was appointed a Justice of Northampton Co. Oct. 11, 1749 (N. C.
Col. and State Records, IV, 966). He was also a Captain in the
militia of the county, as shown by his will, which was dated Dec.
2, 1762 (Will Bk. A, p. 18). The will leaves over 1000 acres
of land and 9 negro slaves to his nine children, who were the
following:

    I. Benjamin Deberry, married and predeceased by his
        father, leaving a son Henry, a widow, and other child-
        ren referred to in Capt. Deberry's will.

   II. Peter Deberry died in Northampton Co., N. C. in 1796,
        his will mentioning children Absalom, Peter and Sarah.

  III. Solomon Deberry

  IV. Henry Deberry

   V. John Deberry

  VI. Drewry Deberry died in Northampton Co., N. C. in
        1794, leaving his property to his daughter Charlotte
        Hollomon.

VII. Mary Deberry m. Robert Cobb.
VIII. Sarah Deberry m. (Abraham ?) Stevenson.
IX. Priscilla Deberry m. _____Pope.

Benjamin Sowerby, son of Lydia (Norwood) and John Sowerby, married Elizabeth_____, and had following children shown in the Albermarle Register:

I. Selah, b. February 8, 1745
II. Allen, b. November 10, 1751
III. Benjamin, b. October 28, 1754
IV. Henry, b. December 18, 1762
V. Hartwell, b. February 2, 1761

340

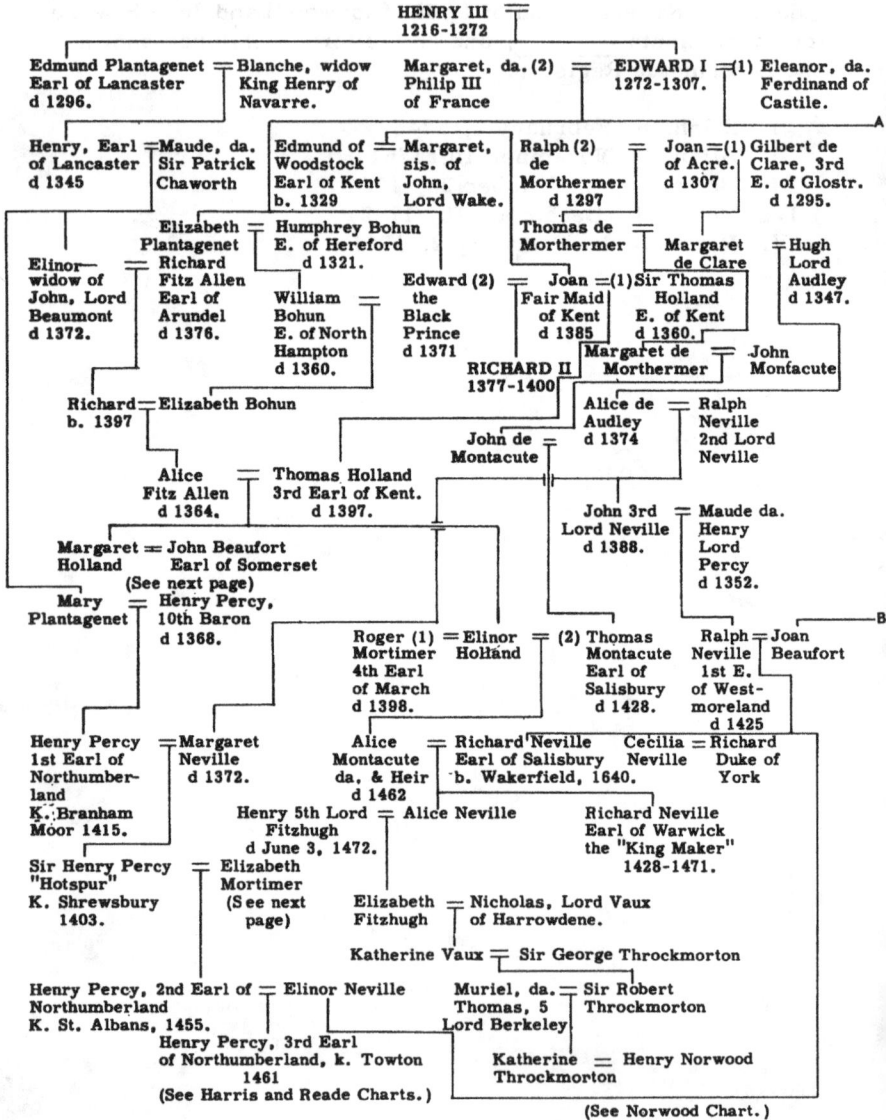

HENRY III
1216-1272

Edmund Plantagenet = Blanche, widow
Earl of Lancaster | King Henry of
d 1296. | Navarre.

Margaret, da. (2) = EDWARD I = (1) Eleanor, da.
Philip III | 1272-1307. | Ferdinand of
of France | | Castile.
A

Henry, Earl = Maude, da.
of Lancaster | Sir Patrick
d 1345 | Chaworth

Edmund of = Margaret,
Woodstock | sis. of
Earl of Kent | John,
b. 1329 | Lord Wake.

Ralph (2) = Joan = (1) Gilbert de
de | of Acre. | Clare, 3rd
Morthermer | d 1307 | E. of Glostr.
d 1297 | | d 1295.

Thomas de
Morthermer

Margaret = Hugh
de Clare | Lord
| Audley
| d 1347.

Elinor = Elizabeth = Humphrey Bohun
widow of | Plantagenet | E. of Hereford
John, Lord | Richard | d 1321.
Beaumont | Fitz Allen
d 1372. | Earl of
| Arundel
| d 1376.

William =
Bohun
E. of North
Hampton
d 1360.

Edward (2) = Joan = (1) Sir Thomas
the | Fair Maid | Holland
Black | of Kent | E. of Kent
Prince | d 1385 | d 1360.
d 1371

Margaret de = John
Morthermer | Monfacute

RICHARD II
1377-1400

Richard = Elizabeth Bohun
b. 1397

Alice de = Ralph
Audley | Neville
d 1374 | 2nd Lord
| Neville

John de =
Montacute

Alice = Thomas Holland
Fitz Allen | 3rd Earl of Kent.
d 1364. | d 1397.

John 3rd = Maude da.
Lord Neville | Henry
d 1388. | Lord
| Percy
| d 1352.

Margaret = John Beaufort
Holland | Earl of Somerset
| (See next page)

Mary = Henry Percy,
Plantagenet | 10th Baron
| d 1368.

Roger (1) = Elinor = (2) Thomas
Mortimer | Holland | Montacute
4th Earl | | Earl of
of March | | Salisbury
d 1398. | | d 1428.

Ralph = Joan
Neville | Beaufort
1st E. |
of West- |
moreland |
d 1425 |
B

Henry Percy = Margaret
1st Earl of | Neville
Northumber- | d 1372.
land |
K. Branham |
Moor 1415. |

Alice = Richard Neville
Montacute | Earl of Salisbury
da. & Heir | b. Wakerfield, 1640.
d 1462

Cecilia = Richard
Neville | Duke of
| York

Sir Henry Percy = Elizabeth
"Hotspur" | Mortimer
K. Shrewsbury | (See next
1403. | page)

Henry 5th Lord = Alice Neville
Fitzhugh
d June 3, 1472.

Richard Neville
Earl of Warwick
the "King Maker"
1428-1471.

Elizabeth = Nicholas, Lord Vaux
Fitzhugh | of Harrowdene.

Katherine Vaux = Sir George Throckmorton

Henry Percy, 2nd Earl of = Elinor Neville
Northumberland
K. St. Albans, 1455.

Muriel, da. = Sir Robert
Thomas, 5 | Throckmorton
Lord Berkeley |

Henry Percy, 3rd Earl
of Northumberland, k. Towton
1461
(See Harris and Reade Charts.)

Katherine = Henry Norwood
Throckmorton

(See Norwood Chart.)

Thomas Plantagenet = Alice,
Earl of Norfolk,   da. of
Earl Marshal of   Sir Roger
England, d 1338.   Halys

EDWARD II = Isabella of France
1307-1327

EDWARD III = Phillippa of Hainhault
1327-1377   d 1360.

Katherine = (2) John of Gaunt (I) = Blanche   Lionel, Duke of   Edmund
Swinford   Duke of Lancaster   da. Henry Clarence, d 1638. Duke of York
              d 1399.   Duke of   d 1402
                                   Lancaster

HENRY IV = Mary, da.   Phillipa = Edmund Mortimer
1399-1413 Humphrey Bohun   Plantagenet 3rd Earl of March
           Earl of Hereford.   d 1381.

HENRY V = Catherine
1413-1422 of France.   Elizabeth = Sir Henry   Roger = Elinor
                             Mortimer   Percy   Mortimer Holland
HENRY VI = Margaret   "Hotspur"   4th Earl
1422-1461 of Anjou.   k. Shrews   of March,
                                         bury, 1403 d 1398.
Prince Edward = (I) Anne Neville
b. Barnet   da. "Kingmaker"   Anne = Richard
                                          Mortimer Plantagenet
                                                    Earl of
         Richard = Cecilia   Cambridge
         Duke of York Neville   b 1415.

EDWARD IV   RICHARD III = (2) Anne   George = Isabel
1461-1483.   1483-1485.   Neville, da. Duke   Neville
                                  "Kingmaker"   of
            EDWARD V   Clarence
            m. 1483 in the Tower.

John Beaufort   = Margaret
Earl of Somerset   Holland,
d 1410.   da. Thomas, 3rd Earl of Kent.

Jane   = JAMES I of   Edmund   = Elinor, da.   Margaret = John, 1st Duke
Beaufort   Scotland.   2nd Duke   Richard   Beauchamp   Somerset
                         Somerset k, Beauchamp.   d 1444.
                         St. Albans, 1455

Alianore (2) = Sir Robert   Edmund Tudor, Earl = Margaret
               Spencer.   Thomas Howard of Richmond, d 1456 Beaufort.
                           2nd Duke of Norfolk HENRY VII = Elizabeth   Edward
Margaret = Thomas   d 1524.   1485-1509   Princess   Earl of
Spenser   Carey.   of York   Warwick
                                               Lord   b 1499.
William = Mary   Edmond =   Last of
Carey,   Boleyn, Thomas Boleyn = Elizabeth   Howard   Plantagenets.
d 1529   d 1543   Earl of Wilts. Howard.   d 1538
Katherine = Sir Francis Knollys
Carey.
                                        Anne = HENRY VIII = Catherine
     Anne Knollys = Thomas West.   Boleyn. 1509-1547   Howard
                    11th Lord   b. 1536   b 1541/2
                    Delaware,   ELIZABETH I
                    d 1556.   1558-1603.

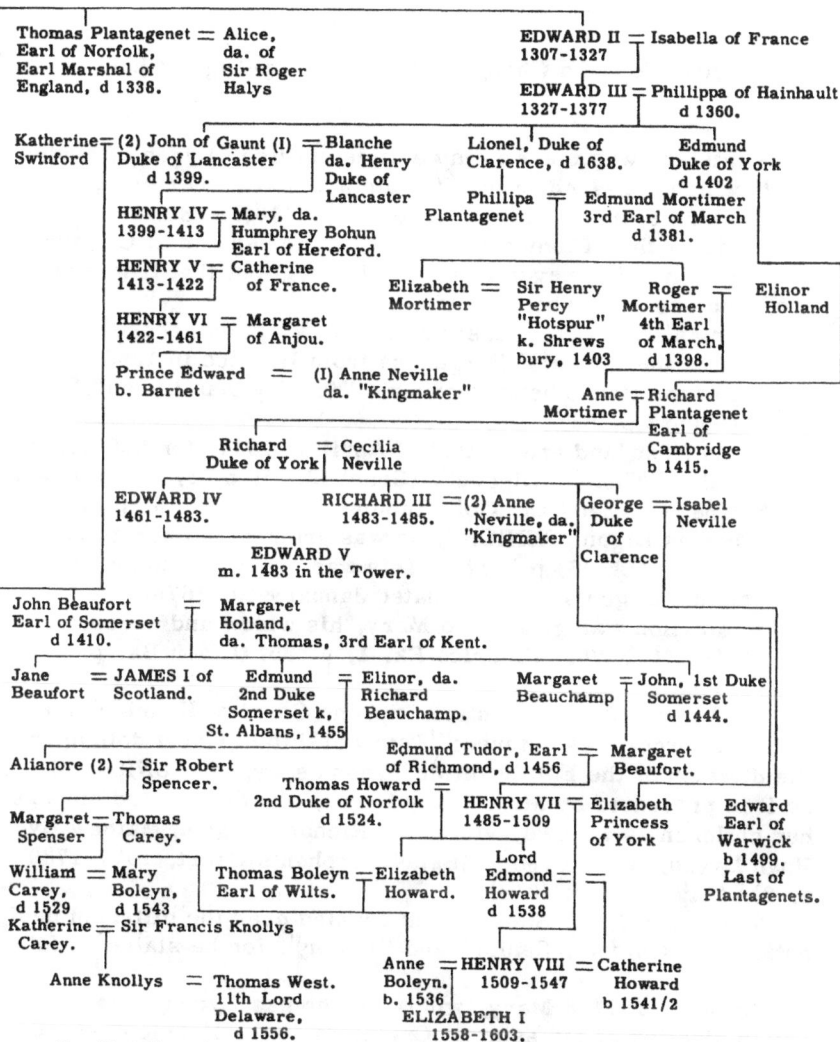

(See West Chart.)
(Under Claiborne)
Abbreviations: b. = beheaded; d. = died; k. = killed; m. = murdered.

Explanation of a Change in the Berkeley-Ligon Chart.

A mistake was made in my article entitled "Lygon of Madres-field" which appeared in the William and Mary Quarterly, April, 1936, which I now desire to correct. (W. 16(2)-289)

It seems that Thomas Lygon, Sr., who resided at Callouden, Warwick, in 1630, never came to Virginia, but that it was his son, Thomas Jr., who did. (do. 308)

Thomas Lygon Jr., first appears in Virginia records as a member of the House of Burgesses from Henrico in 1655. In the journal of the House he is shown as "Mr. Thomas Lygon". (Vol. 1659-93 p. 55)

In his first land grant, that of April 5, 1664, for 800 acres, he is called "Thomas Liggon". (Grant Bk. 5, p. 6). In a patent of 1668 he is called "Lt. Col. Thomas Ligon" (Bk. 6, p. 188). As "Thomas Ligon, SENIOR", he was granted 340 acres March 28, 1672-3. (Bk. 6, p. 447). This was his last land grant.

Thomas Lygon's will was dated January 10, 1675-76 and administration was granted to Mary, his widow and executrix March 16, 1675-76. (Henrico Bk. 1, p. 35) (Ligon Bk. p. 313) (will lost).

On August 20, 1678, in the Orphans Court of Henrico, the following order was entered: "This worshipful Court doth approve the division of the Estate of Mr. Thomas Lygon, JUNIOR, decd., as it is presented by Mrs. Mary Lygon, and distributed amongst her children as follows, viz.: . . Richard Lygon, Mathew Lygon, Hugh Lygon, Mary Lygon."(Bk. 4, Orphan's Court, 1677-1739 p. 3). (Ligon Bk. p. 313)

The beloved Dr. Stanard was puzzled over the different desig-nations of "Colonel, Senior" and "Junior", for he stated as fol-lows:

"In Feb. 1677-8 Mary, widow of Thomas Lygon, was granted administration of his estate. One entry in the Henrico records is rather difficult to understand, or rather identify the person named. On Aug. 28, 1689, Mrs. Mary Lygon, widow of Mr. Thomas Lygon, JR., deceased, returned an inventory of the cattle belonging to Richard, Mathew, Hugh and Mary, orphan's of said Thomas Lygon, Jr. At that time, 'orphans' meant minor orphan's. Unless 'Col. Thomas Lygon' was 'Mr. Thomas

Lygon, Jr.' the children named cannot be placed in other records of the time." (35V48)

So it was wrongfully concluded that Thomas Lygon, "Senior", had come over to Virginia and that he had a son, "Thomas Lygon, Jr." (W 16(2)-312) Therefore, Mary Harris was placed as his second wife. Now it appears that "Colonel" Thomas Lygon, Thomas Lygon, "SENIOR" and Thomas Lygon "JUNIOR" were one and the same person. It also appears that Thomas Lygon, Jr., son of Thomas, Sr., of Callouden, was the person who came to Virginia. Thomas Lygon, Jr., was a comparatively young man as he had four minor children at the time of his death in 1677. According to the Ligon Book the four above orphans were born in the following years: Mathew, 1659, Mary, 1663, (p. 318), Hugh, 1661, (p. 352), Richard, 1657 (p. 328). Richard made a deposition in 1693 that he was aged "thirty-six or thirty-seven years old". (p. 328).

These children were born between 1653 and 1663. Therefore it seems very improbable that Colonel Thomas Lygon, Jr., was born in 1586 as stated in the Ligon book (pp. 105 and 307). He would be 77 years of age on the date of his last child.

It would seem that one more generation should be added to the Berkeley-Lygon chart. "Thomas Lygon Jr.," as evidenced by the above quoted Henrico records.

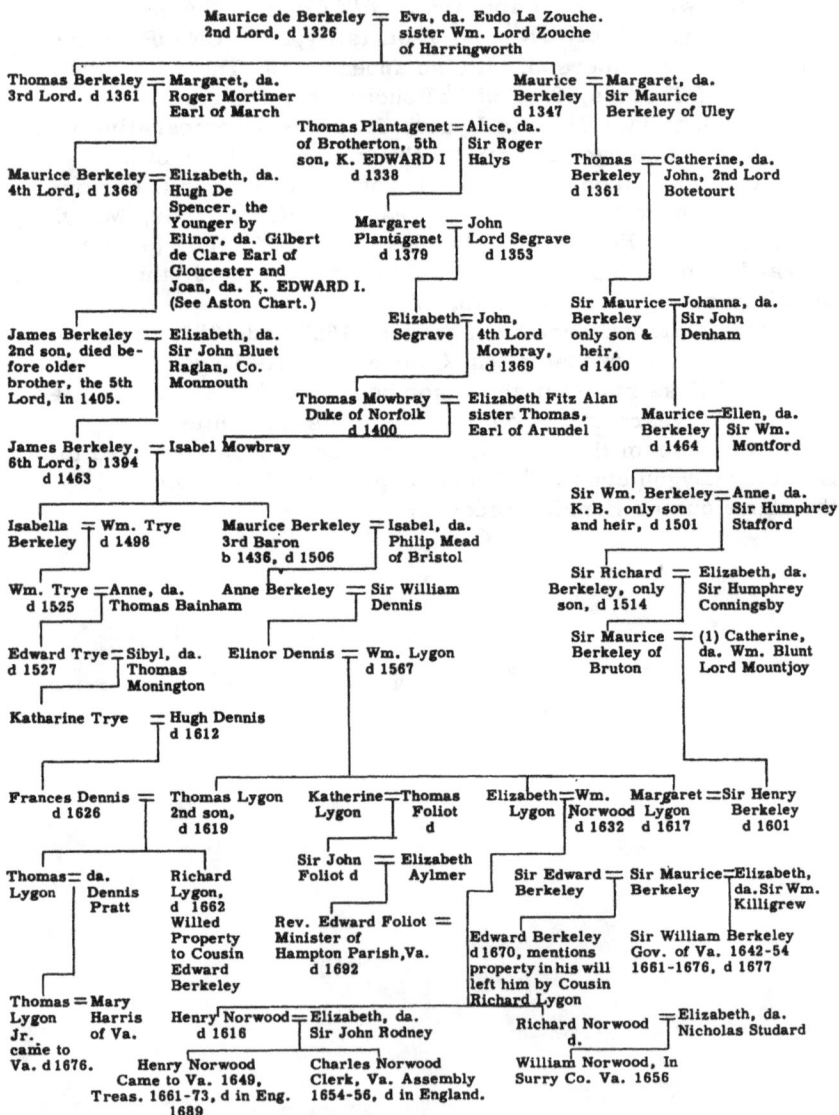

BERKELEY

```
Maurice de Berkeley = Eva, da. Eudo La Zouche.
2nd Lord, d 1326      sister Wm. Lord Zouche
                      of Harringworth
```

```
Thomas Berkeley = Margaret, da.                    Maurice = Margaret, da.
3rd Lord. d 1361  Roger Mortimer                    Berkeley  Sir Maurice
                  Earl of March                     d 1347    Berkeley of Uley
                            Thomas Plantagenet = Alice, da.
                            of Brotherton, 5th    Sir Roger      Thomas = Catherine, da.
Maurice Berkeley = Elizabeth, da.  son, K. EDWARD I Halys        Berkeley  John, 2nd Lord
4th Lord, d 1368   Hugh De        d 1338                         d 1361    Botetourt
                   Spencer, the
                   Younger by     Margaret = John
                   Elinor, da. Gilbert Plantagenet  Lord Segrave
                   de Clare Earl of  d 1379      d 1353
                   Gloucester and
                   Joan, da. K. EDWARD I.        Elizabeth = John,      Sir Maurice = Johanna, da.
                   (See Aston Chart.)            Segrave     4th Lord   Berkeley      Sir John
                                                             Mowbray,   only son &    Denham
James Berkeley = Elizabeth, da.                              d 1369     heir,
2nd son, died be-  Sir John Bluet                                       d 1400
fore older         Raglan, Co.
brother, the 5th   Monmouth       Thomas Mowbray = Elizabeth Fitz Alan   Maurice = Ellen, da.
Lord, in 1405.                    Duke of Norfolk  sister Thomas,        Berkeley  Sir Wm.
                                  d 1400           Earl of Arundel       d 1464    Montford
James Berkeley, = Isabel Mowbray
6th Lord, b 1394                                                         Sir Wm. Berkeley = Anne, da.
d 1463                                                                   K.B. only son     Sir Humphrey
                                                                         and heir, d 1501  Stafford
Isabella = Wm. Trye   Maurice Berkeley = Isabel, da.
Berkeley   d 1498     3rd Baron          Philip Mead                     Sir Richard = Elizabeth, da.
                      b 1436, d 1506     of Bristol                      Berkeley, only Sir Humphrey
Wm. Trye = Anne, da.  Anne Berkeley = Sir William                        son, d 1514    Conningsby
d 1525     Thomas Bainham            Dennis
                                                                         Sir Maurice = (1) Catherine,
Edward Trye = Sibyl, da.   Elinor Dennis = Wm. Lygon                     Berkeley of    da. Wm. Blunt
d 1527        Thomas                       d 1567                        Bruton         Lord Mountjoy
              Monington
Katharine Trye = Hugh Dennis
                 d 1612
```

```
Frances Dennis = Thomas Lygon   Katherine = Thomas    Elizabeth = Wm.      Margaret = Sir Henry
d 1626           2nd son,        Lygon       Foliot   Lygon       Norwood Lygon   Berkeley
                 d 1619                      d                    d 1632  d 1617   d 1601
                                  Sir John = Elizabeth
Thomas = da.     Richard         Foliot d   Aylmer    Sir Edward = Sir Maurice = Elizabeth,
Lygon    Dennis  Lygon,                                Berkeley    Berkeley    da. Sir Wm.
         Pratt   d 1662          Rev. Edward Foliot =               Killigrew
         Willed  Property        Minister of           Edward Berkeley  Sir William Berkeley
         to Cousin               Hampton Parish, Va.  d 1670, mentions Gov. of Va. 1642-54
         Edward                  d 1692               property in his will 1661-1676, d 1677
         Berkeley                                     left him by Cousin
Thomas = Mary                                         Richard Lygon
Lygon    Harris   Henry Norwood = Elizabeth, da.
Jr.      of Va.   d 1616          Sir John Rodney      Richard Norwood = Elizabeth, da.
came to                                                d                 Nicholas Studard
Va. d 1676.      Henry Norwood      Charles Norwood
                 Came to Va. 1649,  Clerk, Va. Assembly William Norwood, In
                 Treas. 1661-73, d in Eng. 1654-56, d in England. Surry Co. Va. 1656
                 1689
```

SLEDGE

The first one of this family in Surry was Charles Sledge whose will was dated November 3, 1725, and probated February 16, 1726-27. He gave his son-in-law, John Ellison, 75 acres on Pidgeon Swamp where he dwells, for life, and at his decease to granddaughter, Judy Ellison, to son, John Sledge, 100 acres in Surry bounded by Samuel Chappell's land on one side and Colonel William Randolph's on the other side; to daughter, Rebecca Ivey, one cow; to daughter, Martha Sledge, one cow. (B7, page 623).

Mary Sledge, his wife, was a daughter of Robert Clarke. (See Clarke.) She made her will January 8, 1726-27, same probated July 17, 1728. Legatees were son, John Sledge; daughter, Rebecca Ivey; granddaughter, Judith Ellison, when 21; daughter, Martha Hay, rest of estate and son-in-law, Peter Hay, executor. Teste: Edward Prince, Elizabeth Prince, Thomas Hay, (B 7, p. 826.)

Children:
   I. John, (see later); II. Judith, m. Ellison; III. Rebecca, m. Ivey; IV. Martha, m. Peter Hay.

John Sledge, son of Charles and Mary Sledge, made his will in Surry, December 17, 1749, same probated December 18, 1750. He gave son, Charles, 150 acres where he now lives; son, Daniel, part of a tract of 200 acres in Brunswick; son, Amos, part of same land in Brunswick; daughter, Ann Griffin, 15; daughter, Sarah Sledge, pewter dishes and cattle; daughter, Rebecca, 200 acres where "I now live" and at her death to my son, John. Teste: Hugh and Thomas Ivey. (B 9, p. 674).

Children:
   I. Charles, m. Elizabeth_____and had the following children shown in Albermarle Register:
      1. John, b. January 1, 1747
      2. Thomas, b. May 18, 1751
      3. Susanna, b. December 14, 1753
      4. Augustine, b. May 15, 1756 (see later)

     5. Charles, b. September 25, 1758
     6. Noah, b. May 22, 1767
     7. Salley, b. August 10, 1770.
II. Daniel. No record.
III. John, m. Amy_____ and had the following children shown in register:
     1. Nathaniel, b. February 22, 1761
     2. Hartwell, b. January 8, 1765
     3. Minns, b. January 7, 1768.
     4. Lucy, b. February 26, 1770
     5. Rebecca, b. April 18, 1775.
IV. Amos, m. Sarah_____ and had following children shown in register:
     1. Martha, b. April 7, 1761.
     2. Robert, b. January 27, 1759.
V. Ann, m. Travis Griffin or Griffith, son of Thomas Griffis whose will was probated in Surry, September 21, 1726. (B 7, p. 649).
Children from Register:
     1. Rebecca Griffin, b. April 29, 1751
     2. Allen Griffin, b. November 15, 1758
     3. Joshua Griffin, b. March 9, 1762
     4. Thomas Griffin, b. April 28, 1770.
VI. Rebecca
VII. Sarah

2. Augustine Sledge, son of Charles and Elizabeth Sledge, was baptized May 15, 1756. He died May 2, 1833, in Sussex. His will was probated in 1833. (Bk. M, p. 1) Children mentioned in will were Augustine, Jr., Henry (see later #3), William P., Thomas B., Martha A., Celea D., Miles C., Susan Bailey Sledge, Elizabeth P. Sledge and Lucy Sledge.

3. Henry Sledge, son of Augustine, married Sarah, daughter of George Ivey, Sr., December 22, 1806, in Southhampton County, Virginia. He died in Halifax County, North Carolina, December 22, 1848.

    Children:
    I. Ann, m. Rev. J. W. Hepinstall
    II. George, m. Sarah Peoples
    III. Rebecca, m. Asa Hepinstall
    IV. William H., m. Judith Peoples
    V. Joseph, no record.
    VI. Sallie, m. Richard Parker
    VII. Mary, m. Samuel Miles
    VIII. James, m. Miss Webb

IX. Thomas W., m. Mary Elizabeth Parker
X. Benjamin Franklin, b. 1836, m. Martha Chappell
Johnston (see later).

4. Benjamin Franklin Sledge, son of Henry Sledge, born
1836, died June 23, 1899, at Weldon in Halifax County, North
Carolina. He married October 26, 1852, at "Quankey", (Johnston ancestral home), Halifax County, Martha Chappell Johnston,
born January 1, 1832, daughter of Margaret (Binford) and
Colonel William Willis Johnston. Colonel Johnston was a colonel
of militia in the war of 1812.

Children:
I. Eliza Cook, b. November 27, 1853, m. R. J. Lewis.
II. (5) John Wesley, b. October 29, 1855, m. Mary Whit-
field Wilkins. (see later)
III. Margaret Sarah, b. April 2, 1860, m. Rev. A. J.
Groves.
IV. Albert Sidney Johnston, b. April 14, 1862, died in
infancy.
V. William Johnston, b. April 27, 1864, died in infancy.
VI. Benjamin Franklin, b. May 4, 1866, died (single) Jan-
uary 26, 1897.
VII. Grance Binford, b. March 25, 1869, m. B. F. Johnson.

5. John Wesley Sledge, son of Benjamin Franklin Sledge,
was born October 29, 1855, and died May 30, 1927, at Weldon,
North Carolina. He married June 20, 1888, at Weldon, Mary
Whitfield Wilkins, born October 4, 1869, daughter of Ida Tem-
perance (Powers) and John W. Wilkins, soldier Confederate
Army.

Mr. Sledge was educated at the Fetter School for Boys. He
owned and published Roanoke News, was a bank director, a member of the School Board of Weldon and a trustee of the Weldon
Methodist Church.

Children:
I. Mary Binford, b. August 5, 1889, m. Philip StJohn
Moore, Captain United States Merchant Marine World
Wars I and II.
1. Philip StJohn, Jr., b. November 4, 1920, m. Ellen
Louise Smithwick. Was educated in Weldon Public
Schools and University of North Carolina. First
Lt. United States Army Medical Corps World War
II; served in the European Theater with First Army-
was twice wounded and given the Purple Heart twice-
was awarded the Army Silver Star for heroism be-
yond the call of duty.

2. Mary Elizabeth, b. June 8, 1922; educated Weldon
Public Schools and North Carolina College for Women;
was employed by United States Navy in Honolulu.
3. John Campbell, b. April 21, 1924; educated Weldon
Public Schools and Riverside Military Academy;
seaman United States Naval Reserve World War II;
served in the Pacific Theater aboard a destroyer
two years.
4. Martha Binford, b. December 7, 1925; educated
Weldon Public Schools and North Carolina College
for Women.
5. Whitfield Sledge, b. September 13, 1927; educated
Weldon and Norfolk Public Schools.
6. Benjamin Franklin, b. Feb. 9, 1929.

II. John Burton, b. August 16, 1894, m. Josephine John -
son - Mill representative for Durham Hosiery Mills;
educated Weldon Public Schools, Trinity Park School,
and Trinity College, now Duke University; was sergeant
United States Army World War I, later assigned to
Officers Training School at Fort Meade, Md., when
war ended.

Children:
1. John Burton, Jr., b. November 13, 1929.
2. Josephine Ann, b. July 3, 1932.

III. William Whitfield, b. June 18, 1898, was educated
Weldon Public Schools, and Universities of Virginia and
North Carolina. He is a lawyer and is also interested
in many civic enterprises. He is President of Durham
Hosiery Mills, President of Security Building and Loan
Association, President of Homeland Investment Company,
Trust Officer of Durham Bank & Trust Company, and
General Counsel of Home Security Life Insurance Com-
pany. He resides at 111 Corcoran Street, Durham,
N. C.

IV. Ida Laura, b. March 1, 1901, m. Emry C. Green,
President of Pilot Life Insurance Company. She was
educated in Weldon Public Schools and Greensboro
College for Women.
1. Emry C. Green, Jr., b. May 20, 1925, was edu-
cated in Greensboro Public Schools, Episcopal High
School and Duke University. Seaman United States
Naval Reserve World War II.

V. Walter, b. June 26, 1905 m. Charlotte Frances Umstead;
was educated in Weldon Public Schools and Wake Forest
College; Treasurer Home Security Life Insurance Company; Lieutenant United States Naval Reserve World

War II.
1. Infant daughter, b. May 29, 1944, d. May 29, 1944.
VI. Margaret Johnston, b. April 21, 1911, was educated in Weldon Public Schools and North Carolina College for Women.

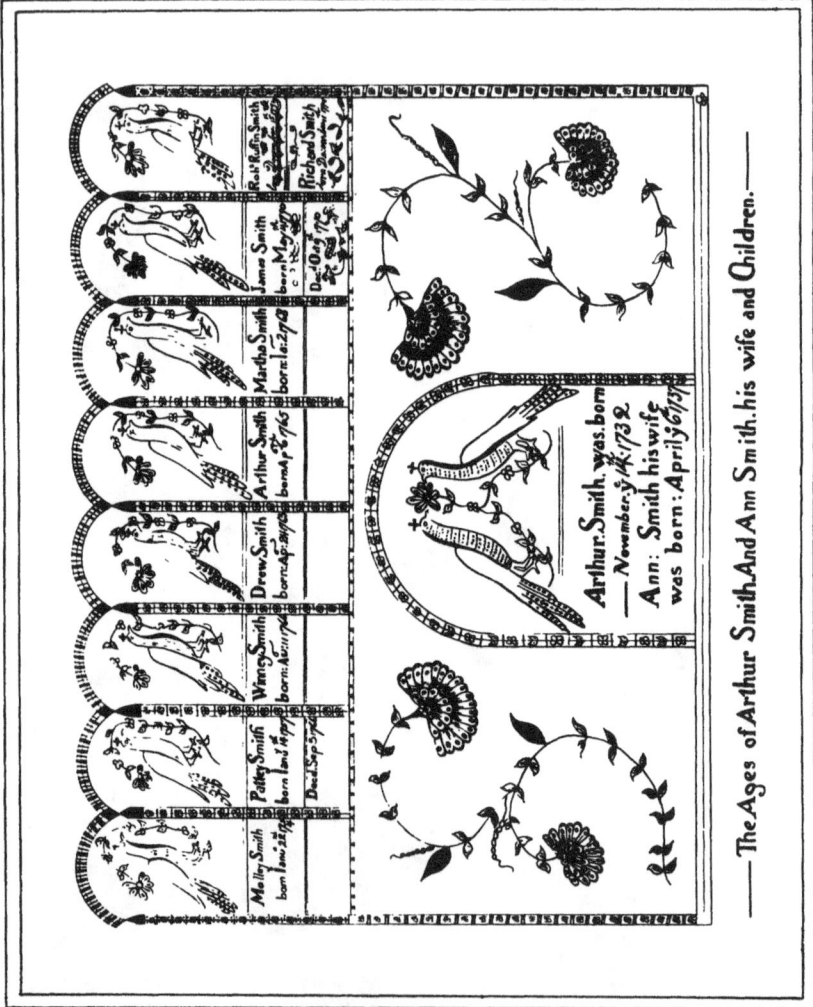

The Ages of Arthur Smith And Ann Smith, his wife and Children.

THE RICHARD SMITH FAMILY
of
Surry, Virginia and Scotland Neck, N. C.

This family of Smiths seems to be descended from the Smiths who owned the Manor of Blackmore in Essex, England. The arms of that family were, "Argent, a crosse gules between four peacocks azure". (17th Cent. p. 247).

Mr. Stuart Smith of Scotland Neck, N. C., has a chart now in his possession, evidently made between 1774 and 1777, showing the names and ages of Arthur Smith, born 1732, and Ann Smith, his wife. On this chart are two large peacocks representing the parents and for each child is a separate panel with a peacock at the head of it. The date of the chart is fixed as not later than 1777, for the reason that their two youngest children, Anne Bennett Smith and William Ruffin Smith, are not shown thereon. They were born in 1777 and 1779 and are mentioned in the wills of both Arthur and Anne.

The first one of this family in Surry from whom the Smiths of Scotland Neck are clearly descended was Richard Smith of who appears in the list of tithables in 1668. In his transactions he is closely associated with a Nicholas Smith and these two may have been brothers or otherwise related.

A Thomas Smith made his will in Surry, March 29, 1669, but only the date is shown; the balance of the page is missing so his children are not known. (Bk. 1, p. 348.)

It is apparent that he may have been Thomas Smith, brother of Arthur Smith I of Isle of Wight County, and son of Arthur Smith of Blackmore who died in 1622. (See 17 C. p. 247.) This would account for the descent of the Peacock arms to the Arthur Smith of the Peacock Chart. Richard Smith (d. 1712) first of this line, had a son named "Thomas", and the name "Thomas", and particularly "Arthur" persisted in this family down to present times. Richard and Nicholas Smith of Surry could well have been sons of this Thomas Smith.

1. Richard Smith, on July 5, 1674, sold Richard Drew some steers (Bk. 2, p. 56). On March 4, 1678, the estate of John Twyford was presented by Richard Smith who had married Mary, the relict. Nicholas Sessums was one of the appraisers

of Twyford's estate and a small neck of land was leased to John Bynum (Bk. 2, p. 199).

In 1687, Richard Smith was a foot soldier in the Militia. In the Quit Rents of 1704, he held 200 acres of land.

He made his will February 24, 1712, and gave to Elizabeth Boon and Richard Sessoms each a cow; to son Richard Smith he gave "the plantation I live on after decease of wife Mary; to sons Thomas and Nicholas Smith the land where Thomas Smith now lives."

Children:

I. Richard II moved to Brunswick County (see later #8). On May 2, 1733, Henry Arthur Smith, son of Richard Smith of Brunswick, Thomas Smith of Isle of Wight, Nicholas Smith of North Carolina conveyed to B. Moody 230 acres of land on Pidgeon Creek, Surry.

II. Thomas, moved to Isle of Wight. On April 2, 1697, Robert Flake, Sr., sold to Thomas Smith, lately of Surry, 250 acres, part of 600, called Flake's Mill (17 C. p. 630). On August 1, 1698, Thomas Smith of Surry sold this mill to William Goodman. Elizabeth Smith, Charles Savidge and Nicholas Sessum were witnesses. Elizabeth Smith signed as wife of Thomas. Robert Flake had bought this land from Thomas Moore, January 1, 1667, for on that date Moore sold Flake land near Surry County "where Flake expects to erect a mill." (17C., p. 556.)

On May 22, 1695, William Goodman announced his intention of "departing out of the Colony" (Surry B5, p. 49). He removed to North Carolina.

III. Nicholas Smith moved to North Carolina (see later).

2. Nicholas Smith moved to North Carolina. In 1723 John Bynum conveyed to Nicholas Smith 450 acres in Chowan Precinct on south side of Maratock River for £ 30. (Bertie Bk. A, p. 160). In August 1725 John Gray deeded him 500 acres in same locality (Bk. B, p. 6). August 1728, John Surginer deeded him 325 acres on Kehukee adjoining land of William Drew. (Bk. C, 6 p. 23)

Nicholas Smith, in August, 1729, conveyed to his nephew, Richard Sessums, for love and affection 100 acres in Bertie in which said Richard lived adjoining lands of Richard Killingsworth, John Gray, etc.

The Morotock River is now the Roanoke and the above lands, then in Bertie, now lie in Halifax County. The last record of Nicholas Smith is in 1737, when he witnessed a deed from William Drew of Surry County. There appears to be no record of his death or division of his estate.

In the above deed of August 1729, Nicholas calls Richard Sessums his "nephew". In those days sometimes "nephew" meant "grandson", sometimes "cousin", and sometimes actually "nephew". "Cousin" then was more often used for "nephew".

Judge Richard H. Smith, born 1812, stated that his great-grandfather Nicholas Smith and his brother were among the first settlers on the Roanoke River. "His family were Church of England people and worshipped in Kehukee Chapel on Chapel Run. The remains of this chapel are still visible. I have obtained some of the bricks which I placed in the northeast corner of the New Trinity Church in Scotland Neck. Dr. Simmons Baker, a former citizen of county, told me that when he first came to the county, about 1795, the old chapel was standing in ruins. In this chapel my father William R. Smith was baptized about 1780. " (Quoted from an old letter.)

Children from will of son Drew Smith:

I. Drew made his will which was recorded in Halifax, 1762, (Bk. 1, p. 57). He mentions his wife, Elizabeth; daughters, Millea, Anne, Temperance and Priscilla; his brothers James and Arthur Smith; his nephews Nicholas Bryant and Needham Bryant, sons of his sister Mary who had married Arthur Bryant.
   Children:
   1. Millea, m. Thomas Barrow and had
      Children:
      (1) Thomas Barrow, m. Mary Duke Lawrence. He was a member of the General Assembly from Northampton, 1828.
         Children:
         (a). Dr. William Barrow, m. October 2, 1841, Eliza R. Calvert and had 4 children among whom was Aletha who married Dr. H. T. Clark, son of Governor Clark and had several children among whom was Rebecca Clark who married Dr. Thurman D. Kitchin, President of Wake Forest College, son of the Hon. W. H. Kitchin.
      (2) William Barrow
      (3) Ferches Barrow, m. Robert Justice
   2. Ann, m. Thomas Whitmel
   3. Priscilla, m. Thomas Hunter of Nash County.
II. Captain James is said to have been married five times. His first wife is said to have been Mary Edwards. Later he married Millie (Emily) Turner, daughter of Thomas Turner. His last wife was Mrs. Sarah (Hill) Ruffin, widow of Thomas Ruffin.

Captain Smith owned large tracts of land on the Roanoke River and in the Piney Woods section of Halifax County, at Scotland Neck, including "Spring Hill", now owned by James B. Hall; "Greenwood", now called the "Ferell Farm", "Gallberry", owned by L. H. Kitchin; and "Albin" owned by J. A. Kitchin.

Children of first wife:

1. Lucy, m. 1. Thomas Langley who died 1764, 2. Reuben Norfleet.

   Children:
   - (a) Penelope Langley, b. 1762, m. 1. Mr. Edwards, 2. Jacob Battle. (See Battle Book)
   - (b) Marmaduke Norfleet, m. Hannah Ruffin, daughter of Sarah(Hall) and William Ruffin and had six children among whom was Louisa Norfleet who married David Clark (See Ruffin Family).

Children by wife Millie Turner

2. Turner, m. Bettie Edwards and had Mary Turner who married Dr. Simmons J. Baker, son of General Lawrence Baker of the Revolution.
3. James, m. Mary, daughter of James Norfleet and had (1) Turner (2) James (3) George Nicholas.
   - III. Mary, m. Arthur Bryant, children Nicholas and Needham Bryant, mentioned in will of her brother Drew Smith.

3. IV. Arthur, b. November 4, 1732, m. Anne RUFFIN.

3. Arthur, b. November 14, 1732, m. Anne RUFFIN, b. April 6, 1737, daughter of Anne (Bennett) and Robert Ruffin. He ówned valuable lands on Roanoke River and in the Piney Woods at Scotland Neck.

An old chart made in India ink about 1775, by Arthur Smith, is now in the possession of Mr. Archibald S. H. Smith of Scotland Neck. It bears the Peacock heads of the Smiths of Blackmore in Essex, England and gives the names and ages of himself, wife, and children as follows:

Children:
- I. Mollie, b. January 22, 1754, m. Lemuel Hogan, son of General James Hogan of the Revolution and his wife, Ruth, widow of Thomas Norfleet. They had nine children. This family moved to Tennessee.
- II. Pattie, b. January 17, 1757.
- III. Winney, b. August 11, 1760.
- IV. Drew, b. April 24, 1762, m. (1) unknown (2) Elizabeth Slatter.
- V. Arthur, b. April 6, 1765.

VI. Martha, b. January 2, 1768, m. (1) Marmaduke Bell
(2) Richard Harrison.
VII. James, b. May 4, 1770
VIII. Robert Ruffin, b. December 15, 1771.
IX. Richard, b. December 11, 1774.
X. Ann Bennett, b. May 22, 1777, m. John Hannon.
4. XI. William Ruffin, b. January 26, 1779.

4. William Ruffin Smith, born July 26, 1779, in Scotland
Neck, died June 22, 1845, married Sarah Walton Norfleet, born
November 27, 1782, died December 9, 1870, daughter of Sarah
(Gordon) and James Norfleet of Gates County.

Mr. Smith acquired large holdings of land in Scotland Neck
and at time of his death owned about 12,000 acres.

Children:
I. Sarah Anna, m. James L. G. Baker
II. William Ruffin, b. Oct. 5, 1803, m. Susan Evans
5. III. Richard Henry, b. May 10, 1812, m. Sallie Hall
IV. James Norfleet, b. June 14, 1817, m. Adelaide Evans
V. Robert Arthur, b. Sept. 22, 1814, never married
VI. Elizabeth Norfleet, b. Sept. 25, 1825, never married.

5. Richard Henry Smith, born May 10, 1812, at Scotland
Neck, died March 2, 1893, at Raleigh, married December 4, 1833,
at Warrenton, N. C., Sallie Hall, daughter of Mary (Weldon) and
Justice John Hall of the Supreme Court of North Carolina. She
died August 14, 1872, at Scotland Neck.

Richard Henry Smith was a graduate of the University of
North Carolina and was for many years a large planter on Roanoke
River. He was trustee in many State institutions. He represen-
ted Halifax County several times in the General Assembly and
was a member of the Secession Convention. He was, also, Pre-
siding Justice of the Halifax County Court of Common Pleas and
Quarter Sessions. For 50 years he was Senior Warden of Trinity
Parish, and attended the National and State Conventions of the
Church.

About 1850, under the leadership of the Reverend Joseph
Chesshire, and largely through the contributions of Richard
Henry Smith and his brothers William Ruffin Smith and James
Norfleet Smith, Trinity Church, the old brick church about one
mile from the present limits of the town of Scotland Neck, was
erected. It was a beautiful building, perfect in its architecture,
and was for years the pride of the community. In 1885, it was
burned. It was restored, later, by Mrs. Martha Clark, widow
of William Ruffin Clark. (Archibald Stuart Hall Smith)

Children:

I. Norfleet, b. January 28, 1839, m. Rebecca Alexander
6. II. Richard Henry, b. September 19, 1841, m. Mary Herbert Cocke.
III. Ann Elizabeth, b. October 2, 1843, m. Major John B. Neal.
IV. Alexander Hall, b. November 5, 1846, m. Ann H. Cocke and Irene Bayle.
V. Isaac Hall, b. January 9, 1848, m. Sarah F. Baker
VI. Sallie Hall, m. Hon. F. H. Busbee
VII. Mary Weldon, b. 1837, m. Dr. James Johnson
VIII. Weldon, b. January 30, 1851, never married.

6. Richard Henry Smith, Jr., born at Scotland Neck, Sept. 19, 1841, died January 26, 1919. He married December 12, 1865 at Petersburg, Virginia, Mary Herbert Cocke, born December 20, 1844, at Aberdeen, Prince George County, Va., died July 3, 1890, daughter of Virginia (Peterson) and Nathaniel Colbey COCKE. Mr. Cocke died of fever while serving in Lee's army.

Mr. Smith was a vestryman of Trinity Church. He left the University of North Carolina in 1862 to join the Confederate Army but was later discharged on account of tuberculosis acquired in service. He recovered and lived to be over three score and ten.

Children:

I. Weldon Thweatt, b. March 4, 1868, m. Dixie Murray.
II. Mary Herbert Smith, b. June 1871, m. Thomas M. Robertson.
7. III. Archibald Stuart Hall, b. November 11, 1876, m. Pauline Ramsey.
IV. Elizabeth Curtis, b. September 24, 1878, never married.
V. Richard Henry, b. September 1881, m. Elizabeth Jeffries.
VI. Nathalie C., b. June 16, 1883, m. Thomas M. Robertson.

7. Archibald Stuart Hall Smith, who collected and kindly contributed all this data about the Smith family, was born at Scotland Neck, November 11, 1876. He married June 19, 1907, at Union Springs, Bullock County, Alabama, Pauline, daughter of Julia (Boyd) and Asa Alexander Ramsay, born January 21, 1875, died June 9, 1927.

Mr. Stuart Smith is an attorney at Scotland Neck. He has served on the Exemption Boards of Halifax County during two world wars, and one term on the Halifax County Board of Edu-

cation. Also, he has been a member of the local school board
for 32 years.

Mr. Smith writes that of the old Smith homes, "Woodstock",
the home of Richard Henry Smith (5) is owned by the children of
his son Isaac Hall Smith (6). "Magnolia", the home of James
Norfleet Smith (5) is owned by his grandchildren. The land on
which Spring Hill was situated is owned by James B. Hall. Both
"Woodstock" and "Magnolia" are in good state of preservation.
Other lands, formerly owned by William Ruffin Smith (5) are
owned by the grandchildren of James N. Smith and by Burton
H. Smith, Walter Johnston Smith (7) and Bertha Albertson Smith
(wife of Dr. Claiborne T. Smith). The family of Peter E. Smith
own the farm on which his old home was situated.

Children:
  I. Julia Boyd Smith, b. October 15, 1910, m. Reverend
      Benjamin T. Brodie.

8. Richard Smith II, son of Mary and Richard Smith I (d.
1712) removed to Northampton Co., N. C. where his will was
probated in 1756. His children were: Richard; Mary, m._____
Aldridge; and Henry Arthur Smith. The last named had a son
Arthur Smith, born ca. 1740, who removed to Wayne County
N. C. where his will was probated in 1808. His wife was Sarah
(last name unknown) whose will was probated in the same county
in 1814.

Children:
  I.   Arthur, Jr., m. Lucretia Luzelle. Their children were
        James, Mary and Avery Smith.
  II.   Sampson
  III. Avery, m. _____ Rouse.
  IV.   John, m. Elizabeth Lancaster. (See later.)
  V.   Drewery, m.____. Children: Thomas, James, Morley,
        William, Drewery and Arthur C. Smith.
  VI.   Benjamin
  VII. Joseph
  VIII. Lazarus, m._____, and had James Smith and one daugh-
        ter.

John Smith, son of Arthur and Sarah Smith, was born in
Wayne Co., about 1770 and died there in 1833. He married
Elizabeth, dau. of William Lancaster of Wayne.

Children:
  I. William, b. Feb. 6, 1806, m. Anne Everitt
  II. John, m. Margaret Kornegay.

III. Everitt
IV. Stephen, b. May 11, 1793, m. Sarah Ann Rhodes (see later).
V. Ezekiel, m. Elizabeth Applewhite
VI. Tabitha

Stephen Smith, born May 11, 1793, near Goldsboro, Wayne Co., N. C., died Sept. 6, 1834, in Wayne. He married Aug. 4, 1811, Sarah Ann Rhodes, born Jan. 10, 1794, in Wayne, died Aug. 9, 1854, at Livingston, Sumter Co., Ala., daughter of Anna (Bass) and General James Rhodes.

Mr. Smith served in the House of Commons from Wayne 1817, 22-23 (Wheeler) and was also Sheriff of Wayne for several years.

Children:
I. Joseph Andrew Smith, b. Sept. 19, 1812, unmarried.
II. James Rhodes Smith, b. Nov. 26, 1814, m. Mary Elizabeth Foy.
III. John Thomas Smith, b. Jan. 10, 1823, m. Cornelia E. Houston.
IV. Edward Ward Smith, b. May 27, 1825, m. Martha Ann Houston (see later).
V. Stephen Uriah Smith, b. Jan. 2, 1817, unmarried.
VI. Sarah Ann Elizabeth Smith, b. Dec. 25, 1829, unmarried.
VII. Mary Amando Smith, b. May 23, 1832, m. James H. Houston.

Edward Ward Smith, born May 27, 1825, in Wayne Co., died Feb. 25, 1874, at Livingston, Alabama, married Nov. 21, 1850, at Livingston, Martha Ann Houston, born Nov. 21, 1831, in Morgan Co., Ala., died April 12, 1858, at Livingston.

Mr. Smith was educated at Princeton University. He served as an officer in an Alabama regiment in the Confederate Army and represented Sumpter in the State Senate.

Children:
I. Addison G. Smith, b. Oct. 1, 1851, m. Florence D. Hopkins, (see later).
II. Stephen Smith, b. Aug. 9, 1853, m. Mary Phifer.
III. Walter Keirn Smith, b. Oct. 31, 1855, m. Susan Tankersley.

Addison Gillespie Smith, born Oct. 1, 1851, at Livingston, Ala., died May 16, 1933, in Birmingham, Ala., married Dec. 1, 1875, at Livingston, Florence Devereux Hopkins, daughter of Elizabeth (Ryan) and Devereux Hopkins, born at Livingston, died at Birmingham, Jan. 24, 1938.

Mr. Smith attended Wetmore and Hoke Academy at Lincoln-
ton, N. C., and Cumberland Univ., Lebanon, Tenn. He practiced law at Birmingham and served in the State Senate from
Jefferson County. He was Chairman of the Democratic Executive
for Ala. when Cleveland was elected president in 1892, and during the Kolb-Jones contest for Governor. He was also Division
Counsel for the Ala. Gt. Southern and Mobile and Ohio Railroads.

Children:
I. Edward, D., b. Sept. 5, 1876, m. Florida Whiting
   Graves. (see later).
II. Kate, b. Oct. 22, 1883, m. J. T. Stokeley.
III. Addison G., b. Feb. 1886, died young.
IV. Sidney Preston, b. June 17, 1890, m. Dorothy Johnson.
   Mr. Smith is now a major in the army (1944) and has
   two sons in service.

Edward Deverux Smith, born Sept. 15, 1876, at Livingston,
Ala., married March 24, 1904, at San Francisco, Calif., Florida
Whiting Graves, born Mar. 27, 1878, at Montgomery, Alabama,
daughter of Florida (Whiting) and Captain William Henry Graves.
Mr. Smith is an A. B. of Univ. of Ala., 1896; L. L. B.
Georgetown, 1898; and a Phi Beta Kappa. He was City Attorney
for Birmingham 1901-1907, Division Counsel for the A. G. S. and
M. &O. railroads until 1919; Democratic National Committeeman
for Alabama 1916-19. He removed to Atlanta, Ga., in 1919, to
become General Solicitor of the Southern Bell Tel. Co. and then
served as General Counsel, Director and Vice Pres. of that
Co. until his retirement in 1941. He is now V. P. of Fulton
National Bank.
Mr. Smith is a member of the Capital and City Clubs and
resides at 134 West Paces Ferry Road, Atlanta, Ga.

Children:
I. William Graves, b. Apr. 11, 1905, d. July 31, 1938,
   unmarried.
II. Addison Gillespie, b. Dec. 25, 1909, m. Rose Mary
   Manry. Mr. Smith is a Lieut. (J. G.) in the U. S.
   Navy. They have one son, Addison G. Smith IV.
III. Edward D. Jr., b. Mar. 12, 1912, m. Laura Maddox.
   Mr. Smith is a Lieut. (J. G) in U. S. Navy. They have
   two children, Louisa Maddox and Florida G. Smith.

INDEX

Middle names are not shown.
Names may appear more than once on a page.
Names on charts are not referred to in index.